The 5 Personality Patterns

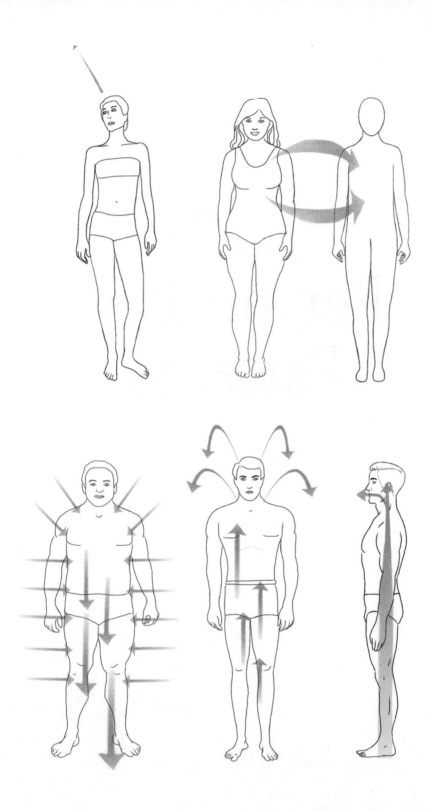

The 5 Personality Patterns

Your Guide to
Understanding Yourself and Others
and Developing Emotional Maturity

STEVEN KESSLER

 BODHI TREE PRESS

Published by Bodhi Tree Press
Richmond, California
www.BodhiTreePress.com

Editing by Jordan Gruber

Illustrations by Christine Chrisman
christinechrisman.com

ISBN- 10: 0996343903
ISBN- 13: 978-0-9963439-0-9

Library of Congress Control Number: 2015908422

For information on speaking, workshops, and trainings on the Patterns, please visit *www.The5PersonalityPatterns.com* or contact the author at *info@The5PersonalityPatterns.com*.

Your experience of life
is determined mostly by
your habits of attention
and the patterned flow
of your life energy.

– *Steven Kessler*

Contents

Acknowledgments

I first want to profoundly thank Lynda Caesara, who first introduced me to character structure and has been my primary teacher of it for over ten years. Much of the material in this book comes from her teaching, supplemented by my own observations and insights. I have also drawn on material from the writings of Wilhelm Reich, Alexander Lowen, John C. Pierrakos, Stephen M. Johnson, Barbara Brennan, and Anodea Judith.

My clients and my fellow students have fleshed out the teachings by providing hundreds of real life examples of the survival patterns in action. They have been a continual source of insight and inspiration, and I want to thank each and every one of them. I especially thank the entire community of students studying the survival patterns for their years of suggestions, feedback, and extraordinary support of this project as it gradually grew from a first draft to a finished book.

I also want to thank Anodea Judith, who first invited me to teach the character structure patterns and has freely offered her help and support as I navigated the publication process.

The creation of this book has taken almost ten years and has turned into a labor of love for me. For his iterative editing, I want to thank Jordan Gruber. And for her months spent helping me find ways to illustrate the energy flows and typical body shapes of each pattern, I thank Christine Chrisman. For her work on the diagrams, I thank Jane Chamberlain. For her proofreading, I thank Sally Boden O'Sullivan. Lastly, I want to thank Camille Clark, who first persuaded me to begin this project.

Introduction

Much of our human suffering is not necessary. It is created by unhealthy patterns of feeling and acting that helped us survive the traumas of childhood, but then got stuck in our bodies. These patterns have shaped us so deeply that now we think that's who we are. But these patterns are not our true self. In fact, they cover up our true self and prevent it from shining out into the world.

Fortunately, there is a map of these survival patterns, a map that shows us both how we got stuck and how we can free ourselves and return to being present in the moment. This book lays out that map and shows you the path out of your suffering and back to your true self. The inner journey still takes time and effort, but once you know where you're going, it will be much easier. Without a map, you may have been walking in circles for years. With a map, you can find your way home.

The Nature of This Map

Other maps of personality, such as the Enneagram and the Myers-Briggs Type Indicator, describe a series of "types" and then refer to people *as* a type, for instance, calling them a "Four" or a "Nine" or an "ENTJ." This map is fundamentally different: it does not describe who you are, but instead describes the survival strategies you automatically go into when you start to feel overwhelmed. It is not a set of types, but a set of survival patterns that come to the fore to buffer you from directly feeling the distress. Consequently, this map does not describe *who* you are, but rather what *obscures* who you are. It focuses not just on which patterns you go into, but also on the difference between being "in pattern" and being "present," and on learning how to get out of pattern and back to being present. As you first learn about the five survival patterns and discover which ones you go into, it's easy to forget this difference. To highlight it, I refer in this book to people *going into* a pattern, being *in* a pattern, or *doing* a pattern, but never say that they *are* the pattern.

Another important difference between this map and most other maps of personality is that the survival patterns are not based on what is happening at the surface — on what people say and do. Instead, they are based on what is happening within — on how the stream of life energy and awareness habitually moves through the body, especially in times of distress. The five survival patterns described here arise out of five different ways that the flow of energy through the body can be shaped in an attempt to cope with the distress. The flow can habitually:

- move away from others

- move toward others

- move in and down

- move up and out

- be constricted

These patterns of energy flow influence how a person perceives the world and, therefore, what he experiences, thinks, and feels. And they influence how the person behaves, especially when too much energy hits his system and he goes into overwhelm. These patterns of energy flow are so fundamental that they even shape the body as it grows. But the survival patterns are not based on body shape or emotions or behavior. They are based on how energy flows through the body.

This book attempts to give you a sense of what each survival pattern feels like from the inside, so that you can understand others more deeply. It will give you a window into their world, enable you to understand how they experience themselves, and help you communicate with them more successfully. It will also give you a window into your own inner world. As you develop a better working relationship with yourself, you will begin to break the hold your patterns have on you, and more easily return to being present.

The Origins of the Map

The map of the survival patterns is part of a larger body of work. It begins with Wilhelm Reich, a star student of Sigmund Freud who began his career as a Freudian psychoanalyst. During the 1920's, Reich observed that his patients displayed shared patterns of "character resistances." He called these patterns "character structures." Over time, as he focused on understanding his patients' character structures, Reich's therapeutic method changed so much that he began calling it "character analysis" to distinguish it from Freud's psychoanalysis.

Reich also noticed that these character structures were held in place by patterns of chronic muscular tension in the body, and he began to look for ways to loosen his patients' muscular armoring. Over time, he found that as their muscular armoring relaxed, their life energy flowed more freely through their bodies. This led to his discovery in 1935 of the orgasm reflex, which caused him to shift the focus of his therapy from the character resistances to the body itself[1] and to change the name of his method to "vegetotherapy." This name proved unfortunate, for while it was accurate in German, it was confusing when translated into English. In 1939, Reich coined the term "orgone" for the life energy flowing through the body and began calling his method "orgone therapy."

Alexander Lowen, one of Reich's early students, championed Reich's concept of character structure and his body-based way of working, and further developed Reich's insights and methods into a form of therapy that he called "Bioenergetics." Another of Reich's students, John Pierrakos, first collaborated with Lowen in the development of Bioenergetics. Later, he added more awareness of the spiritual dimension to create his own form of therapy, which he called "Core Energetics." Still other students, who stayed closer to Reich's teachings, called themselves "neo-Reichians." Many branches grew from these roots, leading to more recent contributions by Barbara Brennan, Stephen M. Johnson, and Anodea Judith, among others.

The Names of the Survival Patterns

The names used for the patterns have evolved over time as various writers attempted to clarify the patterns and find more useful names for them. Because Reich initially perceived them as patterns of resistance, he named them for the associated psychological pathologies, using Freudian terms such as "schizophrenic," "passive feminine," "hysterical," "compulsive," "masochist," and "phallic-narcissist."

As Alexander Lowen extended Reich's work, he defined five clear patterns and renamed most of them, but still used Freudian terms derived from their pathology, calling them "schizoid," "oral," "masochist," "psychopath," and "rigid." In his book, *Core Energetics*, John Pierrakos retained Lowen's five character structure patterns, but renamed the psychopath pattern to "aggressive."

Some more recent writers have tried to get away from Lowen's pathology-based terms by renaming the patterns for their associated talents and skills, giving them names such as "Creative," "Lover," "Communicator," "Inspirer," "Charismatic Leader," "Industrious," and "Achiever." However, such names imply that the patterns are something to aspire to, rather than places we got stuck. They also distract our attention away from the fact that the patterns are created and defined by survival strategies, not by the skills and talents needed to make each pattern work.

For this book, I have used names that highlight what each pattern *does* — its survival strategy — without adding a positive or negative bias. Hence, I have called the patterns: "Leaving," "Merging," "Enduring," "Aggressive," and "Rigid." By using names that highlight each pattern's survival strategy, I am also emphasizing the fact that a pattern is something a person *does* to protect themselves when in distress, not something they *are*.

Seeing Which Patterns You Go Into

While reading this book, you may recognize which patterns you go into. You may have epiphanies and see yourself more clearly. I hope that you do. When attempting to figure out which survival patterns you go into, look especially at how you act when you're upset and overwhelmed. That's when your survival strategies are likely to be the most obvious. You may also want to ask your family and friends for feedback on how you behave when you're upset or overwhelmed. However, don't lose sight of the fact that your patterns are survival strategies — they are not who you are and not your essence. They prevent your essence from shining through and manifesting as presence. We will go into this in more detail in Chapter 2.

Your survival patterns are also not a way to justify your behavior. Identifying them will help you understand what's behind your behavior and how to change it, but they're not an excuse for mistreating anyone, including yourself. I sometimes suggest that clients let themselves be guided by this instruction: "Treat yourself at least as well as you have ever treated your dearest love."

Similarly, understanding another person's survival patterns will help you understand what's behind their behavior, but it does not obligate you to accept mistreatment from them. You may feel compassion for them and want to help them feel safer, but you still need to protect yourself and keep yourself safe.

Managing their behavior is their responsibility, not yours. Being upset is not a license to mistreat anyone.

I hope this book helps you learn how to recognize when you've gone into pattern, take steps to get out of pattern, and return to being present. I hope it also helps you understand others and interact with them more skillfully.

Seeing Which Patterns Others Go Into

However, if misapplied, your new knowledge of the survival patterns can be used as a weapon against those around you, including those you love. As you read this book, you will probably recognize which survival patterns your friends and family go into, and you'll be tempted to turn your understandings into accusations, such as *"You're so rigid!"* or *"You're just leaving!"* I urge you not to impose your insights on others or put them in a box this way. If you label people, they will feel judged, and they won't like the idea that your new understanding gives you power over them.

Instead, use your new understanding to see their needs and fears more clearly and interact with them more skillfully. Use it to get yourself out of your patterned reactions so that you can treat them in a kinder and more compassionate way. Instead of expressing your discoveries in words, try expressing them in new behaviors that work better for the other person, as well as for you.

When you do talk about your insights, instead of telling others what you've discovered about them, tell them what you've discovered about *yourself* and how that has helped you. If they seem interested, give them this book and invite them to explore it with you.

Use your new knowledge to act more skillfully and lovingly toward both yourself and others. Don't use it to judge others or yourself or to justify your own patterned, unhealthy ways of acting. And don't use it to attack others for being stuck in their patterns, or yourself for being stuck in yours. We're all doing the best we can.

How to Use This Book

This book has three main parts. The first part introduces you to the idea of survival patterns in general, lays out the developmental stages that underlie the patterns, gives you a brief overview of the patterns themselves, and concludes with a discussion of the skills needed for any inner work. The middle part starts with a chart to help you compare the five patterns to each other and then fleshes out the chart with five large chapters, one devoted to each survival pattern. The last part of the book goes into how the patterns interact with each other within one person and elaborates on how you can get yourself out of pattern and back to being present.

Don't expect to be able to grasp all the nuances of this map without taking some time to study it. As you read about the survival patterns, you will be attempting to see both the larger picture and how the individual pieces fit together to form it. Most people need to go through the material several times to accomplish that. To help you, this book presents the map three times, starting with a simple version and gradually providing more and more detail. First, it draws the outlines of the map by giving you a brief overview of the five patterns and how they are created. Next, it presents a chart that shows how the five patterns are related. Reading vertically down the chart will give you many specifics on each survival pattern, while reading horizontally across the chart will allow you to compare each pattern to the others. Finally, the book fills in the map by describing each pattern in detail.

You may be tempted to go directly to the chapters that describe the patterns you resonate with so you can learn about yourself. This is fine as a starting point, but don't confuse it with learning the overall map. If you don't yet have the larger map in your mind, you won't be able to see how your own patterns fit into the larger picture, and you won't have anywhere to put the details you're learning. So, after reading about yourself, I urge you to go back to the beginning and read the rest of the book. At the end, I suggest that you also re-read the chapters about your patterns to help you take in any details you glossed over the first time. Or, if you can stand to wait, the most efficient way to assemble the map and flesh it out is to read the chapters in order.

On the next pages, you will find a list of the principles that underlie this map of personality. The essence of the entire book is spelled out there, so a careful reading of the next few pages will help you assimilate the rest of the book much more easily.

Principles

THESE ARE THE PRINCIPLES BEHIND the map of the survival patterns. The heart of how survival patterns are formed, and how you can return to presence, is laid out here.

Our natural state is simply being present. In this state we are relaxed and contented.

When too much energy hits our body and nervous system, we go into overwhelm. If we are soothed, we will discharge the energy, relax, and return to simply being present.

If, as children, we are not soothed but are instead left with overwhelming feelings, we begin to build a defense against those feelings. The defense buffers us from directly experiencing our overwhelm.

As children, we may try out several defense strategies. We stick with the ones that best help us solve the problems we face.

If we use a particular defense strategy often enough, it becomes a habit and then becomes a survival pattern.

All of the survival patterns arise out of feeling unsafe and all are attempts to create some sense of safety for ourselves.

We construct our survival strategies out of whatever talents and abilities we have.

All the survival patterns are skill-based, since the successful use of any pattern depends on having the skills needed to make it work.

Each of us typically settles into a primary survival pattern and a backup pattern. Some of us have two backup patterns.

We then build our sense of self around those patterns. This creates a false self and makes us lose contact with our true self, which is presence.

Being in a survival pattern affects our sensory perceptions, our experience, and the meaning we assign to our experience in ways that validate and reinforce the survival pattern. Because of this, our experiences, beliefs, identities, and survival patterns become a self-reinforcing system.

We may remain in a survival pattern nearly all the time, with it running quietly in the background or running loudly in the foreground. This constitutes much of our personality.

Our false self and survival patterns unconsciously make many of our choices regarding interests, friends, lovers, career, etc.

We can learn to recognize when we are in a survival pattern, and we can acquire the skills needed to shift ourselves out of that pattern and back to being present.

The more we are present, the less we find the pattern useful and attractive. Our identity begins to shift from the pattern to presence.

As an adult, we may do spiritual practices to reconnect with presence as our true self, but until we heal the core traumas in our body that fuel our survival patterns, we will still go into our patterns when in overwhelm.

A healing experience that dissolves the core trauma that created a survival pattern can "break" the pattern. Once broken, a survival pattern loses much of its compelling emotional force.

Since using any of the patterns requires practicing certain skills over and over, each pattern fosters its own particular set of gifts.

– 1 –

Our Eyes Deceive Us

OUR EYES DECEIVE US. EVERY day, every moment, we look out at the world and believe that what we see is the whole world, the only world, the world that everyone else sees. But we are mistaken.

The world we see is a filtered and distorted version of the real world. Some parts of the picture have been shifted to the foreground, brought into clear focus with vivid colors, while other parts of the picture have been moved to the background, dimmed and dulled until we hardly notice them at all. But we aren't aware of these distortions, so we think that the images we see are an accurate picture of the world.

Think of it this way: imagine that you live your entire life in a small room. The walls, floor, and ceiling of this room are made of TV screens, screens so big that they fill the entire wall, ceiling, and floor. Wherever you look, there are only screens. Everything you know about the world — everything that you see, hear, feel, touch, smell, taste, or perceive in any way — comes through the screens. Even how you perceive yourself comes through the screens.

Now ask yourself, *"What channel are my TV screens usually tuned to?"* Are you watching The Fear Channel, the channel which highlights all the dangers surrounding you? Are you watching The Love Channel, the channel devoted to feeling connected to others and pleasing them? Do you spend most of your time watching The Winning Channel, the channel which shows you who's up and who's down and how you can fight your way to the top? Are you watching The Avoid Losing Channel, the channel focused on how to stay small and hidden and avoid getting run over by those fighter types? Are you watching The Rules Channel, the one focused on keeping things ordered and correct and controlled, on doing it the right way and making sure that others do it the right way, too?

Obviously, which channel you watch will make a huge difference in how you perceive the world and how you perceive yourself. And if you watch the same channel all day, every day of your life, you will have nothing to compare it to, no way to know that it is just one slice of the world, just a small fraction of the whole picture. You won't even know that there is a whole picture, a bigger, fuller world that you have never experienced. You won't know what you're missing.

You may notice that some people refer to things that you don't experience, or that they focus on things that don't make sense or just don't seem important to you. But you'll usually explain it by telling yourself a story, like *"They're stupid"* or *"I'm stupid"* or *"They're wrong"* or *"I'm wrong"* or *"They're mean"* or *"I'm not good enough"* — a story that boils down to either *"They're deficient"* or *"I'm deficient."* But, whatever you tell yourself, your stories won't challenge your belief that your view of the world is accurate. In fact, they will usually reinforce it.

So we go through life seeing a filtered, distorted picture of the world and making all of our decisions based on incomplete and distorted information. Then we wonder why life is such a struggle and why it is often so hard to get others to agree with us and cooperate with us.

Some of us try to find safety by being alone. Some of us look for safety through others, either by pleasing them or dominating them. Many of us try to persuade others to be more like we are. But whatever strategy we use, we are all seeking safety.

So how can we ever truly find safety? How can we ever learn to see the world as it really is and navigate skillfully through it? How can we get what we want? This book is about answering those questions.

The first step is to learn to change the TV channel you see in your head. Even one experience of changing your usual channel and seeing the world differently will decrease your certainty that your usual channel is the only channel and is showing you the whole picture.

To change the channel, you have to shift the way you are holding your attention. As you practice shifting how you hold your attention, doing it gets easier. You get better at telling what station you're currently tuned to just by looking at the theme running through what you're seeing. You learn that you have a choice: that you can change what you're seeing out there in the world by changing the channel inside yourself. And you get better at shifting your habitual stance of attention and thereby changing the channel.

But perhaps you find that the channel keeps changing back to your old habitual one. Over and over, you change it to something you like better, only to find that it somehow changes itself back. So you start investigating: what is it that causes it to change back? Gradually you realize that whenever you get distressed or overwhelmed, you go back into your old, habitual survival pattern and the channel goes back to the same old station.

This book is about shifting out of those habitual survival patterns. It is about recognizing those patterns in yourself and in others, shifting yourself out of pattern and back into presence, and dealing with other people when they're in pattern. It is about how to come out of pattern so you can see the world as it really is and become the person you want to be.

– 2 –

About Survival Patterns

Pattern vs Presence

Aʟᴍᴏsᴛ ᴀʟʟ ᴏғ ᴜs ʜᴀᴠᴇ noticed the difference between being present and being in pattern, although we usualy call the two states by other names. Being *present* means that all of our attention is here, in this time and place. Usually, this happens only when we're feeling relatively safe. At these times, our bodies are not in a state of alarm conditioned into them by past traumas, and our perceptions are not filtered or distorted by thoughts and feelings from the past. This allows us to perceive the real situation happening right now and respond to it in a healthy and effective way.

Being *in pattern* means that our perceptions are being filtered and distorted by a survival pattern. A survival pattern is an automatic, body-based reaction that we go into to try to buffer ourselves from feeling overwhelmed. But it's a reaction that was conditioned into us by traumas in the past. It is not a response to the present situation. Sometime in the past, it was the best strategy we could find to deal with a difficult, ongoing situation. Over time, it was so deeply conditioned into our bodies that now it automatically kicks in whenever we feel distressed, making us react as if the past distress is still happening to us, even when it is not.

While in a pattern, we usually feel that our reaction is completely justified. This happens because our mind and body are flooded with the feelings and perceptions of the past situations. It's as if an old tape recording is playing and drowning out our perception of the present situation. At some level we believe that the old trauma is happening all over again. Often this makes the present threat seem much larger than it really is, causing us to overreact to the current situation. Overreacting is one of the major indicators of being in pattern.

A friend who is practicing noticing when she is in pattern and getting herself out of pattern described the two states this way:

> On Tuesday afternoon I had a brief sense of happiness and satisfaction after a meeting with my manager and updating her on my projects. I checked off some major activities and felt good about my work.
>
> About an hour later everything changed. All of a sudden a flood of To Do items overwhelmed me: a charge to my dad's credit card of $1000, insurance claim forms waiting to be completed, my daughter's tuition challenges, being behind on paying my own bills. My office was messy and I couldn't find things I needed. I was late leaving for my dentist appointment. I experienced a huge deluge of everything I had blocked out of my mind because of work priorities.
>
> Instead of taking time to ground myself and address the fact that I was now in pattern, I rushed out of the house to my dentist appointment, forgetting my wallet and that I needed gas. From the moment I left the house, everything became a struggle. People were driving like lunatics. I didn't have any money to buy gas. My dentist's office had over-billed me for a cleaning and couldn't see it even though it was OBVIOUS! Every human encounter was difficult, frustrating, awkward, maddening, and tiring.
>
> Later, when I took time to ground myself and come out of pattern, I felt this rush of what I can best describe as ease. Relief. A wave of harmony and relaxation. I didn't need to fight or struggle. I do think that deep down I felt safer, but that is so primal I often don't recognize it.

This description paints a vivid picture of how feeling threatened and overwhelmed tends to throw a person into pattern and how different that is from being present. However, going into pattern is not the only possible response to a threat. It is possible to stay present while dealing with a real danger in the here and now. The difference is that, when you're present, you're seeing and hearing the real situation around you and responding to the particulars of the actual current threat, not to something from your past. You are composing a new, flexible response based on this particular situation. Because your response is tailored to the current situation, it works better than an automatic, fixed reaction. And, because you are present in the moment, you can monitor how well your response is working and adjust it as needed. Your response is calibrated to this situation; it is not an overreaction based on past situations.

For many of us, however, staying present when we're upset is nearly impossible. Our bodies are so deeply conditioned by the traumas still stuck in them that we go into pattern the instant we feel uncomfortable. In fact, many of us stay in pattern nearly all the time. Our unconscious survival patterns have become so strong that they rule our lives, coloring our every thought and feeling and determining our actions. When asked why we behave that way, our only answer is often, *"That's just who I am."*

However, things don't have to remain this way. Our wounds can be healed. Our old conditioning can be softened. We can learn now the skills that we didn't learn earlier. And we can live most of our lives in the present, rather than from inside a pattern. This book will help you discover when you go into pattern and show you the path back to being more present in the moment.

Your Survival Patterns Are Not Who You Are

As you learn about the survival patterns, the most important thing to remember is that *a survival pattern is not who you really are.* It is what *blocks* who you really are. It buffers you from feeling overwhelmed, but it also stops you from directly experiencing yourself in the moment and expressing that in the world. When you were distressed as a child, you naturally used whatever capacities you had to buffer and protect yourself. This was needed. It was the best you could do at the time. Gradually, the buffering strategies that you used were conditioned into your body and mind. Over time, these buffering strategies developed their own internal logic and structure and became your survival patterns. But they are *not* who you are.

So who are you? You are Presence. And you are the one who is present. You are the awareness, in this moment, of this moment. You are not your thoughts, emotions, or behaviors. Not even your body. You are just a simple, open awareness. In many spiritual teachings, this awareness is called Essence or Spirit. It is also called the True Self, and this term is used to distinguish it from the personality, or False Self. In this book, I will refer to it simply as *presence*, or as *being present*. Presence is who you are underneath all the conditioning, armoring, beliefs, and identities that you carry. You are the experiencer, pure and simple.

It is also important to remember that your survival patterns are not some sort of failing for which you should be punished. You developed them to try to keep yourself safe in difficult situations. And since making your survival patterns work requires that you employ some of your best skills, such as creativity, love, strength, and will, you've also been practicing and developing those skills, even while lost in a pattern. Adopting a particular survival pattern is one way of honing a particular set of skills — perhaps the skills you need to accomplish important things in your life.

Why We Need Defenses

As newborn babies, we are mostly just Presence in a body. We're not thinking or evaluating our experience. We're not remembering the past or imagining the future. We have not closed or armored our body in any way. There is no edge, no inside or outside. No self or other . . . just the flow of experience. It is this pure Presence that makes babies so adorable and so compelling. And remember, this Presence is still there in you, buried under all the layers of hurts and defenses.

But because, as babies, we have no edges or boundaries, we also have no buffer, no way to modulate the amount of sensation we experience. Any sound or emotion that happens near us flows right through us. If the person holding us is feeling a strong emotion, whether it's love, joy, fear, or hatred, that emotion flows right through us. Not as a mental concept, but as a body sensation. We are like little tuning forks, resonating to every note that is played nearby.

But we need a way to regulate the amount of sensation we experience. Any stimulation, whether from outside (e.g., noise, touch) or inside (e.g., hunger, gas pains) creates an energy charge in our body. Our nervous system is designed to go through a regular cycle of charge and discharge, excitement and soothing, tension and relaxation. Excitement is good, but not too much or for too long. After excitement, our nervous system needs to relax and come back down to the ground state to rest.

Since, at this age, we cannot regulate our own system, we need our caregivers (e.g., mom or dad) to do it for us. We need them to shield us from too much noise, too much sun, too much heat or cold. When we do get charged up, whether with excitement or pain, we need them to soothe us and help us discharge the inner tension. Parents spend a lot of time soothing their children by rocking, cuddling, and singing lullabies.

This need for someone else to regulate the charge in our bodies is one of the defining characteristics of childhood. Conversely, the ability to regulate our own bodies is one of the defining characteristics of adulthood. Adults are

15

able to track their own needs and take responsibility for either giving themselves what they need or negotiating ways to get what they need from others. Many happy marriages are based on the fact that the spouses are able to help each other with the charge and discharge process.

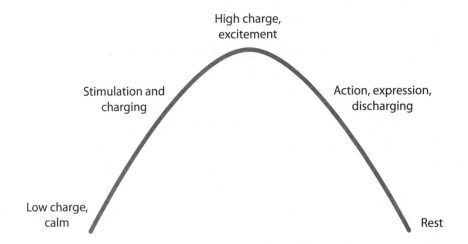

The Charge-Discharge Cycle

Ideally, as each of us grows into adulthood, we acquire all the skills we need to regulate our own charge/discharge process. We feel sufficiently safe in our bodies to fully inhabit them. We learn how to ground ourselves to the Earth and operate in time and space. We learn how to take energy into our bodies and metabolize it. We develop an energetic boundary around our bodies that keeps our own energy inside and other energies outside. We develop a felt sense of the core of our own body and learn to recognize that felt sense as "me." This gives us an embodied sense of self, of "I." We learn to track the sensations in our body and interpret what they are saying about our feelings and desires. This gives us a clear sense of "I feel" and "I want." And we learn healthy ways to get those wants met, which gives us experiences of "I deserve" and "I can." All these skills help us to track and regulate the amount of charge in our bodies so that we are comfortable, rather than in overwhelm.

However, most of us had a childhood that was far from this ideal. Our young, vulnerable nervous systems were not protected and regulated by ideal parents. We often felt overwhelmed and alone, and to buffer ourselves from these recurring feelings of overwhelm, we developed survival patterns.

How Survival Patterns Are Created

As we consider the charge/discharge cycle and our need to regulate the amount of charge in our nervous system, we can see that all traumatic events share one characteristic: they overcharge the body and put it into overwhelm. Survival patterns attempt to solve the problem of overwhelm by buffering us from our direct experience, thereby making it easier to bear. This is the main function of survival patterns. This means that when you've gone into pattern you are no longer in direct contact with your experience: you are no longer present. In that moment, however, buffering yourself in this way may be the best solution you have to the problem of feeling overwhelmed.

Broadly stated, then, the process by which a child develops a survival pattern goes like this:

1. Something happens to you that puts you into overwhelm. Now you have a problem, a need for self-protection and self-regulation. Usually this is a repeated experience, although, if the experience is intense enough, one event can create a survival pattern.

2. You use whatever capacities you have at that age to try to solve your problem. You may copy something that you've seen others do or invent a new strategy. You try it out.

3. If the strategy works, you keep using it. If it fails, you try something else.

4. Over time, you settle into a strategy to deal with your problem. As you use it repeatedly, it becomes conditioned into your body and gradually develops from a survival strategy into a survival pattern.

5. As you grow up, that survival pattern becomes the lens through which you experience life. It influences how you see yourself, how you see the world, and how you try to protect yourself.

Each of us is born with certain talents, and if those talents are useful or rewarded in our early environment, we tend to develop them into skills. For instance, a child born with musical talents and raised in a musical family will tend to develop musical skills. A child born with sensitivity to the psychic realm, who is raised in an environment of random violence, will learn to use her psychic sensitivity to detect danger and get away from it. Another child born into the same violent family, but with different talents, say, for fierceness rather than for sensitivity, will develop a different strategy for dealing with the

How Survival Patterns are Created

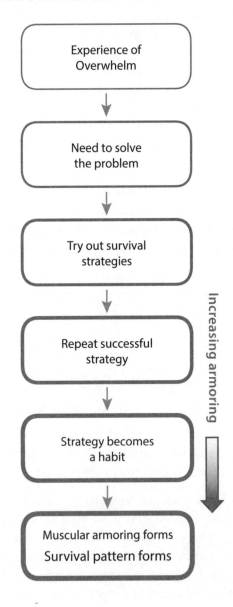

danger. She will likely be more successful at fighting than at avoiding the danger, so her survival strategy will rely more on fierceness than on getting away.

Conversely, if a talent causes us distress, we may learn to suppress it. For instance, if a boy's brilliance intimidates his father, who then humiliates him, the boy may learn to act dumb and thus lose touch with his brilliance. If a girl's beauty arouses jealousy in her mother, she may hide or disown her beauty and think herself ugly.

All the survival patterns are skill-based. You have to have the skills needed to carry out a particular strategy or it won't work for you. If you can't make it work, you'll probably drop it and try another strategy.

Sometimes you can watch a child go through this process of trying out different strategies until she finds one that works for her. Suppose her problem is that her older brother bullies her. First, she may try fighting back. If she has the innate fierceness needed, this strategy may work for her, even against an older, larger brother. But, if she can't make it work, she will most likely try something else. Maybe she will try a connection strategy next, such as befriending the bully and getting him to like her. If she can turn the bully into her protector, she has solved her problem. But if that strategy doesn't work, she may try hunkering down and just enduring it. If that strategy works, she will continue using it. She will naturally repeat whatever strategy works for her. It will become a habit and then a pattern, one which will influence how she relates to her brother (and others) for the rest of her life.

Getting Stuck in Overwhelm

In the previous section, we talked about how survival strategies grow out of ways of coping with feeling overwhelmed. Now let's consider what happens if you get stuck in overwhelm. This can cause a solution to a temporary problem to become a permanent stance toward life. This is when a temporary survival strategy becomes a permanent survival pattern.

When your body has accumulated too much charge, it will try to discharge the extra energy. It will spontaneously go into a natural healing process to try to return to the ground state. But it needs a sense of safety to do that, a situation that is soothing rather than frightening. When a hurt child runs to Mommy's lap, he is running to a safe place. As he cries or rages about what hurts, he is releasing the tension from his nervous system. He is also reaching out for her help in the discharge process. He needs to be held, soothed, and comforted. In order to discharge his fear, he needs to know that he is once again safe.

If he can stay long enough in a place that is safe enough, his body's natural healing process will run to completion and his system will relax back down to the ground state. The hurt will be completely resolved and he will once again feel happy and safe, trusting and open to the world. But what if he is not so fortunate? What if he gets stuck in overwhelm?

There are several ways this can happen. One way is shock trauma, a single event that causes the body to freeze and go into shock. Something bad happens and a high-charge state gets frozen into the body, held there by chronic tension. A full explanation of shock trauma is beyond the scope of our discussion here, but if you're interested in learning more, I refer you to Peter Levine's work, starting with *Waking the Tiger* (North Atlantic Books, 1997).

A person can also get stuck in overwhelm through developmental trauma. This is different from shock trauma in that it is not caused by a shock to the system, but by a repeated failure to get what you need. Instead of something bad happening to you, something good fails to happen to you. Because you can't get what you need, you can't complete that particular developmental stage, and you get stuck there. Again, your body uses chronic tension to manage your distress. We will go into this in more detail in the next chapter. For a more thorough discussion of the differences between shock trauma and developmental trauma, I recommend *Healing Developmental Trauma* by Laurence Heller and Aline LaPierre (North Atlantic Books, 2012).

A person can also get stuck in overwhelm if their natural healing process is repeatedly interrupted. If the healing process can't run to completion, the person's nervous system is never able to relax all the way back down to the ground state, and their body continues to hold some chronic tension. Even worse, if the person's attempts to heal are not just interrupted but punished, an additional layer of tension is added. This happens when a child is mocked or humiliated for seeking safety and comforting. It also happens if he's being threatened with violence for attempting to heal himself, as in *"You stop crying or I'll give you something to cry about."* Now he has two problems: his healing of the first hurt has been interrupted, and if he shows that he's hurting, he will be hurt again. So he's stuck. He can't heal and he can't reach out for help. He's still in overwhelm, but asking for comforting brings more overwhelm. The only way he can stop his body's natural attempts to discharge the extra energy as anger, tears, trembling, etc., is to once again tense his body.

In all three situations, the child gets stuck in overwhelm. In all three situations, he will adapt to his chronic distress by using muscular tension to manage his inner state. His body will learn to maintain that tension, both to suppress the unexpressed emotions and to dampen his awareness of them.

This chronic tension in his muscles becomes body armoring. It shapes how his life energy moves through his body. It shapes where his energy goes and doesn't go, and because more energy flowing to a particular part of the body tends to make it grow larger, it even influences what shape his body grows into. This chronic tension in the body becomes part of the physical foundation for the survival patterns and makes the patterns body-based. It makes them automatic physiological reactions to overwhelm, not just mental beliefs.

How Survival Patterns Become Self-Perpetuating

So far we've looked at why and how we create survival patterns. Now let's consider how they can take on a life of their own and become self-perpetuating.

The main way survival patterns perpetuate themselves is by distorting our experience of reality. They do this by shaping our attention, which leads to a whole cascade of other shifts. Schematically, the process looks like this:

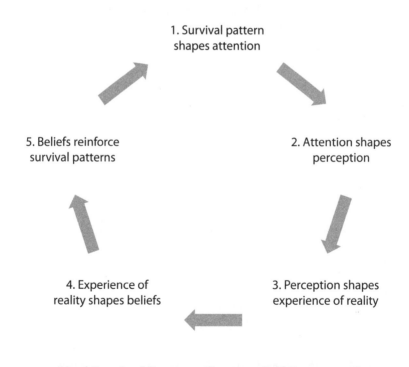

How Survival Patterns Become Self-Perpetuating

Let's go over this in more detail.

1. Our survival patterns shape our attention

This means that when you're in a survival pattern, it determines which details of your experience you attend to and which you ignore. It makes some details seem more important than they ordinarily would be. For instance, if you're in a fear pattern, it makes you more attentive to any signs of danger. If you're in a pattern focused on emotional connection, it makes you more attentive to any signs of approval or disapproval. And if you're in a pattern focused on power, it makes you more attentive to any signs of strength or weakness. We touched on this earlier, when we spoke of watching the Fear Channel versus watching the Love Channel.

To get a sense of how this works, imagine that you're in a dark house on a rainy, stormy night. The power just went out while you were watching a scary movie about the dead rising from the grave, and you're spooked. Now every creak of a floorboard and rattle of window seems like a cause for alarm. Your ears strain to hear any sound of the ghouls approaching. All your attention is now focused outward, scanning for danger. You are unlikely to even notice an internal experience, like feeling hungry or tired. What do they matter if your life is in danger? The fear has shaped where you put your attention and what you consider worth noticing.

Compare this to a similar night in the same house, sitting by a warm fire and reading a love letter from your sweetheart. Your attention is focused inward, on the warmth and fullness of the love in your chest and the sweet sadness of missing your beloved. The rain on the windows only adds to the poignancy of the scene. Your attention is on love, not on danger. It is focused inward, not outward. The ghouls could walk right in the back door and you probably wouldn't notice because your attention is on your inner experience.

Now let's add time to this equation. Imagine that, instead of being temporary, one of these two states becomes permanent in you: you're always focused outward, scanning for danger, or always focused inward on love and relationship. In either case, your attention becomes habituated to that focus. It no longer sees the whole picture, but only a slice of it.

What would cause a temporary stance of attention to become fixed like that? Well, trauma stuck in the body can cause it. Not only does the old trauma cause you to scan for anything similar to the wounding situation, but when you find something, the old trauma is re-triggered and your body is once again flooded with the old perceptions and feelings. In a very real sense, you are stuck in that traumatizing moment of time. Being stuck in that trauma causes that temporary stance of attention to become a more permanent *habit of attention*.

2. Our attention shapes our perception

We saw this illustrated in the examples above. In each scenario, certain details are seen as more important, which moves them into the foreground and makes them appear brighter and more vivid. Other, less important details fade into the background, where they become gray, dull, and flat. And all this happens at the level of raw sensory perception, before you even begin thinking about what you're perceiving.

This process is a natural part of focusing your attention. If the focus is temporary, it is the most efficient way to use your sense organs because it helps you vividly perceive what is important right now. But if your attention gets stuck, it begins to actually distort your perception of reality. It causes your habit of attention to skew your raw sensory perceptions in a more permanent way. Certain details become louder, clearer, and more vivid all of the time. Others fade into the background and stay there. This is how a persistent stance of attention creates a skewed sensory perception of the world.

3. Our perception shapes our experience of reality

We experience the world through our sensory perceptions and from them we build our picture of the world. So a skewed set of sensory inputs gives us a skewed experience of the world, and from this we build a distorted picture of the world. We don't know it's distorted, of course, because we have no other picture to compare it to, but it is distorted, nonetheless.

Because our sensory perceptions are so fundamental to our experience of the world, we usually don't ever question them. It may be hard to imagine that someone else's sensory perceptions could actually be different from your own, so let's look at some extreme examples. Some people are born without a sense of smell. For them, there are no smells in the world. Cleaning up vomit is the same as cleaning up pancake batter. That's a very different sensory experience than the average person has. Until these folks are told about smells, they must think the rest of us are crazy to be so repulsed by vomit.

Similarly, some people dream in color, while others dream in black and white. Some people's dreams include music, even whole symphonies, while others have mostly silent dreams. These four groups of dreamers have very different experiences of what's possible in the dream world. It's easy for us to see these different experiences of the dream world because, in the waking world, we have experienced all four of these states. We've seen movies in both color and black and white, and we've heard both symphonies and silence.

But suppose that in our waking life we hadn't had the full range of these experiences. Suppose we had experienced only one of these four states. Then all we would know of the world would be what we had experienced, and we would find it hard to believe anyone who described one of the other states. And that is exactly what happens to us in life. Each of us assumes that we are experiencing the world as it really is and that we know the whole truth of the situation. But in fact, because our habits of attention distort our raw sensory perceptions, we are experiencing only a slice of the world and mistaking it for the whole.

4. Our experience of reality shapes our beliefs

Since most of our beliefs are based on our experience, whatever shapes our experience also shapes our beliefs. Take the previous example, in which you were alone in a dark house, scared and scanning for danger. If that happened frequently during your childhood, you would probably believe that life is scary, dangerous, and lonely. That would be one of your core beliefs. On the other hand, if most of your childhood was spent in the second example, you might believe that life is mostly about love and longing, and that would be one of your core beliefs. Either way, you would have constructed a whole system of beliefs about the world that was consistent with your core experiences. And you would live inside the world you had constructed, believing it was the complete, real world.

5. Our beliefs reinforce our survival pattern

Now we come to the point where the entire process becomes self-perpetuating. Since what we believe determines where we put our attention and how we sort our experience, our patterned beliefs support and reinforce our habits of attention. If we are sorting for danger, for example, then all evidence of danger seems big and important and confirms our belief that the world is dangerous. This, in turn, makes us even more vigilant, which then further confirms our survival pattern's original view of the world and makes it seem indisputable.

So now the process has come full circle. We have seen how a survival pattern shapes our attention and experience of the world in ways that reinforce the pattern. And we have seen how trauma stuck in the body supplies the fuel that keeps the distorted perceptions and feelings alive and vivid and thereby holds that stance of attention in place.

This is what makes the survival patterns so resilient and self-sustaining. It is what allows a pattern formed in the first years of childhood to persist through the rest of a person's life, even though they long ago left behind the situation that caused them to adopt it. Although the person left the precipitating external environment when they left their family of origin, they still carry that environment inside themselves, in their body armoring, beliefs, and habits of attention. These distort their perceptions and recreate their old experiences for them wherever they go.

While each of the survival patterns distorts our experience of reality, they each distort it in their own particular way. So people who are stuck in different survival patterns actually experience different realities. Of course, we don't realize this. Stuck within our own survival patterns, each of us thinks our own experience is complete and accurate. This leads us to feel justified in maintaining our own view and discounting the views of those in other survival patterns. We may disagree with each other bitterly for years without ever seeing the real source of our disagreement. We will explore this point more fully after presenting an overview of the five survival patterns.

There is one more element that we need to note in seeing how survival patterns perpetuate themselves, and that is the role of identity structures. An identity structure is a self-image, an image you carry inside you of who you are and what your role is in relationship to others. If you were hurt a lot as a child, you might have an image of yourself as a "victim." That self-image will make you more likely to take on the role of the victim in a current situation. Or if you fought back as a child, you might have developed an image of yourself as a "warrior." That self-image will make you more likely now to take an aggressive stance, rather than a passive one, no matter what the situation. Other examples of self-images might be "achiever," "lover," "realist," and "dreamer."

Because a change to an identity structure tends to feel like a threat to the self, we usually resist it. Maintaining our familiar identity structures can actually feel to us like a matter of life and death, so we unconsciously try to eliminate any experience or evidence that would challenge them. People will often reveal that they are guarding an identity structure by saying something like *"This is who I am"* or *"That's just how I'm made."* Our need to maintain our old, familiar sense of "who I am" often makes us want to maintain our survival patterns, even when they are causing us suffering. This is also why we often fight so hard for our limitations. Those limitations have become part of who we think we are.

– 3 –

The Developmental Stages that Underlie the Survival Patterns

As a child grows, she* passes through a series of developmental stages. Ideally, during each stage she develops a new set of skills and uses them to accomplish the main task of that stage. We will differentiate the developmental stages according to those tasks and also name each stage for its main task.

As the child moves into a new developmental stage, new needs arise and she becomes sensitive to feeling deprived in that new area. Before a particular need arises, she is not sensitive to whether that need is being filled or not. For instance, a newborn baby is not attempting to develop autonomy and so will not feel deprived if her caretakers do not support her autonomy. However, a two year old *does* have a need to develop autonomy and is therefore very sensitive to whether or not her caretakers support her in this. If they punish her attempts to assert her autonomy, she will have to find a way to buffer herself from her feelings of frustration. If she is unable to succeed in asserting her autonomy, she may get stuck and be unable to complete this developmental stage.

---

* To avoid the cumbersomeness of having to continually say "he or she," I will say "he" in some parts of this chapter and "she" in others. In this section, I will assume the child is a girl. However, everything said about the girl in this section could just as easily have been said about a boy. When "he" is used, everything said about him could just as easily have been said about a girl.

The Developmental Stages that Underlie the Survival Patterns

Each of the five survival patterns can be seen as the result of getting stuck in a particular developmental stage, unable to learn the skills and complete the main task of that stage. So to understand the survival patterns, we must first understand the developmental stages that underlie them. The main tasks of the five developmental stages are:

1. Embodiment

2. Taking In

3. Putting Out

4. Trusting Others

5. Trusting Self

As a child succeeds in learning each stage's new skills and accomplishing its main task, she completes that stage and can then draw on her new abilities as she faces the challenges of the next stage. In this way, the skills acquired during one stage become the foundation for her success in the next stage.

However, if she fails to learn the skills and accomplish the main task of a particular stage, time does not stop so that she can catch up. Instead, new needs come online and push her into the next developmental stage even though she has not yet mastered the previous set of skills or laid a strong foundation for this next stage. In effect, she now has a hole in her growing set of developmental skills, a hole which makes it even harder for her to learn the skills needed to accomplish the main task of the new stage. Time continues to move on, however. Her body continues to grow, and she has to muddle through as best she can, using the skills she has to improvise some sort of work-around for the skills she lacks.

This does not mean that someone who completed the earlier developmental stages and didn't get stuck until a later stage is a "better" person than someone who got stuck at an earlier stage. It does mean that they have more developmental skills at their disposal for dealing with their feelings of overwhelm. It also means that they're more separated from their raw feelings and perceptions, and so less likely to feel overwhelmed by them. However, this distance from their own raw perceptions also has a downside: while those who made it through the earlier developmental stages and got caught only in the later patterns have stronger developmental skill sets, they also have weaker sensitivity skill sets. While they have more capacity to take action and accomplish things in the world, they have less capacity to connect and relate to other people, to animals, and to nature itself. (In Western cultures, especially here in the United States, we equate growing up with separating from other people, from nature, and even from our own subtle perceptions. When our children see things that we don't see, we invalidate their subtle perceptions, saying, "There's nothing there. Go to sleep." or "Don't be scared. It's only a dream." When we tell them that what they perceive isn't real, we're telling them to stop perceiving it, to shut off their innate sensitivity and subtle perception. This tends to shut down the inner capacities which would make them more energetically sensitive and capable of feeling.)

Whether we develop any particular survival pattern depends on the interplay of several factors. It depends on the depth of the difficulty we experience when our needs are not met. It depends on what talents and skills we have at that time to buffer ourselves from the difficulty. It also depends on whether our environment will allow that buffering method to succeed. If our buffering method succeeds, we will continue to use it. It will become a habit and, eventually, develop into a survival pattern. However, if it fails, either because we don't have the talents to pull it off or because the environment won't allow it, we will have to find another buffering method. So which survival pattern we adopt is a product of both nature and nurture. It is a product of the interaction of our needs, our inborn talents, and our environment.

As suggested earlier, each of us got stuck somewhere along the way, and so each of us has holes in our developmental skill sets. The good news is that our skill deficits do not have to be permanent. The skills that you didn't learn in childhood can be learned later on, even in adulthood. The bad news is that the trauma that blocked your learning of those skills the first time around is probably still stuck in your body and may block learning those skills now. Before you can learn them, that trauma may have to be cleared out of your body. While this may require some serious inner work, you can do it.

In order to heal our patterns and become able to thrive in the present, then, each of us must fill in the holes in our developmental skill sets and finish whatever developmental tasks we did not complete as children. If we got stuck in one of the earlier developmental stages, then we don't have the foundation needed to succeed in the later stages either, so we have to go back to where we first got stuck and re-build from there. Because we're now adults and have more skills and capacities than we had as children, our re-building process can be very rapid, but there is no substitute for building a strong, complete foundation.

People who successfully completed the early stages tend to take the early developmental skills for granted and assume that everyone has them. They often have a very hard time understanding that others might not already have those early skills. They may say to the person, *"What's wrong with you? Why don't you just get a grip and do it?"* But in order to see other people clearly, we must realize that not everyone has the skills needed to "just do it." Seeing this allows us to recognize when someone doesn't yet have those early skills and treat them with compassion.

In general, as we deal with a world full of people who still have big holes in their skill sets, we will be able to act with more skill and compassion if we adopt the attitude that *everyone is doing the best they can.* I suggest adopting this attitude toward yourself as well. Judgment will not help. Criticism will not help. Understanding and healing will help, and it is my hope that this book will promote these attitudes in all who read it.

Now let's take a quick look at the five developmental stages and the survival patterns that are created when a person gets stuck in each one. Later on, we will devote an entire chapter to describing each pattern in detail.

1. Embodiment – Claiming the Body

Embodiment takes place when the incoming spirit/soul is able to orient itself to the physical world, settle into the physical body, and claim it. We might say that the child's incoming spirit *attaches* to the physical world. In order to do that, it needs to experience the physical world as being sufficiently loving and safe.

If her early environment (including the womb) feels safe and loving enough, and if her caregivers are attuned to her and respond well enough to her needs, she will sense that it is safe to exist here in the physical world. She will be able to attach to the physical world, claim her physical body, and achieve embodiment. Her experience will be something like:

"I am safe here. I want to stay."

However, if something in her early environment/womb does not feel safe and loving enough, but instead shocks and scares her, then she won't have this felt sense of safety in her body and she won't be able to fully orient to the physical world and attach to it and her body. She won't believe the physical world is safe and she won't expect that her needs will be filled by anybody. This is the genesis of the *leaving pattern.* Her experience, in this case, is something like:

"I am scared. No one cares. I want to leave."

2. Taking In – Receiving, Holding, and Digesting

This stage occurs during the first years of life, when a baby's main activity is taking in and metabolizing both love and nourishment. If the baby is able to do this well enough, she will feel full and contented.

If her caregivers are able to figure out what she needs, provide it, and help her take it in, her body will have the felt sense that her needs are okay and that they will be filled. She will learn how to take in what she needs, and she will learn how to hold and digest what she takes in. In this case, her experience around needs will be something like:

"I have a need. I ask for it. I get it. I feel full and satisfied."

However, if she is not able to take in, hold, and metabolize what she needs, then she won't have this felt sense of fullness in her body. Instead, she will feel empty and deprived, and she will come to believe that her needs will never really be filled. This is the genesis of the *merging pattern*. Her experience around needs will then be something like:

"I have a need. Maybe I shouldn't. I can't figure it out. I feel empty. You fix it."

If she tries to solve this problem by shifting from being the needy baby to being the nurturing mother, she has shifted into the *compensated merging pattern*. Now her experience around needs becomes something like:

"I have a need. I ignore it and project it onto you. I will fill your needs."

3. Putting Out – Action and Self-Expression

This stage begins at about 18 months, as will and strength first come online, the word "no" appears, and the toddler begins the separation-individuation process. As the toddler begins expressing a self, rather than just a need, "I," "me," and "mine" appear.

If his caregivers are able to allow him to separate from them by exerting his own will and acting to get what he needs, he will learn that he has the power to get what he wants. He will also learn that it is safe to be a separate individual with his own feelings, will, and strength, and that it is safe to express himself. In essence, he will learn how to put energy out into the world, both as action and as self-expression. His experience around needs will be something like:

"I have a need. I figure out what I need. I act to get it."

However, if his caregivers thwart his actions and punish him for acting separately from them, then he won't learn that he can act to get what he needs or develop a felt sense of pride in his own separate abilities. Instead of expecting to succeed in getting what he wants, he will expect to fail. Now the only way he can separate from his caregivers is by resisting their wishes. But obvious resistance only brings more punishment, so he learns to hide his resistance and avoid expressing his feelings or taking any action. This is the genesis of the *enduring pattern*. His experience around needs will be something like:

"I have a need. I can't express my need. I can't act to get it. I can't win. I can only hide and resist."

4. Trusting Others – Outer Support and Guidance

As his will and strength increase during his third and fourth years, even a child who has succeeded at expressing himself and acting to get what he wants will still need to feel contained and protected by something larger than himself. He will need to know that his power is limited by a good, kind, larger force, a force that will keep him safe, even from himself. This allows him to relax and trust the world, knowing that something bigger and stronger is there for him, taking care of him.

If his caregivers are able to tolerate his growing strength and still lovingly contain him, he learns that there are limits on what he can do. And if they are able to protect him, he learns that he is protected and cared for by something larger that he can trust. He will learn both to trust others, and that, while he can have his own power, he does not have to be the ultimate power to be safe. His experience around needs will be something like:

"I have a need. I figure out what I need. I act to get what I need, but there are limits on what I can do. I am contained and kept safe by something good that is larger than me."

However, if his caregivers are not able to lovingly contain and protect him, then he won't have this felt sense of something containing, protecting, and caring for him. He won't expect that anything will contain or protect him, but instead will believe that he faces the world alone and must always be ready to fight to protect himself. Now, being the biggest and strongest fighter is his only hope for safety. Since having needs makes him feel weak and vulnerable, he disowns them. This is the genesis of the *aggressive pattern*. His experience around needs will then be something like:

"If I need something, I take it. I have to do it all myself. No one supports me or cares for me. Nothing contains me. I am alone."

5. Trusting Self – Inner Support and Guidance

As soon as a child learns that she *can* do, she faces a new challenge, and that is deciding *what* to do. She needs a way to make those decisions.

If her caregivers are able to support her in finding her own inner truth and in making her own decisions, she will learn that she can trust her own inner wisdom. She will learn to trust herself and the Source within. Her experience around needs will be something like:

"I have a need. I act to get it. I am guided by something that is good, flexible, and intelligent inside of me. I am a spark of it, and we are in constant contact."

However, if her caregivers are blind to the Source within her, discount her inner wisdom, and insist that she rely only on their rules to guide her, then she won't develop a felt sense of her own inner wisdom. She won't believe that her own feelings are important or that there is a source of wisdom within her. Instead, she will ignore her own inner experience and believe that her only value is in her outer performance. She will believe that all wisdom comes from outside, and she will look only to outside authorities and rules for guidance. This is the genesis of the *rigid pattern*. Now her experience around needs has become something like:

"I have a need. I can act to get it, but I must obey the rules. Everyone must obey the rules. I am guided by an authority that is above me and outside of me. I must obey it."

There are two other themes that deserve attention at this point: first, none of the survival patterns is better or worse than any other — each pattern has its own gifts and its own struggles. Second, from inside its own worldview, none of the survival patterns is able to comprehend the stuckness of the other patterns. Each pattern looks at the stuckness of the other patterns and thinks, *"What is wrong with you? Why don't you stop that? I am not stuck that way, so why are you?"*

This inability to understand and empathize with the difficulties of those who are caught in another survival pattern seems to be more acute the farther the other pattern is from your own in the developmental sequence. Those who do the earlier patterns (leaving and merging) look at those who do the later patterns (aggressive and rigid) and wonder *"How can you be so mean and unfeeling?"* At the same time, those who do the later patterns look at those who do the earlier patterns and think *"What's the problem? Get a grip! Stand up for yourself!"*

So, if you find yourself judging one of the survival patterns while you're reading about it, take a step back and ask yourself, *"What pattern am I in right now? And how is this pattern coloring my view of what I'm reading?"* Noticing what sort of judgments you have about each of the other survival patterns can tell you a lot about which patterns you go into. And shedding the distortions of your own survival patterns will help you see those you love through clearer and kinder eyes.

Other Factors in the Creation of the Survival Patterns

There are many routes an individual child may follow in adopting a particular survival pattern. As she interacts with her environment, she finds her own unique path, so generalizations about which environments create which survival patterns are only generally accurate. They may explain most people's route to a pattern, but they cannot explain every case.

In the last section, we talked about how getting stuck in a particular developmental stage tends to create a particular survival pattern in the body. While that is true, it is not the entire truth. Many parents report that their child was "born that way," meaning that they were exhibiting the talents needed for a particular pattern very early on, probably well before they adopted it as a survival strategy. And extreme circumstances can create a survival pattern in a child before the usual age for that pattern, or in some cases, a survival pattern may be created later, in response to some very difficult life situation.

There are clearly other factors at work here. Some of those factors seem to be inborn, while others are environmental. I believe there are four factors that influence which survival patterns get conditioned into a child's body. They are:

1. A child can get stuck in a particular developmental stage, as detailed above.

2. A child can *template* the pattern, that is, their body copies it from someone else they see using the survival pattern.

3. The child can have an inborn tendency for energy to move through their body in a certain direction or manner, which predisposes them to a particular survival pattern.

4. The child may need a particular survival pattern to accomplish their life purpose.

Because some of these factors exist mostly in the physical world, while others exist mostly in the energetic or spiritual worlds, your own beliefs about reality will naturally influence how you see the situation and which of these factors you see as credible.

If you start with a belief in physical materialism, that is, the worldview that recognizes only the physical world and does not recognize the existence of anything beyond it, you are likely to give more weight to the environmental factors, such as getting stuck in a particular developmental stage and templating a survival pattern from someone else.

If you also recognize the existence of an energy world, or at least believe that there is a life energy that flows through the human body and animates it, you may be open to the possibility that a child can be born with a tendency for his life energy to flow in a particular way, a way which supports the development of a particular survival pattern and discourages the development of others. There appear to be five main ways that the free flow of life energy through the body can be distorted:

1. It can tend to flow *away from others*.
   This predisposes a person to the leaving pattern.

2. It can tend to flow *toward others*.
   This predisposes a person to the merging pattern.

3. It can tend to flow *in and down*.
   This predisposes a person to the enduring pattern.

4. It can tend to flow *up and out*.
   This predisposes a person to the aggressive pattern.

5. The flow can tend to be *constricted*.
   This predisposes a person to the rigid pattern.

Lastly, we have the possibility that there is a spiritual world which underlies and creates both the physical and energy worlds, and that each person is born with a life purpose. This view holds that we develop the survival patterns we need to have in order to accomplish our life purpose.

Those who believe in reincarnation say that the whole purpose of being born into human life is to learn, and that we learn through personal experience. If we can learn through pleasant experiences, that's great, but usually some pain and suffering are required to get us to pay attention enough to learn the next lesson. As the Chinese proverb says, *"A teacher is a problem that you can't get away from."* If we can get away from it, we usually do. But if we can't get away, we have to face the problem and solve it. And that is when we learn something new. This way of thinking says that the earth is a kind of school: our spirit is born into physical life here again and again, and gradually accumulates wisdom through personal experience.

According to this view, we set up the general outlines of each life beforehand to help us learn whatever lessons we have chosen. Each life has a purpose (some important lesson that we are trying to learn through our experiences), and each life has problems designed to push us toward learning that lesson. We then choose to be born into a particular body, in a particular time and place, with particular parents and siblings, because those circumstances will create the problems that will push us to learn this life's lessons. From this perspective, the adoption of a particular survival pattern is not just the result of getting stuck at the associated stage of development, it is also a method of honing a particular set of skills — skills that we will need to accomplish our life purpose.

Eastern religions and cultures tend to espouse the reincarnational view, while Western ones do not. Some teachers of the character structure patterns endorse the life purpose view; others do not. For a Western-based compilation of accounts of the journey between lives, I would recommend reading *Journey of Souls* and *Destiny of Souls* (Llewellyn Publications, 1994 and 2000), both by Michael Newton.

Personally, I do not have a big enough view of reality to know for sure whether this way of thinking is correct, but I have observed several things. First, it is the most elegant explanation I've come across for why there is so much suffering in the world. It says that there is suffering because suffering is needed to focus our attention on what we are trying to learn. However, as we develop the skills to pay attention and learn without suffering, our suffering diminishes. As I look around me at the world, I observe that this seems to be true.

Second, this way of thinking reframes life's problems from "Something has gone wrong" or "Something evil is trying to hurt me" to "What am I trying to learn?" I have observed that adopting this view tends to decrease a person's suffering considerably. Life, then, is no longer a struggle between good and evil, but a movement from ignorance to wisdom. Suffering is only a mechanism for learning. And as soon as we are able, we can let it go and begin to learn through love and joy.

– 4 –

A Brief Overview of the Survival Patterns

EACH SURVIVAL PATTERN GROWS OUT of a strategy that a child employs to buffer itself from the sense of overwhelm it feels when its needs are not being met. With repeated use, the survival strategy gets conditioned into the child's body and becomes a survival pattern. What defines a survival pattern is the particular strategy it uses to manage the sense of overwhelm, not the age when the pattern first appears or the wounding that happened at that time. Although all five patterns perform the same function — they buffer the child from directly experiencing the feelings of overwhelm — they employ five different methods to accomplish this.

People go into their survival patterns to varying degrees of intensity. Some people are caught in a pattern nearly all the time. For them, that survival pattern rules their life. They identify with it deeply and it shapes every aspect of their reality and behavior. Conversely, other people wear a survival pattern so lightly that it shows up in their behavior only in moments of extreme distress, while the rest of the time they are able to stay present. Most people fall somewhere in between these two extremes.

This variation is partly due to the fact that early childhood environments also exist on a spectrum, ranging from the nearly ideal to the unspeakably horrible. A milder, more ideal early environment tends to produce lighter patterning in a child, depending, of course, on the child's sensitivity to that particular kind of wounding. A more extreme early environment tends to produce more deeply entrenched patterning in a child, again depending on that particular child's sensitivity to that kind of wounding. While the severity of the wounding influences whether and how deeply the child goes into the pattern, there is a great deal of variation from person to person in the amount of wounding needed to induce a particular survival pattern. What one child finds intolerable, another may hardly notice. This seems to depend on the sensitivities and talents that we bring with us and, perhaps, on what we came here to do and learn.

Let's look at each of the five survival patterns in developmental order.

Leaving – Here, the wounding happened very early, most likely during pregnancy, when the baby's incoming spirit did not experience the safety that it needed to complete its transition into the physical world. During this time, the developmental task is embodiment, the process by which the spirit re-orients itself from the spirit world to the physical world and bonds with the physical world and the physical body. Ideally, the physical body and the physical world feel safe enough for the baby's spirit to settle into the body and claim it. Then her spirit can use the body as a reference point, a center to return to if it gets lost or shattered. As time goes on, her physical body then develops an energetic boundary that keeps out foreign energies and increases her felt sense of safety.

In the formation of the leaving pattern, however, something in the physical world repeatedly shocks the incoming spirit so badly that its attention fragments, causing it to flee back to the spirit world to protect itself. Being shocked out of the body this way interferes with the spirit's process of orienting itself to the physical world and rooting itself in the physical body. These shocks leave the newborn baby's delicate self so vulnerable that any intense energy directed at her can cause her self to once again shatter into fragments. And without a felt reference point in the body to return to, she finds it difficult to reassemble her self.

Such repeated shattering prevents the child from ever coalescing a strong sense of self, firmly anchoring it in the body, and creating the strong energetic boundary around her body that will make her less vulnerable to future shocks. This means that, even as an adult, she will be easily overwhelmed. Her self will tend to fragment under pressure, which may leave her unable to function because she cannot find a center from which to operate. Most likely she will maintain a strong connection to the spirit world and will be highly creative, sensitive, and aware of energetic phenomena. But she will doubt her right to exist in the physical world and will have trouble functioning here.

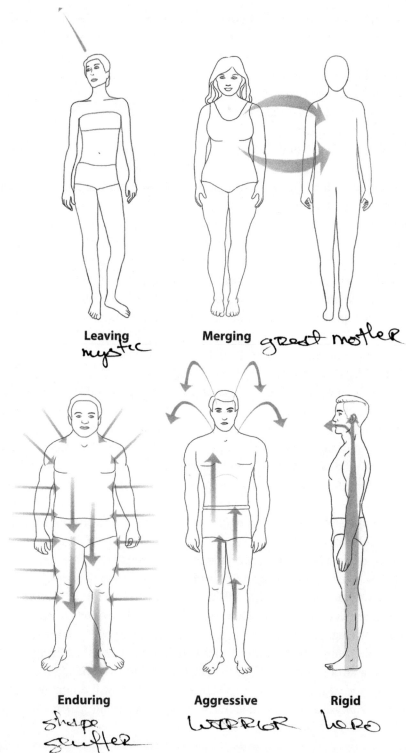

Leaving *mystic*   **Merging** *great mother*

Enduring *shape shifter*   **Aggressive** *WARRIOR*   **Rigid** *hero*

Merging & Compensated Merging – Here the unfulfilled need was for nurturance. The deprivation happened during the first few years of life, usually in relation to nursing and/or bottle feeding. The child didn't get or couldn't take in the nourishment and soothing she needed, so she never felt full and satisfied. The tension of being hungry or otherwise upset was not fully released, so some anxiety always remained in her system. This anxiety further inhibited her ability to take in and metabolize nourishment and she got stuck in a cycle of needing, not being able to effectively receive, and never getting full. This left her feeling hollow and empty inside.

There are two ways that she can handle this situation. She can identify with the need and wait for rescue, or she can project her need onto others and then try to fulfill their needs. The first method leads to the pure merging pattern, the second to the compensated merging pattern. These are fundamentally the same survival pattern, but in the compensated merging pattern the feelings of need and helplessness are covered over by a pretense of self-reliance and power.

A child in the pure merging pattern will be clingy, fragile, and need a lot of attention. A child in the compensated merging pattern will act self-reliant too soon by rejecting her own needs and focusing on helping others instead. While the second child looks more functional, the compensation is only a mask covering the unfinished work of this stage of development. In both situations, she practices referencing others, but avoids referencing herself. The gift of this strategy is that she then becomes skillful at sensing the needs of others and providing what's needed.

Enduring – At around the age of two, a new need arises in the child. He is now walking and talking and grappling with the discovery that he is separate from his mother. This discovery of separateness brings with it the need for autonomy — the need to be in charge of his own body and actions. He begins to say "No!" and to oppose attempts to control him.

While this assertion of his autonomy is exactly what he needs to do to complete this developmental stage, this is also a distinctly new behavior, something a baby doesn't do. If a parent or caregiver cannot tolerate his budding autonomy, a conflict will arise. As the parent tries to suppress his autonomy by controlling and punishing him, he will feel humiliated and enraged.

He will actively resist the parent's domination for as long as he can, but will eventually conclude that he cannot win and will switch to resisting passively. He will withdraw deep inside himself to protect his last shred of sovereign territory and, in a last act of autonomy, turn his will against himself to suppress his own desire to act and even to express himself. He will hunker down and limit his opposition to *"You can't make me."* This method of relating to the world is the core of the enduring survival pattern.

To make this survival strategy work, a child must have the will and strength required to silently persevere, even while enduring hardship and mistreatment. He does this by sending his life energy, even his very self, down into the ground and hiding it there. The difficulty is that he gets stuck down there, unable to move and act in the world. The benefit is that people who do this survival pattern are typically more grounded than others and often have great stamina.

Aggressive – Here, the unmet need was the need to feel contained and protected by something larger and stronger. This child won the battle for autonomy and felt proud of his strength and will. But then, in what felt to him like a life or death situation, he discovered that what he loved and trusted was not there to protect him. So he faced his fear alone and survived by summoning all his internal resources and willing himself through it. He felt betrayed, and it was his trust in others that was shattered. The unfulfilled need was once again safety, but here the focus was on the interpersonal, emotional safety of being able to depend on others.

This feeling of being failed or betrayed by what he thought was protecting him can be created in several different ways. In one scenario, the child simply has such a big energy that his parents are not able to energetically contain him. He wins all the battles, but discovers that he faces the world alone. Conversely, the parent may be authoritarian and dominating, but this child refuses to give in, even though he loses most of the fights.

In a third scenario, one parent seduces him into a coalition against the other. In doing this, the seducing parent is ignoring the child's needs and using the child to meet his or her own needs. The seduction may include sexuality, but it is often purely emotional. When he realizes that his love for the parent was used to manipulate him, the child concludes that loving is dangerous and that it opens the door to being used and betrayed. He closes his heart and unconsciously resolves, "You will *never* do that to me again."

The child who develops the aggressive pattern has developed a cohesive sense of self, a strong will, and the ability to defend his own personal space, but he is always a little guarded. He finds it hard to trust or depend on others, or even to let them have their own space — space that he does not control. He still harbors a deep, unconscious terror that he will once again be used and betrayed.

Dominating every situation becomes his only way of creating a sense of safety for himself. He does, however, become skillful at making things happen in the world, and this becomes one of the gifts of the aggressive pattern.

Rigid – The injury here was that the parents could not value the child's inner experience. Having lost contact with their own inner life, they could not nurture their child's inner life. Instead, they focused on the child's appearance and performance, on things like manners, posture, correctness, and grades. They taught her to follow the rules they followed, and to obey the authority they obeyed. They could love their child for her achievements and performance, but not for her feelings and beingness.

Each of us needs our inner self, our being, to be seen and valued. If our parents see only our appearance and performance, we tend to lose contact with our inner experience and come to believe that our surface — our performance — is all that we are. Without contact with our inner self, we are unable to find our own inner guidance, so we have to rely on an outer form of guidance to help us make decisions.

A child who suffers this injury becomes focused on the forms and rules of life and loses touch with life's essence and substance. She tends to experience the world indirectly, through words, rather than directly through sensations and feelings. Rules replace personal feelings in her decision making process. She may use language well and become a terrific performer, but for her, doing has replaced being, and the map has replaced the territory. In new situations, her plea will be, *"Tell me the rules,"* because without the rules, she has no way to navigate.

When extra energy hits her system, she will attempt to contain it so that it doesn't really affect her and interfere with her performance. Instead of allowing it to emotionally move her, she will shunt the energy into activity — she will get busy and do something. While people who go into this survival pattern may not have much feeling, creativity, or color in their lives, they are often very successful on the outside, living in model homes with perfect lawns.

Primary and Secondary Patterns

Now that we've had a brief first look at the five survival patterns, it's important to also notice that people typically go into more than one pattern. When they feel overwhelmed, they first go into their primary pattern. If that pattern is not solving the problem at hand, they will shift into their secondary, or backup, pattern. Some people even go into a third pattern, although this is rare. So, as you read through the descriptions of the survival patterns, be aware that you probably do two of them, not just one. You may go into one much more often than the other, or you may do them about equally.

This observation that each person does two patterns, arranged as a primary and a backup, came to me through the oral teachings of Lynda Caesara. She received it as an oral teaching from Harley Swift Deer Regen.* I have not seen this insight from any other source. Lacking this piece of the puzzle, some writers have suggested that each of us does all of the patterns to varying degrees. I believe that this is a mistake, which arises out of defining the survival patterns as collections of behaviors, rather than as survival strategies that a person habitually employs to buffer himself from feelings of overwhelm. The thing to watch for, in my opinion, is what strategy a person employs first when distressed and, if that one fails, what strategy the person switches to next. These are the person's primary and secondary patterns.

Simply exhibiting some of the behaviors of a given pattern is not the same as adopting the pattern as a survival strategy. You may have taken on the behavior of a certain pattern because that was what was expected in your family or community, even though you couldn't make the behavior work as a buffer against your distress. Similarly, if your parents did a particular pattern and trained you in its skills, you may have learned that pattern's skills, even though you don't use them as a survival strategy. Or you may have been blessed with the talents of a particular pattern, but never developed those talents into a defense strategy. To determine whether you do a particular pattern, notice how you try to protect yourself when you feel overwhelmed. That's the key.

We will discuss primary and secondary patterns more fully after describing each survival pattern in depth in its own chapter.

People in Different Survival Patterns
Experience Different Realities

Now let's briefly consider how going into different survival patterns affects how we communicate with each other. Have you ever been in a disagreement

---

* Harley Swift Deer Regen said he got this teaching from a psychotherapist, whose name I do not know. Harley Swift Deer is now dead, but his organization, the Deer Tribe, can be reached through their website, *www.dtmms.org*.

with someone and been completely baffled by their description of the situation? Maybe you said to yourself, *"They must be blind,"* or *"They must be crazy,"* or even *"What an idiot!"* Most likely, what was happening was that both of you were in pattern, but in different patterns. Your perception of reality was distorted by your survival pattern in one direction, and the other person's perception of reality was distorted by their survival pattern in a different direction. *So the two of you were actually perceiving different realities.* Each of you was convinced that your own view was accurate, of course, because it matched the way you usually see the world. What neither of you realized was that your usual views were distorted.

So, is there any way that two people can see the same reality and agree on what they're seeing? Yes, there are two ways this can happen. First, this can occur when both people are in the same survival pattern. Second, it can occur when both people are present, that is, not in any pattern.

When both people are in the same survival pattern, their views of reality are distorted in similar ways, so they are seeing similar realities. Neither reality is accurate, but they won't notice that, because they have no accurate view to use for comparison. Instead, they feel reassured by their agreement. They interpret it as support for their belief that they are seeing the whole truth of the situation.

We all like this feeling, so we seek it out. We choose friends who run the same survival patterns we do, and we join groups that validate our patterns. Those who fear that danger lurks around every corner feel safer in the company of others who also see danger (both are watching the Fear Channel). Those who value connection are happiest in the company of others who also value connection (both are watching the Love Channel). And those who believe in following the rules find comfort in the company of others who also value the rules (as long as they value the *same* rules, whether those rules are "law and order" or "free love").

The second situation in which two people can see the same reality occurs when they are both present, that is, when neither of them is in pattern. Now their views of reality are much more accurate and therefore much closer to each other. Obviously, this is a much better situation. It is also the only path to actually resolving disagreements that are based on being in different patterns. This is why it is so important for each of us to recognize when we have gone into pattern and take steps to get ourselves out of pattern.

– 5 –

The Basic Skills Needed for Inner Work

BEFORE WE EXPLORE EACH SURVIVAL pattern in more detail, we need to review the basic skills that we all need to develop in order to succeed when doing major inner work. Unfortunately, few healing methods teach all of these skills, so you may have to seek help from several methods to learn them all. During the process of your inner work, you will need to develop the inner witness, learn how to attend to raw sensory experience, practice the basic energy skills, and disidentify from the inner critic.

Developing the Inner Witness

When you start doing therapy or any sort of self-reflective inner work, your first task is to develop the Inner Witness, also known as the Observing Self. The inner witness does not judge or comment on your experience. Its job is simply to record what you think, feel, say, and do — moment by moment — so that after the fact you can go back and walk through the experience again to see how you got from point A to point B.

For instance, suppose you're remarried after a bitter divorce, and you're going out for the evening with your new husband. But you're not quite ready yet, and your husband mildly says, *"Come on, Honey, we'll be late"* and you suddenly find yourself enraged and screaming at him. What happened? How did you get from "not quite ready yet" to enraged and screaming? You can ask your inner witness to very slowly play back for you all the steps in between. As you review the steps, you can begin to see the connections. Maybe your inner dialogue went something like this:

Uh-oh, it's getting late. But I still have this one more thing to do to get ready. If I don't do it, I won't feel fully dressed for this party.

But if I take the time to do it, I'll be late again. I hate that.

What's wrong with me? Why can't I be on time? [self-attack]

He'll probably complain about it again. I really hate that. He's got no right! [attacking the other]

My first husband used to complain about it, and then, when he left me for his stupid secretary, he pretended that it was because I was late so often. [now furious and lost in the past] *Damn him! It wasn't my fault!*

At this point, your hapless second husband says, *"Come on, Honey, we'll be late"* and you bite his head off, not distinguishing between him and your first husband.

If you have not developed your inner witness, you may believe that your anger must have been caused by something your new husband did, and your mind will get busy looking for the evidence to justify that belief. But if you have the ability to go back through your own experience second by second, you'll realize that what angered you was a hurt from the past and that the present situation only reminded you of it.

Now you know some important things:

1. You are still hurt and angry about the past situation.

2. You are not being hurt right now.

3. You are caught in a reaction based on your past.

4. Your new husband did not cause your upset.

Your inner witness has helped you learn something about yourself and come back to being more present in the here and now.

Developing the inner witness is the first step required for all inner work. It is the mirror you look into to see yourself more clearly. Its job is simply to show you a clear reflection of yourself. It does not judge. It does not comment in any way. It just plays back the movie of everything that was going on, both inside you and outside you.

Attending to Raw Sensory Experience

Along with developing the Inner Witness, each of us needs to be able to perceive our own raw sensory experience, and to do that, we need to learn to tell the difference between our sensory experience and our mind's interpretation of it. Many of us spend most of our lives up in our heads — commenting on our experience, deciding what it means, and telling ourselves stories about it. Those of us who disregard the raw sensations in our bodies, and those who dissociate so that we don't feel them, may live our entire lives with very little direct experience of our own lives, that is, of our raw felt sense perceptions.

This leaves us with an impoverished experience of life. While our minds have great value, they are not where real life takes place. We live in a physical world, and our lives happen at the interface between our awareness and the physical world. It is in our raw sensory experience of the world that we are most alive. That is where real life happens, not in our thoughts about it. And the only way to be present with our raw sensory experience is to take the mind off its throne and put it aside for the moment.

When we are lost in our inner commentary, when we are absorbed in memories or fantasies, we have left our felt sense experience of the moment, and while we are gone, we are missing the Now. The only time real life is happening is Now. And the only place it is happening is Here. So the only way to fully engage real life is to be present in the Here and Now. That means putting your attention on your five senses, on your raw sensory experience, rather than on your thoughts, beliefs, and stories. It means putting your attention especially on feeling the core of your own body. It is in your inner felt sense of your core that you can find your self most vividly. And it is there that you can discover the self that you may have been looking for in your mind.

Let's clarify the distinction between experiencing life through the mind and experiencing it directly, through raw sensory perceptions. The mind is the place of thinking: of reasoning, understanding, evaluating, drawing conclusions, and making decisions. It is the place where we deal with concepts, like up and down, in and out, and cause and effect. It is where we make judgments, like good and bad, right and wrong, and true and false. And it is in the mind that we create the beliefs and stories that define for us who we are and how we interact with the world.

All of these activities share one important quality — they are not the raw data, but things we do with the raw data. They are the results of digesting the raw data. They are derived from the raw data — and so they are one step removed from it.

The raw data exist only in the present moment and only in our own direct experience: in experiences of texture, pressure, movement, size, weight, shape, temperature, location, taste, smell, color, brightness, sound, pitch, vibration, prickliness, tension, pain, pleasure, and the like. In these experiences, there is an aliveness, a freshness and immediacy. They are happening right now, right here, to you.

As an example, let's consider the difference between thinking about a strawberry and actually eating one. In your mind, you probably have a lot of information about strawberries — information like their typical size and color, where they're grown, how they're grown, where you buy them, how much they cost, how you feel about the pesticides used in growing them, how long they stay fresh, and so on. You may have years of accumulated information about them, stories of your interactions with them, knowledge about them, beliefs about them, and even judgments about them.

All of this knowledge has value, but it is not the direct experience of tasting a strawberry right here, right now. To get that experience, you must put aside the thoughts and focus your attention on the sensations of a strawberry in your mouth, right now. The easiest way to do that is to put an actual strawberry in your mouth and bite into it. Try this, if you can, and notice how just focusing on the taste and texture and juiciness tends to turn off your thoughts. Notice how, if you love the taste, your whole body relaxes in order to just take it in. Notice how you are experiencing *this* strawberry *now*, not strawberries in general. You are getting the experience first-hand, as raw sensory perceptions.

If you don't have a strawberry handy, you may be able to call up a sense memory of biting into a juicy strawberry. (A sense memory is a memory in which you recall the raw sensations of the experience, rather than your thoughts about it. Recalling an experience this way is easier for some people than for others, but it is a skill that everyone can develop.) If you are very skilled at recalling sense memories, it may be nearly as vivid as a present moment experience. If sense memory is harder for you, you may find yourself shifting into thinking instead of sensing.

Either way, notice not only how easy it is for you to taste a strawberry, but also how easy or difficult it is for you to stay in touch with your direct sense perceptions while you're upset or when you are attempting to accomplish a task. You may need to practice this skill repeatedly for months to become skillful at it. Begin with simple exercises, like just tasting the strawberry, and gradually add more complexity, like staying with your raw perceptions while performing a task rapidly. As you practice, you will notice that life becomes more vivid, fresh, and immediate for you.

Developing Basic Energy Skills

There are four basic energy skills that are needed for healthy, adult functioning. Ideally, each of us would have learned all four of these skills automatically in childhood, the same way that we learned to maintain our balance, moment to moment. However, very few of us were that fortunate, so most of us need to consciously practice these skills as adults until they become second nature and we do them automatically in every moment. Modern psychology tends to focus on the mind and emotions while ignoring the movement of energy through the body, so it often either ignores these skills or touches on them only peripherally. This is unfortunate, since these four energy skills are fundamental to our optimal functioning, as well as to the healing process itself.

These energy skills are also needed for getting yourself out of pattern and back to presence. In the chapters on the five survival patterns, we will discuss each of these skills in more depth. For now, here is a brief summary of each skill:

Core: This is the skill of holding your attention on and feeling the center of your own body. It is what gives you a felt sense of self. It is required for referencing yourself and perceiving what you actually feel and want.

Ground: This is the skill of energetically connecting yourself to the earth, of having a relationship with what supports you, both physically and energetically. It is what gives you a felt sense of that support.

Edge or Boundary: This is the skill of creating and holding an energetic boundary around your personal space, also known as your bubble. Just as each cell in your body has a cell membrane that regulates what enters and leaves the cell, each of us needs to have an energetic membrane around our personal space that regulates what enters and leaves our space. This boundary is also necessary for building an energetic charge within the body so that you can take effective action in the world.

Me/Not Me: This is the skill of distinguishing between what is you and what is other (not you). Since other people's thoughts, feelings, and energies can get into your space and cause you to be confused about who you are and what you think and feel, you need a way to clean out your body and your personal space, removing everything that is "not me." If you have other people's feelings in your body, mixed in with your own, it can be very hard to figure out what you actually feel.

Disidentifying from the Inner Critic

"The beatings will continue until morale improves."

Inside each of us, there is a voice that criticizes us whenever we do something wrong. This voice is called the inner critic, and it is an amalgamation of all the commands we heard as a child to *"Be good," "Tell the truth," "Stand up straight," "Don't hit your brother," "Don't draw on the walls," "Don't talk with your mouth full," "Don't run with scissors," "Don't talk back,"* etc., etc., etc. Every time Mom, Dad, or whoever had power over us instructed us on what to do or not do, our little brain recorded it. Over time, we built up a library of their voices and mixed them together into one voice that tells us Who We Should Be.

The Job of the Superego

The inner critic is part of something larger that Freud called the "superego." It develops in early childhood, roughly between two and five years of age. The superego's job is to stop you from doing things that will get you in trouble with your parents and caretakers. It tries to keep you inside the Good Boy/Good Girl box they have defined, where you are loved and safe. The inner critic helps out by becoming a kind of inner policeman, interrupting you the moment you have an impulse to do something bad, and scolding you to stop you from actually doing it.

Of course, to stop you it has to beat down an awful lot of your impulses and desires. After all, you *want* that cookie, dinnertime or not. To make you obey, it criticizes and shames you and calls you names. Anything you've seen others do, it copies and uses against you. Its tone can range from merely devaluing to vicious and hateful. This changes you from a free, spontaneous, uninhibited child into an internally censored, well-behaved child. Your parents like this, of course, and praise you for being such a good boy or girl.

Developing a superego is an important and necessary step for any child. Now you have an internal mechanism that can regulate your behavior, and some kind of inner self-regulation is much needed. For the first time, something is able to intervene between having an impulse and acting on it. For the first time, how others will respond to your action enters your decision-making process. This is a real step forward, although ideally it would not include the self-hatred that is so common in Western cultures.

The superego is composed of three parts:

- the ideal self-image

- the inner praiser

- the inner critic

The ideal self-image literally holds all your internalized images of the perfect you — the one that Mom and Dad want you to be, the one that they love best. These are your images of the Good Boy or Good Girl, of *Who I Should Be*.

Each time you have an impulse to do something, that impulse is compared to your ideal self-image. If the impulse fits with Who I Should Be, your inner praiser speaks up and says *"Good boy!"* or *"Good girl!"* In response, you feel worthy and proud. You like the praise, so you act like that more often. Every time your impulse or action doesn't fit with Who I Should Be, your inner critic attacks you. It says *"Bad boy!"* or *"Bad girl!"* In response, you feel unworthy and ashamed. You don't like those feelings, so you try to avoid acting like that.

But the voice of the inner critic is not your own voice. It is only the voices of the people who raised you. For some people, this inner voice is so clear in their head that they can tell you exactly which parent is speaking. For other people, all the voices have been mixed together into one voice that they think is their own. And for some, there isn't a voice at all, but only a bad feeling in the body, as if the voice is speaking in their unconscious and only the bad feeling rises into awareness.

It's important to distinguish here between the inner critic and your conscience. Your conscience is based more on empathy and compassion for others, so it develops later, as those abilities come online. It also offers you advice about what to do, and it matures along with you as you develop. The inner critic, however, doesn't mature much after it is formed, so for the rest of your life it operates with the understanding and maturity of a five-year-old. New situations are measured only against "Will Mom like this? Will Dad be mad?

Will I get in trouble for this?" It is a young part of you, trying to protect you in its 5-year-old way. And the inner critic doesn't just advise you, it attacks you in order to control your behavior. A critic attack always devalues you in some way. It always makes you feel small or stupid or bad in some way. That devaluing is the hallmark of the inner critic and the way you can recognize it every time.

The superego's purpose is to maintain homeostasis in your psyche, which means keeping you within the Good Boy/Good Girl box and not letting anything new happen. Obviously, it is not a fan of inner work. It will attack you for exploring outside the known territory. In effect, the superego is an internalized parent. It holds the image of who you're supposed to be, compares your current state to that, and then corrects you. It attempts to keep you out of trouble with Mom and Dad and helps you get along with other kids. It helps you learn manners and all of the other norms that you need to get along in society. It gives you some ability to regulate your own behavior and conform to social norms. So far, so good. But there is one last major step that needs to happen for the formation of a healthy, mature ego structure.

Separating from the Superego

After your superego forms, it is supposed to separate from your central ego. You will then disidentify from your own inner praiser and inner critic, and begin to hear them as separate voices in your head, voices that tell you what Mom and Dad want, but not what you yourself want. When that happens, you will once again hear your own voice clearly and have lots of information to help you decide what to do. You will be able to hear what your inner critic and inner praiser have to say about your impulses, but you will also be able to hear your own inner voice and feel your own feelings and impulses. Then you can make your own decision. It will be an informed decision, not the unthinking, impulsive act of a two-year-old, nor a decision determined by slavish obedience to the standards set by Mom and Dad. Now you are beginning to form a healthy ego and an authentic self.

But what if this last major step doesn't happen? What if your superego does not separate from your central ego? Then the voices of your superego do not just praise or criticize the self; they drown out the voice of the self. Then the voice of your inner critic is loud and constant in your head, and when it speaks, you think it's your own voice. You do not question it. You think it speaks the Truth. When your inner critic attacks you, you don't realize that it is something separate from you that is attacking you, or that you can defend yourself against its attacks. And you don't realize that your inner critic cannot praise you, but only criticize, so its words are not a fair assessment of your worth.

Unfortunately, this last developmental step does not happen for many, many people. Their inner critic stays fused with their own inner voice, and they can't tell the two apart. They think that the voice in their head — the voice that is correcting them, shaming them, and calling them names — is their own voice.

If you listen closely to these people as they talk aloud, you can almost hear what their inner critic is saying inside their head. It is like listening to one side of a phone conversation and guessing from the side you hear what the other side must be saying. For example, if they are telling you about finding the bathroom flooded when they arrived, they will say something like, *"The bathroom was already flooded when I got here at 10 . . . well, it wasn't right at 10 . . . it was five minutes after 10."* Did you catch that? During each of those pauses, their inner critic was correcting them about the time, even though the exact time was not important to the story.

Failing to disidentify from your inner critic is a real problem. It will cause you to suffer frequent critic attacks, against which you will have no defence. And it will leave you with very little internal space to experience anything new. As soon as a new impulse or feeling arises within you, your inner critic will attack it. It will try to push you back into the Good Boy/Good Girl box that will guarantee Mom and Dad's approval. Its attacks can be quite vicious and leave you feeling worthless and ashamed.

The failure to complete this developmental step is just that — an incomplete developmental step — it is not a survival pattern. While it is a major part of the rigid pattern, it does not guarantee that a person will adopt the rigid pattern. Many people who do other patterns also remain identified with their inner critic and suffer from it greatly, although it is not central to the mechanism of their survival patterns.

To complete the process of separating from their inner critic, most people need training in how to recognize its voice. Some clients I have worked with are startled to realize that they are actually hearing the voice of their mother or father — not only the same intention and tone, but actually the same voice, with the same words, inflection, and accent. Once they can perceive their inner critic as separate from themselves, they can start to recognize its attacks. Some of those attacks may be a voice or thought in their head that devalues them. Others may only be a crummy feeling in their body.

The distinguishing characteristic of a critic attack is that it attacks your value as a person. It doesn't just correct a mistake, it makes you feel bad about yourself for having made the mistake. It isn't the voice that says, *"Hey, you're driving too fast. Better slow down."* It's the voice that says, *"You idiot! You're screwing up again! You always do this!"* It makes you feel small, worthless, and ashamed of yourself.

Bottom line: if you haven't already, you need to find a way to stop your inner critic from beating you up and running your life. To become ourselves, each of us needs to develop our own inner voice, so disidentifying from the inner critic is a crucial step in everyone's inner work. Each of us must learn to reference and feel our own inner experience and desires.

Defending Yourself Against a Critic Attack

Once you can recognize a critic attack, you are ready to learn how to defend yourself against it. You do this by using your own life energy to push back against it instead of letting it use *your* life energy to squash you. Over time, this practice will profoundly change your relationship with your inner critic.

Even though at first your inner critic may seem like an 800 pound gorilla that stomps at will on your small, helpless self, as you practice pushing back against it, the life force that used to feed your inner critic will be redirected into feeding your self. Your inner critic will begin to shrink and your self will grow. Eventually, your self will become bigger and stronger than your inner critic. It will be able to feel an incoming attack and either hold the inner critic off at arm's length or just tell it to *"Sit!"*

As you change your relationship with your inner critic, there is one more thing you may need to do, and that is to stop it from using your mouth to attack others. Just as your inner critic tries to make you behave according to Mom and Dad's Rules, it often tries to make others behave according to those rules as well. It does this by criticizing and correcting their performance. The extent of this varies from person to person, depending on how much outward aggression their survival patterns allow.

In some people, most critic attacks are directed inward, toward the self. In other people, most critic attacks are directed outward, toward others. Some people start with an inner critic directed almost entirely inward, but as they find their inner strength, their inner critic turns outward and begins to attack others. If your inner critic attacks others, you must learn how to control it. You can still express anger, but you must learn to do it cleanly, rather than as an attack.

Once you have disidentified from your inner critic and learned how to defend yourself against its attacks, your inner exploration and growth can proceed much more rapidly. You will have cleared a space inside you, within which you will be able to try out new experiences and find your own voice. While it is unlikely that your inner critic will ever disappear completely, your relationship to it will have been turned upside down. Instead of your inner critic running your life and dominating you, now you will be in charge.

Whenever you open the door to some new experience, especially one outside the Good Boy/Good Girl box prescribed by your parents, your inner critic is likely to squawk and try to stop you. But it won't get to make the decisions any more. In time, you will even come to recognize this kind of critic attack as a sign that you are growing and entering new territory, not a sign that you are in trouble.

For a more thorough discussion of this topic, I recommend Byron Brown's book, *Soul Without Shame* (Shambhala, 1999).

– 6 –

A Chart of the Survival Patterns

For more help in determining which patterns you go into, please visit
www.The5PersonalityPatterns.com.

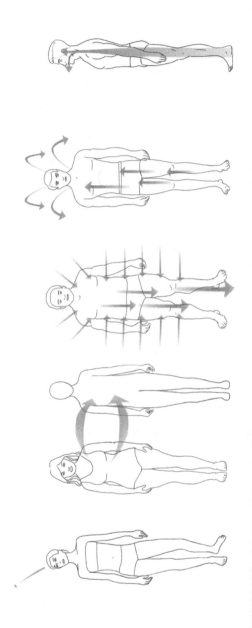

	LEAVING	MERGING	ENDURING	AGGRESSIVE	RIGID
Other names	Schizoid, Creative	Oral, Lover, Dependent, Self-Reliant	Masochist, Burdened, Endurer	Psychopath, Challenger-Defender	Hysteric, Achiever, Industrious
Gifts	awareness of energy	caring, nurturing, loving, pleasure	grounding, stamina	big energy, will, charisma	order, form, structure
Positive aspects	creative, playful, joyful, sensitive	loving, generous, nurturing, giving	steady, patient, diplomatic	strong, competent, resourceful	good achiever, highly functional
Examples	Albert Einstein; Nikola Tesla; Robin Williams	Marilyn Monroe; Oprah Winfrey; Bill Clinton	Eeyore in *Winnie the Pooh*; Samwise Gamgee in *Lord of the Rings*	Jack Nicholson; Tom Cruise; Voldemort; most heroes and villains	Mitt Romney; archetypal librarian

	LEAVING	MERGING	ENDURING	AGGRESSIVE	RIGID
Difficulty with	embodiment	needs: receiving, holding, digesting	expressing self, taking action, claiming own space	trusting others, containing self	feeling self, trusting self
Typical age at wounding	in utero to 6 months	6 months to 2½ years	1½ to 3 years	2½ to 4 years	3½ to 5 years
Developmental task at that age	embodiment: claiming the body and physical life	taking in: receiving, holding, metabolizing	putting out: claiming self and expressing self	trusting others: feeling held by a good, bigger, stronger presence	trusting self: feeling and expressing self
Development of will and strength	will and strength are not yet online	will and strength are not yet online	first personal action taken, but it is thwarted and punished	succeeds in personal action, but is not limited or contained	personal action is divorced from feeling
Typical arena of wound	energetic	physical and interpersonal	interpersonal	interpersonal	interpersonal and spiritual
Typical parent	frightened or angry, insufficiently grounded	depriving, ill, absent	intrusive, dominating, authoritarian	one parent seductive, one authoritarian	rule-bound
Typical wound	hostility shattered attention of the incoming spirit	unable to take in enough nurturance and love	invaded; humiliated; punished for expressing own autonomy	during survival fear, no one was there for them; willed self to survive	taught to ignore or distrust inner experience and trust only outer rules and forms
Effect of wound	self is left fragmented and fragile	can't get full; feels needy and empty; fears deprivation	can't control own body/space; fears self-expression and action	feels powerful, but alone; fears own needs; fears betrayal	fears own inner experience; loss of control

	LEAVING	MERGING	ENDURING	AGGRESSIVE	RIGID
Seeks safety through	leaving	merging	hiding self, resisting other	power	containing and correcting self
Defensive action	limits contact and incoming energy; leaves body; leaves situation	looks to others to fill own needs; *Compensated Merging*: fills others' needs	resists other; turns will against own self; pulls in and hides self deep inside	rejects needs; idealizes power; dominates and controls others	controls experience; references Rules instead of self; acts appropriately
Results of defensive action	self is unable to coalesce and anchor in body; weakness in body and ego structure; self shatters easily	unable to source, hold, and metabolize own energy; collapses easily	resists everything; can't express self or take own actions; sabotages own actions	must guard self; unable to need others, trust others, or ask for help	unable to feel self and trust inner guidance
Typical body shape	thin, may be wiry or waif-like	soft and rounded	strong stocky body; heavy hips and thighs	broad shoulders, narrow hips	fit
Body signs	tension in joints; twist in body; jumpy, clumsy	sunken chest, head forward; too fat or thin; pale, soft, weak	heavy, compressed body	attractive, strong upper body; inflated chest	high head, closed heart, fast rhythm
Flow of energy	away from others	toward others; leaks	in and down; stops	up and out; inflates	flow is constricted
Relationship to Core	tries to function without body or physical core	doesn't have core; avoids it	has core, but feels invaded, so hides	has core, but constantly guards it	doesn't have core; references rules
Eyes	vacant, fixed, scared	pleading, puppy dog	suffering	compelling, commanding	sparkling, bright, anxious
Holding pattern	holding together	holding on (clinging)	holding in	holding up	holding back

	LEAVING	MERGING	ENDURING	AGGRESSIVE	RIGID
Main issues	fear of physical embodiment and existence	needs: taking in, holding, digesting	claiming own space, acting and expressing self	trust of others, control	trust of self, authenticity
Doubts	right to exist; value of physical existence	right to need; right to have	right to act (autonomy)	right to trust others; right to feel safe	right to feel; right to trust self
Fears	living in human body as an individual, falling apart, going crazy	abandonment, rejection, deprivation; not enough of anything	invasion, exposure, humiliation, being controlled	weakness, domination, betrayal, trusting and letting go	chaos and disorder, imperfection, surrender to feelings
Orients to	the psychic realm	connection	space	truth	rules and words
References	mind only	the other only	resistance	self only	rules and forms
Psychological defenses	denial; escape; withdrawal; fantasy	identifies with needs; *Comp Merging:* projects needs, identifies as giver	resisting; hiding; self-negation; self-sabotage; passive aggression	splitting off and denial of needs; active aggression	intellectualization; order and correctness; performance; achieving
Illusion	my mind is my body	need causes abandonment	I'm just trying to please you	it's all a matter of will	I am my performance
Patterned priorities/ values	safety: alone time	relationship; love; being needed	private space	control of the situation	forms; rules; facts; competence
Default emotion	fear	shame	resentment; guilt	anger	criticism; blame; resentment
Mind chatter	gotta get away	I can't; *Comp:* I can	I don't deserve; leave me alone.	I will; let's go.	the "shoulds"; what's wrong; details
Fear reaction	fragmentation; leaving	puddling	resisting	anger; aggression	containment

The 5 Personality Patterns

	LEAVING	MERGING	ENDURING	AGGRESSIVE	RIGID
Shame reaction	flees	collapses	blames self	becomes angry	blames self and/or others
Form of attack by Inner Critic	self-hatred	shame	guilt	anger; ridicule	self-blame
False beliefs	"I don't exist."	"Love will solve everything."	"I can't win." "Life is hard." "I just have to endure it."	"Abuse is normal." "There is no protection."	"All knowledge comes from others." "Love must be earned."
Diagnostic statement	loss of words and language	"I can't."	"You can't make me."	"Knew I couldn't trust you." "I can handle it."	"You're wrong."
Personality symptoms	fragile; lacks sense of self	dependent; needy; gives to get; dramatic	feels stuck; heavy; moody; stubborn	aggressive; wants power; rebellious or authoritarian	rigid and correct; righteous; competitive
In pattern, attention goes	away	to other, to rescue	inside, hunkered down	to the will to survive	to rules, forms, and order
Action under stress	freeze; dissociate; fragment	reference other; accommodate	pull in; resist; refuse	amplify energy and will; inflate	focus on surface, appearance, detail
Patterned sensations and feelings	may not feel body at all; scared	empty, deficient, weak; confused; depressed	heavy, thick, solid; stable; internal pressure	powerful; confident; superior	righteous; efficient; numb
Patterned thoughts	"I don't matter." "No one cares."	"I can't." "I'm not enough." Comp: "I will help you."	"I have to hold it all."	"I can and I will." "You're not enough."	"Something is wrong." "Someone is to blame."

	LEAVING	MERGING	ENDURING	AGGRESSIVE	RIGID
Patterned behaviors	freeze; dissociate; leave	manipulate; cling; collapse; play victim or rescuer	hunker down; resist; endure; complain	challenge; fight; intimidate; dominate	get busy; work hard; clean; organize
Patterned acts	withdrawal from body and from others; self-damaging acts	giving to get; accommodating; pleasing; placating	not acting; self-sabotage; will lash out if pushed beyond endurance	aggression; fighting; blasting others	find what's wrong and fix it
Patterned expression of a desire	"You have it. I want it. I'll just imagine I have it."	"You have it. I want it. I'll get you to give it to me."	"You have it. I want it. I've failed."	"You have it. I want it. I'll take it."	"You have it. I want it. You should give it to me."
Sex	more energetic than physical	generous lover; cuddling feeds infant; merging kills passion	loyal lover, but sex can feel like work; may avoid pleasure	wants control; fears need and vulnerability	becomes a performance; may be mechanical
Time distortion	in universal, non-linear time; does not orient to linear time	never has enough time	time feels stopped, stuck	rushes into the future	experiences time as rigid, mechanical, and predictable
Communication style	psychic rather than verbal – sends pictures and feelings	very verbal, personal, heart to heart; about feelings and melody, not facts and words	slow, reluctant speech; often a partial sentence and a pause; will become confused if you interrupt	commanding, declarative style; very convincing and compelling, even when wrong	preaching, correcting, improving; many words and facts, but few feelings
Form of complaint	dissociates or leaves	"It's too hard." "I can't."	verbal complaining	"It's not good enough."	"It's incorrect or impolite." "It has no rules and order!"

The 5 Personality Patterns

	LEAVING	MERGING	ENDURING	AGGRESSIVE	RIGID
Pattern when requesting help	believes resource/support went away (but actually, their attention went away)	avoids direct requests; references others for answers; waits for rescue	asks, then devalues what is offered, because they want to find it on their own	rarely asks for help; demands or commands instead	organized and justified; often impersonal
Response to a request	confusion	references requester's core and says "yes"	automatically says "no," then considers it	references only self and answers accordingly	whatever the rules dictate; wants to help
Form of anger	psychic attack; white hot rage about unmet needs	little direct anger; resentment at having to grow up	spiteful; no longer cares; can now act on all those boundary violations	an explosion; venting the terror while denying that it is terror	righteousness; sharp words, usually about rule violations
Weapons and tactics used in a fight	leaving; confusion; distraction; psychic attack	accommodating and placating; drama; manipulation	hunkering down and enduring; not responding; passive aggression; baiting	active aggression, bullying and intimidation; blunt force	sharp, piercing words: sarcasm; blaming; condemning
Complimenting the pattern	use a light touch, be soft and warm; note their beauty, fun, creativity, originality	make it personal and emotional; speak to their heart; tell them you love what they did	don't invade their space; softly leave your compliment at the edge of their space	speak from your core to their core; note their competence and achievements	put it in words; make it factual, specific, and verifiable, with examples
Tasks	embodiment, integration, individuation	metabolize own energy; take responsibility	move, express self, act	trust, surrender, receive help	feel and value own inner experience

	LEAVING	MERGING	ENDURING	AGGRESSIVE	RIGID
Relationship to essence	can experience unitive essence; fears individuated essence	experiences individuated essence as not enough	individuated essence is not protected from others	has individuated essence, but fears it is bad or evil	does not experience individuated essence; believes it doesn't exist
Human need	to individuate; to decide to live as a human in a physical body	to nurture self; to know self is enough	to claim own space and the safety to express self	to trust others; to have needs and still be safe	to feel real self; trust it, express it, and act from it
Spiritual need	to experience individuated essence	to experience the infinite source within	to recognize individuated essence as valid and divine	to feel held by a bigger, stronger, loving presence	to experience both unitive and individuated essence within
Energetic skills needed	ground, core, edge, me/not me	ground, core, edge, me/not me	edge, me/not me	ground, edge	ground, core
Can take pleasure in	embodying spirit in the physical world	competence; giving and receiving	owning lots of space, expressing self, taking action	letting go in a safe place	feeling; being moved
How to get yourself out of pattern	re-enter your body; reference your core and ground; reassemble your self	find your core and reference it; act from there	move your body; claim your space and fill it	ground yourself; allow something good and bigger than you to contain you	focus on feelings and sensations as your guidance

For more help in determining which patterns you go into, please visit *www.The5PersonalityPatterns.com.*

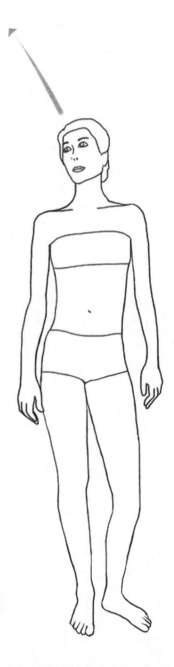

The Leaving Pattern – body and energy flow

– 7 –

The Leaving Pattern

"This place scares me. I want to go home."

LIKE ALL THE SURVIVAL PATTERNS, the leaving pattern is a way to buffer the self from feelings of overwhelm. It is a holding pattern, conditioned into the body by trauma, which creates a particular habit of attention. The original trauma is the shattering of the incoming spirit's attention, usually before birth.

The survival strategy employed here is to move away from whatever is frightening or potentially frightening. This is done by shifting attention upward into the head, away from the body, and even away from the physical world into the spirit world, a shift commonly called dissociation. This allows the person to live in her* head, maintain a strong connection to the spirit world, be highly creative, and be unusually sensitive and aware of energetic phenomena, but it leaves the physical body weakened and less able to protect itself. It also prevents the coalescing of a strong sense of self that is firmly rooted in the body and able to function well in the physical world. Under pressure, her fragile self fragments once again, and since she cannot find a center from which to operate, she may become unable to function.

One woman who does this pattern described her experience this way:

---

* To avoid the cumbersomeness of having to continually say "he or she," I will assign a gender to the child described in each chapter and then stick with that gender throughout the chapter. For example, in this chapter, I will assume the child is a girl. However, all five of the patterns are found in both genders, and everything said about the girl in this chapter could just as easily have been said about a boy.

I get tired of being overwhelmed all the time. Why can't I be like these people who can handle three children and nothing seems to really phase them that much? And me, I'm like the princess and the pea — one little thing and I'm feeling like I'm overwhelmed and I can't handle this.

When I dissociate, my eyes just glaze over and I go into this place of imagination, and not a lot registers around me when I do that. I'm not really here, so I don't feel people coming into my space. Going away is my way of getting refuge. It's safe everywhere else but here. Here is not safe.

A lot of times I feel like a squirrel up in the top of a tree. And I'm safe up here, but down on the ground there are dogs and cats and cars and humans, and it's pretty risky. And I need to remind myself that I'm not that squirrel. I'm actually a human being that can be down on the ground and be safe. I don't always have to climb up this tree and hide up here at the top. And I can be safe down there as long as I'm not in my squirrel body, as long as I'm in my human body. But I keep perceiving myself as the squirrel, which is small and vulnerable and not seen clearly, and I don't feel confident because I don't know what's going on.

Range of Functioning

Each of the survival patterns appears across the entire spectrum of functionality, from those who are completely ruled by the pattern to those who wear it lightly. For those who do the leaving pattern, the variation is mostly in how fragile the person is, in how much intensity it takes to put them into overwhelm and cause the self to shatter. Lower functioning people are more fragile, while higher functioning people are more resilient.

On the low end of the spectrum, we have those who are totally caught in the pattern. It organizes them and rules their life. They are extremely sensitive to any harshness in the environment and are easily overwhelmed and shattered. Because of this, they have a great deal of difficulty functioning in the ordinary physical world. They are constantly afraid of being overwhelmed, and they avoid most social situations in order to protect themselves.

In the mid-range, we have people who are somewhat more resilient, but still wary of social situations. While strong in the skills and talents of the pattern, they have not claimed their bodies enough to use them as a reference point and a refuge from the stresses of daily life.

On the high end of the spectrum, we have people who can generally stay present while using the skills and talents of the pattern. While they are still unusually sensitive and aware of energetic phenomena, they have claimed their bodies enough to use them as a reference point and a refuge from the stresses of daily life. This allows them to tolerate the distress of most upsets without fragmenting. With training, they may be able to navigate skillfully through the non-physical dimensions and bring back many gifts for the physical world.

The Gifts of the Leaving Pattern

As a person uses any of the patterns, she continually practices the skills that that pattern requires. Over time, she becomes exceptionally proficient in those particular skills. As she heals the wounds that created the pattern and becomes able to shift her attention out of the pattern and back to presence, the abilities she has acquired stay with her and become the gifts of the pattern. Now she is able to employ her exceptional abilities as she responds to the needs of the present moment. Even though some of the physical structures remain in her body, she has shifted out of the patterned survival defense and into the gifts of the pattern.

The gifts of the leaving pattern are the gifts of psychic and subtle perception. People who do this pattern are Masters of Psychic Perception, that is, sensitive to psychic impressions and able to read and track energy. Typically they are able to perceive and communicate psychically, sending and receiving information without the use of words. Often they are able to communicate with plants and animals. Sometimes they are also able to communicate with beings and forces outside the physical realm. They may be aware of their psychic skills and use them in their work. They are also energetically nimble. They tend to have a light touch and think of themselves as a "highly sensitive person."

Leaving-patterned people have a very facile attention. They may be able to move their awareness to locations outside their physical body in order to experience an object or event from multiple viewing points — from in front, in back, beside, above, below, or even inside. They are often quite skillful at controlling their attention and are able to hold multiple attentions, that is, able to hold their attention on several things at once.

Their awareness is also multi-dimensional. Often they are able to move through other dimensions and have experiences that are outside of ordinary time and space. They consider time and space to be "just co-ordinates," not limitations to where they are able to go. With training, they can travel to higher spiritual dimensions and bridge to other worlds. They easily shift into the unitive consciousness of higher dimensions and experience themselves as one with everything (but have difficulty becoming a separate self here in the physical world).

Because of this mobility of attention, those who do the leaving pattern are very talented at seeing the big picture and all of its parts (although they tend not to focus on the details). Their attention is non-linear, so they are comfortable in chaos and do not need to force order and organization onto what they see. This gives them an awareness of many possibilities at once. It makes multi-tasking easy and natural for them. And when they're done with something, they're good at moving their attention off of it and letting it go.

This broad, multi-dimensional perception also makes them unusually intuitive and creative. They are able to go to other dimensions to get new things, put them together in new and creative ways, and bring them back here. Most of the world's artists, visionaries, and seminal thinkers belong to this group. Some examples are Mozart downloading whole symphonies and Albert Einstein riding on a beam of light to discover his theory of special relativity.

People who do this survival pattern are curious and fun, and a gentle, joyful playfulness is an easily accessible state for them. They like games and can truly enjoy inventing and playing them. They have rich imaginations, enjoy fantasy, and can easily entertain themselves. For them, the physical world of the Earth plane may appear as just one of the possible games, no more important than any other. They tend to be open and child-like, and there may even be a sprite or fairy-like quality about them. If their psychic abilities are developed, they may be friends with the sprites, fairies, and devas. Often, they have delightful ethereal, mercurial, or magical qualities.

Examples

- Albert Einstein

- Nikola Tesla

- Pablo Picasso

- Wolfgang Amadeus Mozart, as portrayed in the film *Amadeus*

- Robin Williams

- Lisa Kudrow's character Phoebe in the TV show, *Friends*
- Luna Lovegood in the *Harry Potter* films

Alternate names

- Schizoid
- Creative
- the Hated Child

Exercise – Being Caught in the Pattern

Fear of Being Shattered

This exercise is designed to give you a felt sense of what it is like to be caught in the leaving pattern. It may feel very strange to you, or it may feel very familiar. Either way, try not to judge your experience as you go through the exercise, but instead just notice how familiar or unfamiliar this is and what it would be like to live this way much of the time.

Sit down in a quiet place and close your eyes. Take some deep breaths and let your body calm down into a relaxed presence, just feeling yourself and letting your body breathe itself.

Now let yourself imagine that you're a squirrel and you live up in the tree tops. You're a small, agile creature, and you feel at home high up here in the trees. You can run and jump and almost fly from one tree to another. You can play all you want, and it's a lot of fun.

It's safe up here, but down on the ground there are dogs and cats and cars and humans, and it's pretty risky. Bad things can happen. You can get hurt. Before you even know what hit you, you can get squashed or torn apart. You're too vulnerable down there, so you try to stay up in the tree tops as much as you can.

But sometimes you want to see what's going on down there. The people live in warm houses with lots of good smells coming out of them — delicious smells, like hot chocolate and fresh bread baking. Sometimes you creep down the tree and look in the windows and it all seems so warm and happy inside. You close your eyes and imagine living in there in the warmth and good smells and belonging.

But then a dog barks, right near you! And the sound is so loud it scares you right out of your body, and you don't know where you are any more or even which way is up, so you just run madly in any direction! And maybe you go up and get back to safety, but maybe you go down and the dog gets you and tears you apart and just the thought of it is so terrifying that you can't think or feel your body any more for a long time, and you're just frozen right there until you can kind of piece yourself back together and quiet down and get oriented again.

Now take a moment to notice what is going on in your body. Are you breathing fast? Are you tensed up? Are you scared? Do you just want to get away?

Take some deep breaths and let them out slowly through pursed lips, letting the terror flow out of your body on each outbreath. Feel your butt in the seat and your feet on the floor. Shake your body for a while to help it let go of the fear and calm down again. Take as long as you like to let your body settle down into a state of easy, safe presence.

Now take some time to absorb what you just experienced and consider the following questions:

- *What was it like to live up in the trees but look in the windows and imagine being inside?*

- *What would it be like to feel so small and vulnerable all the time? To know that your only safety is in getting out fast, before you get overwhelmed and something bad happens?*

- *What thoughts or feelings arose as you did the exercise?*

- *What thoughts or feelings seemed to get in the way?*

- *What would it be like to live this way all the time?*

Exercise – The Gifts of the Pattern

A Mobile Awareness

This next exercise may seem very easy and natural for you, or it may seem strange and impossible. Don't judge yourself either way. We're just trying out different experiences so that you can see which are familiar to you and which are not. This exercise gives you a taste of the kind of mobile awareness that is a talent of the leaving pattern.

Sit down in a quiet place and close your eyes. Take 5 or 10 deep breaths and let yourself settle with each exhalation. Notice where your awareness is located. Is it in your head, behind your eyes? Is it somewhere else in your body? Is it outside your body?

Move your awareness into the middle of your head. You can do this just by intending, sensing, or imagining it. It's the same process you use when you move your hand: you simply intend to move your hand and it goes. With practice, you can move your awareness in the same way, just by intending to move it.

Let's practice moving it some more.

Move your awareness to the left side of your head, just inside your ear. What is this like?

Now move it back to the center of your head.

Now move it to the right side of your head, just inside your ear. What is this like?

Now back to the center.

Now move your attention to the back of your head, against your skull. What is this like?

Now back to the center of your head.

Now try going into your eyes, into the eyeballs themselves. What is this like?

Now back to the center.

Now move your awareness up to the top of your head, right at the crown. What is this like?

Now let it move up a few inches more, until it is just above your head. What is this like?

Now let it move further outside your body, up to the ceiling and over to a corner of the room. What does the room look like from up here? Can you see your body below you? If you can, what is the effect on you of looking at your body from outside it?

Now move your awareness to a different corner of the room. How does changing your viewing point change the appearance of things? If you are able to move your awareness around independently from your body, how does that affect your relationship to your body?

Now bring your awareness back down into your body, perhaps through the crown of your head or just by intending it to be back inside. Feel your body from the inside. Feel your butt in the chair and the soles of your feet on the floor. Breathe into your body, feel the many sensations within it, and let your awareness fully reconnect with your physical body.

Now, notice what this whole experience was like for you and consider the following questions:

- *How easy or difficult was it for you to let your awareness move around within your head? How about outside your body?*

- *How easy or difficult was it for you to come back into your body? Do you feel at home there? What does this tell you?*

- *How did you feel about letting your awareness go places outside of your physical body?*

- *What thoughts or feelings arose as you did the exercise?*

- *What thoughts or feelings seemed to get in the way?*

- *What would it be like to have access to this skill all the time?*

The Origins of the Leaving Pattern

Entering the physical world

In order to understand the origins of the leaving pattern, we must first understand the process that a spirit goes through as it shifts from living in the spirit world to living in a human body in the physical world. Here in the physical world, we know ourselves as separate entities, which exist in specific places in space and time. Our awareness has a boundary around it which makes it local, and we are aware only of this particular place and time. Because of this, most of us think of ourselves as a thing in a world of other things. This kind of existence is all we know, so when we think of how a spirit transitions from the spirit world to life in a human body, we naturally imagine that the spirit also starts out as a thing, as a bounded, local entity in the spirit world, which then simply travels somehow to the physical world, where it takes up residence in a human body.

But this understanding is not quite accurate. Spirits in the spirit world do not exist as things in the same way that we do here. They do not experience themselves as entities in the way that we do here. The awareness of a spirit in the spirit world is not localized or bounded. Linear time and space do not exist, and awareness is not confined to any particular place or time. Instead, it exists everywhere at once. It is open and expanded, more like a boundless field of awareness than a point of awareness, more like aware space than an aware entity. Think of a drop of water in the ocean that has melted into the ocean and is no longer a drop, no longer a local, bounded entity, but diffused throughout the entire ocean. This is the experience that is known as Oneness or Unitive Consciousness.

This must all change for the spirit to enter the physical world of space and time. The spirit must become an Individuated Consciousness. It must focus its awareness more into a point of awareness. It must coalesce its attention enough to orient itself to a particular human body, a body which exists only at a particular place within the linear space-time of the physical world. It must differentiate itself out of the ocean of awareness and become a single drop, a drop which can experience a human life.

This coalescing process has already started before the spirit first enters the fetus in the womb, and it helps the spirit re-orient itself to the physical world. Ideally, what it finds there is a warm, welcoming, holding love, a love which makes it feel safe there. For a while, it moves back and forth between the spirit world and the body, but eventually it settles into the body and takes up permanent residence. It attaches both to the physical world and to this particular body. It claims the body as its own. Ideally this happens either before birth or soon after.

Many spiritual traditions recognize this process in some way, though they speak of it in their own terminology and from their own point of view. In the field of somatic psychology, this process is commonly called "embodiment," and it is a baby's very first developmental task.

Attaching to the physical world

To facilitate the embodiment of the incoming spirit, the ideal mother also provides grounding for it. This means that she provides an energetic and emotional connection from her own body to the earth and to the earth plane. Her baby connects to her body, and through her the baby feels a connection to the earth. This helps give the incoming spirit the feeling that the earth plane is friendly toward it, making it much easier for the incoming spirit to feel safe enough to claim the new body as its own.

Grounding is a lot like attachment, a term that is used in psychology to describe the emotional connection of one person to another, usually of a baby to its mother. Like psychological attachment, grounding is a form of energetic and emotional connection that provides a felt sense of safety and belonging to the one who attaches. However, grounding is not attachment to a particular human being or even to human beings in general. It is attachment to the physical plane, and specifically to the physical and energetic earth that supports and nurtures all life here. Being grounded to the earth conveys to the human body the felt sense that "I am welcome here. I am safe. The earth likes me." Native cultures all recognize this connection to the earth and our universal need for it, which leads them to refer to the earth as "mother earth" or "grandmother earth."

Until a child is around six, she needs to ground through her mother or some other caretaker. This is part of the reason babies and young children become distressed when separated from their mothers. Somewhere between ages five and seven, if the child has acquired a felt sense of grounding and has been able to template how to ground from her mother or caretakers, she becomes able to ground her own body directly into the earth. This gives her a new felt sense of safety, even when separated from caretaking adults.

Embodiment

Once an incoming spirit has claimed the body and securely attached to it, the body becomes its protection and refuge. When disoriented or fragmented, it can reference the body as the place to come back to. As the body grows, it develops an energetic boundary around itself. This boundary helps to shield the spirit from damaging energies in the environment. This is part of the reason that people who have completed the process of embodiment are much less vulnerable to being shattered by others' anger and hostility than those who have not.

However, the amount of safety, grounding, and welcoming love that is sufficient to allow the incoming spirit to complete the process of embodiment depends greatly on the needs of that particular spirit. What is enough for one is not necessarily enough for another. At the very beginning, the newly focused awareness of the incoming spirit is very vulnerable. It has not yet fully coalesced, and angry or hostile energies hitting it can shatter it into fragments. This is when the wounding that leads to the development of the leaving pattern first occurs.

How the Leaving Pattern Forms

So far, we've talked about the ideal situation, in which the mother's body is grounded to the earth and she holds the incoming spirit in a welcoming, nurturing love. But what happens if things are not so ideal? What happens if Mom is herself disconnected from her own body or from the earth? What if she runs the leaving pattern or another ungrounded pattern and cannot provide a felt sense of groundedness for her child? Further, what if she is unattuned or inattentive to the infant because she is overwhelmed by other difficulties, such as illness, poverty, domestic violence, or even war? What if she does not want the child? What if the larger environment is not safe, or is hostile to the child? What if hatred or anger in the environment energetically impacts the incoming spirit? What if this happens repeatedly?

Being shattered

When the newly focused awareness of the incoming spirit does not have enough support to keep itself together, or when it gets hit by energies that shock it, it shatters into fragments. This is extremely distressing to the incoming spirit, especially since it has very little ability at this point to re-assemble itself. And the fragments don't necessarily stay nearby, in the vicinity of the body, or even in the physical dimension; they can be scattered through many dimensions. For those caught in the leaving pattern, the fragmentation was typically so bad that they have never been able to retrieve all of their fragments and re-assemble themselves completely. But they have to get through life as best they can, even though parts of their attention remain scattered in other dimensions.[1]

Being shattered is terrifying — when the self fragments, the felt sense is that "there is no there, there," and the person may find herself floating in a black, empty void, unable to find any point of reference. Without the body as a reference point from which to begin the process of recollecting and re-assembling itself, the self may stay fragmented, floating, and terrified for a long time.

One person put it this way:

> *There is a great fear of being alone, lost in space. There's no one there. There's no universe and no world. I don't have a body, so I can't do anything, but I still have an intellect, so there's kind of a craziness to it. Even "floating" sounds too sensuous. There's no body to float. There's just a point of mind.*

This vulnerability is why people who do this survival pattern want to spend a lot of time alone in environments of low stimulation. They are protecting themselves from shocks to their system and giving themselves time to recover from the shocks that do occur.

This is the core wound of the child who develops the leaving pattern: at the very beginning of her existence as a separate consciousness, her attention was shattered so badly that she has not been able to assemble a unified, integrated self and anchor it firmly in the body. Even as an adult, parts of her attention may remain lost in other dimensions.

Of all the survival patterns, the wounding that creates this pattern is the most difficult for the rest of us to observe from our usual viewing point in the physical world. Why? Because it is not something that happens to the infant's physical body, but only to the awareness of the incoming spirit.

Defensive Action

To try to protect itself from further shattering, the incoming spirit learns to flee at the first sign of trouble. Each time it becomes frightened, it leaves the body and goes back to the safety of the spirit world. This weakens its connection with the body and strengthens its connection with the spirit world at a time when just the opposite should be happening: it should be strengthening its connection with the body and shifting its sense of "home" from the spirit world into the physical world and the physical body. It should be learning to reference the body as home and the place of safety and nurturance. Instead, the incoming spirit learns that the physical world is not safe or caring and that its best defense is to immediately leave any upsetting situation. As the person uses this strategy over and over, it becomes self-reinforcing and gradually grows into the leaving pattern.

Results of the Defensive Action

The self remains fragile and vulnerable

The repeated shattering of the infant's awareness and its flight back to the spirit world to protect itself prevent it from ever completing the process of coalescing a unified, integrated self. Instead, the self remains fragile and fragmented. It does not develop a reference point in the core of the body or a strong protective boundary around the body. This makes it more vulnerable to later shocks than it would normally be, and less able to re-assemble itself after such shocks. Even as an adult, the routine stresses of life can still shatter the self into fragments.

The physical world seems unsafe

The spirit's action of repeatedly leaving the body, rather than claiming it, has many consequences that make the physical world seem even less safe than it actually is. To begin with, instead of the child's energy and awareness being distributed evenly throughout the body, it is habitually shunted upward into the head, where the mind interprets this extra energy as fear. This means that any increased energy in the body brings with it a surge of energy into the head and a feeling of fear.

Not fully inhabiting the body also inhibits the development of a strong energetic boundary around the body. Without the protection of a strong boundary, the body is easily penetrated by energies from other people and the environment. This makes the child unusually sensitive to energies and psychic impressions, and often leads her to label herself a highly sensitive person. Being frequently penetrated in this way is frightening and overwhelming and makes the physical world seem even less safe to her.

Having a weak energetic boundary also makes it harder for her to differentiate inside from outside, to separate what is "me" from what is "not me." Because she is frequently penetrated by the energies of others and not able to discern that these new energies within her system are "not me," she is likely to accumulate lots of energies within her body that don't belong there and only confuse her. Having all these foreign energies within her makes it even harder for her to coalesce a self than it would normally be.

A friend who does this pattern described her experience of being in pieces this way:

> It's like you're trying to put together a jigsaw puzzle of your own face, but you don't have the box top with the picture of how it should look, so you have no idea where the pieces fit. And the pile of pieces you have is all messed up. Lots of your puzzle pieces are missing, because they're lost somewhere in some other dimension or stuck inside someone else's body. And lots of the pieces you have inside you aren't really your pieces; they're just junk that floated in from somewhere else. So you don't have the right pieces, and you don't know where they go, and it just seems impossible.

Difficulty orienting to the physical world

Another consequence of not claiming the physical body is that this child has difficulty learning about herself through her interactions with the physical world. Ideally, as a child is creating her sense of self, she is getting constant feedback from the physical world about what is "me" and what is not. A toddler who bumps into a coffee table is getting feedback about the size and shape of her body and exactly where its edge is located. But if that toddler's awareness is not in her body at the time of the bump, she may not even feel it, and so may miss that bit of information entirely.

Feeling the body from the inside is one of the main ways a child comes to know herself and form a stable sense of self. Of course, the sense of self in any young child is very delicate and fragile, as demonstrated by how easily a child falls apart when shocked or overwhelmed. Even a loud noise may be enough to cause a baby to burst into tears. But if the child has succeeded in claiming the physical body, this fragility gradually diminishes as her connection to her own core grows. Over time, her sense of self coalesces around her core, and she forms a cohesive, unified self that is anchored in the physical body. She becomes more resilient and falls apart less frequently. If a shock does cause her to fall apart, she is able to more rapidly re-assemble herself around her own felt core. And if, after falling apart, she can reach out to an adult who holds and comforts her, she also learns that connection with other humans is safe. She learns that it offers her a refuge within which to re-assemble herself.

Now, as she struggles to put herself back together after a shock has shattered her, she has two crucial forms of support: she has a safe place within which to re-collect herself, and she has a reference point around which to re-assemble herself. She is on the road to coalescing a unified, integrated sense of herself as a separate individual in the physical world. But a child who develops the leaving pattern did not have these supports, or didn't have them enough.

As this experience of leaving the body happens over and over, it becomes a habit. But, while it solves the problem in the moment, it prevents the incoming spirit from completing its first developmental task, from settling into and claiming the body. Without claiming the body, the child's spirit cannot use the body to orient herself and find protection in the physical world.

All this leads to difficulty functioning in the physical world. Her physical sensing of the body is diminished, which makes it harder to develop physical coordination and strength. There is less life energy and vitality in her body than there would otherwise be, which makes it harder for her to feel connected to her body and to physical life in general, especially when the spirit realm seems so much more vivid and interesting.

The physical world feels cold and hostile

Because reaching out to others for comfort and soothing did not work for them, leaving-patterned people have no model of a safe, nourishing human connection and no expectation that turning to others will help them now. Instead, they experience the world as cold and hostile.

Those who do this pattern are used to experiencing themselves as part of a larger, unitive consciousness, but they haven't finished the process of separating from that unitive consciousness and coming to know themselves as a personal, individuated consciousness, as an individual human in the human world. Typically, they don't like or value the physical world, and they're not sure they want to be here. Even as adults, many who do this pattern have not yet decided to stay and live in the physical world. They don't have the impulse toward life here.

As they withdraw to protect themselves, a self re-enforcing cycle develops. They expect hostility from others, may see it even if it isn't there, and flee as soon as they see it. Leaving their body so frequently weakens it and also tends to draw anger from others, who feel abandoned when they disappear. Then their own sense of weakness and the anger from others combine to re-enforce their belief that the world is not safe. As this cycle repeats, it creates the leaving pattern.

In summary: something happens that shatters the awareness of the incoming spirit. Fleeing this, the infant's spirit takes refuge in the spirit world and doesn't fully claim the body. The task of embodiment is not completed and the self remains fragile and un-integrated. The physical world is experienced as cold and unwelcoming, and human contact is seen as always potentially dangerous. A habit develops in which the person flees at the first sign of conflict or hostility. Even as an adult, the person's self fragments easily, and this tendency to fragment becomes the hallmark of the leaving pattern.

The Leaving Pattern in Full Bloom

Body Signs

Since the flow of energy in the body helps shape the body as it grows, this person's failure to fully inhabit the body actually deprives the body of the energy it needs to become robust, leaving it weaker than it would otherwise be. It may be wiry, but would rarely be called muscular. The wrists and ankles are often weak and thin. The body of someone with this structure tends to be slender, especially if their other pattern also tends to create a slender body.

To the extent that life energy has been blocked or withdrawn from certain parts of the body, the person will have less physical sensation there. Since the defensive action of this pattern is to move up into the head and exit the body from there, their life energy is strongest in the head and weaker farther down in the body, becoming weakest in the feet. The extra energy built up in the head may create headaches, while the hands and feet are often cold, reflecting the decreased blood flow and life energy available to them.

The body is more like a collection of parts than an integrated whole. It appears to be tense and jumpy, and there is tension in the joints because energy builds up at these areas of transition, rather than flowing freely through them. The holding pattern in the body is one of holding everything together, a manifestation of the energetic effort required to hold the un-integrated self together.

This lack of integration of the self is also reflected in the way the body moves. Instead of the grace displayed by a body moving from its center as a unified whole, the movements of someone who does this pattern tend to have an uncoordinated, jerky quality, as if the various body parts are not fully connected to each other. Sometimes the person will acknowledge this by calling herself clumsy or a "klutz." Movements and speech are often quick. Overall, the person tends to be hyperactive and ungrounded.

Frequently there is a twist in the spine, as if the person is twisting away from life, not wanting to face it directly.[2] The head is often tipped to one side, as if not quite connected to the body. This is a physiological manifestation of the disconnection between the head and body, as if the head does not quite recognize the body as part of itself.

The eyes may look scared, even in repose, and may be open extra wide, as if startled. When a shock has caused the person to fragment, the eyes may be fixed and vacant, betraying the fact that no one is home at the moment. The voice may be unusually high pitched, with a thin, young-sounding quality.

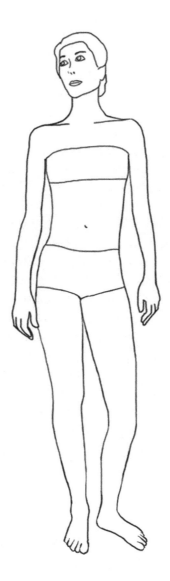

The Leaving Pattern – typical body shape

Because they don't really value the physical body or live in it, people who do this survival pattern often neglect their bodies. They may not notice that they are hungry, thirsty, or tired, and may frequently have accidents that injure their bodies.

Psychology

The main issue for leaving-patterned people is existential terror, that is, a terror that it is not safe for them to physically exist. Since they felt attacked while coming into the physical world, they doubt that they have the right to exist here. They remain caught at the place where the spirit transitions from living in the spirit world to living in a human body, frozen by their shock and terror in a developmental arrest at the very beginning of their human life.

This leaves them developmentally in a very young state, with a weak ego structure and weak energetic boundaries, continually vulnerable to energetic penetration and overwhelm. The fragmenting of the self is an ever-present threat. At a minimum, the experience of fragmenting is disturbing and disorganizing. At worst, it is terrifying. This vulnerability accounts for much of the fear that these people feel and for their avoidance of potentially overwhelming situations.

Frequently, they see themselves as "a leaf, blown in the wind." This self-image speaks volumes about their inner experience. A leaf being blown by the wind is not anchored to anything in the physical world. It cannot move itself, but is frequently moved by outside forces. And it has no power to change its situation or even call out for help.

One person who does the leaving pattern put it this way: *"I think of myself as a shadow, not solid or permanent like other people. Just a shadow that might be there sometimes and not other times. When I leave, I'm surprised when other people make such a big deal about it, 'cause, after all, I'm just a shadow. What does it matter if I'm there or not?"*

Beliefs

The beliefs of leaving-patterned people reflect their fears that the physical world is unsafe and unloving. Some of their typical beliefs are:

"I am not my body; I am my mind."
"I don't physically exist."
"My actions don't matter."
"No one cares."
"I am out there alone."

"I am not safe here."
"The physical world is cold and loveless."
"The physical body and physical world are not mine and not important."

By contrast, their beliefs about the spirit world are mostly positive. They see it as the place of safety, connection, and loving presence.

Fears

Falling apart and going crazy

Typically, the biggest fear of people who are caught in this survival pattern is that they will fall apart and go crazy. This fear is a recognition that they do, in fact, shatter under pressure and that the inner experience of being shattered feels like going crazy. When their self is shattered into fragments, they lose much of their ability to think and function. They cannot orient themselves in space and time, and they may become unable to organize their thoughts enough to speak coherently or even understand language. If they cannot find a reference point around which to re-assemble themselves, they may be left floating helplessly in a cold, black void. There is literally "no one there," not even themselves. Just a point of awareness suspended in the cold blackness, utterly helpless. Eventually their psyche is able to re-assemble itself, but that may take hours or even days. This is why they are so vigilant in their efforts to avoid situations that might shatter them.

Fear of being an individual person in the physical world

People who do the leaving pattern are also afraid of the physical world in general and of being a physical person in it.[3] For them, being a physical body means being vulnerable to physical and emotional injury, a vulnerability that they do not face in the spirit world. Being unable to protect themselves in the physical world makes them want to avoid it by fleeing to higher spiritual realms, where they can shift into a state of loving, unitive consciousness. This feels safer, but it gives them no practice at experiencing themselves as a single, individuated entity, which is one of the essential steps in ego development and in navigating the physical world.

What is the effect on them of living in so much fear? When a person's early life is lived in a state of chronic fear, her nervous system becomes acclimated to the fear and begins to treat it as the normal state of affairs. Vigilance in the mind and arousal in the nervous system become familiar, even re-assuring, inner states. She comes to believe that hyper-vigilance and feelings of fear are what keep her safe. In the extreme, this belief becomes paranoia. In a healing situation, where she is actually safe and her body begins to relax, she may initially feel even more uncomfortable because she isn't able to find the old familiar feelings of fear in her body.[4]

Psychological Defenses

As with all of the survival patterns, the psychological defenses used by leaving-patterned people are all attempts to make some safety for themselves in an unsafe world. But because the leaving pattern is developmentally so young, those who do this survival pattern have few options to choose from when they need to protect themselves psychologically. Their main defenses are denial, projection, withdrawal, and fantasy. Let's look at each one in turn.

Denial

Denial is the most obvious of their psychological defenses. They deny the needs of their own body for food, rest, and warm, human contact. They may not even notice when their body is tired, hungry, or in danger of injury and may run themselves ragged and have frequent accidents. Frequently, they also deny the needs of their heart, including the fact that they needed love as a child and that they still need love now. They may begin therapy believing that they had a wonderful, happy childhood, but for some reason just don't have or want any close human relationships as an adult.

Projection

Another psychological defense used by people who do this survival pattern is projection. This means that, instead of feeling an upsetting emotion inside themselves, they imagine that someone else is feeling it. Scary and dangerous emotions are the ones most often projected onto others, so it may seem to them like someone else is feeling angry or hateful, when in fact, they are. Since these people are also talented at psychic perception and may be able to actually perceive the inner states of others, this tendency to project their feelings can distort their perceptions. Their projections get mixed in with their accurate perceptions, which makes the projections seem to be accurate, also. Because they have a real gift of perception, learning to differentiate perception from projection is especially important for them.

Withdrawal from others and from the body

Two other psychological defenses often used by leaving-patterned people are withdrawal from others and withdrawal from the body into the mind.

Withdrawal, whether from others or from the body, is a way to buffer themselves from the distress building up in the body. Each of us needs a way to regulate the amount of distress in our body, but since these people are less protected by strong ego structures and energetic boundaries than others, they need some additional way to protect themselves. Since they can't shut out the noise, they need to get away from it.

Withdrawal from others usually shows up as avoidance of physical contact and emotional attachment, often justified as "independence" or "spiritual detachment." The shadow side of independence is a fear of dependency. As infants and children, we are all dependent on those who take care of us. Ideally, if our caretakers are present, attuned to us, and lovingly meet our needs, we learn that dependency on others is safe. As we grow, we become capable of caring for others, and our dependency matures into interdependency. We see ourselves as part of a group in which we all take care of each other. However, those who developed the leaving pattern did not have such an idyllic childhood experience. They found others to be the source of their pain, not the salve for it. So, as adults, they tend to avoid emotional attachments and even contact with others.

As you can imagine, joining a monastery or going on long, silent retreats can provide the perfect cover for this psychological defense. Claims of spiritual detachment can mask real fears of personal attachment. When choosing an inner work practice, it is always important to explore what you're avoiding, as well as what you're pursuing. I have known of people who were able to meditate alone for years in a monastery cell, opening deeply into states of bliss and boundless love, but then felt terror when they returned to the world and fell in love with a real, live, physical human being. Letting their ego boundaries dissolve was tolerable, but the attachment needs aroused by sex and personal love were terrifying.

The withdrawal of awareness from the body up into the mind is essentially the same strategy, but used internally, rather than externally. Since the body and heart seem to be the source of the pain, the person moves her awareness away from her body and up into her head. Verbally, this withdrawal from the body will appear as a tendency to talk in abstractions and generalizations, instead of talking about specific personal needs and feelings.[5] The illusion of the leaving pattern is "I am my mind, not my body." In psychology, this withdrawal of awareness from the body is called dissociation.

Fantasy

Fantasy is a further withdrawal into the mind. In this case, all of physical reality is left behind and an entirely new world is created to replace it. Usually, that new world is a much more appealing one, a place where the person can be creative and even magical.

On the other hand, this facility with abstract thought, coupled with the ability to collect ideas from other fields and even other dimensions, also accounts for the fact that most of the seminal thinkers in every discipline do this survival pattern. These extraordinary people have both the need and the ability to leave behind the personal realm and devote themselves to assembling the larger picture. They may be famous worldwide, but still remain largely unknown to their own families. Albert Einstein was an example of this.

Relationship to Self and the Inner Critic

Typically, leaving-patterned people are comfortable being a spirit in the spirit world, but fear being a separate individual in a physical body. To them, the physical world is just one of many possible worlds, so they see little value in a body that is so easily hurt. Since they are used to moving through time and space at will in the spirit world, physical time and space seem unimportant to them. In daily life here, they tend to lose track of linear time and space, which causes them to get lost, run into things, and not show up on time. These are the people that others refer to as "spaced out."

Self-hatred

The fear that is so obvious in those who do this survival pattern is accompanied by a less obvious feeling of self-hatred. The self-hatred actually comes from their inner critic. (For a more thorough discussion of the inner critic, see chapters 5 and 11.) Since anyone's inner critic is a distilled version of all their parent's negative attitudes toward them, a hostile parent tends to create in their child an even more hostile inner critic.[6] The voice of such an inner critic can be more than just critical; it can be hateful. While anyone can develop a hateful inner critic — no matter which survival patterns they do — the target of their inner critic's hatred is determined by their patterns. Simply put, a person's inner critic will attack her for whatever her patterns say is wrong with her. Furthermore, if she has not succeeded in separating her own voice from the voice of her inner critic, she will experience its hatred of her as her own hatred of herself. This leads leaving-patterned people to hate their physical body for its weakness and vulnerabilities, and to hate themselves for having to exist in a physical body at all. Psychologically, the hostility that they initially experienced as coming from the outside has now been taken in and turned against themselves: "They hate me" has morphed into "I hate me."

Self-harm

Hatred is an emotion that wants to annihilate what it hates, to remove it from existence, so "I hate me" becomes "I should not exist. I should be destroyed." This can lead those who are caught in the leaving pattern to engage in self-damaging acts. These can range from simple self-neglect, like failing to eat or sleep as needed, to active self-injury. Their self-hatred is a very early imprint and therefore hard for them to oppose. Self-destruction is always an imprint. Life wants to live.

Self-damaging acts are also a way for them to express their anger without risking conflict and possible retaliation from another. Instead of being directed outward at what is currently hurting them, their anger is directed inward at themselves for being unable to prevent it.

Rage

Leaving-patterned people are stuck in a terrible dilemma. Buried underneath their self-hatred is an enormous rage at their early mistreatment. This rage is life affirming; it is a natural response to being hurt. Ideally, when we are being hurt, our life energy arises to protect us. It may arise as strength, anger, or even rage to say "No!" and protect the self. It is a self-unifying force. But because they don't have a strong enough energetic container to hold this amount of charge or a strong enough self to ride this big wave of feeling without falling apart, consciously feeling this rage would be overwhelming to those caught in the leaving pattern. It would shatter the very self that it is trying to protect. So their own strength energy, which arises to protect them, instead frightens them. Their unconscious belief is "My strength threatens me," or "My life force threatens my life."[7]

To cope with this dilemma, they tighten and stiffen the body to reduce the amount of life force moving through it. They disown their own strength. They may deny that they even have anger, and instead see themselves as being only loving and spiritual. This suppression of their own strength energy produces weakness in the body and many of the other body signs mentioned above. It leaves them feeling weak, helpless, and unsafe, and accounts for much of their difficulty protecting themselves in their interactions with others. Without strength and boundaries, they have no way to say "no" or push back.

Since the rage at how they were treated cannot be felt or expressed directly, it stays buried in the unconscious. However, it does not disappear. It is instead turned inward, against the self, and fuels the self-hatred and self-destructive acts described above. The rage cannot be safely opened up, however, until after the person has done a great deal of inner work to strengthen her self and her energetic container. Then she can turn it back toward the outside and begin to gradually feel it and release it in a safe way. We will go into this in more detail at the end of this chapter, in the section on healing the leaving pattern.

Personality Traits

Now let's look at the personality traits associated with the leaving pattern. These are the way a person who does this survival pattern will tend to look when she is caught in the pattern. When she is simply present, these qualities may be muted or even absent, but when she is in pattern, her appearance will be more like what follows.

Most likely, the first thing you'll notice will be a general sense of anxiety and fear. Often this shows up behaviorally as hyper-vigilance, a belief that danger is just around the corner, and a readiness to flee at the first sign of increased emotional intensity (even positive intensity). On the other hand, if the person is feeling safe when you first meet her, she may appear more as a playful sprite, with a childlike sense of lightness and magical wonder. Either way, there is a general impression of fragility. She is highly sensitive, in both positive and negative ways, and because of this, easily over-stimulated and overwhelmed.

Over time, you will notice a tendency to avoid social situations, personal feelings, and emotional intimacy, coupled with an even stronger need to avoid anger, confrontation and conflict. Instead of the vulnerability of sharing personal experience, you'll notice a preference for mental abstraction. These are all attempts to keep herself safe by avoiding anything that might over-stimulate and overwhelm her.

You may also notice a distrust of human connections and a belief that there is no safety or warmth to be found there. Instead, there is a preference for spiritual or non-human connections, often appearing as an easy sense of connection with divine love, nature, or nature spirits. She may be good friends with plants, animals, angels, and fairies, all of which are much safer than humans, since they don't have an ego or an inner critic, like humans do.

During meditation, she may feel an easy connection to spirit and may drop into deep inner states of oneness. But she has difficulty navigating in the physical world and operating as an individual in a separate, physical body. She may seem aloof or arrogant, especially if she claims to be more spiritually evolved than others, but this is only meant to keep them at a safe distance, not to control them.

You may also notice an extraordinary flow of creativity. She may invent, draw, paint, write, compose music or otherwise bring new creations into the world. Sometimes, this flow becomes a flood that is astonishing to watch, as it was with Robin Williams.

How They Recreate Their Early Wounding

As with all the survival patterns, leaving-patterned people tend to recreate their own early wounding through the very things they do to try to keep themselves safe. This tendency is unconscious, of course, but it very effectively maintains the kinds of relationships and experiences they had in childhood and therefore perpetuates the survival pattern.

One way they recreate their childhood wounding is by leaving their own body, which scares it on a cellular level. When they return, that cellular level fear is the first thing they encounter. This reinforces their belief that the physical world is not safe.

Another way they recreate their childhood wounding is by breaking the connection with others and leaving at the first hint of an emotional disturbance. When they leave, the other person feels abandoned and protests in some way, which creates the very sort of emotional disturbance that they feared. The other person's frustration and anger then seem like proof that the world is hostile and unsafe.

Because they are usually in denial of their own aggressive impulses and acts, they are not aware of how they use their aggression against others. Their aggression is almost always expressed in non-physical or passive ways, such as provoking aggression in others and then using the other's aggression as an excuse to break the connection. This maneuver allows them to withdraw from the relationship, while blaming the other person for causing the disconnection.

Patterned Thoughts

For people who do the leaving pattern, thinking is frequently separated from feeling. This makes them more capable of pure, abstract thought (as in the way Albert Einstein imagined himself riding on a beam of light in order to understand relativity), but less capable of thinking in a way that is informed by feeling and the heart. They prefer abstract, impersonal thinking to specific, personal thinking and feeling. One person described it this way: *"My attention goes to ideas, concepts, possibilities. I live a lot of my life in ideas and inspiration. I love the constant flow of inspiration."*

If we look at how they process their experience — at whether they prefer the visual, auditory, or kinesthetic channel for their mental processing — we see that they typically prefer the visual channel. This is the channel that is the least connected to the physical body as well as the one in which mental processing happens the fastest. As a result, people who do this survival pattern have a fast rhythm of thought, movement, and speech. They can rapidly process new information, work out all the possibilities and options, and see the implications. They are able to connect the dots and get to conclusions faster than other people. However, if they don't lay out how they got to a conclusion, others who aren't able to follow them are likely to become frustrated and impatient. This rapid thinking also leads them to talk faster than the average person. From the outside, it often looks like the motor inside them simply runs faster than it does in most people. Those who use the kinesthetic channel, the slowest of the channels, to process their experience often have a hard time keeping up.

Leaving-patterned people are even able to handle multiple mental threads at the same time. One man put it this way: *"I'm able to walk into a room, stand there, and listen to many different conversations at once throughout the room. Receiving and processing all of that is no problem at all. However, if I'm lost in listening to all those conversations, people who approach me see that no one is home and they don't stay to talk."* I have a reliable report of someone in this pattern who was able to play piano in a band onstage while simultaneously studying calculus from a book on the music stand.

The mind chatter of those caught in the leaving pattern is "Gotta get away," and when they go into pattern, their attention does actually go away from their body and from personal, present moment experience. This means that they lose touch with the sensations in their own body that would help them figure out "what I feel" and "what I want." It also disconnects them from the resources that could help them get out of their distress — both the resources already within them and the resources of others that they could ask for help. For them, however, the internal experience is not that they themselves went away, but that the resources went away. This makes them feel abandoned, when in fact, they are the ones who left. All this makes it especially hard for them to figure out what they need and ask for it.

Each of the survival patterns tends to create a characteristic sequence of thoughts when a person in that pattern sees that someone else has something that they want. For leaving-patterned people, the sequence goes something like, *"You have it. I want it. I'll just imagine I have it."*

Patterned Behaviors

Leaving

When people who are caught in the leaving pattern become uncomfortable, they try to manage their inner state by somehow leaving the situation. They may become more mental and abstract, leave the room, or completely dissociate by energetically leaving their body. Since they can't stand and fight or even ask for what they need, leaving is almost their only option when in distress.

Creativity

Their attention tends to go away from the physical body sensations and feelings, and often also away from the physical realm entirely. When this happens, a lot of their activity is taking place only in the mind and in other realms, activity which is not apparent in the physical world. It isn't until they return, bringing new music, mathematics, ideas, solutions to problems, etc., that their activity becomes apparent in this world. They literally go to different planes, gather lots of pieces, assemble them into something new, and then bring their creation back here.

Playfulness and curiosity

This is the most playful of all the survival patterns. Those who do this pattern can truly play and take delight in the experience. Because they are also very creative, they love creating new games and having new experiences. These are the people who want to go to a new restaurant and try a new dish they've never tasted before, the people who will try out a new route home from work just to see what will happen. Getting lost is not as scary for them as it is for some people — it's just something new to explore. People who do this pattern are comfortable in chaos and do not need to put things in order. They can relax into the chaos and let things unfold however they will. This is an extraordinary talent.

They are also very curious. They want to see something from every point of view: front, back, sides, above and below. Pablo Picasso's cubist art is an example of seeing something from all sides at once. If they want to know how you just did something, they will take you apart and reverse engineer your actions. This is an invasion, of course, but they will most likely do it so lightly that you will not feel it.

Difficulty functioning

Under stress, they may freeze, dissociate, or fragment, causing them to lose some functionality. In order to decrease their distress and manage their internal state, they then withdraw from what disturbs them. As mentioned earlier, their hatred of their own vulnerability and helplessness can lead to anything from self-neglect to active self-harm.

Patterned Experience of Time

For people who do the leaving pattern, time and space are "just coordinates," not a rigid structure that has to be obeyed. They are used to living in the all-time of the spiritual realms, not in the linear space and time of the physical world. The upside of this is that they can sometimes warp time and space to suit their own needs. The downside is that they may easily lose track of physical time and space, which means they can easily get lost or arrive late.

Patterned Emotional Life

Avoiding feelings

Generally, leaving-patterned people tend to avoid feelings, especially ones that are personal and negative, such as anger, need, or intense grief, and they especially avoid such feelings when around other people. On the other hand, when they're alone, they often review what has happened and feel it much more deeply than they did while it was happening. When in the presence of others, their attention goes to their fear of being hurt, but when they're alone, they feel safe enough to let themselves feel more. They may also preview a planned experience before it happens and feel it much more deeply during the preview than during the actual experience.

When they're feeling safe, they can be very playful and happy. Typically, this happens only when they're alone or with others who also do the leaving pattern.

When they are able to give voice to their anger, it usually takes the form of a white hot anger about unmet needs. The white hot intensity of this expression testifies to how much anger it takes to overcome their inner terror and express their needs to the outside world. Any anger that they are not able to speak may get broadcast psychically, whether intentionally or unintentionally. Others who are not psychically sensitive won't notice anything, but those who are psychically sensitive may react as if someone is yelling at them.

Fear

Each of the five survival patterns has a default emotion. This is the emotion that a person who does this particular pattern feels whenever too much energy hits her system. The kind of energy hitting her system doesn't matter — it could even be something positive, like pride or joy — but if it is enough to put her into overwhelm, she will start to feel her default emotion.

If you know what your own default emotions are, you may be able to avoid being swept away by the wave of emotion that hits you when you go into overwhelm. If you can say to yourself, *"Oh yeah, there's my usual feeling again. So is this what I'm really feeling right now, or is this just my default emotion kicking in?"* you have a much better chance of re-orienting yourself and not getting lost in the emotion.

The default emotion for leaving-patterned people is fear, and even a small increase in the level of energy around them can trigger it. The extra energy hitting their system is shunted upward in the body to the head, where the mind interprets it as fear. The mind then looks for the cause of the fear, but because it is constrained by its patterned beliefs, it looks only outside itself, sifting through all its perceptions of the outside world for any signs of danger. Usually it is able to find some evidence of danger, which reinforces the patterned sense of fear and the belief that the world is dangerous.

Interacting with Others

Sensitivity

Leaving-patterned people tend to be more energetically sensitive than others. Often this makes them very perceptive, although as with anyone, their perceptions can be totally distorted by projections of their own unconscious material. The upside of this perceptiveness is that they can be incredibly sensitive and attuned to others. The downside is that they may trust their own impressions so much that they don't bother to check them against reality, and so may feel certain about a "perception" that is not accurate.

When dealing with someone who does this survival pattern, you must keep in mind her extraordinary sensitivity to energy and her inability to tolerate very much of it. Because her own energetic boundaries are so weak, any energy you are radiating can easily penetrate her. This means she may sense how you feel before you do, but her interpretation of what she senses in you may or may not be accurate. If you are energetically merging with her, she will likely feel invaded. If you are angry — even if it has nothing to do with her — she will feel scared. On the other hand, if you're loving her silently from the next room, she is likely to feel that, too.

Vulnerability

Since people who do this survival pattern feel so vulnerable, their main priority in all interactions is safety. Everything else is secondary to their need for safety. Remember that their parents did not show them that human connections can be safe and loving. Instead, they were shown that human connections are often cold or hostile. So if you have an agenda when you approach them, they will tend to interpret your agenda as a threat, even without having any idea of what your agenda actually is.

Energetically, the process goes like this: when you focus your attention in order to initiate an action, your awareness shifts from a soft, wide field of diffused attention to a more narrow, contracted attention. Just by focusing your attention, you create a tension in your energetic field. This is one of the ways that prey animals detect the presence of a predator who is hunting them. For instance, when a lion is hunting gazelles, in the moment when the lion picks out his prey, his energy field contracts. The gazelles feel the contraction in the energy field around them, and they all bolt away from the contraction. On another day, when that same lion has a full belly and is not hunting, he may walk through the same herd of gazelles without causing a disturbance, because his attention remains diffuse and field-focused.[8]

Similarly, when you focus on an agenda, your energy field contracts. People who do the leaving pattern will notice this contraction in your energy field and interpret it as danger. If you want them to trust you, you must offer a soft contact without an agenda. Depending on which survival patterns you yourself do, offering such a soft contact may not be easy for you, because you may habitually hold your attention in a contracted state, focused on an agenda.

Because people who do this survival pattern actually were totally helpless when they got stuck in this early state, they typically continue to think of themselves as helpless. They don't think of themselves as having the ability to cause change in those around them, so it does not occur to them to make demands or put pressure on others to change. Instead, they tend to just accept the current situation as a given.

Others typically experience this lack of complaint as acceptance of their behavior, and may take the lack of opposition as permission to continue doing things which are invasive or abusive. So, if you want to know how safe someone who does the leaving pattern feels around you, notice how long they stay in contact with you, not whether they complain. They're more likely to manage their inner state by leaving (physically or energetically) than by complaining or demanding that you change your behavior.

Style of Contact

People who do different survival patterns usually have very different styles of making contact with others, which is one of the reasons that intimate relationships can be so confusing. In order to interact skillfully with other people, then, you need to first understand what styles of contact work for them, and then adjust your approach to fit their preferences.

The preferred style of contact for leaving-patterned people is essentially an avoidance of contact, unless it is done with a very light touch. So to help them feel safe, you must keep your touch light, both energetically and physically. For them, the safest kind of contact is in the mental realm, in the world of ideas, so the person is most likely to feel safe when the contact is made through the mind (artist's mind, not lawyer's mind), rather than through the body or the heart. If you want to make physical or heartful contact, make sure you are offering a warm, comforting energy, without an agenda.

When they need to process their experience, they will want to go away and do it by themselves. When alone, they can feel safe enough to relax into the experience and actually experience it, usually by reviewing it in their mind. This may be the first time they are able to actually be present in the experience, because while it was happening they may have been somewhat out of their body. Reviewing it afterwards may be the first time they are able to fully experience it. The richest times of their life are often when they are alone, either previewing or reviewing favorite experiences. Readers who are familiar with the terms introvert and extrovert will notice that this is the introvert's way of processing their experience. One of the reasons that people who do this survival pattern need so much time alone is simply so that they can process their experiences.

Romance

In romantic relationships, as in all others, leaving-patterned people will want to be approached without an agenda and with a light touch. Playful engagement will almost always work better than seriousness, and any expectations you have will feel to them like pressure and may scare them away.

Because they often have little felt sense of their own physical body, they may not be getting signals from their body about desiring contact or physical pleasure. Remember that you're dealing here with someone who does not expect connection with other humans to be a positive experience. For them, safety is in separateness, not in connection.

When in distress, they will need to pull away in order to feel safer, and they may even need to pull away just to relax. For instance, in order to relax into sleep, they may need to move over to the other side of the bed and not have you touching them. If you wanted the two of you to sleep in each other's arms, this may be difficult for you.

Sexuality

When it comes to sexuality, we find that many people who do this survival pattern began masturbating quite young, well before puberty. In masturbation they found a way to safely increase their feelings of pleasure and aliveness in the body and get some of the warmth that they were not able to get through connection with others.[9] As adults, they may need to use some solitary physical activity, such as running or swimming, to help them come more into their body before they are able to tolerate the intensity of sexual arousal. They may also need non-sexual stroking of their skin to help them focus on their body and find their edges before they are ready for sexual touching.

For some people who do this survival pattern, sex is more an energetic than a physical experience. Some women have reported that they can orgasm just from being penetrated by the energy emanating from their boyfriend's open palm when it is not even touching them, but held a few inches below their genitals.

Their Approach to Conflict

People who do this survival pattern typically want to avoid conflict at almost any cost. They have no history of winning confrontations or of conflict leading to anything positive, so they want to avoid all conflict. When anger or conflict arises, they will leave the situation physically or energetically (dissociate). Their only thought is "Gotta get away."

If they are unable to get away fast enough, the intensity of the conflict may shatter them, rendering them unable to function. Falling apart like this is terrifying. Now they feel even more scared and helpless than before they fragmented. Now there isn't even an "I" who is terrified; there is just the terror.

While shattered, they may be unable to follow the thread of the conversation, and may go off on a tangent, as if trying to move the focus of the conversation away from the conflict. From the outside, this may appear voluntary and intentional, but it is probably only an unconscious effect of their internal confusion and loss of center.

Weapons used in a conflict

They usually do not feel or express their own anger, but when they do, it will appear first on the psychic airwaves as a feeling of anger that floods the room. Although they avoid conflict in the physical world, they can be quite angry, vicious, and hateful on the psychic airwaves. They can even attack others by sending angry, hateful energy toward them. They can also control the psychic space by occupying all of it. This is a little bit like someone verbally filling the room with their anger by yelling hateful things and shouting over anyone else who tries to talk. However, others who are not psychically sensitive will most likely not notice anything.

The only physical-realm weapons at their disposal are leaving, confusion, distraction, and becoming invisible — if those can even be called "weapons." Their inability to stand their ground and fight for their needs, as some of the developmentally older survival patterns would, does not mean that they don't have needs. It only means that they don't have the aggressive skills that a child acquires during the later developmental stages. Do not think that, because they cannot fight for their needs, they don't have needs.

When they do finally give their anger verbal or physical expression, it typically appears as a white hot rage at their unmet needs. They have not had any practice at expressing anger, let alone rage, so they are unlikely to be skillful at expressing their rage when it does surface.

Communication Style

Leaving-patterned people are good at rapid, multi-channel communication. There are several channels of non-verbal communication happening between people all the time, and people who do this pattern are more skillful than the average person at using these additional channels. For them, the main channels of communication are energetic and psychic impressions, not language and words.

When listening to you, they will read the energy of your communication, but they may not listen closely to — or even really hear — your words. If the energy of your communication does not match your words, they will put their attention on the energy and disregard your words.

When speaking, their attention will be on the energetic and psychic impressions they are sending, not on the words. Because of this, their words may be jumbled, ungrammatical nonsense, if read literally. There may be big gaps in the words, where the most important part of their communication was not said in words at all, but only sent psychically. Often, they will neglect to name the person or subject they are talking about, assuming that you know it already, since they sent it as a psychic impression.

Two people who both have this psychic communication talent can talk to each other using hardly any words at all. It goes something like this: the first person says *"You know that time when . . . (send picture) . . . well, I went back there and it was so . . . (send feeling). What a bummer."* The listener gets the pictures and feelings on the psychic channel and understands completely, even though the main part of the communication was never expressed in words. The words just fill in the gaps. Their conversation may even be conducted silently, by simply tossing pictures and feelings back and forth. One friend of mine refers to this as "speaking dolphin."

To a third person, who does not have their shared psychic talent, such a conversation will be incomprehensible. For him, it's as if the other two are talking in some sort of code that he cannot decipher. He's likely to feel confused and left out, and may become frustrated and angry. Many fights between lovers arise out of these differences in communication styles, coupled with our belief that everyone uses the same way of communicating that we use, so if they misunderstood us, it must have been intentional.

Communicating with Them

When you communicate with people who do the leaving pattern, send your message on the psychic channel, if you can, as well as in the words. If you can't send it psychically, at least make sure that your energy matches your words, rather than contradicting them. Keep in mind that they will attend more to your energy than to your words, so pay attention to your feeling state and the energy in your body as you speak. If the energy in your body does not match the message you want to send, take the time to shift your feeling state before you try to speak to them.

When listening to them speak, don't focus too much on the words. Instead, put your attention on the emotions behind the words. Let the words just flow over you and feel for their flavor, instead of their literal meaning. Let the details go and focus on the feeling tone of what they're saying.

If you can't listen in their style, and you really need them to use words, then ask them to shift into your style . . . but do it gently. You might try saying something like: *"I'm sorry, I'm just not able to follow this, and I really need you to put it into words. Can you do that for me?"* When you say this, be sure that you're being kind and sincere, or they won't even hear your words.

If you're so frustrated and angry that you can't be kind and sincere, know that your anger is all that is coming across to them, so they're scared and probably half way out the door or out of their body already. In that situation, it's wiser to take a time out so that both of you calm yourselves before trying to continue the conversation. If your bodies are upset, neither of you is able to be present or skillful right now.

Their Way of Complaining About Something

For leaving-patterned people, the main way of complaining about something is to dissociate or "space out." Since this isn't an active form of complaint or even a physical act, it's easy for you to miss. Mentally and energetically, they just leave.

A slightly more noticeable way they may show their discomfort with the current conversation is to shift the focus from something personal to something impersonal and abstract. This is the same move they make inside their own body when they shift their attention up into their head. You are seeing that move mirrored in how their attention moves during the conversation. Typically, neither of these actions — spacing out or becoming less personal — are conscious or intentional. Often, they are not aware that they're uncomfortable; their patterned reaction just kicks in and moves them away from whatever is making them uncomfortable.

The most obvious way they will express a complaint is by physically leaving. But since they want to avoid conflict, they will probably slip away as quietly as possible.

Since they don't believe that actively complaining will cause anything to change, doing so rarely even occurs to them. Instead, their complaint is expressed in actions, often unconscious actions. It is expressed simply in some form of leaving. If you want to know when they're unhappy, you will most likely have to track this yourself, since they're not able to track it or put their complaints into words.

Their Way of Asking for Help

When people who are caught in the leaving pattern do ask for help, they usually believe that the resource or support they need has gone away and they want it back. Typically, it is still present, but they have moved their attention away, which makes them think it has disappeared. You can help them by gently bringing their attention back to their body in the here and now, where the resource or support actually exists. As they reconnect with their body, help them look around and find the resource or support that they wanted.

Making a Request of the Pattern

Again, keep your energy calm and your touch light. This can be especially difficult in this situation, since you do have an agenda or you wouldn't be making a request in the first place. It will help a lot if you can shift yourself into a playful feeling and present your request as a fun possibility. As you speak, go to the psychic channel if you can, and put a picture of your fun idea there, as well as in the words you're using. If you can't put your request on the psychic airwaves, at least make sure that your energy matches your words and conveys your intention that this can be a fun possibility.

Their Response to a Request

If a leaving-patterned person is not able to reference her body to assess whether she wants to agree to your request, she will instead use her mind to assess it. If her mind can figure it out, she will answer you from there. However, if the request can be answered only through referencing her body sensations (*"Are you tired?"; "Are you feeling sexy?"*) she is likely to go into confusion. And if that confusion is sufficiently distressing, she may dissociate.

Complimenting the Pattern

When you want to compliment someone who does the leaving pattern, try to keep your energy calm and your touch light. If you can, send softness and warmth to her on the psychic airwaves. Then, express your compliment in her language, by referencing what she values and pays attention to.

This is an important principle to keep in mind when complimenting anyone. If you want them to take in your appreciation, put it in terms that they understand, and reference what they value. Since those who do the leaving pattern value beauty, creativity, and originality, they're more likely to feel valued if you remark on how original and beautiful their creation is than if you focus on its correctness or on how well it functions. They probably don't care how correct it is or how well it functions, so your appreciation of those qualities will mean less to them. Similarly, appreciating how much fun you're having with them is likely to mean more to them than complimenting them on how well organized they are.

As with all things relating to the survival patterns, this is not a one-size-fits-all principle. In addition to considering what patterns the person does and what those patterns value, you'll also need to consider their personal values. If you watch their responses closely, you'll probably be able to tell when they took your compliment in and when they didn't.

Getting Yourself Out of the Leaving Pattern

Whenever you realize that you've gone into a pattern, your first job is to get yourself out of pattern and back to being present. At first, this may seem counter-intuitive. After all, you went into pattern to buffer yourself from a difficult experience. Why would you want to remove that buffer and have to face the upsetting experience without it?

There are several reasons. First, the survival pattern is distorting your perceptions and your experience. The upset may not be nearly as bad as it looks through the filter of the pattern. And even if it is, you need to see it clearly to find the best way to respond to it. Following a distorted map will not take you where you want to go.

Second, as long as you're in pattern, your response will be dictated by the pattern. It will be the pattern's automatic response, even if that response is not a good choice right now. In fact, the patterned response is likely to make things worse, not better. Since the survival pattern was formed when you were much younger and had fewer resources, it is very likely that you have better options now.

Third, when you get out of pattern and back to being present, you will once again have access to all the help, resources, and maturity that you have worked so hard to develop. Once you are back in presence, you will be able to find the best way to respond to this current situation.

So, as soon as you realize that you're in a survival pattern, start to figure out which one you're in and how to get out of it.

Signs you're in the leaving pattern

- you have lost connection with your body
- you are fragmented or "out there"
- all you can hear in your head is "Gotta get away!"

The solution: You need to come back. Your body did not leave you.

To get out of the leaving pattern

Shift your attention from the fear in your mind to your bodily sensations and your connection to the earth

Exercise:

Bend your knees and take a deep breath, keeping your eyes open.

To reorient yourself, say your own name out loud:

- notice the frequency of your name — that is your personal frequency.
- look for that same frequency in the core of your body. That is where you want to come back to. That is your home in the physical dimension.

Gently ask all of your fragments to come back. Consciously intend to bring yourself back in through the top of your head. Feel your awareness coming into each part of you as you move down your body. Start with your head and face and then move down through your neck, chest, back, arms, belly, pelvis, thighs, calves, and feet.

Look for evidence that the earth likes you and wants to connect with you. Connect down deep into the core of the earth.

Allow the energy of the earth to flow up into you and fill you, just as it flows up through the roots of a tree and into the trunk and branches. Let it fill you, nourish you, and support you.

Feel the core of your own body.

Feel that your body likes you and wants you here.

Look around for signs that others like you and want you here as well.

For more information on how to get yourself out of pattern, please see Chapter 13, *Getting Yourself Out of Pattern*, on page 358.

Remember: whenever you realize that you're in a pattern, your first job is to get yourself out of pattern and back to presence.

Healing the Leaving Pattern

Each of the survival patterns grows out of a situation where the child gets stuck in a particular developmental stage, unable to learn the skills of that stage and then use those new skills as the foundation for learning the skills of the next developmental stage. Because the leaving pattern is developmentally the very first of the survival patterns, the healing of this pattern requires that we return to the very beginning of life and build from there.

People who use this defense are comfortable with experiencing themselves as part of the divine oneness of the spirit world, but afraid to separate from it and become an individual, divine spark in a human body. Their unmet developmental need is to feel safe here in the human world — welcomed, loved, and nurtured by other people. Their developmental task is embodiment: orienting their awareness to the physical dimension, claiming the physical body as their own, coalescing an integrated sense of self, and then anchoring it in the body.

To feel safe enough to complete the process of embodiment, people who defend this way need a bridge to experiencing the physical world as friendly, rather than hostile. They cannot do this by themselves. They need someone to gather them up, provide a human connection that is safe, warm, and welcoming, and help them claim their body. They need support and instruction in many, many skills that they missed as an infant and child. They will be developing a variety of different skills at the same time, and the details will vary from person to person, but the process will generally look something like the following.

Sensing the body

One of their first tasks is simply to learn to put their attention on and feel their raw body sensations. As they begin to value these sensations as a source of information about themselves, their sensing will expand to exploring their feelings and emotions and to valuing these as sources of information about themselves, as well. Gentle bodywork can help to gradually relax the chronic tightness in the body and increase their bodily sensations.

103

Rosen Method bodywork is particularly useful in this process because it is very gentle. The practitioner simply puts his hands on those parts of the client's body that are not moving with her breathing, but frozen into stillness. The practitioner's touch helps her pay attention to the frozen parts of her body, and helps her release the hurts and fears that have been locked into those tissues.

Ortho-Bionomy is another form of bodywork that is particularly good for someone who is caught in the leaving pattern. The practitioner notices how the client is tensing her body to try to protect it, and then provides support for that tension. As it feels the support it needs coming from the outside, her body naturally relaxes into that support. Most of us, no matter what survival patterns we adopted, are deeply hungry for a real, felt sense of support. We usually don't feel this hunger, because the chronic tensions we carry keep it buried, but it will come to the surface as soon as we feel held and supported.

Grounding

Early on, people who were wounded in this way will need to learn how to ground and form a friendly connection to the earth. To do that, they will typically need to connect with another person who is well grounded. They will need to see that being grounded is actually good for that person and might be good for them, too. Then they will need clear instruction in how to ground themselves, followed by daily practice. The goal here is for them to personally experience the earth itself as safe, friendly, and welcoming, and to develop a strong energetic connection to it.

I have found that, for those who do the leaving pattern, modeling how a tree grounds itself is often a good way to begin learning these grounding skills. Trees show us how the core of the body (the trunk) can be deeply connected (rooted) into the earth. And trees are safe: because they don't have an ego or an inner critic, a tree will never criticize you for doing it wrong. Often, leaving-patterned people have used their psychic skills to communicate with trees before, so connecting with a tree is not a new idea for them. I ask them to connect with a big, strong, friendly tree and then ask it to show them how it grounds into the earth. Learning from a tree this way is a body-to-body transfer of knowledge, not a mental experience. It's like copying someone's dance moves, rather than talking to them about their moves. After they've done this with a tree once, I suggest that they make it a daily practice, trying it out with lots of different trees.

After they've established a connection to the earth, I ask them to start getting to know the earth. Is the earth friendly? Is it nourishing? Is it glad they're here? The first time they experience the earth as safe and welcoming to them, they may burst into tears, both from the relief of finally feeling this and from the grief of never having felt it before. As their system gets stronger, they will eventually be ready to move on from modeling the grounding of a tree to modeling the grounding of something bigger, like a mountain.

Core

Along with learning how to ground, leaving-patterned people need to develop a felt sense of their physical core. They may have a sense of self as a spirit, but they don't yet have a sense of self as a physical being. To develop this, they need to develop a felt sense of the core of their physical body.

The core of the body is a column that runs vertically through the center of the torso, like the trunk of a tree. If you sit up straight and imagine a line from the crown of your head down to your perineum, this is where your core is located. (Your perineum is located at the bottom of your torso, between your anus and your genitals.) Your core is the part of your body where you are the most you. When you want to feel your self, this is the place to look. When you want to know how you feel, this is the place to sense into. Your thoughts arise in your head, but your sensations and feelings arise in your body, and mostly in your core. If you want to build a stronger felt sense of self, putting attention on your core is the place to start.

Your core is shaped like a column and includes your spine and the space just in front of it. You may experience it as having any width, from very narrow to wider than your body. The way you sense your core may be mostly kinesthetic, mostly visual, or even auditory. How you sense it is not so important, as long as you're able to sense it somehow. I suggest that you make sensing your core a daily practice. You can begin by letting large trees teach you about their core, as discussed above. Many movement and bodywork techniques also support awareness of your core, particularly ballet, Pilates, Gyrotonics, Alexander Technique, Aston-Patterning, and Body-Mind Centering. For help in feeling your core, I recommend taking classes or sessions in any of these methods.

Physically sensing your own core is both a subtle and a profound experience. It is subtle in that the felt sense will never be as vivid as poking your palm with a finger or grabbing your own wrist with the other hand. At first it will probably be hard to tell whether you're actually feeling something or only imagining that you're feeling something. Don't let that discourage you. As you continue putting your attention on your core, the sensations will gradually become stronger. Remember that you're also strengthening your attention by doing this practice.

Just like a muscle, your attention becomes stronger the more you exercise it. As your attention becomes stronger, you'll begin to feel your core more vividly.

Sensing your own core is profound in that it gives you a direct experience of actually existing here in the physical plane as a physical being. You no longer have to infer your existence from seeing your reflection in a mirror or from others' responses to you. Instead, you have a direct and undeniable experience of feeling and knowing yourself. For some, this is an entirely new experience.

Remember to put your attention on the entire length of your core, from the crown of your head down to your perineum, not just on one point, like the heart or the belly. Feeling yourself so vividly may trigger many different emotional reactions within you. You may simply feel present and calm, or you may feel elated to know that you actually exist. You may feel afraid that you're doing something wrong, or you may feel empty, as if something is missing. You may feel spacious, which is like emptiness but without a sense of lack. All sorts of thoughts and feelings may arise. Don't let those throw you. Note them, but bring your attention gently back to the practice of sensing your core. Each of those feelings contains information for you, and it may take some time for your body to process them and distill that information for you, but you can let that happen at its own pace and in its own time. No need to rush, and no need to worry that you're doing it wrong. Just let the experience unfold within you, gradually, over time. If you need help in processing the feelings that come up, then go and get that help. There is no need to do this all alone. And the fact that your felt sense of your own core will start out being faint and grow slowly will give you time to work through the feelings that come up as you do this practice.

Reaching out for soothing

People caught in this survival pattern also need to learn both how to reach out to others for soothing and how to receive soothing when it is offered. They need a safe, non-sexual situation in which they can allow themselves to feel their need for contact and comforting, reach out for it, latch on to the other person, and then snuggle in and let their body drink in what they need. Of course, reaching out is exactly what they learned to avoid, since that did not go well for them early on. So there are likely to be many fears and tears in the way of reaching out now. But, with help and support, these can be faced, felt, and allowed to pass through. Eventually, people who have been caught in this pattern can learn to turn toward others for comforting, instead of turning away. This will allow them to develop healthy emotional attachments to other people.

Feeling soothed and nurtured by others also teaches their body how to soothe and nurture itself. These skills were probably missing in the parenting they received, so they do not have this template in their body. Every child needs to learn how to soothe and nurture themselves, of course, but this skill is particularly lacking in leaving-patterned people.

Developing strong boundaries

Since much of the overwhelm experienced by those who adopted the leaving pattern is caused by having weak boundaries around their body, they need to develop stronger boundaries. There are two ways to look at boundaries: psychologically and energetically.

The field of psychology has produced many books on the importance of *psychological boundaries*. These books show the reader the difference between living with healthy boundaries and living without them. They help you distinguish between what is my feeling and what is your feeling, my responsibility and your responsibility. They teach you how to say "no" when you need to, even though you may disappoint someone else. And they show you how to deal with the long list of objections that often arise — both in you and in others — when you first begin to assert your boundaries.

These books also teach you that, for your boundaries to be effective, you must be able to enforce them. You do that by stating to the other person what action you will take if they violate your boundary. It must be an action that you are able and willing to carry out. For instance, if your lover frequently yells at you, you may decide that you're no longer willing to accept this behavior and that, if he does it, you will leave the room. Your boundary is "no yelling at me" and your consequence is "I will leave the room."

Before announcing your new boundary, however, you must think through all of the ways this scenario might play out so you can be sure that you mean what you say and that you're willing to enforce your new boundary. By setting a new boundary, you are changing one of the norms of the relationship. Your lover may respond to your boundary by changing his behavior, proposing a compromise, or even leaving the relationship, so you have to be clear about how important this boundary is to you before you take action.

Then, you have to tell your lover what you have decided and that you will leave the room if he yells at you again. Finally, you have to carry out your action each time he violates your boundary. It is very likely that he will cross your boundary just to see whether you're really willing to carry out the consequence you've named, so be ready for a test. In fact, be ready for several tests. Your lover probably does not want to give up the privilege of yelling at you and whatever benefits it gives him, so you will have to show him, by your repeated actions, that you're serious about this. When he gets that you can and will enforce your boundary, he will have to decide how to respond to this new reality. The process of developing strong, healthy psychological boundaries is a big topic, too big for us to do it justice here. But it is very well covered in many self-help psychology books, so I suggest that you get two or three of them and begin working through the steps that they advise.

Developing strong *energetic boundaries* is not so well covered in books, so I will lay out the basic practice here. Begin by imagining that you have an egg-shaped bubble that surrounds you. It extends out about two or three feet beyond your body in all directions, including above and below you. At the edge of this bubble, imagine that you have a membrane, like the membrane that surrounds a cell. The cell membrane is what separates "inside" from "outside" for the cell. It regulates what enters the cell and what leaves the cell. The membrane at the edge of your personal bubble should be doing the same for you. It should contain your personal space and regulate what comes into it. By putting your attention on this membrane, you can strengthen it. It has intelligence, just like a cell membrane does, so you can actually talk to it and instruct it to allow into your space only what is good for you. I recommend spending 5-10 minutes several times a day on this practice until it becomes second nature. Just hold in your mind an image of the bubble around you and highlight the membrane at the edge of your bubble. Experiment with talking to your membrane, telling it how you want it to protect you and serve you, and thanking it in advance for its help. Then notice what effect your practice has on your experience, moment to moment.

Because our culture is so unaware of the energy world, this idea of holding an energetic boundary around yourself may sound strange to you. Don't let that prevent you from practicing this exercise. Fortunately, leaving-patterned people are usually sensitive to energy and familiar with it, so this exercise doesn't sound as strange to them as it does to those who adopted the later survival patterns.

Differentiating me from not me

Along with learning to differentiate what is me from what is not me in the psychological sense (my needs vs. your needs, my responsibility vs. your responsibility), all of us need to learn how to clear out foreign energies that have gotten into our space. This is especially important for a person who does the leaving pattern, since her weak energetic boundary is not able to stop foreign energies from coming into her space. Having other people's energies and feelings inside her space makes her feel invaded and confused. She will feel much safer when she has only her own energies and feelings inside her space.

In order to clear the foreign stuff out of our space, each of us needs to learn and practice the skill known as "me/not me." The practice goes like this:

1. Say your own name. Notice the frequency of your name: that is your personal frequency. If the idea of frequency doesn't make sense to you, think of it as your note, your taste, your scent, your feeling tone, your is-ness, or whatever works for you.

2. Look for that same frequency in the core of your body.

3. Use one of the following methods to clear out of your body and your bubble anything that doesn't match your own frequency.

    a. Talk to the edge of your core, that column in the center of your body, and tell it that it is going to push out ahead of it anything that doesn't match your frequency. Then imagine your core gradually expanding in diameter and pushing everything that is "not me" out ahead of it, the way a glacier pushes rocks ahead of it to form a moraine. This method seems to work better for people who are more kinesthetic.

    b. If you're more visual, try this. Decide that everything that is "not me" within your space is going to light up so you can see it. Then imagine using a vacuum cleaner to go around and vacuum out all the lit up stuff. Or highlight each one and then delete it, the way you do on a computer. Or blow up each piece that is lit up, if that appeals to you.

    c. Or, since each piece that is "not me" came from someone else and really should be there instead of here, you can imagine that there is still a thread that connects each piece to wherever it came from. Then you just instruct all the threads to become elastic and pull their pieces out of you and back to wherever they belong. Many people like the "putting everything back in order" feeling of this one.

    d. Or, invent some other method for clearing all the foreign energies and feelings out of your space. Let your imagination go and be as creative as you like. Your method can be anything that gets the job done.

Developing social skills

Since people who protect themselves by leaving have mostly avoided interacting with others, they usually need social skills training. A social skills training group can be very helpful for this. It will give them both instruction in social skills and the opportunity to practice those skills with others in the group. Typically, such groups are offered by therapists and educational institutions; an internet search will likely reveal a group near you.

Returning to the body

People who use leaving their bodies as a defense strategy also need to learn to sense the difference between being in their body and being out of it. They can learn this skill by practicing intentionally leaving (dissociating) and coming back (re-associating), while tracking how they do this and what it feels like. With enough practice, returning to the body can become automatic, like the way we unconsciously maintain our balance, moment to moment. As with all the other skills, it will be easiest to practice this with the support of someone who can track what you're doing and support you in your efforts.

Recovering from shattering

A more advanced skill is learning how to recover more rapidly from being fragmented. The best way for a person to do this is to put her attention on her felt sense of her own core and use that as a center to return to and re-assemble herself around. Bodywork and Reichian breath work can be helpful to her in building that felt sense of her own core. These methods build and move energy in the body in ways that support becoming more embodied.

To completely re-assemble herself, the person must also retrieve all of the pieces that were lost during her original shattering, and then re-integrate those pieces into her sense of self. Since finding all those pieces, still scattered through many dimensions, requires a very high level of psychic skill, she will need the help of someone who has those skills to complete the retrieval process.

Dissolving the terror

People who were conditioned into this pattern also need to gently and gradually unfreeze the places where they froze in shock a long time ago. They need to feel safe enough for the shock to melt and for their system to digest whatever has been frozen. They will need the help of a skilled therapist to accomplish this, however. The therapist must be able to manage the client's intensity so that she doesn't go into overwhelm and get retraumatized. She has already experienced far too much overwhelm, and additional experiences of overwhelm will not be helpful.

This part of the work is best left until the person has developed a felt sense of her body and is able to reference it during the therapeutic work. She will need support to stay in touch with her body sensations moment by moment during the process as her body digests the frozen trauma. I have found that the newer energy psychology technologies, such as Emotional Freedom Technique ("tapping") and Matrix Reimprinting, can facilitate this process rapidly and with a minimum of difficulty, but again, the practitioner must be skilled at managing the client's level of intensity so that she doesn't go into overwhelm again.

Strengthening the self

All of the above practices, taken together, will help the person develop a strong, integrated ego. This includes developing a felt sense of her own core and her own self in the body. It also includes restoring the flow of life force within the body and establishing boundaries around the body. This development of a stronger container and sense of self will make her more able to tolerate states of strong emotion without leaving or shattering. It will also enable her to more easily say "no" and stay connected with another person, rather than physically or emotionally leaving.

Disidentifying from the inner critic

To the extent that she is still identified with her inner critic, she will need help in learning to disidentify from it, recognize its attacks, and defend herself against them. Being able to hold it at bay will clear a space inside her and make it easier for her to hear her own voice and feel her own needs and impulses.

Since listening to her inner critic's voice has been the primary source of her self-hatred, disidentifying from that voice is the key to freeing herself from that feeling. This change in her relationship to her inner critic will also free her from its demands for perfection. (We will go into this in more detail in the chapter on the rigid pattern).

Deciding to live

Somewhere during her healing process, she will come face to face with the fact that she has not yet chosen human life — that she is still ambivalent about living in the physical plane as a human being. At some point, she will have to choose life. With the help of a therapist who is firmly rooted here in the physical plane and who offers her a warm, welcoming human connection, she will have to actively decide to cross over the bridge into individual human life here in a physical body. This is the moment in which she claims her own life, her own body, and her right to exist here. For some people, there is also a wave of grief about giving up the spirit world as their primary home.

Anger work

Because they are usually in denial of their own aggressive impulses and acts, people who run this survival pattern need help in identifying how they unconsciously use aggression against others. They may be totally unaware of how they are throwing anger at others in the psychic realm, so they will need help in recognizing this, taking responsibility for it, and containing it.

In the physical realm, their aggression is almost always expressed in passive-aggressive acts, such as provoking aggression from others and then using their aggression as an excuse to withdraw from the connection. Once they are able to recognize their own aggression, they can usually follow the thread back to discover what they need and then act more directly to get it. Self-assertiveness training can be helpful for them at this stage so that they can learn how to ask for what they want more directly.

But anger work is tricky for a person who uses this survival pattern. As discussed earlier, she faces a dilemma: the child inside needs to rage at how she was mistreated, but the child is so small and the rage is so big that actually feeling the rage too soon will shatter her. Instead of unifying and protecting her, the strength of her own energy arising threatens and frightens her. Because of this, opening up her anger must be postponed until she has done a great deal of the other work outlined above, that is, until she has developed a strong sense of self that is firmly rooted in the body, and she can tolerate a strong flow of energy through her body. Only then is it time for her to begin touching her anger energy directly, and then only gently, in tolerable doses. If she is ready and the dose is not too large, the experience will leave her feeling a little stronger and more self-confident, not weaker or self-doubting.

Within the rage, there is a self for her to experience and express. Within the rage, there is also the strength to defend that self and act in the world. She needs to express her rage and strength and see that no one dies from it. She needs to see that expressing her rage and strength brings something good, and that she can have an effect on others and get what she needs. She also needs to see that if she makes a mistake and hurts someone, she can apologize and not lose the relationship and the love that comes with it. In short, she needs to learn that she can let her energy flow freely through her body and things will work out alright.

Feeling her own strength rise in her body to support and protect her also makes the world seem safer. As more energy flows through her, she will feel more warmth in her body. This opens up her deepest, earliest need: the need to feel held by a warm, nourishing, human love. Since infancy she has felt the physical world to be a cold and hostile place, and to cope with that she has had to minimize her own need for human warmth and connection.

As the possibility of human connection returns, the grief at its loss will also return. She will likely cycle through waves of rage, longing, and grief. But each wave will allow a little more life energy to circulate through her system. Her body will feel warmer and stronger, her physical sensations more alive and vivid. Gradually, as her own strength and warmth increase, the physical world will also seem warmer and more inviting to her, and her self-care and orientation in physical time and space will improve. Her increasing self-esteem and self-love will lower her barriers to loving and attaching to others. She will retain the talents and skills of the leaving pattern, but she will now have the capacities needed to complete the tasks of embodiment and individuation.

Energetic skills needed

Leaving-patterned people are very talented at perceiving energy, but they still need to develop all of the basic energy skills: ground, core, edge, and me/not me.

Their human need and spiritual need

Ultimately, the human need of people who do this survival pattern is to feel welcomed into the physical world and the body, to feel safe here, and to develop an integrated ego which is able to function here. Their spiritual need is to become an individual, divine spark in a human body. As they succeed, they can take pleasure in being an embodied spark of the Divine.

For more help in determining which patterns you go into, please visit
www.The5PersonalityPatterns.com.

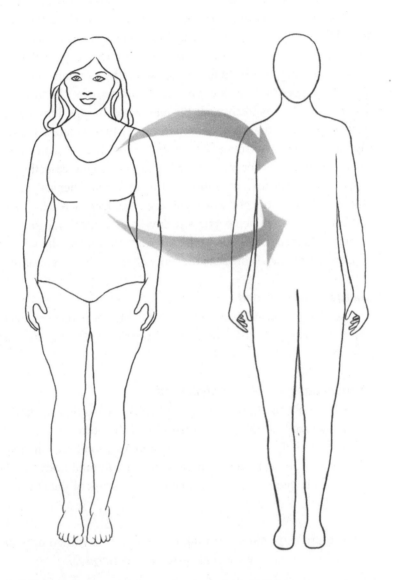

The Merging Pattern – body and energy flow

– 8 –

The Merging Pattern

"I can never get full. I'm not enough."

LIKE ALL THE SURVIVAL PATTERNS, the merging pattern is a holding pattern in the body, conditioned into it by trauma, which creates a particular habit of attention. The habit here is to shift attention away from the self and internal resources and toward others and external resources. This pattern develops in response to a feeling of deprivation during the nursing stage, when the child is so young that she* actually has very few internal resources and really does need others to do everything for her.

The difficulty arises when the child gets stuck in that mindset and continues to believe that she must get others to meet her needs instead of learning how to meet her own needs. So her attention stays focused on her connection to others and on pleasing or manipulating others to get what she needs, instead of on developing her own internal capacities.

Range of Functioning

Each of the survival patterns exists across a broad spectrum of functionality, from those completely ruled by the pattern to those who wear the pattern

---

* To avoid the cumbersomeness of having to continually say "he or she," I will assign a gender to the child described in each chapter and then stick with that gender throughout the chapter. For example, in this chapter, I will assume the child is a girl. However, all five of the patterns are found in both genders, and everything said about the girl in this chapter could just as easily have been said about a boy.

lightly. For this pattern, the variation occurs mostly in the person's capacity to reference her own needs and act to get those needs met. Lower functioning people are able to reference only others, while higher functioning ones are also able to reference themselves and act on their own behalf.

On the low end of the spectrum, we have people who are totally caught in the pattern: it organizes them and rules their life. They have no capacity for self-referencing and no belief that their own actions can result in getting their needs met. When they have a need, they automatically pull on others to give them what they need, or, if that fails, they collapse in a puddle of tears.

In the mid-range, we have people who still live within the worldview of the pattern, but who can, with guidance and support, reference themselves and begin to act on their own behalf. They still automatically turn to and rely on others, but can allow their attention to be directed back to themselves and their own capacities.

On the high end of the spectrum, we have people who can generally stay present while making use of the pattern's skills and talents. While they are still very skillful at referencing others, they are also able to consistently reference themselves and act to get what they need.

The Gifts of the Merging Pattern

As a person uses any of the patterns, she continually practices the skills that that pattern requires. Over time, she becomes exceptionally proficient in those particular skills. As she heals the wounds that created the pattern and becomes able to shift her attention out of the pattern and back to presence, the abilities she has acquired stay with her and become the gifts of the pattern. Now she is able to employ her exceptional abilities as she responds to the needs of the present moment. Even though some of the physical structures remain in her body, she has shifted out of the patterned survival defense and into the gifts of the pattern.

The gifts of the merging pattern are the gifts of the heart: love, compassion, nurturance, and generosity. People who use this survival pattern are typically heart-centered, and at their best, they can actually radiate love energy.

They are always aware of the emotional connections between people. For them, it is the flow of love between people that matters most. They are Masters of Connection, and it is relationship that organizes their life — not ideas, not rules, not power. This applies to all kinds of relationships, not just romantic ones.

These are the people who want to make sure that everyone in the group is feeling included and happy. They are very attuned to the feeling states and needs of others and very generous in filling those needs. They are good at listening and are kind, supportive, and helpful. They are aware of other people's likes and dislikes and enjoy making them happy. They enjoy being with other people and are good at bringing people together and creating community.

When merging-patterned people are in the gifts of the pattern, there is a sense of abundance, nurturance, and generosity about them. Their generosity takes many forms, from feeding, calming, and caring for others, to graciously accommodating them. One person put it this way: *"I feel like a warm, soft, comfy bed with huge comforters with beautiful colors and patterns and textures, and there's room for lots of cuddling and laughing and coziness there."* They are very focused on the issue of nourishment, and are especially good at nourishing others with both love and food. The love that flows out of them gives them a quality of being downright yummy. At its best, the merging character becomes the Good Mother.

Merging-patterned people are very strong in right brain functioning. At their best, they display emotional intelligence, receptivity, and sensitivity. They are open-hearted — accepting and trusting, innocent and impressionable. Because they're so accommodating and compassionate toward others, forgiveness is easy for them. They are slow to anger and unlikely to judge others or hold a grudge.

They tend to focus their awareness outward on to others, rather than inward on their own feelings and needs. While both men and women do this pattern, energetically the merging pattern is the most feminine of the five survival patterns, and therefore the one that tends to be the most receptive and responsive to others' words and behaviors.

People with this structure are also Masters of Pleasure and are adept at enjoying pleasure in all its forms. They enjoy intimacy through both touch and feeling, and can tune in to the other person's inner state as well as their own. They enjoy the reciprocity of feeling that is sometimes referred to as "limbic resonance" or the "pleasure loop." This means that they can surrender into both their own pleasure and into the joy of pleasing the other. Given these gifts, it's no surprise that they have a reputation for being truly wonderful lovers. Their sensuality extends to enjoying all the senses and all the good things in life. They find life delicious. They love good food, good sex, and all the comforts life can provide, both for themselves and for others.

At their best, merging-patterned people are also lots of fun. They enjoy life and laugh a lot. They are able to find delight in most things and are good at finding something to be glad about in every situation. They still have the gifts of childhood — an ability to be happy, bubbly, playful, and simply present in the moment. They tend to focus on Being, rather than Doing, on the present-moment sensory experience, rather than on abstract ideas or on plans for the future. Their emphasis is on play and the present moment, rather than on work or accomplishment in the future.

As Masters of Connection, they can feel that everything is connected to everything, so they understand that they are connected to all the rest of the Universe, and that everyone else is, too. One person described it as, *"I have my own individual sunbeam. We all do. It feels very real to me, like of course we all have a sunbeam. I'm my own individual piece of the rainbow, too."*

The radiant love that is one of the gifts of this pattern is attractive to all who come in contact with it. If you want to attract people, whether for social or business reasons, switching on this radiance will do the job. At their best, merging-patterned people are capable of radiating so much love that they can shift the energy of an entire group. A friend told me of a Thanksgiving dinner during which members of her birth family began sniping at each other. Her merging-patterned husband quietly dropped deep inside himself and began radiating such a strong love energy that the sniping stopped and everyone returned to enjoying dinner together.

As we will see later, the key to consciously moving into the gifts of the merging pattern is good self-care — learning to love and nourish yourself first.

Examples

- the archetypal Good Mother
- the heroines of romance novels who wait for rescue
- Pollyanna in the film *Pollyanna*
- Drew Barrymore's character in the film *50 First Dates*
- Marilyn Monroe
- Oprah Winfrey
- Bill Clinton (compensated merging)

Alternate Names

- Oral

- the Lover

- the Dependent personality (for pure merging)

- the Self-Reliant (for compensated merging)

- the Giver (for compensated merging)

- the Undernourished Child

Exercise – Being Caught in the Pattern

Getting Life from Others

This exercise is designed to give you a felt sense of the experience of someone who is caught in the merging pattern and has to turn to others for every need. As you go through this exercise, try not to judge it, but instead just notice how familiar or unfamiliar the experience is and what it would be like to live this way every day.

Standing with your feet about shoulder width apart, begin pulling the center of your chest back into your body, as if you're trying to protect your heart. As you do this, notice how pulling your heart center inward like this causes your pelvis and head to move forward. Seen from the side, the line of your torso has now shifted from being a straight vertical line to being concave, like this:)

Now let your shoulders also round forward, as you pull your heart center in even farther. Notice how your breathing has become shallow, since you can no longer fully expand your chest to inhale.

Now imagine that all the muscles in your body have become soft, weak, and puffy. Let your whole body become soft and diffuse, sort of like the Pillsbury Dough Boy. If you normally hold an energetic boundary around yourself, let it dissolve until you can't really tell any more where you end and others begin. Let all the structures inside you dissolve until you're just fluid inside, almost like a cloud of mist.

If you tend to ground yourself to the earth beneath you, let that connection dissolve until you're just a floating bubble. Notice how the loss of that

119

grounding and support makes your legs feel soft and weak, and how much harder it is now to stand on your own two feet.

Now notice how vulnerable and needy you feel. There is no structure or strength inside you. There is no solid ground under you to support you. There is no edge that defines you or protects you. Since there is no container to hold it, any energy that comes into you drains right out again. Notice that you feel empty inside.

You need something from somebody. But even trying to lift your arms to reach toward them brings a wave of shame at how empty and needy you are. Asking brings the risk of judgment and rejection. So don't do anything physical to try to get what you need. Just wait until someone comes into view and then use your eyes to get them to help you. Make your eyes into pleading, helpless, puppy dog eyes. Send out your need through your eyes until they can't resist you anymore. At the same time, send out a feeler from your belly with a suction cup on the end of it. Try to plug into their belly and drink from them.

It's all about the connection. Only connection to someone else will fill you up. You can't do it for yourself. All you can do is try to get them to do it for you. But how can you do that? How can you get them to like you? How can you get them to give you what you need?

Let yourself just walk around like this for a while. Imagine that this is your experience of life, all day, every day. Feel into what it would be like to go through life this way.

After exploring this for a while, relax, shake out your body, and take some time to absorb what you just experienced:

- *How easy or difficult was it for you to shift your attention this way?*

- *Did it seem familiar to you? Or did it seem strange and unusual?*

- *What was it like to feel so weak, empty, and needy?*

- *How was it to try to get everything you needed from someone else?*

- *What thoughts or feelings arose as you did this exercise?*

- *What thoughts or feelings seemed to get in the way?*

- *What would it be like to live this way all the time?*

Now, let's make sure you're completely back from the exercise. Stand up and plant your feet firmly on the floor. Feel the pressure in your feet of the earth supporting you. Bring your attention to a line drawn from the crown of your head down to your perineum. This is your core, the part of your body where you are the most you. Breathe into your core and feel yourself from the inside. Now let your core extend downwards into the earth, like the roots of a tree. Feel how these roots connect you with the earth, how they both support and nourish you. Any time you need more energy, strength, or confidence, you can ask the earth to send what you need up through your roots and into you, filling your body. Take as much time as you like to experiment with these sensations before moving on to the next exercise.

Exercise – The Gifts of the Pattern

Radiating Love

This exercise is designed to give you a felt sense of one of the gifts of the merging pattern. As you go through this exercise, just notice how familiar or unfamiliar the experience is and what it would be like to have this skill always at your disposal.

Sit down comfortably, with your spine relatively straight, and close your eyes. Take several deep breaths down deep into your body and release them. Once again, breathe into your core and feel yourself from the inside. While continuing to feel your core, let yourself recall a moment when you felt a profound love flowing through your body. Perhaps it was a moment with a newborn baby, or a time watching your child sleep. Perhaps it was a moment with a parent or spouse who was near death, a moment when all the hurts and disagreements of the past seemed to melt away, leaving only the love between the two of you. Perhaps it was a moment with a dearly beloved pet. Or a moment when you felt a profound love for yourself. Or a time when you felt wrapped in the love of something greater than yourself.

However it comes to you, let yourself tune in to that moment deeply. As you keep part of your attention on your core, feel how the love flowing through you shifts your internal state. Let that happen. Breathe that love in. Marinate in that love. Let your body tune itself to the frequency of love. Just as if you were turning the dial of a radio to a particular station, let your attention open to this love. If it hasn't already, let the love start to fill you. Let it seep into every corner of your body, gradually filling every cell with its sensation.

Notice especially how the love fills the core of your body, and as it does, let it gradually begin to radiate out from there. Perhaps it first fills your own body and then spills out and fills the space around you. However it happens, notice that you are now embodying and emanating Love. It is filling you and radiating out from you in all directions.

Let this happen easily and gently, while still respecting others and their own personal space. Don't impose it on them or attempt to change them. Just let it flow out from you as an offering to any who want it.

Let yourself enjoy this experience as long as you like. You may want to try moving about or just sitting still. You may want to be by yourself or out in nature or interacting with others.

Let yourself take some time to absorb what you have experienced. When you're ready, consider the following:

- *How easy or difficult was this exercise for you?*

- *Did it feel familiar or strange?*

- *This exercise asked you to shift your state of being, but not to do anything physically. What was that like for you?*

- *What thoughts or feelings arose as you did this exercise?*

- *What thoughts or feelings seemed to get in the way?*

- *What would it be like to have access to this inner state all the time?*

Exercise – The Gifts of the Pattern

The Pleasure Loop[1]

This is a partner exercise designed to help you experience the pleasure of giving pleasure. It's not about performance. It's not about technique. It's just about enjoying giving your partner pleasure. It's about noticing how your partner's pleasure feeds you and gives you pleasure.

Find a partner for the exercise.

Choose who will be the Giver and who will be the Receiver.

Giver: You will be touching the Receiver in a simple, non-sexual way that feels good to them. You might be stroking their arm or face or hair. You might be gently rubbing their feet. Ask the Receiver what they want, and work out something that's comfortable for both of you.

Both: Figure out a way to position yourselves so that both of you feel physically comfortable and supported. This is important — if either of you is uncomfortable, you will be unable to focus on the pleasure.

Giver: Try giving the Receiver exactly the touch they want. Ask for feedback and adjust what you're doing until you get it just right. When they begin to feel the pleasure, you will feel their body relax. It may take a while for them to relax into it. That's okay. Give it time.

Receiver: Keep giving your partner feedback until their touch is just the way you want it. Then just relax and let it in. Feel free to moan and sigh.

Giver: Can you feel the pleasure flowing through your partner? If you can, does that give you pleasure?

Receiver: Can you feel your partner taking pleasure in giving you pleasure?

Giver: Can you feel your own pleasure in giving pleasure to your partner? This is the pleasure loop.

After 5–15 minutes, stop and take some time to share with your partner:

- *How was that for each of you?*
- *What did you discover?*

Switch roles and repeat.

The Skill of Referencing

In order to understand the merging pattern, we must first understand referencing. Referencing is a fundamental skill, one that each of us must learn to become an emotionally healthy adult. Simply stated, it is the skill of sensing inner experience. When you are self-referencing, you are sensing your own inner experience. When you are other-referencing, you are sensing someone else's inner experience. Many people have grown up without this skill or with the ability to reference only self or only other, so this idea may sound strange to you at first.

To reference yourself, put your attention on the core of your body, the place where you are most yourself. When you want to find out something about yourself, this is the place to put your attention. When you wonder how you are feeling, this is the place to look for the answer. When you have a question about what you want, this is where you will find your answer. Whether it is a small question ("Do I want chocolate or vanilla?") or a big question ("Do I want to marry him?"), as long as it is about you, this is where to put your attention to find your answer.

So how do you get the answer? First, you put your attention on your core. Then you make a clear statement *("I want chocolate"* or *"I want vanilla")* and sense whether the statement resonates with your core. Resonating might look-feel-sound like one of these: "it fits," "it matches," "it clicks into place," "it rings," "it sounds right," "it shines," "it's clear," or something similar. This is a "yes" signal. Not resonating might look-feel-sound like "it doesn't fit" "it's not right," "it sounds wrong," "it doesn't feel right," or something similar. This is a "no" signal.

If you're not sure what your own personal "yes" and "no" signals are, try testing them with statements that you know are clearly true or false. For instance, say out loud, *"My name is _____"* and then say your name. Sense your core. Now say out loud, *"My name is Mickey Mouse"* or anything that's not your real name. Again, sense your core. What difference do you feel in your core between a true statement and a false statement? Practice this by trying out lots of clearly true and clearly false statements, going back and forth until you can sense the difference in your core's response to a true statement versus a false statement.

If you're finding it difficult to sense anything inside your torso, you may need to practice simply putting your attention on your body sensations until they become perceivable. Many families, and even whole cultures, consider it selfish or self-centered to want anything for yourself, and they condition their children out of sensing themselves and knowing what they want. If this happened to you, there may be an unconscious part of you that steers you away from feeling yourself. As you attempt to sense your core, a lot of feelings may surface, feelings that you were not allowed to have when you were a child. If this happens, it will be very helpful to be in therapy or have some sort of support to help you process those feelings as you practice sensing your core.

If you were conditioned out of sensing yourself, it is likely that you were encouraged to sense the feelings and needs of those around you. You may well be a champion at referencing others, while being clueless at referencing yourself. This almost compels you to please everyone but yourself because that is the only information you have to guide you in what to do.

Referencing others is basically the same process as referencing yourself, except that you put your attention on the other person's core instead of on your own. You notice what he is feeling by sensing his core, whether he speaks or remains silent. You may not have known that it is even possible to sense others in this way, and you may not have developed this skill. If the idea of directly sensing another person's feelings seems strange to you, you may have been raised in a situation that supported you in sensing yourself but didn't require that you also learn to sense others. You may even be a champion at referencing yourself, while being clueless at referencing others.

The Origins of the Merging Pattern

There are many routes an individual child may follow in adopting a particular survival pattern. As the needs of the child interact with her situation, she will find her own, unique path, so generalizations are only generally accurate. They may explain most people's route to a pattern, but they cannot explain every case. Still, generalizations are valuable because they give us a sense of most people's experience.

The merging pattern usually forms during the time of nursing, the time that Freud called the oral stage of development, when the infant is totally dependent on her mother and caregivers and is mostly a bundle of needs. At this age, there is almost nothing she can do for herself. "You have to do it for me" is her reality. Her very survival depends on receiving from others.

As soon as the infant is born, she needs nourishment; she needs to receive food and love from others. Taking in milk and love gives her a sense of being filled. There is a sequence of needing, receiving, and filling that the infant's body is instinctively programmed to expect. The wound that creates the merging pattern arises from an inability to complete this sequence.

When it is working optimally, the sequence goes like this: the infant experiences an internal need or distress and cries out for help, she receives soothing/nourishment/love until her body feels full, and then she relaxes into happy contentment. The process doesn't have to be perfect; it only has to be good enough for that particular infant to complete the sequence and return to a state of relaxed contentment. Then the infant experiences this:

I need → I ask → I receive → I feel full and happy.

In real life, it often looks more like this:

> *The infant becomes distressed → she fusses or cries → her mother holds her or nurses her → she feels the milk and/or the love energy flowing easily into her body → her body drinks it in until she feels full → her nervous system relaxes back down to the ground state → she stops sucking.*

Her need is completely satisfied. She may even push away, more interested now in separation and autonomy than in merging and filling.

In an ideal infancy, as this experience is repeated over and over, she forms an image of the mother/world as full of love and nourishment for her. She can trust it and depend on it. She can relax into the process of needing and receiving. She can drink her fill and then push away, confident that more is available whenever she wants it. Her needs are welcome and effortlessly met. She is good, her needs are good, and the mother/world is good. She develops an attitude of *confident expectation* regarding her needs and the world. Getting is just a matter of asking.

Not Getting Enough

For the child who adopts the merging defense, however, whatever happened was not good enough. She did not arrive often enough at feeling full and happy. Instead of feeling full and pushing herself away, she repeatedly experienced difficulty filling and then lost the source of nourishment without feeling full. Instead of feeling satisfied, she wound up feeling deprived and abandoned. For her, the sequence became:

> *I need → I ask → something bad happens → I feel worse.*

Many different circumstances might lead to an infant's difficulty with taking in nourishment from her mother. Her mother might be ill, exhausted, or terrified for some reason. She might be overwhelmed or too busy with other obligations or other children. She might have difficulty producing milk or be too anxious to wait until the infant finishes feeding. She might have been taught to ignore the baby's cries and feed her only according to a schedule. She might even leave or die during the child's first years. The infant herself may be unable to nurse or digest the mother's milk for some reason. She may be lactose intolerant or unable to digest the formula used for bottle-feeding. Whatever the cause, she was unable to complete the process of needing, receiving, and feeling full. Over and over, needing led to feeling empty and helpless.

The Healthy Taking-in Sequence

The Not-Getting-Enough Sequence

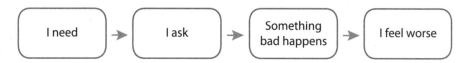

When her need is not fully satisfied, the infant's nervous system cannot fully relax back down to the ground state, but instead stays somewhat aroused and anxious. This residual anxiety interferes with her ability to take in and digest nourishment the next time, and a self-reinforcing cycle develops. It becomes harder for her to relax into the process of receiving, nursing takes even longer, and the process becomes more frustrating for both mother and child. Gradually, the infant loses trust in the mother (and the world) to meet her needs. She starts to feel that she is bad, that her needs are bad, and that her mother and the world are depriving and abandoning. She develops an attitude of *anxious expectation* regarding her needs and the world.

Emotional deprivation can have the same effect. If the child is very heart-centered and needs to feel loved in each moment, but her parents withdraw their heart connection whenever they are displeased or just busy with something else, the child feels emotionally abandoned and deprived of the love she needs. This loss is devastating, and she will begin to organize herself around ways to get and maintain the heart connection she needs.

Whatever the cause, the baby's repeated experience is that she doesn't get enough. Instead of a confident expectation that her needs are welcomed and will be filled, she develops an anxious expectation that she will be left empty and wanting. Instead of feeling relaxed and happy, she feels empty, needy, and anxious.

Defensive Action

Because she feels so empty and needy, this child puts her attention on others and on trying to get them to fill her up. She is developmentally far too young to act to fill herself, so her only option is to stay focused on her connection to others and try to get them to fill her. The only thing she knows how to do is to plug into others energetically and try to drink from their bodies.

In order to mute the feelings of emptiness and longing inside her, she learns to abandon herself, that is, to shift her attention away from the core of her body, where these difficult feelings are strongest. She learns to habitually avoid referencing herself and instead focus on referencing others.

Notice that the defensive action here is not to withdraw attention from the body itself, as the leaving-patterned person does. Rather, it is to withdraw attention from the core of the body, where the felt sense of self develops, and instead put that attention on maintaining the connection to others. *The defensive action here is to abandon self in the search for love.*

Results of the Defensive Action

Difficulty referencing self

This habit of abandoning the self to focus on others has major consequences for the child. Without referencing her own core, she is unable to perceive her own feelings and needs. This makes it difficult for her to discover and define herself through her own feelings and needs. Referencing others tends to fill her body with their feelings and needs, so most of the feelings in her body are not her own feelings, but ones imported from others. This is very confusing and makes it nearly impossible for her to sort out what is "me" from what is "not me" and then use the "me" to form a strong felt sense of self.

The habit of other-referencing instead of self-referencing means that when she asks herself "What do I want?", the response she gets from inside herself will be mostly other people's thoughts and feelings, not her own. But she will not realize this. Since these imported thoughts and feelings make up most of what she experiences, she will think they are her own thoughts and feelings. And she will act on them, thinking she is being herself, when in fact, she is being who the people around her want her to be. From an early age, she will become very skillful at pleasing others by being who they want her to be, but woefully inept at pleasing herself or even knowing herself.

Not having enough and not being enough

The attitude of anxious expectation also has consequences. As mentioned above, it inhibits the process of receiving. The chronic fear and tension in her body make it harder for her to take in and metabolize the love and nourishment that are available.

Her fixation on getting energy only from others doesn't allow her to move on developmentally, establish her own direct connection to the earth (grounding), and learn how to take in and metabolize her own energy directly from the environment. This leaves her without a way to get enough energy for herself. It leaves her stuck in the experience of not having enough and not being enough. Without enough energy flowing through her, she tends to easily get tired, discouraged, and depressed.

When she tries to get more energy, the way she goes about it only makes things worse. Since she is stuck in the nursing stage, the only method she knows is to get it from someone else's body. So she energetically plugs into someone near her and starts sucking. If she plugs into you and you are energetically perceptive, you may be able to feel exactly where on your body she has plugged in, and you may actually feel a pulling sensation as you are being drained. If you're like most people, you will only notice that you feel tired of being around her. You may become annoyed or angry, and your mind will find some reason to get away from her. When you leave, she will naturally feel abandoned. And while it is true that you left her, she is completely unaware of how she contributed to your decision to leave.

So, merging-patterned people typically conclude that it is their neediness that leads to being rejected and abandoned, not their attempts to siphon off other people's energy. Numerous repetitions of this cycle make it seem like the world is bent on depriving them of nourishment and then abandoning them. They may feel cheated of their birthright[2] and blame the world for this injury. Frequently they have a conscious or unconscious attitude of "Life owes me a living,"[3,4] accompanied by a half-buried resentment at being deprived of it. And in a way, they are correct. When you're an infant, life does owe you a living. Their mistake is only in thinking that this is still true for an adult.

Getting stuck in the infant state

In a very real way, a merging-patterned person is stuck in the infant state: empty, helpless, and needing to be cared for. The very real fact that she hasn't yet learned the skills required to care for herself, combined with a belief that she must stay the helpless infant in order to finally get what she needs, keeps her stuck. She is still trying to get filled from the outside so that she can finally complete the receiving task of the oral stage. However, her attempts to remain the helpless infant tend to get in the way of acquiring the skills she needs to finish growing up.

The Merging Pattern in Full Bloom

Body Signs

The body tends to be soft and rounded, much like the body of an infant. The hands and feet are small relative to the rest of the body, while the mouth tends to be large, with full lips. The musculature is under-developed and does not project a sense of power or capability. Instead, the body often appears flaccid, without strength or backbone, and the person may be too fat or too thin.

The chest tends to be sunken and the shoulders rounded forward, as if the heart center is being pulled back into the chest for protection. The pelvis may be thrust forward when standing, and the head may also be thrust forward, further accentuating the pulling in of the chest. This posture breaks the flow of energy moving up and down the body, further contributing to its sense of weakness. This posture also restricts the breathing and thereby suppresses feeling in the body. The decreased breathing and energy flow contribute to the emotional depression that is common for merging-patterned people.

The feet are not planted firmly on the ground and the body is not energetically grounded and receiving support from the earth, making the person feel unsupported and unable to "stand on their own two feet." Being ungrounded in this way also makes the person a "pushover."

In terms of physical attractiveness, a person who does mostly the pure merging pattern is more likely to be cute and adorable, rather than glamorous or hot. That is, her attractiveness is more like that of a puppy in that it evokes mothering, rather than sexual arousal. When she is present and in the gifts of the pattern, she may also radiate a wholesome joyfulness. By contrast, a person who does mostly the compensated merging pattern is somewhat more

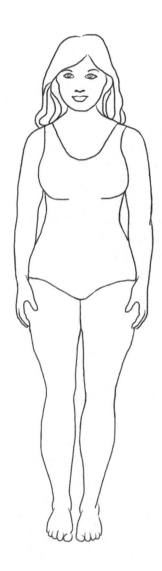

The Merging Pattern – typical body shape

likely to be glamorous or hot, although she may often appear to be cute and adorable, too. (We will differentiate between the pure and compensated forms of the merging pattern later in the chapter.)

In contrast to the dryness of the leaving pattern, there is a sense of wetness and fluidity in the merging pattern — of tears, sadness, and of flowing emotions in general. These are manifestations of both the inherent juiciness of this pattern and of the way that the body leaks energy, since it has weak psychological and energetic boundaries. This leaky container and difficulty in containing energy are part of the reason that people with this structure have such difficulty getting to the state of feeling full.

Merging-patterned people will usually make eye contact easily, but their eyes may have a pleading, puppy dog look, as if begging "Take me home and feed me." Their voice may be sad, childlike, or too soft for you to hear them clearly. Speaking this way draws you in and gets you to energetically reach out to them. When they have a problem, they will typically talk about it a lot, often in a long, rambling saga. But they will take little or no action to solve the problem. Instead, they will act helpless and wait for you solve it. This is the essence of the merging survival strategy: trying to get the other person to give them what they need.

The holding pattern in the body is one of *holding on*, in the sense of clinging to the other, as if the body is unable to support itself and must hold onto something external for its support. The overall impression is of insufficient energy in the system, of depletion and need, and sometimes of full-blown depression.

Psychology

The main issues for merging-patterned people are around taking in and metabolizing the food and love that they need. Instead of expecting to get what they need, people who do this pattern have come to expect deprivation. As infants, they did receive some warmth, love, and nourishment from others, but they did not get enough, or they were unable to hold and metabolize enough. They had a glimpse of paradise, but they didn't get enough of it, and now they feel deprived. Because of this, they were unable to complete the main task of the merging stage, which is to take in until they feel full and satisfied. Feeling full would allow them to move on to the task of the next developmental stage, which is pushing away and exploring their strength and independence. Instead, they are stuck in the merging stage, feeling perpetually dependent and needy.

Coping with not getting enough

Living with the frustration of an unfilled need is too painful for a baby to tolerate forever. A baby in need will cry at first, but eventually will fall into an exhausted sleep. The need has not disappeared, so why does the baby stop crying?

Studies of how a child responds to being separated from her mother have shown that the child goes through three distinct stages as she deals with the loss. Initially, she will protest more loudly, believing that a more vigorous appeal will bring help. Then she will give up crying out in protest and fall into a passive despair, still hoping for help but no longer actively pursuing it. Finally, she will give up hope and adjust to the continuing frustration by detaching internally from her awareness of the need, that is, by muting her own aliveness.[5]

At this point the child appears to have adjusted to the loss, but internally she has paid a high price: she has lost contact with her own core. In order to dull the feelings of being abandoned by her mother, she has abandoned herself. In order to cope with her overwhelming feelings of frustration and helplessness, the child has diminished her own life energy and power, and identified with the helplessness. She has accomplished this by diminishing her own breathing and physical activity and by shifting her awareness away from the core of her body, thereby reducing the flow of energy through her body and dulling her experience of herself. The active, angry protest of the healthy infant has been replaced by a passive despair and self-deadening. In the words of Stephen M. Johnson, the child *"chooses depression over expression."*[6]

If the mother returns and repairs the breach by allowing the child to express her upset at being left and then filling her with love, this incident may have no lasting effect. But if the breach is not repaired and the child has to live in a continuing state of unfulfilled need, an internal state of anxious expectation will become the norm. The child must find a way to cope with this situation. If she focuses on trying to get Mom to come back and fix everything, she will develop the merging survival pattern.

Notice that the child has now learned to cope with her bad feelings by diminishing the flow of her own life energy in order to dim her awareness of all sensations and feelings. When upset or overwhelmed as an adult, she will resort to the same survival strategy and again diminish her life energy to try to dim her bad feelings. The result will be depression.

Just as a leaving-patterned person doubts her right to exist, a merging-patterned person doubts her right to have needs and to receive what she needs.

She fears that, because of her needs, she will be rejected and abandoned and will never get enough. One merging-patterned person put it this way: *"I don't believe I can get my needs met. Things are too hard and harsh. There is too much effort. And I don't trust that anyone would want to meet my needs."*

While a person who develops the leaving pattern rejects the body, a person who develops the merging pattern rejects the needs of the body. She may (or may not) have succeeded in the task of embodiment, but she has failed in the task of taking in what the body needs. In order to dull the pain of not getting what she needs, she disconnects from her own core. She learns to shift her attention off of herself and onto the other person. She learns to focus on what the other needs, hoping that filling the other's need will somehow lead to someone filling her needs. This makes her an expert at referencing others and reading their emotional state and needs (which is a very valuable skill), but leaves her unable to self-reference and read her own emotional state and needs.

Because she got stuck in the dependency of the oral stage, she did not go on to explore her own strengths and learn how to do things for herself. She got stuck in the time when connection with others really was required for survival, when all problems were solved by someone else, and all goodness was received from someone else. So now, she continues to look to connection with others to solve all her problems. In essence, merging-patterned people believe that they must stay helpless to attract the nourishment they need, so they avoid acquiring new skills and learning how to do things for themselves.

Coping without strength and will

Another way to think of the behavior of people caught in the merging pattern is that they are stuck in a "pre-strength" state. Since they have never developed their own core, strength, and will, they have not been able to learn how to take direct action to get what they want. Unable to use direct, active-aggressive means to get what they want, they must use indirect, passive-aggressive means, such as manipulating others into giving them what they want.

Without strength and will, they are not able to go on to develop self-confidence. A child develops self-confidence by doing, that is, by trying and succeeding. Stuck in a stage before doing comes online, merging-patterned people have never had the experiences that create self-confidence. Instead of practicing "I can do it," they have practiced "I can get you to do it for me."

They also have difficulty saying "no" when they need to. Without the ability to self-reference, they do not even realize that they want to say "no." And without direct access to their own aggressive energy, they find it difficult to oppose another person's wishes, even when they know they want to. They also fear that displeasing others might once again lead to being abandoned and deprived.

Growing up without access to their own aggressive energy, people who adopted this survival pattern weren't able to psychologically separate from Mom and Dad and develop strong boundaries. They still tend to merge with others, rather than maintaining their own personal space. This merging is the natural state for a baby, but as the baby grows into a child with her own will and strength, she begins pushing away and separating from others so that she can grow into a separate individual. Even nursing babies will naturally display this behavior by pushing away from their mothers after they have finished nursing. The problem for those caught in the merging pattern is that they were not able to finish nursing. They never felt full and ready to push away and separate, so they still tend to merge.

Ideally, as a child grows, she discovers that the best way to get her needs met is to separate from mother, develop her own strength and autonomy, and move toward adult-adult forms of relationship. However, a merging-patterned person believes that the best way to get her needs met is to stay in the infant-mother relationship and make it better this time. She believes "Love will solve everything." However, the "love" that she envisions is not the love of individuated adults — the love of two separate, equal, adult partners. Rather, it is the love of an infant for her mother, the love in which "I relax and melt into you and you take care of me." Because of this, she often appears to others to be downright clingy.

The desire to stay a child shapes the person in many ways. She values being over doing, connection over achievement, and love over power. Her weak energetic boundaries tend to create a soft, puffy body, without clear edges and definition. Her weak energetic container makes it hard for her to build a charge in her body and then use it to accomplish a goal. So play is easy for her, but work is not.

The Value of a Strong Energetic Container

Doing anything in the physical world requires building a charge in the body and then directing that charge into action. However, in order to build a charge, a person's body has to be able to contain the charge. That requires strong energetic boundaries. Without them, the charge leaks out before it can build up. So in order to function effectively in the world, a person must have a strong energetic container.

You can think of the body as a container that holds energy just as a jar holds water. A large, strong jar can hold a lot of water. However, a leaky jar can't hold much water, because it keeps leaking out. (Keep in mind that the size of someone's energetic container is not determined by the size of their body. A 200-pound body cannot necessarily hold more energy than a 100-pound body. It is the size and strength of the person's energetic container that matters, not the size of their body.)

If we think about water contained in a jar, we realize that the water can escape from the jar in several different ways:

1. The water can leak out.

2. The water can overflow.

3. The jar can burst.

4. You can open a valve and direct the flow of water where you want.

Now let's use this analogy to explore how energy can escape from a person's body. For people in general (not just merging-patterned people), energy leaking from their container will often take the form of small emotional displays. If the energy is anger or resentment, it may take the form of snide comments, sarcasm, or complaining. If the energy is grief, it may manifest as a quiet sniffling or tears. If the energy is joy, the person has to tell you about it, rather than just quietly feeling it. The main point here is not how the leaking energy manifests, but that the person does not have voluntary control over the leakage.

If you suspect that you habitually leak energy via some behavior, try stopping that behavior and see what happens. For instance, if you frequently complain, try going without complaining for a week and see what happens. Are you able to stop complaining? Does stopping cause the energy to build up inside of you until you get outright angry? Or does that energy leak out in the form of some other behavior, instead?

Energetic overflow, the second option, is like leaking, but on a bigger scale. There is a feeling of a rush of energy, of a torrential flow, and a need to "get it off your chest." As the emotional waters rise above the lip of the jar, they spill out. Again, this overflowing energy can take the form of any behavior or emotion, from an angry volcanic eruption to jumping for joy. Following the release, there is a sense of relief, as if an internal pressure has been vented. Indeed, what we call "venting" is often this same sort of release of internal emotional pressure, but in a manner that is more or less voluntary. Overflow is involuntary venting.

When the container bursts, the outflow of energy is bigger still, more like a dam breaking. And the disintegration of the container brings with it a disorientation or disorganization of the self, making the person temporarily unable to function. Panic and hysteria are examples of this: the container of the self has disintegrated and the person is overwhelmed by chaotic feelings and unable to function. An intense orgasm is another example, but with more positive feelings. For a moment, the ego container dissolves as the person is overwhelmed by pleasure and loses track of everything else.

The fourth option, voluntarily opening a valve and directing the flow of energy in the way you choose, is the method used by a healthy adult taking action in the world. A person with this capacity can choose how and when she sends her energy out into the world. She can choose the timing and the form so that her self-expression and actions accomplish what she intends. Her ability to hold an internal charge is what gives her this voluntary control. Because she can contain the charge that arises within her, she can choose when and how to express it. She is able to feel great fear and yet act courageously, to feel a strong sexual attraction, but not act on it, or to carry an enormous reservoir of joy or love or strength, but not have to brag about it. Depending on the needs of the moment, she may choose to act, or she may choose to remain silent. In order to develop this capacity, she must have her own source of energy, a strong container that can hold it, and voluntary control over how and when she sends that energy out.

Another way to say this is that a strong energetic container gives a person control over her charge/discharge cycle. It gives her the freedom to build and hold energy in her body and then use it when she wants to, rather than having to discharge it immediately. A child does not have control over her own charge/discharge cycle and relies on her parents to regulate it for her. Ideally, as she grows into adulthood, she learns how to manage it for herself. This gives her control over her own behavior.

Merging-patterned people don't have control over their charge/discharge cycle. Their weak container allows the charge to leak out, typically in the form of small (or large) displays of emotion. This is what creates the frequent emotionality that is characteristic of this pattern. Because they can't hold much of a charge, when they do try to act, they don't have much energy to put into the action. Since holding a strong energetic charge within the body is necessary for the internal sensations of strength, expansiveness, and confidence, these sensations are not easily available for them. They find it difficult to persevere through obstacles and complete a task, because they have difficulty containing the tension that goes with feeling frustrated. This difficulty with containing and channeling energy is one of their main issues.

Those who adopted the merging pattern also face another challenge relating to their energy. Because their development was arrested while they were still nursing, that is, while they were still taking in predigested energy from others, they did not go on to learn how to absorb and metabolize their own energy directly from the environment. This means that, even as adults, they continue to believe that they must get their energy from others. Together, these difficulties create the low energy levels, muscular weakness, mild chronic depression, and the habits of clinging and sucking energy from others that are characteristic of the merging pattern.

Shifting into the Compensated Merging Pattern

So far, we have seen that the survival strategy of merging-patterned people is to avoid a clear awareness of their own core, identify with their neediness, and try to get what they need from others. This is a description of the merging pattern in its pure form, and up to now, this is what we have been discussing.

However, for some children, this strategy was not enough. Perhaps they could not stand feeling so needy, or perhaps in their family having needs was shamed, while helping others was praised. They may have been told, "Don't be so selfish. Take care of your brothers and sisters." In church, they may have been taught, "It is more blessed to give than to receive." So they developed an additional layer of defense against their neediness by shifting from playing the infant to playing the mother. The child is still caught in the infant-mother relationship, but now, instead of being the helpless, needy baby, she can be the helpful, giving mother.

Rather than denying or condemning her troublesome needs, she simply projects those needs onto someone else. Now, instead of feeling that *she* needs something, she feels that *you* need something. Her conscious experience shifts from "I need you to give to me" to "I can give to you." Now she can feel big and strong, instead of small and needy.

Becoming "the Giver"

Now "giving to get" has expanded from a strategy into an identity, and the person now sees herself as "the Giver." Though she is still without a felt sense of her own core, and still unaware of her own needs, she has shifted from the role of rescuee to the role of rescuer. As the Giver, she no longer experiences herself as deprived and needy. Instead, she experiences others as deprived and needy, and herself as the one who can fill those needs. It is not *she* who is dependent, but someone else. Since this new state is a way of compensating for the deprivation experienced in the merging pattern, it is called the compensated merging pattern. In psychology, this strategy has long been referred to as the co-dependent personality, in which the helper's attention is not grounded in herself, but focused on the person she is helping.

Because her giving is serving a defensive function, it differs from simple generosity. To maintain the compensation, this person needs to keep giving to someone. So she finds situations where she can play the caregiver role, such as nursing, childcare, or working in a homeless shelter. Instead of hoping someone will save her, she makes it her business to save others.

And since the impulse to give is not fueled so much by the other's need as by her own need to be the Giver, the giving inevitably goes too far. The person playing the Giver feels overly responsible for keeping everyone else happy, gives more than she can afford, and drains herself dry. She may be providing a truly wonderful service to others, but her service is not supported by good self-care. She is ignoring her own needs even more strenuously than a person in the pure merging pattern. This makes it very difficult for her to ask for help, or even to accept help when it is offered.

Having a pretend core

The shift into the compensated side of the merging pattern is an attempt to grow up. It is an attempt to practice the strength and will needed to become a capable adult. But because the compensation is not built on a felt sense of the body's core, it does not have the foundation needed to succeed, and the person can create only the pretense of strength. She will present herself as very competent and self-sufficient, saying things like *"I don't expect anything"* and *"I don't want to be a burden,"* but inside, she often has a gnawing feeling of falseness and may even say to herself *"I feel like a fake."* Without a felt sense of core, she cannot self-reference and self-measure, so she does not have a clear sense of her own needs and limits. She tries to be "all things to all people," over-estimates her strengths, under-estimates her needs, ignores her self-care, and then periodically crashes and burns.

In many parts of the world, the compensated merging pattern is culturally sanctioned, while the pure merging pattern is not. Here in the United States, for instance, we applaud self-reliance and self-sufficiency, but we tend to shame people for being needy and dependent. A child raised in this sort of environment is encouraged by her culture to shift into the compensated side of the merging pattern.

Flavors of the compensation

When a person creates the extra defensive layer that shifts her into the compensated merging pattern, she employs the defense strategy of one of the other survival patterns, since those are the only other survival strategies available. Consequently, her compensation will usually take on the flavor of the enduring, the aggressive, or the rigid patterns. Sometimes, it will have the flavor of the leaving pattern, but this gives her less protection, so it is rarer.

A person who runs the compensated merging pattern may even learn to imitate all of the other survival patterns and display a chameleon-like ability to match the style and appearance of different groups of friends while with them. In high school, for instance, she may be able to hang out with the cheerleaders, the bikers, and the honor students, energetically shifting to fit in with each group while with them. When she is able to be present and use it consciously, this fluidity becomes one of the pattern's gifts. It gives her the ability to shift rapidly from one skill set to another as the situation demands. Of course, when interacting with people who run other survival patterns, she will never be able to beat them at their own game, but she can at least get into the game and connect with them.

Cycling

When a person who is in the compensated merging pattern crashes, the compensation dissolves, the false sense of strength disappears, and she returns to the collapsed state of the pure merging pattern. If she feels more comfortable in the compensated side of the merging pattern, she will immediately start rebuilding it. Over time, she will cycle between these two states, rising from depression into heroic efforts to rescue others, and then collapsing back into depression.

The cycling typically looks like this:

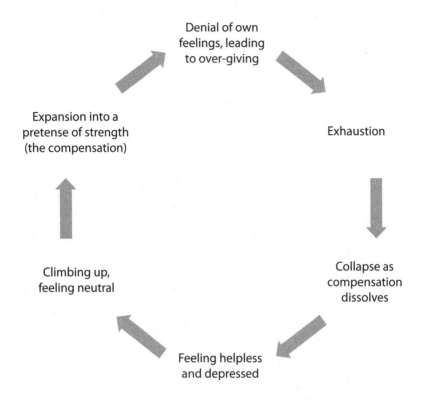

Denial of own
feelings, leading
to over-giving

Exhaustion

Expansion into a
pretense of strength
(the compensation)

Collapse as
compensation
dissolves

Climbing up,
feeling neutral

Feeling helpless
and depressed

The Compensated Merging Pattern's Expansion-Collapse Cycle

The climb out of feeling helpless and depressed is usually a slow process, requiring days or weeks, whereas the collapse of the compensation is more of a crash and can happen in just minutes.

A merging-patterned person will most likely experience both the pure and the compensated sides of the merging pattern. However, she will typically identify with one role more than the other, and spend most of her time in that part of the cycle, visiting the other role only briefly. Fundamentally, they are the same survival pattern and require the same process for healing. However, the compensated merging pattern includes an extra layer — a pretense of strength — that must be relinquished before the process of healing the merging pattern itself can begin.

Under pressure, people in both the pure merging and compensated merging patterns will collapse, but they do so differently. A person who is in the pure merging pattern collapses more easily and frequently, but since she wasn't inflated to start with, her collapse is less severe. It's more like a young child having a melt down — it may be emotionally dramatic, but with the proper support, she can rapidly recover from it.

On the other hand, a person who is in the compensated merging state has farther to fall. She is inflated by a false sense of strength, so she can overshoot her inner resources much farther before she collapses. This means that her deflation happens less frequently, but when it does happen, it is more severe. As her compensation dissolves, the sudden loss of the strength she felt only a moment ago disorients her. Then her inner critic attacks her for being so weak and she feels a wave of self-hatred, which only intensifies her collapse. Because she is less willing to accept support, it may take her days or weeks to recover from her collapse.

This tendency to collapse under pressure is one of the hallmarks of the merging pattern. It is different from the tendency of the leaving-patterned person to fragment under pressure, which involves a silent, internal disintegration of the self and a loss of connection to the body. The collapse of the merging-patterned person is a more outwardly emotional and dramatic event. It is more of a meltdown into tears and complaints (a response to distress that would be appropriate for a child still in the oral stage of development). Since they are developmentally so young, merging-patterned people who have collapsed typically need the help of others to re-connect with their inner resources and get out of the collapsed state.

Beliefs

The beliefs of merging-patterned people are mostly a reflection of their difficulty with taking in and metabolizing love and nourishment, combined with their attempts to maintain their heart connection to others at all costs. Some of their typical beliefs are:

"There is never enough."
"I am not enough."
"I am deficient."
"I can't do it alone."
"My needs are not okay."
"If I need, I will be abandoned."
"If I am strong, I will be abandoned."
"If I disappoint you, I will be abandoned."

"You should love me totally and unconditionally, the way you would love a baby."

"Love will solve everything."

Fears

The empty feeling

The main thing that merging-patterned people fear is the empty feeling that arises when they are not connected with someone else. This makes them fear being alone, rejected, or abandoned.

Because the empty feeling arises when they are alone, they think it is caused by a lack of connection to others. But in fact, it is caused by a lack of connection to themselves, by an inability to feel the core of their own body. When a person cannot feel their own core, it literally seems like "there is no one here." In contrast, when a person can feel their own core, there is a sense of a palpable self, of "I am here." The self that is here may be happy or unhappy, but it is here. There is "someone here."

But feeling their own core brings with it the feelings of need and helplessness, so they avoid it. If they were taught that referencing their own core is a "selfish" and "self-centered" act that will be punished by the withdrawal of love, they avoid doing so even more.

The loss of the heart connection

People who do this survival pattern also fear the withdrawal of the heart connection by others. While no one likes feeling unloved, those who do the other survival patterns can tolerate the loss of a heart connection more easily because they are not using it to orient themselves in the world, which means that losing it is not disorienting for them. For someone who is caught in the merging pattern, losing the heart connection can be not only disorienting, but devastating. Let's explore how this happens.

Within the infant-mother scenario, the infant can get what she needs only through her connection to her mother or whoever stands in for her mother. For the infant, this connection is actually necessary for survival, so infants instinctively orient themselves to it. During the oral stage, this form of orientation is healthy and necessary, because it serves the real survival needs of the time. But because merging-patterned people are stuck in that developmental stage, they continue to use the human love connection to orient themselves in the world, even as adults. While this makes them experts at monitoring their love connection with others, it also makes them feel that maintaining the love connection is necessary for their survival, even when it is not.

Since they are using the human love connection to orient themselves in the world, when it is withdrawn, they become disoriented. Without a reference point, they feel lost and unable to get their bearings. Instead of simply shifting their attention to referencing themselves and noticing how their own heart feels without that connection, they do not know where to put their attention. Since they unconsciously avoid putting their attention on themselves, it tends to flit about randomly, looking for something to latch on to.

Moreover, since they were using the heart connection as the internal sensation around which to organize themselves, when it disapears they tend to become internally disorganized. If the heart connection is withdrawn suddenly, they may become so disorganized that they cannot continue to function as an adult. Suddenly, their adult capacities have disappeared, and they feel like a child — helpless, deficient, and needy. This brings on a wave of shame and an attack from their inner critic, which makes them feel even worse. So they try very hard to avoid disappointing others or doing anything that might lead to losing the all-important heart connection. One person described it as trying to be *"All things to all people."* Another said, *"I think my biggest fear is that when I displease someone, the love goes away."*

Psychological Defenses

Developmentally, people who adopted the merging pattern are a little bit older than people who adopted the leaving pattern, so they have a few more psychological defenses to choose from as they attempt to navigate a world that feels unsafe. Their psychological defenses are mostly focused on maintaining their connections with others and getting what they need from others. Let's look at each of these defenses in turn.

Playing the baby

The two most obvious defense strategies used by merging-patterned people are playing the baby and playing the mother. When playing the baby, they identify with the needy, helpless state and try to get other people to fix it for them. When in this role, they will typically act helpless, play the victim, and avoid responsibility for their actions and overall life circumstances. They are staying the baby in an attempt to finally attract the nurturance of the Good Mother. This role is the essence of the pure merging pattern.

Playing the mother

When they shift into playing the mother, they project their need and helplessness onto someone else and declare "I will fix it for you." Then they start tending to the other's needs and playing the rescuer to the other's victim. They are giving what they need to get, which somewhat diminishes the pain of not getting it, and creates an unconscious hope that the other will reciprocate. This role feels better because they get to feel like the big, helpful one, but it is still a survival strategy, rather than a real service, because it is motivated more by their own need to give than by the other's need to receive. Shifting into the Giver role also diminishes their fear of abandonment, because now the other needs them. This role is the essence of the compensated merging pattern.

Not feeling their own core

People with both forms of this survival pattern avoid feeling their own core in order to not feel their own needs. This allows them to avoid self-referencing and focus only on referencing the feelings and needs of others. Since their own needs cannot be felt directly, those needs are often somaticized, surfacing instead as psychologically-based aches, pains, and illnesses.

Accommodating, placating, manipulating

Merging-patterned people are stuck in a time before they could act on their own behalf, so instead of using active-aggressive means to get their needs met they must use passive-aggressive means. In simple terms, this means that they cannot ask directly for what they need and they cannot even imagine taking action to get it for themselves. What they can imagine is getting the other person to take action for them. This means that they must accommodate and placate others to stay on their good side, and then try to manipulate or seduce them into providing what is needed.

Relationship to Self

As we have noted earlier, merging-patterned people have very little capacity to self-reference and discover what they feel and want. Instead, they have learned to other-reference and to feel what others want from them. This means that, inside them, their own voice is very faint, while the voices of others are very loud, telling them what to do and who to be. Often they cannot hear their own voice at all.

They essentially see themselves through the eyes of others. They may even psychically go inside the other person's body and look back at themselves to find out "Who can I be for you?" When the other is pleased with them, they see themselves as wonderful, beautiful, and lovable. But when the other is not pleased with them, they see themselves as deficient, ugly, and unlovable. So they try very hard to be and do everything that the other wants. But of course they fail, because this is an impossible task.

And when they fail, they hate themselves for their own weakness. It does not occur to them that no one could have succeeded at such a task, and that it is unfair to expect so much of themselves. Instead, they see it as further proof that they are not good enough and not lovable. They approach the task with the open-hearted innocence of a child who loves her parents totally and just wants to please them, so their desire to be everything the other wants is enormous, and their failure is devastating.

Relationship to the Inner Critic

A merging-patterned person has not made much progress in developing her own voice, so what she hears in her head are mostly the voices of everyone else telling her what they want her to be and do and want. When she fails in that, her inner critic shames her, saying things like "You're not enough. You're deficient." For a person with this survival pattern, the form of a critic attack is typically shaming.

And shame, of course, drains energy out of her body, making her feel small and powerless. So her reaction to the critic attack is to feel smaller inside, helpless and ashamed of her deficiency. Then her inner critic will attack her for having those feelings. So, once a critic attack starts, it feeds on itself and she spirals downward into despair and depression. "I can't please you" can quickly grow into "I can't please anyone," and then into "I'm worthless. No one will ever love me."

Personality Traits

Now let's look at the personality traits of the merging pattern. These are the way a merging-patterned person will tend to look when she is actually in the pattern. When she is simply present and not in pattern, these traits may be muted or absent. At those times, she will likely still exhibit the gifts of the pattern, such as a radiant joy and love, but when she is caught in the merging pattern, her appearance will be more like what follows.

The first thing you are likely to notice is how warm and emotionally expressive she is. If she is happy at the moment, she may be bubbly, joyful, and playful. If she is unhappy, she may be tearful and clingy. But you will always feel an emotional flow from her.

Her main focus will always be on the connections between people and on trying to keep everyone happy. Behaviorally, she will be very contactful — very talkative and touchy-feely. She will immediately tune in to what you want and try to give it to you. In a group situation, she will be the one who is tracking everyone's emotional state and making sure everyone's alright. If someone in the group needs help or attention, she is likely to be the first to point it out.

She herself may want lots of attention and may maneuver skillfully to get it, but her moves will usually be subtle, not obvious or demanding. When she needs something, she is more likely to express her need indirectly than as a direct request.

When she's playing the victim (hurt, helpless, looking for rescue), you may notice an almost physical pulling feeling in your belly. This is her pulling on you energetically. When she's playing the rescuer (Helper, Giver, needing to please you), you may feel very well cared for, but if you are honest with yourself, you will also notice that it is out of proportion and probably more than she can really afford to give.

How They Recreate Their Early Wounding

As with all the survival patterns, merging-patterned people tend to recreate their own early wounding by the very things they do to try to keep themselves safe. This process is unconscious, of course, but it is very effective in perpetuating the pattern by maintaining the kinds of relationships and experiences that they had in childhood.

Their habit of anxious expectation inhibits their receiving and metabolizing of the energy and love that is available to them, so even when they are taking in love and nurturance, they still feel empty. Then they blame others for their lack and push them away. Or they attempt to suck energy from them, which drives them away. Either way, they end up once again feeling abandoned and deprived. When they're in the compensated merging pattern, even though everyone around them is getting nurtured, they themselves are not, so they still feel deprived.

Patterned Thoughts

Merging-patterned people focus most of their attention on their heart connections to others. They use their heart connections with other people to orient themselves in the world. This is what makes maintaining the heart connection so crucial for them, and what makes the loss of it so disorienting. Internally, they are constantly checking *"Who am I connected with?" "Is the connection good?" "Do they like me?" "Do they love me?" "What do they feel toward me now . . . How about now? . . . How about now?"*

If we look at their thinking in terms of left brain vs. right brain functioning, we see that they spend more time in the right brain, which deals more with feelings and relationships. They are not strong in the left brain functions, such as logical thinking and analysis, and do not cognize and track their own experience well.

Their attention and thoughts tend to have a positive bias. This skews their perception of reality, making everything look more safe and loving than it really is, as if they were looking through rose-colored glasses. While this is probably better than having a negative bias of attention, it still distorts the picture that they see and makes it harder for them to navigate successfully through the world. Further, their positively skewed picture of reality makes it difficult for them to recognize real threats to their well-being, such as physical danger or the presence of an enemy. It makes them more trusting of other people than a balanced perspective would support. It also makes them especially susceptible to feel-good addictions, such as food, sex, romance, and certain drugs. Because it gives them a good feeling, they may think, "Alcohol is my best friend," or "Sugar has never let me down," without being able to see how getting their good feeling that way can lead to problems.

The mind chatter of people in the pure merging pattern is *"I can't,"* which leads to internal collapse and the plea *"You do it for me."* When in the compensated merging pattern, their mind chatter switches to *"I can,"* but without measuring whether they actually can, which of course leads to over taxing their own abilities and then to collapse.

You may recall that each of the survival patterns has a characteristic sequence of thoughts that arise when a person caught in that pattern sees that someone else has something that they want. For the leaving pattern, we said that the sequence goes something like *"You have it. I want it. I'll just imagine I have it."* For the merging pattern, it is more like *"You have it. I want it. I'll get you to give it to me."* Their efforts to "get you to give it to me" are the source of much of their patterned behavior.

Patterned Behaviors

Connecting

Since merging-patterned people believe that the source of love and life energy is not inside themselves but within others, they naturally go looking for it. Connection to others therefore appears to be the key to survival, so they want to connect a lot and in every way possible. They are typically very talkative, with the talk mostly focused on creating an emotional connection, rather than on exploring ideas or accomplishing a task. They are champions at engaging strangers and connecting with them, and in any setting, they are the people most likely to strike up a conversation with whoever is near them. In a group, their attention goes to including everyone and building a sense of community. They also build community by throwing parties, and they are typically very good at it. They will do everything they can to keep the good feelings flowing.

Merging-patterned people also like to touch a great deal. For them, it is just another way to connect and create warm, fuzzy feelings for everyone. They also love to hug and cuddle, and are often able to do so from a simple desire to promote feelings of warmth and safety, without any sexual overtones.

Giving to get

In trying to get their needs filled, merging-patterned people often engage in "giving to get," a strategy in which they track and fill the needs of others in the hope that these others will then give them something in return. They give a "gift" (which in their mind is really a trade), and then wait for the other person to reciprocate. If the other does not give a gift in return, they will become hurt and angry. Often the care they give to others is exactly the sort of care that they, themselves, need to receive, but cannot ask for directly. Their "giving to get" is often accompanied by pleasing, placating, and accommodating. They are attempting to give you what you want so that you will give them what they want.

Their desire to please you may expand into trying to be whoever you want them to be. Without a word from you, they may have the skills needed to reference you, sense who you want them to be, and then morph into that person. They may also use this talent as a means of seduction. As you can imagine, becoming "whoever you want me to be" can be very hard to resist. At its best, this is a love-gift from an amazingly talented lover. At its worst, this is self-abandonment in order to get your approval, and they will be devastated if you reject them, since they will have lost not just you, but themselves as well.

When moving between circles of friends, their strategy of "being whoever you want me to be" may cause them to change like a chameleon as they move from group to group. In a high school setting, this might mean being a cheerleader when with the jocks, being smart when with the studious kids, and being a stoner in the drug crowd. The merging-patterned person may not even realize that she is transforming this way until several of her circles are thrown together for some event and she becomes confused, not knowing who to be now.

Clinging

Merging-patterned people also try to get their needs met by clinging for support: they find someone strong and then attach to that person. However, getting support this way leaves them feeling jealous if the connection is threatened, or needy if it is lost. Again, this is a healthy stage for a child to pass through on her way to developing her own strength and core. However, here it is being used as a survival strategy rather than as a stepping-stone for growth.

Because they are unable to feel their own core, merging-patterned people tend to feel hollow and empty inside, lost and confused. When they are more in the pure merging pattern, they will tend to emphasize their helplessness and wait for rescue. Because they have renounced their own power, they feel weak and deficient when faced with a task. Believing that strength and ability reside in others, their attention goes to others and to the hope of being rescued. Their thought is not *"How can I do this?"* but *"Who will do it for me?"* In order to attract the help they believe they need, they may act like a baby by appearing cute, helpless, or sick. Or, when they are more in the compensated merging pattern, they will tend to cast themselves in the role of the rescuer and be the one who cares for others.

Difficulty with self-care

Because merging-patterned people are developmentally so young, they are not good at self care. Developmentally, self-care skills have not yet come online, so people stuck in this stage do not yet have access to them. Behaviorally, the situation usually looks like the following:

- Poor boundaries: difficulty saying no, difficulty separating self from other, a tendency to merge and feel what the other person feels, rather than what she feels.

- Little sense of strength, will, and autonomy.

- Difficulty recognizing an enemy or danger, such as dangerous drugs and dangerous people.

- Attachment to what provides soothing and support, often manifesting as addictions to food, drink, sedating drugs, an object, a person, a place, or even a season or holiday.

- Being prone to illness, both real and psychosomatic. Emotional distress is often somaticized and expressed through body symptoms. Somaticized emotions and hypochondria are classic symptoms of the merging pattern.

Patterned Experience of Time

Their experience of time is that they never have enough time. Their inability to reference their own core and measure their own desires and abilities makes planning ahead nearly impossible — they just don't have the data needed to do it. So, they tend to live in the moment and just deal with the future when it arrives. Being so much in the moment gives them access to a childlike sense of wonder and spontaneity, but because they can't measure ahead, they are frequently late and unprepared.

Patterned Emotional Life

More feelings than self

Their weak boundaries give merging-patterned people an increased sensitivity to the feelings of others, but also make it harder for them to differentiate their own feelings from those of others. The combination of weak boundaries and little ability to sense their own core creates a situation in which they have many feelings, but little sense of self. So while they typically experience a lot of emotions, they have difficulty sorting out whose emotions they are and what they mean.

Merging-patterned people are often able to literally feel another person's internal state and therefore know what that person is feeling and needing without any outward clues or communication. This leads them to not only be aware of everyone's feelings, but to also feel responsible for everyone's feelings. Trying to keep everyone happy can become a crushing load. On the positive side, it means that when they make someone happy, they can feel that happiness inside themselves, which makes them happy, too. Now the giving *is* receiving, not giving to get. This can create a positive feedback loop in which each person's happiness increases the other's happiness, and the cycle feeds on itself.

Being heart-centered

The merging pattern is the most heart-centered of all the survival patterns, and it is typically adopted by people who are heart-centered (although their other pattern may tend to pull them away from their heart). Merging-patterned people experience life and the world more through their heart than through their mind or their body. They don't plan life so much as feel their way through it. In a mostly head-centered culture, such as the United States, they may feel like they just don't fit in, but may feel at home in a more heart-centered culture, such as Italy.

Love, happiness, joy, and sadness are often abundant. Of all the survival patterns, the merging pattern has the most positive bias of attention, and those who adopted it can find real joy in even the smallest of things. Play and delight are easily accessible. Even forgiveness for real injuries is not far away. Grudges and resentments are not nursed in secret and maintained for years, but just arise and flow through.

Everything in the system is fluid and changeable, just as it is in a child. This also means that merging-patterned people are prone to mood swings and experience a big range of moods, sometimes shifting rapidly from one to another. Anxiety is always nearby, however, since their anxious expectation of rejection and abandonment underlies everything.

Shame and self-doubt

Whenever a person's system gets overloaded and goes into overwhelm, the extra energy is shunted into its default emotions. For merging-patterned people, the default emotions are shame and self-doubt. Whenever their system gets overwhelmed, they will start to doubt themselves, feel deficient, and fall into shame. With practice, they can realize that this wave of feelings does not necessarily mean that they are deficient, but only that their system got overwhelmed.

Anger

Typically, one feeling is missing, and that is anger. Anger is a developmentally older emotion. It creates separation and differentiation — it says "No." It arises out of the impulse to act to get what you want. It supports the development of the self by asserting "I do not want that." But asserting themselves will put a merging-patterned person right back into the scene of their original wounding: *I want, I try to get, I fail.* So knowing what they want and acting directly to get it are avoided and replaced by unconscious and indirect methods of trying to get their needs met.

Interacting with Others

The merging pattern is all about connecting with others. It's the most relational of the five survival patterns, and its focus is on how people feel about each other. It is not focused on who's better, who's stronger, who's right or wrong, who's up or down, or any form of competition. Instead, it wants to know: "Do you like me?" "Do you need me?" "Are we connected?"

Feeling connected and close to others is the source of safety for merging-patterned people. Since those caught in the other four survival patterns typically want less closeness, those in the merging pattern often find themselves in the role of the pursuer, constantly trying to get closer to the other person. If their pursuit of connection and love is done consciously — by touching into their deep emptiness and need, reaching out for comfort, and then completing the filling process — merging-patterned people can gradually heal their original sense of deprivation and create an abiding felt sense of fullness in themselves. However, their cuddling is typically done unconsciously, so their deep need is not touched, they don't ever feel full and ready to push away, and their belief that all nourishment comes from outside remains unchallenged.

Merging-patterned people are very good at accepting others just as they are, and they long for a similar unconditional acceptance from others. When they feel deeply loved and accepted, they're in heaven. Unfortunately, it is difficult for them to stay in that state, because it does not match their internal experience of emptiness and deficiency, but instead tends to highlight it. In abandoning themselves, they have also abandoned the self-love and self-esteem that would provide a container for the love and acceptance received from others. As David Wilcox put it in a song, *"There's a break in the cup that holds love inside of me."*[7]

Because of their self-abandonment and inner sense of emptiness, it is generally difficult for merging-patterned people to spend time alone. With no one else to focus on, they are left with the longing and loneliness of their original wound. And when someone else is present, they will typically want lots of attention and reassurance. If the other's attention shifts away from them, they will feel the loss of the other's attention as a loss of support and may easily become hurt or jealous.

Romance

Of course, in romantic relationships, all of the above themes will show up with even greater intensity. The main theme, moment to moment, is often the fear of displeasing their mate and losing the heart connection, even temporarily.

In the context of romantic relationships, the fear of being alone usually manifests as a tendency to go directly from one relationship to the next, with no alone time in between to digest the last relationship and grieve its ending. This behavior is usually accompanied by entering the new relationship too rapidly, without first getting to know the other person well enough to evaluate the match. In attempting to secure the new relationship, the merging-patterned person will typically over-accommodate her new partner's needs and lose herself in the relationship. She will abandon her usual interests and do only whatever her mate does, trying to be whoever her mate wants her to be. Ultimately, of course, this does not work, because her self-abandonment actually prevents the formation of a healthy, adult-to-adult connection. If she is not really present, then a real connection is not possible.

Similarly, merging-patterned people tend to fear that they will be abandoned by their lover. This fear may show up as panic attacks when separated, or as the use of teddy bears, stuffed animals, and the like to hold onto while the lover is absent. It may also manifest as jealousies and drama about possibly losing the relationship, accompanied by demands for more attention, nurturing, and reassurance. Or it may show up as giving the lover too much attention, nurturing, and reassurance (giving to get), and then feeling overwhelmed by the demands of maintaining that much giving.

Their need to feel connected and full may cause the merging-patterned person to attach an energetic cord from their own belly to their lover's belly, so that they can suck energy through it. (For drawings of this, see Barbara Brennan's book *Light Emerging* (1993), figures 15-10 through 15-14.) The lover may experience this as a slight tug on their belly, a general sense of frustration with the relationship, or a vague need to get away.

Sexuality

In sex, those who do the merging pattern tend to be attentive and generous. As long as they're feeling confident, they can be wonderful lovers. They have a very real and genuine desire to please their lovers, accompanied by real skill at perceiving the other person's inner state and desires. As they give their lover pleasure, they can share in it. This sets up a feedback loop in which giving the lover pleasure also gives them pleasure. This pleasure loop feeds both lovers and fills them both with love and satisfaction.

During sex, merging-patterned people tend to be more interested in feeling connected than in building a big charge and releasing it. This makes them more focused on cuddling and sharing love than on mind-blowing orgasms. Since they don't have a strong container and can't hold much charge, they may also have difficulty achieving orgasms. For them, sex is more about feeling filled by love than about a charge/discharge event.

Early in the relationship, their sexuality will be geared towards attracting and cementing the relationship connection. Then, as the commitment deepens, younger, more infantile parts of their psyche will come to the surface. This is true for all people, but for those caught in the merging pattern, it may bring to the surface the infant's desire to merge into her mother, rather than a desire for adult sexuality. The spark that ignites sex is created by an energetic difference between the two partners — by the tension of a masculine/feminine polarity. Merging tends to erase that polarity, so when less polarity creates less spark, the result is less sex.

Their Approach to Conflict

When involved in a disagreement with you, a merging-patterned person will typically respond first by accommodating and placating you. Instead of moving away, as a leaving-patterned person would, she will move closer. She will become more agreeable, trying to calm you down. She may even become entertaining to distract your attention away from the disagreement. One of my clients described this strategy with the motto: *"As tension rises, increase cheerfulness."* Those who do this pattern do not like direct conflict and will avoid it, if they can.

Weapons used in a conflict

When trying to get their own way, their main tactic is usually manipulation. Often this involves offering you something you want to make you more tractable to their wishes. They may offer praise, food, sex, love, or anything that will make you feel good. Their idea is that if they make you feel good, you will make them feel good. They believe that, somehow, you will just know what they need and supply it to them, without them ever having to ask for it.

From their perspective, this makes sense, of course. They are masters at reading the unspoken feelings and needs of others and then giving what is needed. And if they can do it, why can't you? *"If you loved me, you would"* is a favorite phrase in these moments. And, from their perspective, it makes sense because if they loved you, they would do what you want. Their mistake here is the same one we all make: we believe that everyone else experiences the world the same way that we do and has the same abilities and needs that we have. Unfortunately, this is not the case, as we will see over and over during our discussion of the five survival patterns.

Also, as they try to set up this kind of reciprocal exchange, they will typically not include any mention of a deal or any verbal negotiation of its terms. The negotiation will be done behaviorally, not verbally, and what they are offering will initially be presented as a gift, not a trade. If you don't do this survival pattern yourself, you will probably not notice this behavioral negotiation or realize that a bargain is being struck. You will simply think that they're being really nice to you and giving you lots of goodies. Later, when they expect something in return, you may be surprised and feel you've been tricked.

Another tactic that merging-patterned people use during a conflict is drama. When they shift into creating drama, they have replaced the carrot of offering gifts with the stick of throwing a tantrum. Their demand becomes stronger, and their tone shifts from positive to negative. The term "drama queen" refers to this tactic. (Note, though, that the term refers to the tactic of throwing tantrums to get what you want, which may also be used by people who do not do this survival pattern.)

Another form the drama can take is playing the martyr. At this point, the merging-patterned person may actually say out loud, *I did everything for you and now you owe me.* The bill is coming due. The "gift" is being revealed as an unspoken trade. Now the manipulation is obvious to everyone . . . except the person playing the martyr.

There is a great deal of interior drama as well. Their anger is frequently turned inward on themselves, as their inner critic berates them for being so weak and needy, so stupid, so deficient in a thousand ways. Inside, they may well be collapsing in shame, overwhelmed by their own flood of feelings, and hoping that you will see this and come to save them.

If all the above strategies fail, and they are totally unable to get what they need, a merging-patterned person will be thrown back into their early experience of deprivation — back into all those thousands of unmet needs — and their anger may rise into a rage about all those unmet needs. In their pursuit of your love, they have abandoned themselves and changed themselves into what would please you, so if you reject them, they are devastated — they have nothing left and nothing left to lose.

Communication Style

Merging-patterned people typically talk a lot. They are very verbally oriented, but mostly use words to connect with others emotionally, rather than to communicate facts or accomplish goals. Therefore their speech tends to be about feelings rather than actions, and to be indirect rather than direct. Because of their positive bias of attention and desire to be liked, they often compliment and flatter the listener. This may be sincere generosity, or it may be a manipulation to get you to like them or do something for them.

Communicating with Them

When you speak with someone who does this survival pattern, make it personal. Let your heart speak to her heart. Tell her what you feel and what you want. Make it specific to the two of you, here and now. Don't wander off into generalizations or abstractions. Don't think you have to build a case or justify your feelings. Don't think you have to prove that some big authority somewhere approves of what you're saying or asking. Merging-patterned people don't care about any of that. They care about you and about pleasing you right now, so stick with that. The more personal and emotionally vulnerable you can be, the more you will touch their hearts and make them want to help you. But be careful not to use this approach to manipulate or harm them. Since they are typically unable to reference themselves, they may not be able to say "no" when they need to. You may need to reference their needs along with your own, notice what is good for them, and support them in practicing good self-care.

If you think about speech as being composed of both facts and feelings — words and melody — then merging-patterned people are much more interested in the melody and the feeling flow than in the words. They will be listening for the feelings in what you're saying and may miss the facts entirely. If you're speaking in an angry tone, anger is what they will hear, no matter what words you're saying. And don't expect them to hear your words clearly when you're upset with them. For them, their failure to please you will be so loud inside them that they won't even be able to hear your words.

Similarly, when they speak to you, they will be attending more to the feelings and melody they are sending than to the words they are saying, so their words may get jumbled up. Don't get distracted by inconsistencies or even contradictions in their words. Focus on the melody and the feelings.

Since they habitually reference the relationship and the other but not themselves, they will often refer to "you" and "we," but only rarely make direct "I" statements. If you need them to reference themselves so they can tell you what they want, reframe their self-referencing as something that will be helpful to you. Say something like, *"It would help me a lot if you could tell me more about what you want."* It will be much easier for them to reference themselves to help you than to help themselves. Remember, referencing themselves is exactly what they were trained *not* to do as a child.

Their Way of Asking for Help

When requesting help, a person caught in this survival pattern will typically avoid making a direct request. Her form of complaint about something will be more along the lines of *"I can't"* or *"It's too hard."* She may describe her problem and her distress about it endlessly, without ever stating what she wants instead. She will not reference her own core to find out what she wants and then ask you for it. Instead, she will reference you for clues to what she should want and do. Her assumption is that all actions and all solutions come from others, not from herself. Essentially, she will act helpless and wait for you to solve her problem.

When help or a solution arrives, if it is not in the form she expected, she may not recognize it. (However, this tendency to not recognize help unless it arrives in the form we expected is not limited to merging-patterned people. We all do this.)

Her theme is *"You have to do it for me,"* which, of course, is true for an infant. Believing that she is still in that state, she will try to force the world to do things for her by acting helpless, keeping her energy level low, pleading, complaining, and waiting. Friends and lovers may be drained by this process and come to see her as a bottomless pit of needs.

The difficulty is that, at a deeper level, a merging-patterned person is pursuing two mutually-conflicting goals. She is maintaining the identity she formed in the oral stage while simultaneously trying to get filled up and move on from that stage.

Making a Request of the Pattern

Merging-patterned people value the personal, so make your requests explicitly personal. Appeals to reason, rules, or morality will fall on deaf ears, but an appeal from your heart to theirs will be irresistible. Ask them *"Would you do this for me?"* On the other hand, if you are a merging-patterned person, be aware that you are vulnerable to being manipulated by others who approach you in this way.

Their Response to a Request

People who are in the merging pattern want to say "yes" to your request. They have a genuine desire to please you. When you ask something of them, their automatic response will be "yes." But they typically have skipped the crucial step of referencing their own core to see if they want to comply or if they are even capable of complying with this specific request. Instead, they have referenced your core, and of course, the answer in you is "yes" because this is what you want from them. As a result, they will say "yes" to lots of things that they actually don't want to do or aren't able to do. Then, when the time comes to deliver, reality will catch up with them as they realize they can't or don't want to do what they promised. However, it is unlikely that they will come back to you and re-negotiate the agreement. Avoiding conflict is much more important to them than keeping agreements, so they may not even remember their commitment. Instead, they will be late or busy or forget — anything but a direct *"No, I don't want to."* Facing your disappointment is even harder for them now, since they have also misled you.

On the other hand, since people who adopted the merging pattern are heart-centered and really do want to make others feel good, their "yes" can arise from a truly sincere and generous impulse. They can take real pleasure in doing something for you just the way you want it done — without judging your way, without trying to improve it or substituting their own way, as people in other survival patterns often do. When merging-patterned people are in the gifts of the pattern, the combination of their sincere desire to please and their skill at tracking the other person's internal experience can make them exceptionally gifted at giving what is wanted or needed.

Complimenting the Pattern

When you want to compliment someone who does the merging pattern, keep in mind that she is tuned in to your inner feeling state. So first put your attention on your own good feelings from whatever she's done, and then speak from those feelings. Make your appreciation personal and emotional, and speak from your heart. Tell her how whatever she has said or done makes you feel inside. Tell her that you love it. Tell her it's beautiful or yummy. Let your heart speak directly to her heart about how wonderful she is, or her creation is. Remember, she wants to please you, so go ahead and tell her just how pleased you are with her.

Typically, merging-patterned people care the most about love, connection, pleasure, harmony, and happiness in general, so when you are complimenting them, focus your appreciation on those things, rather than on correctness or achievements. However, as with all things relating to the survival patterns, this is not a one-size-fits-all prescription. In addition to considering what patterns they do and how those patterns tend to focus their attention, you'll need to also consider the individual person before you and her personal values. If you watch her responses closely, you'll probably be able to tell when your compliment really went in, and when it didn't.

Getting Yourself Out of the Merging Pattern

Whenever you realize that you've gone into pattern, your first job is to get yourself out of pattern and back to being present. The pattern is distorting your perceptions and your experience. In fact, the patterned response to your distress is likely making things worse, not better. Once you are back to being present, you'll be able to find the best way to respond to the current situation.

Signs you are in the merging pattern

- you have collapsed

- you have no felt sense of your own core, and you cannot reference your self

- you are referencing only the feelings and needs of others at the expense of your own

- you are trying to be *all things to all people*

The solution: You need to find your core and reference it.

To get out of the merging pattern

Shift your attention from others and their needs to sensing your own core and your own feelings and needs.

Exercise:

Get up and stand on your own two feet.

Bend your knees and take a deep breath.

Ground down into the earth:

- notice that the earth likes you — even loves you

- notice that it wants to nourish and support you

- relax into that love

- allow the energy of the earth to flow up into you and fill you and support you

Say to yourself, *"I am enough. I can do this, and I can ask for help."*

For more information on how to get yourself out of pattern, please see Chapter 13, *Getting Yourself Out of Pattern*, on page 358.

Remember, whenever you're in pattern, your first job is to get yourself out of pattern and back to presence.

Healing the Merging Pattern

Each of the survival patterns involves getting stuck in a particular developmental stage, unable to learn the skills needed to complete the tasks of that stage, and unable to use those new skills as a foundation to stand upon when facing the challenges of the next stage. Because the merging pattern is a very young pattern, those who are stuck in it will need help and guidance to learn the skills that they missed and complete the tasks of this stage.

The unmet need of merging-patterned people is to feel full of themselves and ready to use that fullness to act on their own behalf. They are stuck in the belief that they must get what they need from others, instead of learning how to meet their own needs. So their attention stays focused on their connection to others and on pleasing or manipulating others to get what they need, instead of on developing their own internal capacities.

To heal, they need a warm, loving connection to others who support them in developing their own capacities by gently directing their attention back to their own core and to their own strengths and abilities.

Getting enough

People who are caught in this pattern need to complete the sequence of needing, asking, receiving, filling up, feeling full, and pushing away. They also need to learn how to take in energy directly and let it fill them. These experiences of fullness will begin to give them feelings of strength, expansion, and self-confidence. And they also need to learn how to reference themselves — their own core — so that they can measure what they have and what they need and then ask for it directly. In psychological terms, they need to reclaim the right to have needs, to get those needs met, and to value themselves as a separate and independent being, rather than for what they can give to someone else.

In order to do all this, they need to feel held by an unwavering love. Because they are developmentally still so young, their own will and strength have not really come online, and they cannot complete these tasks by themselves, any more than a young child could. Their patterned habit is to reference the other person for guidance, instead of referencing their own core. So they need someone to repeatedly direct their attention back to their own core, their own needs, and their own abilities. Someone who can measure their real abilities, pace them, and have realistic confidence in them. Someone who can guide them to tasks they are ready for and reassure them as they struggle that "you can do this." Over and over, they need to confront a challenge, struggle some but not too much, and then succeed. During this period, they will feel like they're slogging through mud. It is really hard work, and they may often want to quit, so they need the support of a steady, encouraging human connection to keep going. During this time of slogging, they will be learning many of the basic skills required for healthy, adult functioning. Let's go through the list of these skills.

Developing core and learning to self-reference

The most basic skill needed by those who do the merging pattern is the ability to self-reference, that is, to feel the core of their own body and put their attention on it. They will need to repeatedly practice bringing their attention back inside themselves and focusing on their own internal sensations. Core-focused physical activities such as ballet, Pilates, Gyrotonics, Body-Mind Centering, Aston Patterning, and Alexander Technique can help them do this.

However, part of them really doesn't want to sense their core because that's where the empty feeling is strongest. So they will need frequent support and re-direction to bring their attention back, over and over again, to feeling their own core. If you have taken on the task of supporting them in this, you will find that they can get very wiggly and squirmy during this process, trying to distract your attention away from helping them feel their core. They will typically throw out objections, fears, drama, and even tantrums to distract you. To effectively help them, you will have to accurately measure — second to second — just how much they are able to do right now and then lovingly hold them to that with an attitude of "you can do this."

Grounding

Merging-patterned people also need to learn how to ground themselves. This is the skill of connecting energetically to the earth and feeling supported and nourished by it. Instead of trying to get their energy from other people, they need to transition to getting it directly from the earth. They do this by developing a personal relationship with the earth, a relationship in which they are able to receive the support of the ground beneath their feet, holding them up and giving them a place to stand. This support allows them to stand on their own two feet and stand up for themselves.

Boundaries and me/not me

Another skill needed by merging-patterned people is that of creating healthy boundaries around themselves. This requires learning what a healthy boundary is, how to create it, and how to enforce it. It requires psychologically and energetically separating from others, which means giving up the habit of merging with others and practicing being a separate person instead.

They also need practice differentiating what is "me" from what is "not me," that is, differentiating my feelings from your feelings, and my responsibilities from your responsibilities. Merging-patterned people need to develop all the basic energy skills — ground, core, edge, and me/not me. (For more detailed descriptions of each of the four basic energy skills, please see *Healing the Leaving Pattern* on page 103.)

Developing will and strength

Merging-patterned people also need to practice using their own will and strength. Because they have not been supported in exercising their own will, it is typically still weak. They will need to practice using it — intentionally exercising their will over and over, strengthening it through exercise the way one strengthens a muscle — until they can push through difficulties, instead of collapsing. Again, they will need support and guidance, both to acknowledge their current limitations and to celebrate their accomplishments. As they work to increase their real abilities, they will learn about commitment, discipline, and perseverance. Gradually, developing their will and strength will enable them to claim their power, ask directly for what they need, and make arrangements to get it.

Dropping the compensation

For those who are caught in the compensated side of the merging pattern, there is an additional step that must occur before they can touch the depth of their wound and heal it. They have to discover that their compensation is only an imitation of the real capacities they want, and they have to decide to give it up, at least for a moment, and drop into the helpless neediness that it has been masking.

As we said earlier, creating the compensation was an attempt to grow up and become capable. But because the compensation was not built on a felt sense of the body's core, it does not have the foundation needed to support real strength and will. In order to develop a real felt sense of her own core, and then real strength and will, someone who does the compensated merging pattern must first let go of the false core that she has created, return to the pure merging state, and then build from there.

This can be very difficult, because the more successful her compensation has been, the more capacities she will lose when she first lets go of it. Being without it will be frightening, and she will likely need to go back and forth many times before she is ready to give it up for good. But every moment of giving it up and surviving counts, and as those moments accumulate, she will be able to gather more courage and move forward more rapidly.

Developing good self-care

Learning these basic skills will enable merging-patterned people to do something that they have never before been able to do, and that is to practice good self-care. Good self-care is the key to getting out of the merging pattern and returning to being present.

Good self-care includes being able to measure their own needs and feel their real tiredness, hunger, loneliness, etc. It includes measuring their own real capacities and energy by feeling their own core. It also includes asking for help directly — even literally reaching out for it. And finally, good self-care includes caring for their own inner child: noticing what the child needs and then arranging for those needs to be met.

Strengthening the self

All the above practices, taken together, will help the merging-patterned person develop a strong, integrated sense of self. This will allow her to finally know herself from the inside out, from a felt sense of her own core, rather than through the eyes of others. It will allow her to claim her own intrinsic value and stand up for herself. And it will allow her to accomplish the main task of the oral stage, namely to take in, hold, and metabolize her own energy.

In order to become happy with herself, she will also need help in disidentifying from her inner critic, learning to recognize its attacks, and learning to defend herself. Being able to hold it at bay will open up a space inside her within which she can hear her own voice and feel her own needs and desires. Since listening to the voice of her inner critic has been the source of much of her shame, disidentifying from it is the key to freeing herself from that feeling. This change in her relationship to her inner critic will also free her from its demands for perfection.

Anger work

Merging-patterned people actually have an easier time with anger work than those who do other survival patterns. They must have enough felt sense of their core to connect to their real self before anger work can begin, but they typically do not have a large reservoir of stored anger, so releasing it is not a big task. Instead, their anger work will focus more on learning to express any dissatisfaction that they feel in their current relationships. This will bring up fears of rejection and abandonment, of course, so the real work will be in learning to value themselves and speak up anyway.

Their human need and spiritual need

When in the grip of the pattern, a merging-patterned person experiences her own essence as not being enough. What she needs to discover is that, in fact, her essence *is* enough. Her human need is to experience herself as being able to fill and care for herself. Her spiritual need is to experience the divine source within filling and supporting her.[8]

By doing the work described above, the merging-patterned person will develop a reality-based self-confidence. She will be able to take responsibility for her own actions, connect without merging, and tolerate being alone.

Addendum — the Oral Stage and Romance

When an infant's needs are met and its nervous system has relaxed back down to the ground state, it feels wonderful. It feels totally relaxed and safe, filled with a golden love as its body melts into its mother's body. Unconsciously, we all remember this heavenly experience and want to return to it. And because, as infants, we experienced the love arising in response to someone else's presence, now as adults, we commonly believe that love must come to us from another person. These two elements — the experience of merging love, and our belief that it comes from others — combine to form our image of romance. We think, "If I just had so-and-so, my life would be perfect." Then we get so-and-so, and of course, life is not perfect. We still have to go to work and pay the bills, plus now there is someone leaving the cap off the toothpaste tube. Our mistake is in thinking that love comes from another person, rather than from relaxing and opening ourselves as profoundly as an infant does to the current of love that flows inside us.

For more help in determining which patterns you go into, please visit *www.The5PersonalityPatterns.com.*

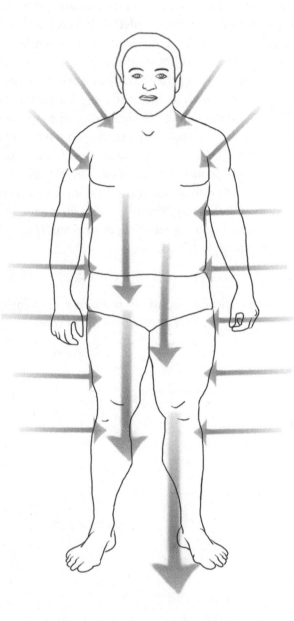

The Enduring Pattern – body and energy flow

– 9 –

The Enduring Pattern

"You can't make me. Leave me alone."

LIKE ALL THE SURVIVAL PATTERNS, the enduring pattern is a holding pattern in the body, conditioned into it by trauma, which creates a particular habit of attention. The defense strategy is to hunker down by pulling their energy in and sending it down into the ground beneath them. By stopping all internal movement and action, enduring-patterned people become able to tolerate almost anything. All their energy goes into resisting, and they become impossible to budge from their silent stance of *"You can't make me."* But this constant resistance also makes it hard for them to move their own energy to act or express themselves, and it makes them feel slow and heavy inside. They hide by sending their energy down into the ground, but then get stuck down there. One enduring-patterned person described it this way:

> *I am heavy. Life is a heavy coat over me, and it gets heavier and heavier throughout the day. The Things to Do list grows longer and longer, but I cannot move. I am stuck in thick molasses. I push and struggle, but barely move. I push harder and harder, but I can't move. Finally, I see that I am holding myself back. I have poured the molasses. I realize I can drain it, so I open the spigot. It starts to drain slowly, very slowly. I want to hope things will get better. I continue to struggle, but it is so slow. I keep the spigot open, hoping. I fall asleep from the struggle. I wake up. I have on a heavy coat. I am in a vat of molasses. I struggle.*

Range of functioning

Like all the survival patterns, this one exists across a broad spectrum of functionality, from those completely ruled by the pattern to those who wear the pattern lightly. With this pattern, the variation is mostly in how much they are able to mobilize their own energy to act in the world, to express themselves and get what they want. Lower functioning individuals are stuck in their resistance to everything, including their own desires, while higher functioning ones can act to get what they want.

On the low end of the spectrum, we have people who are totally caught in the pattern, people who are very stuck in the hunkered down place. They are unable to take action to express themselves or get what they want, and they compulsively resist every idea, even their own. They feel heavy and stuck, and their life shows a pattern of self-sabotage.

In the mid-range, we have people who still live within the world view of the pattern but are able to tolerate more movement, self-expression, and action to get what they want. They are strong in the skills and talents of the pattern and may be able to achieve some small successes, as long as they do not attract attention. Resistance to the agendas of others is still a major theme.

On the high end of the spectrum, we have people who can generally stay present while using the skills and talents of the pattern. While they are still very aware of others' agendas, they do not automatically resist them. They are able to express themselves, take action, and accomplish their goals. Instead of seeming heavy and stuck, they appear to have a deep inner strength and patience.

The Gifts of the Enduring Pattern

As a person uses any of the patterns, he* continually practices the skills required to make it work. Over time, he becomes exceptionally proficient in those particular skills. As he heals the wounds that created the pattern and becomes able to shift his attention out of the pattern and back to presence,

---

* To avoid the cumbersomeness of having to continually say "he or she," I will assign a gender to the child described in each chapter and then stick with that gender throughout the chapter. For example, in this chapter, I will assume the child is a boy. However, all five of the patterns are found in both genders, and everything said about the boy in this chapter could just as easily have been said about a girl.

the abilities he has acquired stay with him and become the gifts of the pattern. Now he is able to employ his exceptional abilities as he responds to the needs of the present moment. Even though some of the physical structures remain in his body, he has shifted out of the patterned survival defense and into the gifts of the pattern.

The gifts of the enduring pattern include a deeply grounded strength. At their best, enduring-patterned people are embodied, stable, and steady. They have more capacity than those in other patterns to hold a grounded space for themselves and others. Frequently, these are the people who are grounding the family, the office, or even the entire community. They have a deep, intuitive connection with the Earth, and may sometimes seem to resemble a mountain in their depth and silent strength. At their best, their bodies and psyches exude a quiet strength and stamina, the kind of presence that people refer to as "the strong, silent type."

They are also Masters of Space. They are very aware of their own personal space and whether it is being invaded or respected. When in the gifts of the pattern, they are able to hold their own space and also hold space for others. Of all the survival patterns, they put the highest importance on respecting others' space and will not invade their space or impose on them.

They are able to just Be, with no need to Do. They enjoy silence and stillness, and while they may be very observant, they feel no need to share their observations with others. They are able to leave you alone and prefer that you leave them alone, too.

There is a patient, tolerant quality, an ability to accept others just as they are and allow them to be that way. They can be very diplomatic, acknowledging all sides of a dispute, while staying grounded and unreactive. While others yell and storm around, they are able to wait patiently until the storm has passed and then help everyone continue on toward the original goal. They can be excellent at mediating disputes and maintaining diplomacy.

Although they are quiet, they have a large capacity for energy, and when doing is required, they can call up a great deal of strength and stamina. This allows them to carry on for a long time in the face of great adversity without fanfare or recognition. In fact, they usually prefer to stay in the background and avoid attracting attention.

They are slow in making decisions, but once they have chosen, they are strongly committed to their choice. Similarly, they are slow to start moving in a new direction, but once they are moving, their momentum is formidable. And they are able to multitask well, while staying anchored to what's important. These qualities make them loyal, low-maintenance workers and spouses, especially if those around them are willing to leave them alone.

Because people in the gifts of the enduring pattern have a strong sense of their own core and self, there is a steadiness about them. They know who they are, and they are able to distinguish between self and other. They do not become disoriented by the storms of life swirling around them.

The key to the gifts of the enduring pattern lies in claiming your own power and will and filling your own space with your own energy.

Examples

- Eeyore in *Winnie the Pooh*

- Charlie Brown in the *Peanuts* comic strip

- Hagrid in the *Harry Potter* series

- Samwise Gamgee in the *Lord of the Rings*

- George Costanza (played by Jason Alexander) in the TV show *Seinfeld*

- Michael Caine's character in the film *Secondhand Lions*

Alternate Names

- Masochist

- Burdened

- the Endurer

- the Over-Managed Child

- the Defeated Child

Exercise – Being Caught in the Pattern

Having to Hide Yourself

This exercise is designed to give you a felt sense of what it is like to be caught in the enduring pattern, feeling stuck and burdened, and having to hide yourself to protect yourself. As you go through this exercise, try not to judge your experience, but just notice how familiar or unfamiliar it is and what it would be like to live this way every day.

Sit down comfortably, with your spine relatively straight, and close your eyes. Take several deep breaths all the way down into your body and release them. On the out-breath, let any extra energy leave your body on the breath.

First, let yourself notice that you have a big bubble of energy that surrounds your body like a giant egg. This bubble extends out about two or three feet beyond your body in all directions, including above and below you, in front of you and behind you, and on both sides. This is your own personal space, and, ideally, it is filled with your own energy.

Now imagine that you're pulling all of your energy inwards, inside your body, and sending it down into the earth below you. Pull in the edge of your bubble, also, until it reaches your skin or even comes inside your skin. Now you have no space around you protecting you.

But you need protection, so imagine that you can send your self down into the earth below you, down where you can hide from anyone who wants to mess with you. Keep sending your energy down into the ground until it feels like all of your energy is down there, until nothing is moving anymore and no energy is circulating through your body. Keep doing this until everything feels kind of dense and thick, like sludge.

Notice that now you're stuck. You're hunkered down, alright, but now you're stuck down here. Maybe you want to take some action or express something, but there isn't any energy moving in you to help you do it.

And you know that, pretty soon, someone's going to come around wanting you to do something for them. They're going to come buzzing into your space, bugging you to do something for them. And they won't even notice that they're trespassing in your space. They'll just walk right in and plunk down some expectation, something they want from you. And then, half the time, they won't even have the grace to leave. They'll just stand there, waiting for an answer, bugging you with their presence until you give them one.

And how can you even figure out what you want anyway, with them in so close, shoving their agenda in your face? It's hard enough to figure out what you want when you're all alone, but when there's someone else in here, filling up your space with all their own wants and feelings, it's even harder to feel yourself. It just gets too crowded. Too much pressure.

Notice the resentment building up in your body. Notice how much you want them to go away, how much you want to retreat into your cave and lock them out, and how much you want to just get away from them so they can't mess with you anymore.

Now gently let your awareness return to the room where you're sitting. Take a few deep breaths and let all these feelings leave your body on the exhalations. Stand up and shake out all of these feelings until your body has returned to feeling safe and relaxed.

Now take some time to notice what this whole experience was like for you:

- *How easy or difficult was it for you to pull your energy inside your body? To send it down into the ground?*

- *How did you feel about being heavy and stuck? Did it seem familiar?*

- *What thoughts or feelings arose as you did the exercise?*

- *What thoughts or feelings seemed to get in the way?*

- *What would it be like to live this way all the time?*

Exercise – The Gifts of the Pattern

Deep Grounding and Strength

In the previous exercise you experienced being caught in the enduring pattern: stuck, hiding, and resisting everything. Now let's shift into experiencing the gifts of the pattern. As you go through this exercise, just notice how familiar or unfamiliar these experiences are, and consider what it would be like to have these skills and gifts always within reach.

Sit down comfortably, with your spine relatively straight, and close your eyes. Again, take several big breaths deep down into your body and release them. Let any extra energy leave your body with each out-breath. Feel your entire system calming and slowing down, and let any unwanted energy within you begin to flow downward and into the ground beneath you.

Now gently and easily imagine that you're an enormous tree. Feel the immense weight and strength of your trunk and limbs. You don't walk; you don't talk; you just stand and watch. Just hang out with this experience for a while.

Now let your attention move downward to your roots. Feel your roots stretching down and outward under the ground and notice that they are just as big as the trunk and the limbs, with just as much weight and reach. If your roots are not this big already, let them grow downward and outward until they are. Let yourself hang out with this for a while.

Now let your roots grow down even deeper, down through the soil and into the bedrock. Let your roots become twice the size of your trunk and limbs, and feel that enormous mass of you under the earth — waiting, unmoving, unaffected by events on the surface. Again, let yourself just hang out with this experience for a while.

Now let your roots reach down even farther, doubling in size again. Feel into this huge mass of you that reaches down so far into the Earth. Notice that now 80% of you is below ground, down deep in the earth, and only 20% of you is above the surface. Notice how much safer this feels than when all of you is up on the surface, where everyone can see you and mess with you. Just let yourself rest here, safe in the arms of the dark, silent bedrock, where no one can bother you. Take all the time you like to just relax into this deep, silent refuge.

Now, while keeping all of your felt sense of silence and strength, of deep groundedness and safety, let the image of yourself change from being a tree into being a mountain that rises out of a plain. Now your whole body is made of rock and earth. Again, notice that the roots of the mountain stretch down deep into the earth so that nearly all of you is underground, with only a small part of you rising above the surface. And yet, when people look at you, they see only that small part. They don't even notice that you extend downward below the surface. They don't see that the roots of this mountain reach down deep into the bedrock. They have no idea how safe and strong and unmovable you are in your rocky depths.

You have become an immovable object, an enormous, effortless, unmoving strength. Maybe you have trees growing on your slopes, maybe not. It doesn't matter. You can stand for centuries, for millennia, while things come and go around you. Such things do not concern you. No one can influence you or make you do anything. You can wait forever.

Now let your awareness gently return to the room where you're sitting. If it's comfortable for you, you may want to keep this sense of yourself as an enormous, effortless, unmoving strength and let it stay with you. If it is not comfortable, simply let it go, but keep the awareness that this is possible and that some people feel this way.

Now take some time to notice what this whole experience was like for you:

- *How easy was it for you to let yourself become the tree? How about the mountain?*

- *How easy was it for you to grow down deep into the earth, to let most of you be hidden underground like that?*

- *How did you feel about being an immovable object?*

- *What thoughts or feelings arose as you did the exercise?*

- *What thoughts or feelings seemed to get in the way?*

- *What would it be like to have access to this skill whenever you needed it?*

The Origins of the Enduring Pattern

While the main difficulty for merging-patterned people is with "taking in," the main difficulty for enduring-patterned people is with "putting out," with expressing the self in thoughts, feelings, and actions. As toddlers and children, their attempts to act and do things for themselves, in their own way and on their own schedule, were thwarted and often punished, so they came to doubt their right to act.

Even when we're young, our bodies have their own rhythms and they know what they want and when they want it. Ideally, our parents are able to support us in becoming aware of our needs and rhythms by letting us express ourselves and by allowing us to do things in our own way and in our own time. However, the parents or environment of a child who develops the enduring pattern were not able to be so attuned and accepting of his rhythms and self-expression. Instead, they were intrusive and over-controlling, at least in that child's experience. Instead of accommodating *his* natural rhythms, they forced him to accommodate *their* rhythms. Instead of respecting his personal space and body, they invaded and controlled it, treating him as one of their possessions, rather than as a separate human being.

Remember that each child has his own level of sensitivity to each kind of difficulty, and what feels deeply wounding to one child may hardly be noticed by another. Some say that we are each most sensitive to the difficulties that help us learn whatever we need to learn to accomplish our life purpose. So the process by which a child develops any of the survival patterns is not a one-way street. It is not a story of simply being the victim of cruel and brutal parents, although sometimes it seems so (especially in the creation of this particular pattern). It may also be seen as a collaboration, in which both parent(s) and child learn through their experiences whatever they are trying to learn. I emphasize this now to give you some perspective on what we will explore next. In listening to some of the stories of how children who developed this survival pattern were treated, it is very easy to lose this perspective and instead see only cruel victimization.

Will, separation, and self-expression

The wounding that creates this survival pattern begins at about the age of two, because at that time the child enters a new developmental stage, a stage focused on the development of autonomy and a separate self. The child begins the process of psychological separation from the mother and begins to want to do things for himself, in his own way. He discovers the word "no" and the power it holds to show that he is different from his parents. He delights in saying "no" just to feel that amazing power in his body.

For the first time, his own will arises and he begins to express it. At 18 months, if he was toddling off in a possibly dangerous direction, his mother could simply pick him up and turn him, and he would happily toddle off in the new direction. No more. Now when his mother picks him up and turns him, he turns back. He feels the change as a challenge to his own budding will, and he asserts his own will by turning back and continuing in his original direction. And so the battle of wills begins. He has entered the "terrible twos."

His self-expression also changes. Before, he was simply expressing needs, whether for food, love, or something else. Now he is expressing HIS needs. In his psyche, a small, fragile sense of self has emerged and each expression has become an expression of that self. If his self-expressions are allowed and reflected back to him by his parents, he can begin to see himself in that mirror: he can begin the arduous process of sorting out "me" from "you" and discovering "this is Me!" He can begin to develop self-awareness.

This is a crucial step in any child's development. We do not discover ourselves solely by an internal process. We see ourselves first through the eyes of our parents, in the reflections we get from them. It's as if they hold up a mirror for us, and we see our own face in that mirror. If the mirror is clear, we see ourselves clearly. If the mirror is distorted, we see a distorted reflection of our self. Let's look at some examples of both clear and distorted reflections.

Suppose the little boy is pounding his fists on the floor in frustration and Mom says, *"You look angry."* The little boy puts the word and the feeling together and learns to refer to that feeling as "anger," perhaps even "my anger." He has gotten a clear reflection and he has learned something accurate about himself.

On the other hand, if Mom says, *"You stop that at once! No child of mine will behave like that,"* the little boy doesn't learn what it was he felt, only that it was somehow bad. The reflection is distorted. The little boy doesn't know himself any better, and now actually fears a part of himself.

Suppose, on another occasion, he announces, *"I hate my brother!"* and Mom replies, *"And why do you hate your brother, Sweetie?"* Now two things have happened. First, Mom has accepted his statement *"I hate my brother,"* which validates his feeling. Second, he has been asked *"Why?"*, so maybe he puts his feelings and thoughts into words and understands them better. Maybe he discovers why he hates his brother right now, and Mom helps him feel better about it and the hatred dissolves. Maybe the hatred doesn't dissolve, but at least he knows more clearly what he feels.

But suppose, instead, Mom responds by saying, *"You don't hate your brother, Sweetie. You love your brother."* Now he is confused. This doesn't feel like love, but Mom says that it is love. Now he's not sure what he feels. He only knows what Mom says he feels. Mom's view of him has been substituted for his own experience of himself.

Similarly, if his abilities and autonomy are reflected back to him, he can begin to develop self-confidence. He can begin to trust himself and his abilities. If he draws a picture with his crayons and his mother says, *"What a wonderful picture you made,"* he thinks *"I made that"* and *"It is good"* and he feels proud of himself. He starts to think *"I make wonderful pictures"* and he wants to make more of them.

On the other hand, if his mother says, *"What a wonderful picture my son made,"* the little boy still thinks *"It is good,"* but now it is no longer quite his own. Now it was made by Mommy's son, instead of by him. He didn't quite achieve psychological separateness that time, because his Mom took credit for his self-expression. The picture became a reflection of Mom (*"my* son"), not of him.

But things can get much worse. Suppose Mommy says, *"Bad boy! We do not make pictures in this house! You should be ashamed of yourself!"* Now he thinks *"I am bad; my picture is bad,"* and he feels ashamed. Now he does not want to make pictures any more. Making pictures leads to bad feelings and doing things leads to shame, not to pride. The more this happens, the more he doubts himself and the more reluctant he becomes to express himself again.

When children are punished, humiliated, or shamed for their natural attempts to develop their own will and establish a separate sense of self, they find it very difficult to complete the tasks of this developmental stage. Instead, they get stuck here. They have to avoid completing these tasks just to survive. Time moves on, and their bodies continue to grow, but their psyches cannot expand along with their bodies. They have to find a way to stay safe in a world where self-expression is shamed and punished. They have to learn to hunker down and endure.

Child-rearing to break the child's will

You may be wondering, "Why would any parent treat their child like that? Why would they punish their child for expressing a separate self?" To answer that, we need to recall that, for many centuries, most human societies were organized around a strict power hierarchy. Everyone believed that all power and authority flowed down from the top: God(s) ruled kings, kings ruled the masses, masters ruled slaves, men ruled women, and parents ruled children. No one believed that the individual had any inborn authority or that the individual person should be respected or nurtured. Instead, a person's authority came from his position in the social ranking, and often that authority was absolute: someone above you in the hierarchy could hurt or kill you, and no one would object. Displeasing your superiors could be punished by beatings or death. There were no individual rights or laws to protect you, so you remained alive only at the pleasure of those above you in the hierarchy. Within that system, the ability to gracefully submit to authority was a survival skill. Parents knew that they had to prepare their child for a life of submission to authority. Allowing their child to develop his own will could become a death sentence. Naturally, that social reality shaped the methods used in rearing children.

Until around 1950, most child-rearing books stated very clearly that the parents' job was to break the child's will in order to prepare him for a life of obedience. In 1748, Jay Suzer wrote in *An Essay on Education and Instruction of Children:*

> One of the advantages of these early years is that then force and compulsion can be used. Over the years, children forget everything that happened to them in early childhood. If their wills can be broken at this time, they will never remember that they had a will . . . it is impossible to reason with children; thus willfulness must be driven out in a methodical manner . . . If parents are fortunate enough to drive out willfulness

from the very beginning by means of scolding and the rod, they will have obedient, docile and good children . . . one must not cease toiling until one sees that all willfulness is gone. . . . Obedience is so important that all education is actually nothing other than learning how to obey.[1]

Another author from the same period wrote:

If your son . . . insists on having his own way: then whip him well. . . . Such disobedience amounts to a declaration of war against you. Your son is trying to usurp your authority and you are justified in answering force with force . . . The blows you administer . . . should convince him that you are his master.[2]

While these ideas are outdated and no longer part of the mainstream, they live on in many of our child-rearing practices. Many people still believe these ideas, and still practice and preach them. We still have many sayings that espouse this attitude, such as "spare the rod and spoil the child" and "children are to be seen and not heard." Many parents still believe that a good child is a quiet, obedient, submissive child. To them, differentness and disagreement are not signs of a healthy, budding self, but instead are "talking back," a challenge to the parent's authority that must be crushed.

Child-rearing when your own will was broken

Let us also take note of the fact that parenting any child is a very difficult and demanding task. Most children repeatedly test the limits set by their parents, push back against every prohibition, and continually try out new artful dodges to get what they want. They are amazingly resourceful and creative in this. Nurturing your child's sense of his own separate power requires that you have a grounded, stable sense of your own power. You have to be able to tolerate his constant challenges without taking them personally, without collapsing, and without hitting back. This is a huge task. It is much harder than raising a docile child.

Another factor in the persistence of these child-rearing practices is the fact that parents who were raised this way are often still stuck in this developmental stage themselves. They weren't allowed to develop their own inner sense of authority and self-confidence, or even to separate psychologically from their own parents, so as adults they aren't able to tolerate separation and assertiveness in their child. When their child challenges their authority, the fragile sense of self that they did manage to cobble together starts to come apart. It feels like their whole inner world is crumbling. In a panic, they turn to the only model of control they have, the one that was drilled into them in childhood — and even if they swore they would never do to their child what their parents did to them, that's exactly what they do. They may react in fury, like the mother of this woman: *"My Mom couldn't stand for me to have different tastes from hers in movies, in food, in clothes, in things that really should have had nothing to do with her. She would get enraged."*

Or the parent's response may appear very calm and logical, but still be meant to break the child's will. They may even patiently explain to the child that what they are doing is "for your own good," but the motivation and action are the same: because the parent cannot tolerate the child's separate self, will, and power, the parent attempts to crush them out of existence. In the Harry Potter stories, the character of Dolores Umbridge is a perfect example of this kind of adult in action. She, herself, is so conditioned into this system of dominance and obedience that she can drink tea and giggle while she tortures Harry for his acts of self-assertion.

Deplorable as such behavior is, it is a common consequence of having endured the same treatment as a child. The sad fact of human existence is that, if we do not heal our wounds, they live on in us and control our thoughts, feelings, and actions for the rest of our lives. We may block our wounds out of our awareness, but they live on under the surface, shaping everything we think, feel, and do. One way or another, we act out our unhealed wounds on our children. We do unto them as was done unto us. This is how we pass our fear, anger, and shame down through the generations. If our own will was broken, we fear our child's will. If guilt and shame were used to punish our own assertions of separateness, shaming will rise up in us when our child asserts his own separateness. If we have buried our own fury, it may erupt at our child, along with the thought, *"I didn't get to do that, so why should you?"* We may find ourselves unable to offer choices, tolerate objections, or support differences. If our own attempts at autonomy were thwarted, it is simply too scary for us to witness the emergence of autonomy in our child. Although this is bad parenting, it does not mean that we are bad — it only means that we are still wounded, still prisoners of our own childhood.

Over-control and invasion

Whatever the parents' motives, for the child who develops the enduring pattern, the early environment was in some way too controlling. The main mechanisms that parents use to control their children are denial of separateness, guilt, shame, conditional love, and violence. Let's look at each method in turn to see how it is used.

First, the parents may be narcissistic and therefore treat the child as an extension of themselves, rather than as a separate being. This might show up as finishing the child's sentences for him, instead of letting him say what he means in his own way. Or it might show up as claiming for themselves anything the child creates, referring to it as "what my child did" rather than "what you did." After years of having everything he produces stolen from him, the child may decide that it is useless to try to do or claim anything, since it will just get taken away.

Parents can also control their child through shame, guilt, and making their love conditional on the child's submission to their will. They might say, *"You don't want to disappoint your Mommy, now do you?"* or *"I could never love a child who acted like that."* These statements put the child in an impossible dilemma: to keep the parent's love, he must give up his own will and self-respect. To keep his own will and self-respect, he must give up his parent's love. He can have one or the other, but not both.[3] But he needs both, as surely as he needs both food and water. One of my clients spoke about his choice this way, *"I gave Mom my balls, my will, my power, because that's what love looks like."*

But neither choice is a real solution to the problem, so the child goes into despair and non-action, as we will see. Such parents are forcing their child to choose between love and growth, pitting his need for love against his developing self. The child's only defense is to try to hide his small, fragile self to save it. That same client said, *"Every kindness is a setup for betrayal. I close my heart to protect my heart."*

And finally, the parent may employ violence to force the child's compliance. The degree of violence can vary from inadvertent energetic invasions to intentional, systematic torture. On the lighter end of the spectrum, I know of a case where a younger sister felt constantly invaded and controlled by her older brother, unable to get enough safe space to just feel herself. So she developed the enduring pattern as a way to keep him from controlling her.

On the violent end of the spectrum, there are some parents who methodically control even the most basic bodily functions of their child. They dictate what the child eats and when he eats it. If he balks, they literally force it down his throat. They dictate his toileting, even resorting to enemas to force the evacuation of his bowels. These are physical invasions, and the child experiences them as a humiliating loss of control over his own body.

When a child is not allowed to move and act in his own rhythm and timing, he has no way to discover his own rhythm and timing. He has no way to discover when he wants to take something in and when he wants to put something out. To understand this child's experience, think of him as a small, scared, captured animal. He is held down and force-fed. Then he is held down and force-evacuated. He is not allowed to sleep or wake when he wants, but only at someone else's command. His body rhythms are violated and his body space is violated. This illustrates an extreme case, but it gives you a sense of how dramatic the childhood violations may have been for some who adopted the enduring pattern.

Defensive Action

So what actions can a child take to defend himself when his body is invaded and violated? When he is punished and shamed for acts of self-expression, or for attempting to separate and assert his autonomy and his own will? Over and over, he struggles against the control. Over and over, he fights until he collapses in exhaustion. But it doesn't do any good. He never wins. Fighting back only brings harsher punishment.

Self-hiding and self-negation

Eventually, he concludes *"I can't win."* And then a change occurs. His attention shifts from *"How can I win?"* to *"How can I avoid losing?"* And in one last act of autonomy, he turns his own will inward to suppress his impulse to act and fight: he defeats himself.

If he cannot prevent his defeat, he can at least be the one who causes it. So he directs all of his force inward and downward, suppressing and hiding his self and his reactions, burying his self where it cannot be found or hurt. And to keep it hidden, he must forget where he buried it. As one of my clients put it, *"I had to hide my self and my power somewhere Mom could not find it. But what I know, she knows, so to hide it from her, I had to hide it from me. She'll take anything I know. I had to bury the treasure and burn the map."*

Now he is stuck. He cannot initiate anything. He has the will to stop, but not the will to move — the will to hold his energy in, but not the will to put it out. Now his expression of his own will has been reduced to either compliance or resistance to his parents' will. On the outside, he complies. But inside, he secretly resists. So his compliance gets laced with sabotage — sabotage of those who would control him and even sabotage of himself. One of my clients described it like this: *"Mom said, 'I own you and everything you do.' I will not forgive. I swore an oath to never surrender. My only weapon is to hurt myself, to disappoint her. This is my prison."*

183

Remember that each of the survival patterns is a strategy to buffer the self from feeling overwhelmed in an unsafe situation. For people who adopted the enduring pattern, it was the process of creating and expressing a separate self that brought the attack. So to protect their budding self, they learned to negate their self. This self-negation is a profound act, and it becomes the core of their identity. They begin to identify themselves not as the one who does, but as the one who resists and refuses. One of my clients put it very succinctly: *"I am No. I am Refusal. I am Shutdown. There is no part of me that is Yes."*

Results of the Defensive Action

The results of this self-negation are profound and far-reaching. Now the oppressor has been internalized. Let's look at the effects of that.

Automatic resistance

Because enduring-patterned people were not able to practice differentiating self from other, even as adults they have difficulty holding on to their own agenda as their own, rather than seeing it as something imposed on them from the outside. A desire that they initially know to be their own can gradually lose its connection to them and become a free-floating desire, at which point it starts to look like someone else's desire that is being imposed on them. And because they hate having anything imposed on them, they feel compelled to resist it. So they find themselves resisting everything, even things that they themselves desired and initiated.

Hiding

Since enduring-patterned people lived through a kind of slavery as children, as adults they can find themselves still mired in the slave mentality, facing the dilemma of the freed slave. Although the external slave-master is gone, he still lives on inside them. So they long for freedom, but are afraid to claim their freedom by expressing themselves to the world in words and actions. Hiding is the only safety they have ever known, so coming out of hiding is terrifying. Self-expression is exactly what brought punishment, so self-expression is terrifying. As one client put it, *"I was raised in a slave mentality. My only safety is a slave safety."*

When your only safety is a slave safety, you can't fully engage in life — you can't stake out a position and claim it as your own. If you overtly rebel against your master, you will be punished. You will lose big. On the other hand, if you wholeheartedly comply with your master, you will lose any remaining sense of yourself. It will be more private, but you will still lose big. The only way to minimize your losses is to outwardly comply while inwardly resisting.

Since their reference point is the other person's desires, instead of their own desires, people who are caught in the enduring pattern often have a hard time fully engaging or really taking pleasure in any activity that involves other people.

Fear of self-expression and action

People caught in the enduring pattern have a deep-seated fear that any form of self-expression will bring punishment and humiliation. And, of course, this was often literally true for them during their childhood. So to protect themselves, they avoid any direct self-expression, such as taking any personal action or position. They avoid revealing their preferences or acting on personal impulse. Instead, they express their desires and actions passively. So when they do act, their actions have a passive-aggressive flavor, rather than an active-aggressive flavor.

Self-sabotage

Their fear of self-expression also leads them to actively avoid success. They believe that success brings attention and exposure, and exposure brings humiliation. Although avoiding success may seem strange, it is actually an attempt to keep themselves safe. In order to maintain plausible deniability, the methods used to avoid success tend to have a passive or accidental quality, but they all serve the same end: avoiding the expected humiliation. So accidents, mistakes, forgetting, failure to complete the task, and myriad other forms of self-sabotage are common. We will discuss this in more detail in the sections on psychological defenses and patterned behaviors.

Holding on and enduring

The strength of people in the enduring pattern is in resisting, not in initiating action. They have the will to hold in and hold still, but not the will to move, so their strength is the strength of a rock. They are the immovable object, not the irresistible force.

In fact, they often take pride in being able to "take it," to continue to endure long after everyone else has collapsed. One thing that they do know to be their own is their ability to endure hardship, and they even nurse a secret sense of superiority about this. This form of strength makes those in the enduring pattern able to be steady, hard workers in difficult, plodding situations. As long as they are not asked to make a decision or initiate an action, they can go on forever.

In short, those who adopted the enduring pattern were punished for self-assertion and lost the childhood fight to establish a separate, autonomous self. They were not allowed to develop pride in their own actions and expressions, and now they feel inadequate and ashamed. To protect themselves, they learned to pull in, hide, and resist, which they now do automatically. To heal, they need to feel safe enough to come out of hiding and passive-resistance, claim their own space and self, and approach life pro-actively.

The Enduring Pattern in Full Bloom

Body Signs

When children who use this survival strategy hunker down to weather a storm, they do so by sending their energy and awareness down into the lower half of their body and into the ground beneath them. This adds extra energy to the lower half of the body, which tends to give people with this pattern heavy hips and thighs. Their hips are dense and armored, rather than soft like the hips of merging-patterned people.

The muscles that are normally used for movement and self-expression are instead mostly used for holding in that movement and self-expression.[4] This gives them a solid, heavy, dense body, one that is strong and muscular, but without pride or expansion. Their body tends to be short and powerful, with a short neck and torso.[5]

Their posture tends toward the posture of shame: not quite erect, but instead slightly slumped, with a slight collapse in the mid-torso, and with the tail tucked in and the head lowered. Movements such as expansion and reaching out are limited or blocked.

Instead of filling the space around their body for two or three feet in all directions, as it normally would, the person's energy field is pulled in closer, sometimes to the skin or even deeper. Claiming the space around them attracted attention and punishment, so to fly under the radar, they have learned to avoid claiming it. Since they are not filling their own space, other

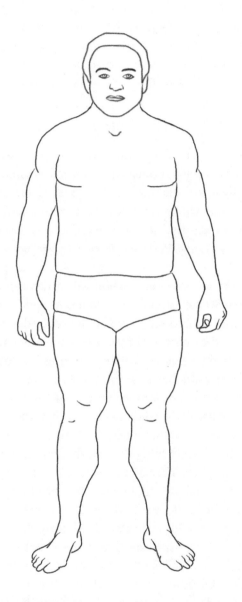

The Enduring Pattern – typical body shape

people have an unconscious tendency to invade their space. So the strategy that once helped to protect them from invasion now draws invasion.

Their eyes tend to look suffering and confused. Their body's holding pattern is that of holding in. They give an overall impression of stuckness, of things not moving or flowing. If you look at their entire being and notice what goes in and what comes out (ideas, sounds, movements, actions, etc.), you will see that, compared to what goes in, not much comes out.

Psychology

Enduring-patterned people typically have a history in which their unique acts and expressions were either punished or claimed by someone else. Because of this, they doubt their own right to act. Their main issue is with putting out energy and information: with expressing the self, taking action, and even with fully occupying their own psychic and physical space. Several of my clients have described this by saying, *"It's like driving with one foot on the gas and one foot on the brake."*

They fear that any act of self-expression will attract some sort of punishment or humiliation. So they stop the outward flow and instead send all that energy downward, into their lower body and then deep down into the ground beneath them, where they hide. Over time, this survival strategy becomes a habit and then eventually a holding pattern, keeping everything in. It is then no longer conscious or volitional; it is "just the way I am."

The unmet developmental need was the need to express their budding self and see it reflected back. They did not have the opportunity to explore and clarify their self by sending out their ideas, feelings, and creations (such as the drawing we talked about) and having all those things reflected back to them as their own. Because they have not had much practice at doing this, they often find it difficult, even as adults, to figure out what they think and feel and put those thoughts and feelings into words. Instead, they have lots of vague, undifferentiated thoughts and feelings stuck inside of them.

They do not experience themselves as being strong or worthy, or even entitled to claim their own body and their own space. In fact, they still find it difficult to know themselves as separate individuals unless they are resisting something. Resisting at least gives some sense of being different and separate, whereas compliance does not. A client who was facing this difficulty said it this way: *"I refuse. I will destroy your plan, or even my plan, since it might be your plan. I can't differentiate between your plan and my plan."*

The developmental tasks that were not fully accomplished were those of individuation and autonomy. Individuation means learning to know yourself as a separate individual, including learning to reference your own thoughts, feelings, and desires and express them as your self. Autonomy means developing a healthy will so that you can act by yourself and for yourself. This allows you to develop a healthy sense of pride in your accomplishments and your self, and even develop a healthy self-confidence.

But if your own will is not allowed to develop, you are not able to reference yourself and act for yourself. You are left with only two choices: submission to the other's will or rebellion against it. Both of these options start by referencing the other, not the self, so they provide no practice in referencing the self, no reflection of the self, and no increase in self-awareness. And while submission to the other's will only emphasizes your own powerlessness, resistance at least gives you some sense of power and separateness, so it becomes your habitual response. As we will see later on in this chapter, the default response of this survival pattern to any request is "No," usually without the individual actually checking inside to see what he wants.

When a child wins at something or succeeds at something, he naturally feels a sense of power and competence. If he had to work hard at it and persist over time, he also sees how applying his own will and effort leads to success. This makes him more confident that he can apply himself and succeed in the future. But if that child always loses and is humiliated in his defeat, he never gets to feel a sense of power, competence, or confidence in himself. Instead, he feels shame and a helpless rage. That rage may be deeply buried, but it is there and it is big. When it finally erupts, the enduring-patterned person has no skill at managing or expressing it, since he has never been allowed to practice expressing his anger.

Beliefs

The beliefs of enduring-patterned people arise mainly out of being controlled and humiliated. Some of their typical beliefs are:

"I can't win."

"Life is hard."

"I have to carry it all."

The illusion of the enduring pattern is *"I'm trying to please you."* People in this survival pattern often sincerely believe that they are trying to please you, not realizing that they are also inwardly resisting you. This is another manifestation of their basic strategy of outward compliance and inner resistance.

Fears

The biggest fear for enduring-patterned people is the fear of being "messed with" by others. To protect themselves, they try to both fly under the radar and physically get away from others. They fear that, if they are found and exposed, they will again be hurt and humiliated.

They also fear personal success, since they believe that the attention it would attract would lead to being invaded, humiliated, or punished. So they avoid it by any means possible, including self-sabotage. This allows them to stay hidden and safe.

Psychological Defenses

As with all the survival patterns, the psychological defenses of the enduring pattern are all attempts to create some sense of safety in an unsafe world. The main defenses of people caught in the enduring pattern are hiding, enduring, resisting, passive-aggression, self-negation, and self-sabotage. Let's look at each one in turn.

Hiding

Hiding and enduring shape their general way of being in the world. Hiding means that their energy and self-expression are kept inside. Anything that would reveal or expose their inner world and self is held in.

Enduring

Enduring means just "taking it." It is a natural consequence of not outwardly responding, since any response would include some self-expression and therefore expose them to humiliation or defeat. If you expect that responding will only bring more pain, then not responding seems like a safer way of being.

Resistance

The only way for them to maintain some sense of self that has not been taken over by the outside authority is to resist that authority. Complete submission would mean losing all sense of a separate self, so to keep some separateness and autonomy, their compliance is mixed with some resistance or sabotage. *"Only my rebellion is authentic,"* was the way one client put it. Their resistance is usually accompanied by a hidden spitefulness and a secret pride in being morally superior to the oppressor, of being able to endure more than the oppressor ever could.

Passive-aggression

This is the solution to the problem of needing to resist, but also needing to not appear to be resisting, so as to avoid the crushing retaliation that active-aggression would bring. It is a way to take action while disowning responsibility for that action. To understand this need, imagine for a moment that you're part of the French Resistance to the Germans during World War II. The Germans have invaded your country and occupied your town. At first, you and your comrades shot back, but the Germans quickly killed whoever shot at them. Then you blew up their headquarters, but they retaliated by rounding up 100 townspeople and publicly shooting them. Now you want to destroy the town's only bridge across the river to prevent the Germans from using it to move their tanks into your town. But if you blow up the bridge, they will know you did it, and they will kill more of your people. So you devise a plan to weaken the bridge just enough that when they drive their tanks across it, the bridge will collapse under the weight. If you're skillful enough, you can sabotage the German war effort without letting them know you were involved. When they question you, you can say, *"Gee, it must have been an accident. Sorry about your tanks."* You can act, but not be seen as responsible for the results of your act. This is the essence of passive-aggression.

Self-negation

The signature psychological defense of the enduring pattern is self-negation: the turning of the person's will against their own impulses and actions. This is the core of this pattern's survival strategy. In effect, the person says "I will defeat myself before you can defeat me. I will make myself lose small before you can make me lose big."

Self-sabotage

Self-sabotage is the outward expression of the enduring-patterned person's self-negation. It is a way of winning through losing. It must be done in passive-aggressive ways, of course, since he must not appear to be responsible for it. That is, it must seem like bad luck or an accident, something that is "not my fault." In daily life the self-sabotage will show up as procrastination, accidents, unfinished projects, incomplete degrees, repeatedly quitting or failing at the last minute — anything that prevents standing out and thereby drawing attention.

This self-sabotage is not conscious or volitional. The body of someone who does this pattern has been so deeply conditioned to avoid any situation that might draw attention and punishment that it moves at the unconscious level to prevent success and the attention it draws. While all the survival patterns operate unconsciously through the body in this way, the process becomes most starkly obvious here, as this survival pattern's unconscious action actually undermines and sabotages the person's conscious attempts at success.

When enduring-patterned people enter therapy, their presenting problem is usually a history of incompletion and self-sabotage. In therapy, they will agree with the therapist's observations and comply with her suggestions, make some slow progress toward their stated goal, but then inexplicably relapse just before reaching it. After several rounds of this, the therapist will typically become frustrated and annoyed, and the client will feel this and use it as an excuse to declare themselves a failure and quit.

Notice that this client has just sabotaged his own goal, despite having invested considerable time, money, and effort. He has also recreated his relationship with his punishing parent. By inducing the expected disapproval and anger in his therapist, he has confirmed his belief that he is a failure, felt punished, changed nothing, and gone back into hiding.

These are the clients that defeat therapists, over and over, all the while believing that they want to change. In order to work effectively with a client like this, the therapist must realize that this surface problem is actually a solution to a much deeper problem, which must be addressed before the client can tolerate any external success.

Relationship to Self

The core act of self-negation is so powerful that the person's identity forms around it. It becomes their relationship to their own self. The oppressor has been internalized, and the person now mistreats themselves in the same ways they were mistreated by others. In order to stay hidden and safe, enduring-patterned people defeat and shame themselves. This can lead to self-abuse and self-harm. At a minimum, it leads to the general sense of heaviness and stuckness that they often feel.

Relationship to the Inner Critic

Since any person's inner critic is made up of the recorded voices of their parents and caregivers, it acts and sounds much like they did. If their parents and caregivers were angry, the inner critic's voice is also angry. If they were shaming, it is shaming. If they were abusive, it is abusive.

When an enduring-patterned person is attacked by their inner critic, the attack will usually sound something like *"You don't deserve anything. You're a loser and a failure. You're nothing."* Of course, this makes the person feel small and ashamed and want to hide.

Personality Traits

Now let's look at the personality traits of the enduring pattern. These are the way an enduring-patterned person will tend to look when he is actually in the pattern. When he is not in pattern, but simply present, these traits may be muted or absent. At those times, he will likely exhibit the gifts of the pattern, such as a solid, strong, grounded presence, unruffled even by the anger of others. But when he is caught in the enduring pattern, his appearance will be more like what follows.

The first thing you'll notice is that the person looks and feels heavy and stuck. He may even use those words to describe himself. Not much is moving energetically, physically or emotionally. There is a sense of moodiness and misery, but without a lot of drama. There may be some complaining, but little or no action to change the situation.

If you watch closely, you'll notice that certain things are missing from his behavior. There will be very little direct self-expression, i.e., very few statements such as "I want . . . ," "I feel . . . ," or "I decided to . . . ." Statements that reveal a personal feeling, position, or action will be absent. There will be a general avoidance of responsibility for the current situation and an absence of proactive moves to change it.

Even when describing a success or a pleasurable event, he will likely not express pleasure or pride, or even acknowledge his success. This is because doing so creates anxiety in him. Historically, he was punished for expressing pleasure and pride, and he still fears punishment if he expresses — or even feels — such things now.[6]

You may notice that the strength of his will varies, depending on whether he is initiating motion or stopping it. His will toward initiating action is weak, so he shows poor self-discipline and follow through. But his will to resist action is very strong, so he can endure forever.

When under pressure, he will pull in, hunker down, hide his feelings and desires, resist all movement, and just endure the situation. His general demeanor will be that of someone who is trapped and feels lonely, humiliated, and resentful. However, the resentment will not be overt and blatant, such as we will see later on in the rigid survival pattern. His silent resentment is just the tip of an iceberg of deeply buried rage at how he was treated. It is the visible sign of a secret, spiteful hatred and desire for revenge.

In *Character Styles*, Stephen M. Johnson has described the secret stance of the enduring pattern very eloquently:

> *You will never conquer me. I am indomitable. I have fooled you. You think you have suppressed me, but just you wait. You think you have beaten me, but just you wait. I will get even. And you won't even see it coming. Vengeance will be mine if it takes forever. You will pay for this. My spirit will be avenged. I can wait as long as it takes. You have taught me forbearance; some day you will regret it. I will never give in, I will never trust you or love you again. I will defeat you if it kills me.*[7]

However, you must look very closely to see all of this, because all that shows on the surface is a passive resistance, masked by the appearance of cooperation.

How They Recreate Their Early Wounding

As with all the survival patterns, enduring-patterned people tend to recreate their own early wounding by the very things they do to try to keep themselves safe. This process is unconscious, of course, but by maintaining the kinds of relationships and experiences they had in childhood, it is very effective in perpetuating the overall pattern.

This is part of how the survival patterns become self-perpetuating. They partially solve the old problem, but also recreate it, which continues the cycle. If they simply solved the old problem, it would be gone and the need for a survival strategy would disappear. Then the person would be healed and return to simply being present. That can happen, and when it does, it's a wonderful thing. However, the survival patterns grow out of survival strategies that did not manage such a complete healing, but rather recreated the wounding situation along with their defense against it.

For instance, enduring-patterned people want to have a space around themselves, like a moat around a castle. They want a big space, free of all intrusion. But they do not occupy or claim that space themselves, since claiming anything is exactly what drew attention and punishment during childhood. Instead, they pull their attention in and shrink their energy field as much as possible to avoid drawing attention to themselves. The problem, of course, is that leaving the space around them unfilled and unclaimed leads other people to think that no one lives there. So others tend to move in on them, without even realizing it. Others think, "Oh, you're not using that space, so it is free for me to use." In this way, their attempt to avoid invasion actually draws invasion to them.

Another way they recreate their childhood wounding is by passively provoking, even baiting, the other person into an expression of anger. The other's anger then recreates in them the feeling of being attacked and punished as a child.

But most of the time, their current feeling of oppression comes not from the outside, but from the inside — from their own will oppressing them. Remember that, in their final attempt to protect themselves, they became their own oppressor. They turned their own will against their own self and began negating themselves, defeating themselves before someone else could. While this maneuver did offer some protection during their original wounding, now it only perpetuates the feeling of being oppressed.

Patterned Thoughts

Each survival pattern shapes and limits the attention of those who do that pattern in certain specific ways. With the leaving pattern, we saw how attention tends to move away from the physical situation to the mental plane and even to other dimensions. With the merging pattern, we saw how attention tends to leave the self and fixate on everyone else and what they want. Here, with the enduring pattern, attention tends to go inside and down, and then gets stuck there. So the attention of enduring-patterned people is not on other people (except for how they might be intrusive), not on accomplishing some task in the world, and not even on the self and personal desires. Instead, it is hunkered down inside, just trying to endure it all and wishing that everyone would just go away.

The mind chatter of those caught in the enduring pattern is *"I don't deserve to take up space"* and *"Leave me alone."* This is a natural result of the fact that their early attempts to expand attracted punishment, rather than affirmation, and that only shrinking and hiding brought any sense of safety. It is part of the general sense of *"I don't deserve"* that pervades this survival pattern.

You may recall that each of the survival patterns has a characteristic sequence of thoughts that arise when someone in that pattern sees that someone else has something they want. For the leaving pattern, the sequence goes something like *"You have it. I want it. I'll just imagine I have it."* For the merging pattern, it goes more like *"You have it. I want it. I'll get you to give it to me."* Here, for the enduring pattern, the attempt to get something collapses into *"You have it. I want it. I can't get it."* or *"You have it. I want it. I've failed."* Or, if the person also runs some aggressive energy (perhaps because of his gender or another survival pattern), the sequence may become *"You have it. I want it. F*** you. (I didn't want it anyway.)"*

For each pattern, the third thought in the series is the patterned solution to the problem of "How can I get that? How can I satisfy my desire?" Notice that, for the enduring pattern, by the third thought the idea of taking action to get what I want has vanished. In its place, there is only fruitless resignation, shame, or anger. This is a snapshot of the self-sabotaging undertow that people in this pattern encounter every time they try to move toward something they want.

Patterned Behaviors

Carrying the burden

Enduring-patterned people often feel that they are carrying an enormous burden, which in many cases is true. They frequently wind up doing the energetic grounding for every group of people they are part of, since they are the only ones who perceive the need for grounding and have the capacity to do it. They are typically better at grounding energy than anyone else — it is one of the gifts of this pattern. This often means that they are working hard all the time, doing something that supports the group, but which goes unnoticed and unappreciated by others. Because of this, they believe "I have to hold up the world. I have to hold it all." While there is some truth in this, it also supports their resentment and secret sense of moral superiority.

Moving slowly

The inner pace of someone who adopted this pattern is typically slower than it is for most other people. This means that they need more time to feel their way through something than the average person does. Being rushed was part of their original wounding, so being rushed now scares them and sends them even deeper into resistance. This is why they need time and space to figure out what they are feeling and what they want.

When anyone gets scared and goes into the fight or flight response, that person's heart closes and they can't feel it anymore. This is a natural and adaptive response to the danger; it helps the person focus on physical survival without getting distracted by a rush of feelings. Once the danger has passed, the person's body needs time to calm down so that their heart can open again. When an enduring-patterned person wants some time and space by themselves, part of what they are doing is trying to come back to safety so that they can feel their feelings again.

Resisting all movement

Another patterned behavior is to automatically and stubbornly resist any outside attempt to get them to move. Enduring-patterned people are famous for this. Their basic stance is *"You can't make me. Leave me alone."* And they're right. You cannot make them. As we said earlier, they have the strength of the Rock, the power of the immovable object.

They may try to please others and comply with their requests, but their compliance tends to be self-effacing, subservient, and appeasing.[8] And, because they need to rebel some just to reassure themselves that they are acting from their own will, their compliance usually has some rebellion hidden in it.

Self-sabotage

However, enduring-patterned people *also* automatically resist impulses from the inside — their own impulses to move and act. So, "you can't make me" turns into "even I can't make me." As soon as they form an intention and begin to marshal their will to act on it, it starts to look like someone else's intention forcing them to do something against their will, and they feel compelled to resist it. This is the mechanism behind their automatic self-sabotage. It causes them to resist all attempts to move them, even their own attempts.

This confusion is created by their deeply-conditioned habit of self-negation, their habit of turning their will inward to suppress their own impulses, instead of outward to act on impulses. Because reactive resistance is the only impulse that they know to be their own, proactive impulses rapidly begin to seem foreign. An idea that begins inside as "my idea" can easily morph into "your idea." When this happens, their automatic resistance mechanism kicks in and compels them to oppose it. A client put it this way: *"Mom broke my will and implanted her own. Any exercise of will serves her, not me."*

This is essentially a "me/not me" problem (see *Differentiating me from not me*, page 108, for a description of this energy skill). Because they are unable to recognize their proactive will as their own, their survival mechanism tries to fight it off. This is an auto-immune disorder of the psyche, in which *the mechanism that should attack what is invading the self, instead attacks the self.*

Since personal impulses take on the appearance of oppression by some outsider, enduring-patterned people have a hard time with questions like "What do I want?" and "What action do I need to take to get it?" As soon as the possibility of taking action comes into their awareness, it starts to look like some new demand from outside them and their attention gets distracted away into a false choice between resisting this new demand or submitting to it. While they are tangled up in that confusion, no action can happen. This is what creates their frequent procrastination.

Tolerating and enduring

Action is also undermined by their assumption that bad situations must be tolerated rather than changed. Because they lost so many battles during childhood, enduring-patterned people have become experts at tolerating difficult situations, but not at changing them. So there's very little impulse inside of them to create a change, even when that's what they want. Typically, they believe that they have no right to ask for something different, and they are often not even sure what they would want.[9] But they are sure that any attempt to create a change will lead to failure, exposure, and humiliation, so why risk it? It seems better to just endure the current situation.

Living in fantasy

However, their buried needs still exist and still exert pressure within them to get those needs met. That pressure is real and constant, even when it is buried in the unconscious. So if asking and acting to get their needs met are out of the question, what is left? Only a few options are left. One option is taking action only inside their head, in fantasy, where no one else can know about it or punish them for it. So enduring-patterned people have a tendency to do things internally, in fantasy, as a substitute for doing them in the outside world. They may even mistake their actions in the fantasy world for taking action in real life. This strategy provides safety, but nothing has changed on the outside.

Passive complaining

Complaining is the second way that they try to get their needs met without asking or taking direct action. Complaining is a way they can draw attention to what they want changed, but without actually referring to themselves or their needs. For instance, suppose an enduring-patterned person says to you, *"I'm angry that you're late. I want you to be on time. When you're late, I'm afraid that you don't care about me."* With these words, he has revealed a lot about himself, including his wants and feelings. If you're inclined to use that information to mock or shame him, you now have plenty of ammunition. And if he fears that you might use that information against him, why would he reveal it? Instead, he can protect himself by keeping things indirect and impersonal, by only saying something vague like *"Oh, you're always late."* Such a statement draws attention to the problem, but reveals nothing about him.

To be sure, complaining is used by many people for many purposes. The important thing here is that enduring-patterned people use complaining as a way to get their needs met while revealing as little as possible about themselves. Since direct action must be avoided, complaining is one of the few options left.

Passive aggression

A third way that enduring-patterned people try to get their needs met without taking direct action is by using passive aggression rather than active aggression. Passive aggression gets the job done, but doesn't leave their fingerprints on it. Since they expect retaliation for any direct action, passive aggression is a way to obscure the trail back to them and thereby minimize the likelihood of retaliation.

Patterned Experience of Time

Time feels stuck for enduring-patterned people. They live in the now, without much of a future.[10] They are in touch with the personal here and now, but have a hard time envisioning their own future. This is not surprising, since envisioning the future involves planning and taking action, two skills that they were never able to develop.

Patterned Emotional Life

Holding it all in

Emotions are "energy in motion," or energy moving within the body. When an emotion is expressed, energy moves out into the world. This energetic expansion out into the world is likely to attract the attention of others and elicit a response from them. When a person thinks the response from others will be positive, he will want to express himself to get that response. Conversely, when he thinks that the response from others will be negative, he will want to avoid expressing himself so as to avoid that response. And in the extreme case, when he thinks that the response from others will be punishing or humiliating, he will try to avoid attracting any attention at all. He will instead try to create some sense of safety by shrinking and hiding himself.

This is the situation for people who are caught in the enduring pattern. Their greatest fear is of expansion and exposure, and of the humiliation and punishment that they expect will follow. So, to protect themselves, they dampen down the flow of energy and emotions within the body and hold in their self-expression.

Feeling stuck and numb

Then, because things aren't moving, they feel stuck and numb inside. But they may not experience this as a problem. If you ask them how they are, they will usually say *"I'm fine."* They say this partly because things are always hard for them, and partly just to get you to go away.

Enduring-patterned people do not like big emotional swings and drama. They do not fall desperately in love or surrender into ecstatic flights of fancy.[11] They do not erupt in anger to get their way, and they will avoid conflict if they can. They are essentially conservative, and are distrustful of hope or change.[12]

Heaviness, burden and pressure

Underneath it all, they feel a vague, chronic dissatisfaction, or in more extreme cases, they feel downright miserable. As we said earlier, they tend to avoid pleasure and feel guilty when they do feel it. Instead of lightness or delight, they usually have an internal feeling of heaviness, burden, and pressure. The person quoted at the start of the chapter said, *"I am heavy. Life is a heavy coat over me, and it gets heavier and heavier throughout the day."*

Resentment, guilt, and shame

The default emotions for those in this survival pattern are resentment, guilt, and shame. Their resentment is a stuck, passive manifestation of the deeply buried anger they feel at all those invasions and humiliations. It is the tip of an iceberg of fury. Their guilt arises from a suspicion that they have somehow brought all of this on themselves, and their shame comes from a suspicion that since this is what they are getting, maybe it is also what they deserve. Any failure, then, can provoke a shame attack — a feeling of intense self-loathing that can spiral down into depression.

On the other hand, any success can provoke an anxiety attack, which arises out of their fear that they will now be exposed and punished. So they are caught in a dilemma, in which both success and failure bring up difficult feelings. Their solution is to neither succeed nor fail, but to remain suspended in between. To do this, they have to find ways to not act, not take a position, and not express themselves. And the only way to do all that, of course, is to suppress all movement of energy and emotions within their body.

Buried emotions

If we think of enduring-patterned people in terms of energetic charge, we see that energy goes in, but it doesn't come out. Where does it go? It goes down into the lower body and then into the ground, creating a situation in which it's almost as if their center of gravity is below their feet.

This can make them very grounded and stable, almost impossible to move or push over. But it also means that they have an enormous reservoir of deeply buried emotions down there. And the biggest emotion in that reservoir is anger, anger at all the defeats, punishments, and humiliations that they've suffered. As we will see later in the section on their approach to conflict, it is rare for their anger to reach the surface, but when it does, it can be huge.

Interacting with Others

The enduring pattern is all about *not* attracting attention, and enduring-patterned people can be masterful at this, so you may not even notice that they are present. A friend who does this survival pattern tells a story from her childhood about a time after dinner when the discussion around the table turned to something that her parents wanted to talk about privately. They told her and her sister to go up to bed, but although her sister left, she did not. Instead, she sat there motionless for an hour, silently listening to the conversation, until one of her parents finally noticed her and said, *"Are you still here? We told you to go to bed."* This is a great example of both passive defiance and the ability to hide in plain sight.

Avoiding self-expression

Remember that the attention of enduring-patterned people goes inward to keep themselves hidden, not outward to interact with others. This accounts for the minimal responsiveness that those in this survival pattern are famous for. They tend to feel without expressing themselves, since self-expression is exactly what brought attack when they were young.

Because they were not allowed their privacy when they were children, as adults they may think that everyone can hear their silent thoughts and know what is going on inside them. So, they may be *internally* holding a conversation with you, unaware that they are not speaking out loud and that you cannot hear them.

Avoiding risk

In general, enduring-patterned people want to avoid risk and play it safe. This is another part of their defense strategy of hiding. Often, even making a decision feels like too much of a risk, since it might lead to exposure and humiliation. So playing it safe means kicking all decisions down the road or referring them to someone else — anything to avoid personally taking initiative and acting.

If you've ever dealt with a bureaucracy in which no one would make a decision or take any action, where every solution you proposed was "not our policy," you were likely dealing not just with individuals, but with an entire institution based on the enduring pattern. In such a bureaucracy, everyone knows that the only way to stay safe is to keep your head down and let someone else handle whatever needs attention. There is typically a boss who uses threats and fear to control the employees, and everyone has seen that drawing the boss's attention can lead to getting fired. So the only employees left are the ones who know how to lay low and stay out of sight. People who run the enduring pattern are more able than others to survive in such jobs, and over time, the workers and the institution reinforce each other's risk-aversion and create the state of affairs that we mean when we speak derisively of "bureaucracy."

Silence is not agreement

Playing it safe also means that enduring-patterned people will tend to be passive, rather than active, in all interactions. They will let others take the initiative and then quietly go along. If they don't like something, they will quietly resent it, but not object out loud.

Other people frequently mistake their silence for agreement. It is not; it is just a way for them to stay off your radar. Getting to agreement is a much longer process, as we will see in the section on communication. If you want to know how much they like the path you have chosen, notice how easily things proceed. Since their method of protest is passive, not active, their objections will more likely show up as obstacles than as overt disagreement.

Their need for space

Their style of contact is to avoid contact. They prefer being alone, since that is the only time they can fully relax, the only time that no one is messing with them. Their minimal responsiveness to contact from others is designed to get you to leave them alone and stop bugging them. It's an unspoken request for more space. The subtext is often *"I'm fine. Go away."*

In psychology, the term "optimal distance" is used to refer to how emotionally close or distant from others a particular person likes to be. It is the distance at which their need to be "a part of" is in balance with their need to be "apart from," the place where their need for belonging is in balance with their need for autonomy. For enduring-patterned people, belonging was too much like being captured, and they never got enough autonomy, so their optimal distance tends to be large. One young woman laid it out this way, *"There's your space and there's my space and there's a moat between them. Don't ever cross the moat."*

This large optimal distance also provides a way of differentiating self from other. Enduring-patterned people were not able to complete the childhood tasks of differentiating self from other, and of establishing a strong energetic boundary around themselves, so being physically close to you can bring up confusion for them about which feelings are theirs and which are yours. Moving away — out of your physical space and energy field — can help them get a clearer sense of their own feelings.

For all these reasons, people who adopted the enduring pattern usually like having plenty of space around them. Space creates safety. It means they are safe from invasion, punishment, and control. Space means it might be okay to come out of hiding and feel themselves a little bit. *Space is the most valuable thing you can give to someone who runs this survival pattern.*

It is very hard for those of us who do other survival patterns to understand how important space is to someone who does the enduring pattern. We're likely to take his movement away as a personal rejection. We're likely to feel fear, hurt, or anger, which we then direct right back at him. He will feel the wave of emotion hitting him as one more invasion, one more time that someone is trying to force him into compliance by pushing on him, so he pulls in and moves even farther away. This simple misunderstanding can easily turn into a self-reinforcing cycle. It can push a couple into divorce or therapy. This cycle also illustrates how those who run the enduring pattern draw to themselves the very same behavior that they're trying to escape.

Romance

Love relationships bring up another fear for enduring-patterned people: the fear that the love offered to them will come at a high price. They fear that it will cost them their autonomy, and that being loved means being invaded, controlled, and disempowered. One way they handle this fear is to simply refuse love, taking the stance that one of my clients described as *"I am on strike. I'm not letting any love in. You have to love me and make me receive it and I refuse to receive it."* The other way they handle their fear that love will disempower them is to accept the love, but disempower themselves by being passive and submissive in the relationship. Again, this recreates their situation in childhood and validates their fear.

At the same time, enduring-patterned people usually make loyal mates and partners. Typically, however, they won't take action to either begin the relationship or end it, but rather will go along with what their partner initiates. Since they can endure a great deal of hardship, they may become the suffering wife or husband who stays in the relationship far too long.

Sexuality

They may experience sex more as work than pleasure, as one more way that they're expected to serve someone else's agenda, and they may feel inadequate in this realm, also. As mentioned above, they may prefer to be sexually submissive, rather than assertive.

Their Approach to Conflict

Enduring-patterned people will almost always try to avoid conflict. Remember that their past history with conflict was a long series of defeats and humiliations. They're the ones who always lost the fight, so they will avoid getting into another fight, if they can.

When an adversarial situation arises, they will hunker down and wait out the storm. People in this pattern will not challenge you or escalate the conflict, but they will get stubborn. As always, their position will be "You can't make me."

Weapons used in a conflict

Each of the survival patterns has its own set of weapons that it turns to during a conflict. What characterizes the set of weapons favored by enduring-patterned people is that they are all passive or passive-aggressive in nature.

Their first weapon will typically be to just not respond. This will be accompanied by the weapons of delay, such as waiting, resisting, hiding, hunkering down, and enduring. These weapons can be used to sabotage the other person's goal, but more often they're just a place to hide from the storm. All of these weapons are purely passive in nature.

If sabotage is their intention, they're likely to add in some of the "accidental" weapons, such as forgetting, making mistakes, and having accidents that can't be blamed on them. These weapons are more passive-aggressive in nature. Now, the person in the enduring pattern is behaving like the French resistance fighter that we spoke of before. He wants to sabotage the Germans, but he must not leave his fingerprints on any actions he takes, for fear of retaliation. So he makes his resistance look like an unfortunate accident: "The bridge? The bridge didn't blow up, it just collapsed while your tank was driving over it. Obviously, the tank was just too heavy for the bridge. It's unfortunate, but it's no one's fault. Sorry about your tank."

Another favorite passive-aggressive weapon is that of baiting you until you get angry. There will not be one big, obvious provocation — that would be too easy to spot. Instead, there will be a drip, drip, drip of small annoyances and provocations. These serve to punish you and get revenge on you, even if you never react to them. And if you do get angry, not only will the enduring-patterned person then feel morally superior and justified in his actions, but he'll have an excuse to get away from you.

Blowing up

All of the above is true for as long as the enduring-patterned person can endure whatever is being done to him. And since his capacity to endure is enormous, that is nearly forever. But it is possible for him to hit a limit inside, and then everything changes. When that invisible line is crossed, he no longer cares — he is done with the relationship, permanently. Now he can switch into active-aggression and become openly furious. Now his deeply buried ocean of anger surges up to the surface and he can react to all those defeats and humiliations.

His anger is not measured and strategic, as it might be for someone else. He has no strategy. It is just an explosion of pure, out of control fury. And since he has so little experience with expressing anger, he doesn't know how to modulate it. It surprises and scares him. Sometimes, he does something really awful while he's out of control. More often, he is so terrified that he rapidly flips back into shutdown mode, horrified at his own fury.

If you see an enduring-patterned person explode this way, remember that he is in a very young, overwhelmed, out of control place, just like a child having a tantrum, and he deserves the same kindness and compassion that an overwhelmed child would deserve. He does not deserve being blasted back into submission, even though your own patterns may want to do that. Despite his lack of skill, he is finally defending his space and his life.

Communication Style

Enduring-patterned people are typically quiet, even silent. They don't like talking, especially when they are in pattern. Their view of the world is pragmatic, and they like facts better than ideas, particularly big, abstract ideas.[13]

When in pattern, their speech tends to have a heavy, slow, serious tone, and they may sound like they are depressed or suffering. You may even find yourself feeling responsible for their suffering, as if you are somehow controlling what they experience. They will speak of "us" or "you" more than "I."

A partial thought and a pause

Since, in childhood, it was not safe for them to put their feelings into words and express them, most enduring-patterned people have never quite mastered that skill.[14] They will often bring out a partial sentence with a partially formed thought, then pause and go back inside to find the rest of it. The pause can be quite long. It is genuine and needed by them to find the rest of their thought, but it is also an unconscious test to see whether you really want to hear what they have to say. If you can't wait through the pause, you will jump in with a suggestion or finish their sentence for them. This interrupts their creative process once again, and reinforces their belief that you don't really want to hear from them. Then they will pull in farther and be unable to find the rest of their idea. Once again, they feel controlled and thwarted by the other. And once again, they have used a passive action to avoid exposure and to protect themselves. Plus, they can blame it all on you.[15] This is another example of how they elicit from others the very behavior that they fear. If you really want to hear from them, you have to remain silent and patiently wait with them until they come out with the rest of their thought.

The goals of their communication

In addition to having its own communication *style*, each survival pattern also has its own communication *goals*. People with different survival patterns may perform the same behaviors, but have completely different goals in mind. Let's take complaining as an example. For people in most of the survival patterns, complaining is a way of saying, *"I don't like this; I want this changed."* So, if you offer to change it for them, they will accept your offer, you'll change it, and they will stop complaining.

However, for enduring-patterned people, complaining may actually be more of a way to connect and share a feeling than to get something changed. This is especially true if their parents also did the enduring pattern, in which case, complaining may have been a family norm.[16]

So if an enduring-patterned person is complaining to you, don't take it personally, and don't assume that he wants the same response that you would want. Stop and ask yourself how complaining works for him and what sort of response he might want. Maybe even ask him what sort of response he would like. You'll be handing power and control back to him, which will make him feel safer. On the other hand, he may also be asking for help, so we'll have more to say about this below in the section on how people with this pattern ask for help.

Enduring-patterned people also use their communication to seek permission for their own self-expression and autonomy. However, since it would be too risky to ask for that permission directly, their request is passive and implied. It's up to you to perceive the implied request and invite their self-expression — without demanding or requiring it, of course. You might simply say, *"I'd like to hear whatever you have to say, too."*

A third goal of communication for those who run this pattern is simply to get more space for themselves, that is, to get you to go away and leave them alone. When they pronounce their usual *"I'm fine; go away,"* it can be very tricky for you to figure out whether that is simply their automatic first response, or they really want you to go away. They may well not know themselves. Below are some tips on how to approach them.

Communicating with Them

When communicating with enduring-patterned people, the main thing you must remember is that you are working to overcome their distrust, their belief that others will always invade and abuse them. Showing them that you can respect their space and timing will build their trust in you. They operate on a point system, based on your behavior. When you respect their space and their timing, you get points. When you invade their space or rush them, you lose points.

You cannot *make* them trust you. You cannot make them come out of hiding. You cannot make them do anything. But if you demonstrate over and over that you can respect their space and their timing, they will take notice and gradually open up to you more. If they are stuck in their distrust, it may help to gently remind them that perhaps they were born into a body here because they actually wanted to be here and participate in life. When discussing this inner conflict between wanting to stay hidden and wanting to come out and participate in life, a friend who does this survival pattern put it this way:

> We never want to come out of our deliberation chamber. I call my hiding place my deliberation chamber. It's the place where I'm way deep down there somewhere, where no one else can ever find me or get me. And when things get really bad, that's where I go, and I'm totally alone and no one can mess with me and the whole world is gone.
>
> And so, when somebody brings me something that says 'Hey, you made an agreement to actually live in the world and be fully engaged and fill your space and be in a relationship and be present and all these things,' it's like, there's a part of me that just hates that. Why don't you just leave me the fuck alone? I'm finally in my deliberation chamber and why don't you let me stay here? I'm happy here. Go away.
>
> So we don't like it when somebody brings that information to our edge and says 'Hey, you should come out. You actually made an agreement to not live down there in that place, but to be out here.' We hate it at first. But then we need space to work through . . . to find our own way out. You'll never be able to pull us out, but if you remind us that we made an agreement to come out, then we'll find our way out.

Respecting their space

So what do you do? How exactly do you respect their space and their timing? First, let's deal with their space. Imagine that they have a bubble around them that extends three or four feet out from their body in all directions, about as far as they can reach. (All people have this bubble, no matter what survival patterns they do.) This is their personal space. Ideally, people fill their bubble with their own energy so that it provides a buffer between them and the world, and they will object if you enter their space without their permission. In this way, they claim their personal space.

However, as children, enduring-patterned people were not allowed to claim their personal space. Over and over, they were invaded and their efforts to repel the invasion were defeated. So they gave up trying to defend the space around them. They pulled in their energy field to the edge of the body or even deeper. This was the only way they could make some safety for themselves. As a result they are both very sensitive to the energetic invasion of their space and unable to oppose it. If you want them to trust you, it is up to you to recognize their space and not enter it, even though they are not claiming it or filling it.

So your first job is: DO NOT invade their space. How? Again, imagine that they have a bubble around their body extending three or four feet in all directions. Hold the image of that bubble in your mind. Notice especially the edge of the bubble: this is the edge of their space. When you approach them, do not come any closer than this edge. In fact, since your own bubble extends out about the same distance, stay twice that far away. If you have any skill with your energy field, pull it in so that it does not enter their space. If you don't know how to do this, just imagine pulling it in. Intending to pull it in will do a lot, even if you can't perceive it.

When you speak to them, send your words only to the edge of their bubble, not straight into the core of their body. You can do this either by intending that your words stop before reaching their bubble, or you can turn slightly and send your words into the space beside their bubble, rather than directly into it. It may be better to not look at them while you speak to them, since your energy will go where your attention goes, and your attention will typically go wherever you look.

By doing this you are honoring their space. This may be a new and weird experience for them, but they will like it. They are used to people just running over them, people who unconsciously notice that they aren't filling their own space and think "Okay, if you're not using that space, I'll use it."

When you don't run over them, when you keep your energy out of their bubble even though they're not defending it, you're showing them that you are *not* the same as all the people who have previously invaded them. They will then feel safer around you. And it will be easier for them to hear your words, because they won't be in overwhelm as you speak. If they feel invaded by your words, they will be preoccupied with that and won't be able to focus on the meaning of your words.

Respecting their timing

The way to respect their timing is simply to give them time to go through their own internal process at their own pace, rather than requiring that they do things at your pace. Remember, being pushed and hurried was part of how enduring-patterned people were hurt as children, so they are very aware of your impatience, and it distracts them from going through their own internal process and responding to you. The more you push them, the slower they go, both because you're distracting them and because they need to resist your attempts to control them. Always keep in mind that their motto is "You can't make me."

If you need them to respond to you or to act on something, just wait at the edge of their bubble. Don't invade it; just wait there. Your presence will annoy them, and after a while they will respond just to get rid of you.

If you want them to decide something, you will have to give them enough time to work their way through to their real answer, not just their patterned first answer.

If you need them to come out of their deliberation chamber and join you in the outside world, try reminding them that there is something out here that they want, but keep it light. Don't try to persuade them, just reference it for them. If you want them to go to the gym with you and they have previously said they might like that, you can say something like, *"I'm leaving for the gym in 10 minutes, and I remember that you said you might like to go, so I'm just letting you know."* Then walk away. Just leave it at the edge of their space and walk away. If you wait for an answer, you are intruding on their internal deliberation. By walking away, you give them the space they need to find their own answer.

This "Would you like to join me?" technique is very useful when communicating with enduring-patterned people. They don't like to be left behind, so they have an incentive to join you. And they feel much safer joining your plan rather than initiating a plan of their own. So if you want them to do something, don't try to persuade them to initiate it by themselves. Instead, announce that you're going to do it, and then ask them if they would like to join you.

A word of warning, though: this must be an honest offer, not a manipulation. If they say "no," don't push it. A friend described her way of using this technique as, *"Just leave something delicious on the doorstep, something that smells great. Just go away and leave it there, and then they'll follow the scent."*

Another way you can respect their timing is to avoid surprising them. They hate being surprised. Warn them about what is coming so that they can prepare for it. If you have a question, announce that you have a question and ask if this is a good time for them to hear it. If you need an answer, let them know that you need an answer and when you'll be back to ask for it. Give them enough time for their internal deliberation. If you don't know how much time to allow, ask them. You can also observe their long-term behavior for more clues as to how much time they are likely to need.

Walking side by side when talking

When you need to present something new to an enduring-patterned person, try to set up the situation so that the two of you are walking side by side, not facing each other or sitting down. If you do it this way, it is much easier for him to take in and process what you're presenting, for two reasons. First, he is moving. Remember that his survival strategy involves stopping the flow of his energy by sending it down into the ground, where it gets stuck. If he is up on his feet and his hips are moving, his energy cannot get stuck like that. It will keep flowing, which will help him process whatever you're presenting. Second, while walking next to him, you are not in his face. You are beside him, which helps you stay out of his energy field and gives him more sense of space.

Authenticity and anger

When you speak to enduring-patterned people, be authentic. They watch for authenticity. If you're authentic, it moves them. They also watch for manipulation. Don't do it. They've had far too much of that already, and they don't like it. It will only stiffen their resistance to whatever you're presenting.

When it comes to anger, things get easier. They can tolerate your anger, as long as you aim it at the edge of their space, rather than at their core. They have more ability to just listen to anger than those in any other survival pattern. They can just hunker down and ride out the storm, whereas people in other survival patterns will tend to go into fear, collapse, retaliation, or argument.

Their Way of Asking for Help

Remember that, for enduring-patterned people, most of what came from the outside was an attempt to control them, so asking others for help now seems like it will only open the door to more control. Because of this, they find it very difficult to either ask for help or receive it.

But, of course, they still have problems and still need help to solve them. So, to protect themselves, they will generally avoid making a direct request, and instead just complain about the problem. (Keep in mind that, while complaining may be a passive request for help, it also may be only a way for them to connect with you and share a feeling.) You will probably respond to their complaint by suggesting a possible solution to their problem. They will dismiss it. You will offer another. They will dismiss that one, also. As you offer solutions, they will dismiss and devalue every single one of your suggestions. The conversation will sound something like this:

"Why don't you . . . "
"Yes, but . . . "
"Okay then, maybe you could . . . "
"Yes, but . . . "
"Huh, okay, well then, how about if you . . . "
"Yes, but . . . "

This pattern of offer-and-refusal will be repeated over and over, until you feel totally frustrated and thwarted.

What is going on here? Why would anyone ask for help and then reject every bit of help that is offered? There is a lot going on here. Let's unpack the layers so that we can understand it all.

Recall that enduring-patterned people were unable to complete the task of establishing their own autonomy by learning to do things for themselves and by themselves. This is an incredibly important developmental task, and a person's psyche will keep trying to complete it for the rest of their life, just as it does with any unfinished developmental task. So enduring-patterned people are still trying to learn to do things for themselves, just like the child who protests, *"Mom! I'd rather do it myself!"* But they are also trying to avoid *appearing* to do anything for themselves, because that's exactly what was punished in childhood. So they're stuck in a bind: they want to do things for themselves, but they cannot show that. Often, they cannot even consciously know it without arousing a lot of anxiety.

So what can they do? They can know what they *don't* want. It is safer and easier for them to know what they *don't* want, than to know what they *do* want. And they have to shoot down every suggestion you make because, in reality, they want to solve the problem and find a solution for themselves, not get one from you.

They really just want a sounding board

If you're able to not take it personally, but just play the game, you can help them find their own solution for themselves. The first step is to let them say "no" to several of your suggestions. Play a few rounds of *"Why don't you . . . ?"* "Yes, *but . . ."* with them. They are practicing differentiating themselves from you, separating from you by saying "no!" Remember the "terrible twos," the time when a child glories in saying "no!" just for the power and autonomy in it? That is exactly what this person didn't get to do. So let him practice with you now.

If you find that you have an agenda about what should happen, let it go. If you really can't let it go and just hold space for him, admit that you're too invested in your agenda and bow out of the interaction. Respecting your own limits is an honorable act, even though admitting that you have limits may not always be flattering or easy for you.

Holding space for them

On the other hand, if you can put your agenda aside and just hold an open, accepting space for the person, you may be able to help him find his own solution through the following process. First, don't take ownership of the problem. His complaining is designed to lure you into this, but don't take the bait. Instead, acknowledge it as *his problem.* You can say something like, *"Gee, that sounds really awful."* Empathize with him and his distress, but keep your emotional charge smaller than his. If your emotional charge even approaches his in size, you will start to take up his space and crowd him out of his feelings, which will shut him down. So keep your emotional charge noticeably smaller than his, even as you empathize with his distress.

Next, sincerely ask how he might solve the problem, while holding a silent, internal conviction that he *can* solve it. Say something like, *"What can you do about that?"* He will feel your confidence in him, and it will bolster his own confidence in himself. Continue to quietly hold space for him while he cycles through avoiding the problem, returning to it, sorting through possible solutions, and going around in circles.

Remember that he has never had much opportunity to practice this, so of course he isn't good at it. He's just learning it. And, as with any adult who is going back to fill in a hole in his developmental skill sets, don't let his adult body fool you. When it comes to this particular skill, he is learning it exactly the same way a child learns it: by doing it over and over again. Each of us must do this when learning the skills that we missed in childhood. He will need time and repetition to learn this new skill, so just settle in for the long haul (but remember to take good care of yourself along the way).

Expressing confidence in them

After you have witnessed him finding his own solutions a couple of times, you may be able to bump up your encouragement a notch by referencing those successes. You might say something like, *"Well, I recall that you figured out how to _____, so I'll bet that you can find a solution to this one, too."*

But be careful. Praise can make him uncomfortable. You're venturing into a very sensitive area here. You are referencing his autonomous action and success, the very thing that probably brought punishment and humiliation during childhood. Being exposed in this way may alarm him, so watch his response to see what effect your statement has on him. He may well discount it or deny it — that is just his habitual way of trying to stay small and fly under the radar. Don't argue with his denial; let him do it. But watch carefully whether your statement seems to make him grow or shrink. Does he then step up to the problem and solve it, or does he deflate and get stuck? His response tells you whether your statement helped him or hindered him in his attempt to find his own solution to this problem, today. Use this information to guide your response the next time.

And, like everyone else, he may not recognize the solution to his problem and the help he needs when it first arrives. If he's watching for it only in the form he envisioned, he may have difficulty recognizing it in any other form. So he may well complain that help has not really been offered, just because he doesn't yet recognize it.

The biggest mistake I've personally made when working with people who do this pattern has been in thinking that my praise and celebration of their successes would make them feel good, the way it does for people in the other survival patterns. I have found that I must wait and let them take the lead in congratulating themselves. If I take the lead, they tend to feel exposed and may get scared, unconsciously expecting that they will once again be attacked or humiliated. And even when they take the lead, I must not let my energy get bigger than theirs, lest I intrude on their space and make them retract. So, I encourage you to support them in celebrating their successes, but make sure it stays *their* celebration, not *your* celebration.

Always, when dealing with enduring-patterned people, remember that they are like small, scared animals hiding in a hole. That hole is their only safety. Helping them come out of their hole requires being trustworthy and patient. You can't *make* them come out, but you can learn to be worthy of their trust.

Making a Request of the Pattern

First, do what is described above: stay out of their space, speak to their edge, and be authentic. If possible, make your request while walking side by side. When they're up and walking, their energy is already moving, so they can more easily take in your request and process it. When they're planted in a chair, the flow of energy in their body may already be blocked, which means that your request will simply hit that block and die. If walking is not an option, at least turn your body a little sideways so you aren't face to face, bearing down on them.

Second, be responsible for yourself. Ask for what you need, but don't make it their problem. Remember that they already feel like they're carrying the world on their shoulders, so acknowledge that this is your problem and take responsibility for it.

Third, present your request at their pace, not yours. Their pace is likely slower than yours, so they will need time to orient themselves to what you're asking. Remember that they've been conditioned to expect punishment from those close to them, so if you're in a relationship with them, it can be very helpful to start by saying *"You're not in trouble."* This will quiet their fear and open some space within them to hear your request. Then, give them only a short summary of your request, maybe something like *"I want to ask you to help me with something"* or *"I want to ask you to do something for me."* This will help them orient themselves to your request. Pause and watch for signs that they have taken this in and are ready for the next piece. If you're unsure, ask them to let you know when they're ready.

When they're ready to hear your actual request, place it at the edge of their bubble. Do not put it inside their bubble or aim it at their core. Tell them calmly and clearly what it is that you're asking of them. If your request is large, present only one, small, do-able part of it. Then wait while they orient to that, evaluate it, and decide whether they can do it. If they fear they can't do it (can't win), they won't want to engage it, so help them feel that they will be able to succeed, one step at a time. It may be hard for you to slow down and do all this at their pace, but remember, if you rush them, you are recreating their childhood wound, and they will automatically have to resist your request.

After you've finished making your request, let them know when you'll be back for their answer, thank them for listening, say good-bye, and then just walk away. Don't look back. Take your attention off of them. Don't track their compliance; let them give you their answer at the appointed time. If you track them, it feels to them like you're hunting them, and they are your prey. In their past, being tracked preceded being attacked, so it alarms them.

Their Response to a Request

When they do give you an answer, notice what kind of answer it is. If they are accommodating you and abandoning themselves, it's not the real answer. Instead, it's the automatic answer that comes from their survival pattern. Recognize it as the pattern, not their real answer. Their real answer to your request will likely progress through several stages, and it is important that you recognize those stages so that you'll know what meaning you should assign to each of their answers.

Their first answer will be an automatic "no." This answer is intended simply to buy time so that they can consider your request. That is its function. It is not really the answer to your request, so acknowledge it, but don't take it personally and don't assume it's their final answer.

If they later say "yes," be aware that the function of this first "yes" is probably just to stop resisting. It's not yet an agreement to your request, but more like an agreement to open up to actually considering your request. Real agreement won't come until their second "yes," and even then, the process may not be complete. If they haven't yet had time to go off by themselves and consider how they feel about your request and whether they want to comply, they probably haven't yet arrived at a real answer.

Along the way, keep in mind that, for them, complaining about your request doesn't mean "no"; it means, *"I don't know yet."* So, if they're complaining, just give the process some more time. Remember that even though they probably want to join you or please you, they still need time to find their own answer.

Complimenting the Pattern

When you want to compliment an enduring-patterned person, first, pay attention to his personal space. If you've accidentally wandered into it, pull back into your own space. If you're intruding on his space, he won't be able to receive your compliment, so before you say anything, attend to his space and make sure you're not in it.

Then softly leave your compliment at the edge of his space. Tell him what you admire and why. Maybe cite an example or two. But keep your level of enthusiasm at or below his. If your energetic charge is much larger than his, your appreciation can easily feel to him like an intrusion. It can morph inside him into a requirement that he perform at least that well from now on, which will turn your compliment into a burden rather than a support. So keep your level of excitement low and out of his space.

As with all things relating to the survival patterns, this is not a one-size-fits-all prescription. In addition to considering what patterns the person does and what those patterns value, you'll also need to consider his personal values. But, if you watch his responses closely, you'll probably be able to tell when your compliment really went in and when it didn't.

Getting Yourself Out of the Enduring Pattern

Whenever you realize that you've gone into pattern, your first job is to get yourself out of pattern and back to being present. The survival pattern is distorting your perceptions and your experience. In fact, your patterned response to this distress is most likely making things worse, not better. Once you're back in presence, you'll be able to find the best way to respond to this current situation.

Signs you're in the enduring pattern

- you're hunkered down and just enduring the situation

- you feel heavy and stuck

- your attitude is "You can't make me"

- you resist every suggestion and action, even ones that originally came from you

- you are sabotaging your own goals

The solution: You need to get your energy moving again and reclaim your space.

To get out of the enduring pattern

Move your body, especially your hips. The movement of your body will get your energy moving. Shift your attention from hunkering down and resisting to letting your life energy flow outward.

Exercises:

Stand up and move your hips: walk, run, dance, or just jump up and down.

- notice the energy starting to flow through your body

- let your feelings and emotions flow, too

Do some Doubt Shouts (explained in the next section).
Let your energy flow out of you in all directions until it completely fills your space.

Once you have filled your space with your own energy, claim your space:

Say to yourself, *"This is mine. This is my space. I claim it as my own."*

For more information on how to get yourself out of pattern, please see Chapter 13, *Getting Yourself Out of Pattern*, on page 358.
Remember, whenever you're in pattern, your first job is getting yourself out of pattern and back to presence.

Healing the Enduring Pattern

Enduring-patterned people need to develop autonomy and self-confidence so that they can complete the tasks of separation and individuation. To do that, they need to turn their personal will around: from pulling in and down in self-negation, to pushing up and out in self-expression and action. This will allow them to bring their energy back up out of the ground and use it to take action in the world. They also need to learn to claim their own space and defend it from intrusion. Along the way, they will need to heal the traumas of childhood that conditioned them into this survival pattern, as well as grieve the losses they have suffered.

Learning to move

First and foremost, enduring-patterned people need to just get their energy moving. One thing that I recommend is doing about 30 minutes of vigorous exercise each day, especially exercise that moves their hips, such as walking, running, cycling, or dancing. Most enduring-patterned people find that doing this in the morning makes the rest of their day flow much more easily. Since their muscular armoring is held mostly in their hips, getting their hips moving is the key to getting their energy moving.

Filling their space with their own energy

Once their energy is moving, they need to fill their body and personal space with it. One practice that accomplishes this is called the Doubt Shout[17]. It is something anyone can do to ward off doubt and give themselves a more embodied sense of strength and power.

To do a Doubt Shout, stand erect with your feet about shoulder-width apart and your knees unlocked or just slightly bent. Starting with your arms hanging loosely at your sides, inhale deeply as you swing your arms out to the sides and upwards in a big circle, with your palms up. Intend and imagine that you are gathering energy from the space around you in each hand. As your palms meet — above and in front of your head — grab that energy between your palms. Holding your full in-breath, pull that energy straight down inside your core and in front of you to the level of your navel. Finally, explode your hands forcefully apart, palms down and out to each side, sending that big energy out into your space in all directions with a loud shout. I was first taught to shout *"Kee-aii!"* — but any forceful sound that works for you will do. When you send the energy outward, intend that it fill your personal bubble and remain around you, rather than dissipating.

Try doing a Doubt Shout and notice the change in your felt sense of yourself. Do several in a row, if that feels okay. You are working directly with the charge in your body — taking in a charge, holding it, then explosively discharging it. Feel the increased sensations of aliveness and strength in your body after doing one or more Doubt Shouts. By doing this practice, you can create these sensations of aliveness and strength in yourself any time you want them.

As the name implies, this exercise is designed to shift you out of the paralysis of self-doubt. It is an excellent daily practice for anyone who has a lot of self-doubt or has difficulty holding and intentionally using an energy charge, typically including those who do the leaving, merging, or enduring survival patterns.

Defending their space and boundaries

Those who are caught in the enduring survival pattern also need to learn about healthy boundaries. There are several good books available on psychological boundaries, and reading one or more of them is a good place to start. (For a more detailed discussion of boundaries, please see the section called *Developing strong boundaries* on page 107.)

However, enduring-patterned people also need to physically practice defending their own space in a safe and supportive setting. In order to really learn any new skill, we need to practice doing it with our bodies. Until you have embodied the new knowledge, you haven't really learned it. It's just an idea in your head, and the moment you go into overwhelm, what your body knows will take over. To have access to the skill when things get intense, you must practice it in your body enough to embody it.

One exercise that helps people practice defending their own space is the Pushing Out exercise. The exercise makes use of a group of people to give the person doing it a physical experience of pushing out invaders. The enduring-patterned person stands alone in the center of the room and feels the open space around him. Then, one at a time, each of the other participants walks up to him and stands too close, even right up against him. He then physically pushes the intruder back out of his space, or even all the way across the room. To help him get into it, I encourage him to verbalize his feelings and intention by using sounds and words. Depending on what suits him, these can range from gently firm words like "no" and "back" to strong exclamations like *"No! Back! Out!"* — or even growling. Typically, an enduring-patterned person has historically just endured these invasions and never actively said "No" before, so being supported and encouraged to do so opens up a whole new world for him.

When setting up this exercise, it is important to clearly state that there will be no physical violence and no one is to be hurt. This is not about who is physically stronger. It is about giving the person in the center the experience of responding to intrusion by actively using his own will and strength to push out the intruders and defend his space. It is a chance for him to practice safe, controlled, active-aggression as opposed to silent, resentful enduring and passive-aggression.

The Doubt Shout and the Pushing Out exercise help people practice moving their energy and their bodies into action. The defense strategy of the enduring pattern is to hold everything in, that is, to prevent their energy from moving out into the world by sending it downward into the ground. Both of these exercises help the person practice sending energy horizontally out of the body, either to fill their own space or to push others out of it. These exercises are useful for anyone who needs to develop these skills, whether they do the enduring pattern or not.

Moving toward a goal

Enduring-patterned people also need to learn to move pro-actively, rather than only reactively. They must learn to direct their energy toward accomplishing their own agenda, instead of just resisting the agendas of others. The basic practice is simple: first, they reference their own core, then notice what they want, and then outwardly express their desire by physically moving toward what they want. Although simple, this practice is likely to bring up many old hurts and fears because these actions are exactly what brought on attacks and humiliation during childhood. Even now, any overt self-expression or self-action may bring up a wave of emotion that must be felt, acknowledged, and allowed to pass through. Doing this practice repeatedly in a safe, supportive environment will enable them to gradually relax their compulsive holding in and become accustomed to putting out energy by expressing themselves and taking action to get what they want.

Anger work

The practice of saying "no" to others has a big brother called anger work. In anger work, anger that has been buried and held in is gradually expressed and moved out of the body. This kind of work is especially important for people who do the enduring pattern because they are sitting on a mountain of buried anger from all those past attacks and humiliations. Up to now, that anger has only leaked out sideways as passive aggression and sabotage. Now, that indirect expression must be replaced by direct expression. Complaining must give way to direct anger, held within a safe, conscious container.

Many enduring-patterned people have never seen anger expressed in a clean, healthy, responsible way. The only anger they've seen was abusive, so they're afraid that if they let out their anger, it will consume them, and they will become angry, abusive people, just like the ones who hurt them. This fear is natural. After all, what other model of anger do they have?

So it is important that they do their anger work with the guidance of someone who knows the territory and understands the value of clean, healthy anger. This person must be able to help them modulate the amount of charge that is coming to the surface, increasing or decreasing the flow as needed, so that they can gradually vent their internal pressure in a way that strengthens and empowers them, rather than frightens them. As their internal pressure goes down, their fear of their own anger will also go down. With practice, they will learn how to feel, manage, and express their anger in safe and productive ways. Gradually, all the energy that was bound up in their anger and in containing it will become available for them to employ in getting what they want in life. In the end, they will feel lighter, freer, and happier.

Energy skills

If we look at what's needed in terms of the basic energy skills, we see that grounding is already present, although not in an open, flowing way. Enduring-patterned people tend to clutch the ground rather than relate to it. The only energy flow is downward, into the ground. To create a healthy groundedness, they need to learn to relax their death grip on the ground and allow energy to also flow upward into them. This will give them an experience of the ground as supportive and nourishing, not just a place to hide. It will also help them feel their own strength and confidence, since now energy is coming up into them and filling them.

Typically, those who run this survival pattern are already able to feel their own core. However, they still need to learn how to hold an energetic boundary around their own space, and they need to learn how to differentiate their own energy from that of others, the skill known as me/not me. (For more detailed descriptions of each of the four energy skills, please see *Healing the Leaving Pattern* on page 103.)

Defending against the inner critic

Like most people, enduring-patterned people also need to change their relationship with their inner critic. They need to recognize the voice of their inner critic and realize that it is not their own voice. Then, they need to learn how to defend themselves against its attacks. Since their inner critic is very shaming, and since shame is a disempowering emotion, this is an especially tricky stage for them. It's likely that a great deal of healing will need to occur during this stage of their inner work.

Once they are able to defend themselves against their critic's shame attacks, they will be able to regard their inner experience less as proof of their inherent deficiency and more as useful information about themselves. This will make it much easier for them to accept their own present-moment feelings and even begin to express them.

Differentiating from others

By identifying and expressing their own feelings and contrasting them with the feelings of others, they will gradually complete the task of differentiating themselves from others. But, before they can allow this, they will need to know that it is genuinely safe to be different, and that they will not be attacked or humiliated for it.

They will also need the time to find their way through things at their own pace. They need to be witnessed as they feel their way to their own truth, but they need time to do it in their own way. Remember that being rushed was part of their original wounding.

Their human need and spiritual need

Those who are caught in the enduring pattern have succeeded in individuating to the extent that they experience their core essence as separate from that of others; however, they have not experienced their essence as being protected from others. They are not used to others respecting their essence, and they are not used to defending it themselves.

They have not been able to extend their separation outward to include their own personal space, feelings, and actions. To do that, they need to come out of hiding and express themselves. They need to project their energy outward, saying to the world, *"I am here!"* This is their human need. Their spiritual need is to recognize their core essence as valid and legitimate, and to claim the divine energy within it as their own.

As enduring-patterned people gradually work their way out of the pattern, they can take pleasure in using their will to show up, rather than to hide. They can celebrate their successes at getting what they want and completing what they start. Their feelings of heaviness and misery can turn into delight. And they can enjoy claiming their personal space and being seen and known by others.

For more help in determining which patterns you go into, please visit
www.The5PersonalityPatterns.com.

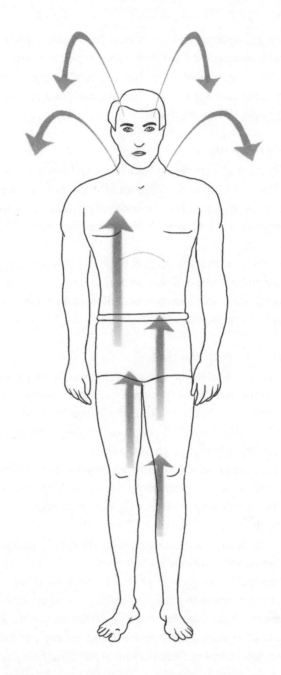

The Aggressive Pattern – body and energy flow

– 10 –

The Aggressive Pattern

"There's no safety anywhere.
It's a jungle out there."

LIKE ALL THE SURVIVAL PATTERNS, this pattern is a holding pattern in the body, conditioned into it by trauma, which creates a particular habit of attention. The aggressive pattern develops in people who were in such distress that they feared they would die, but made it through by willing themselves to survive. Instead of leaving, looking to others for help, or simply enduring, they turned inside to their own resources, to their own will and strength, and fought their way through. Those fights conditioned them to survive by ignoring their fears and weaknesses, while focusing only on their own strength and will. There wasn't real help from others when they needed it, so they learned to distrust others and rely only on themselves.

In a very real sense, they have never come out of that early life-or-death struggle and continue to perceive life as a fight for survival. They believe they are alone, without love or support, so they try to be bigger and stronger than everyone else in every situation. The only safety they know comes from having power and control. They see the world as a battlefield or jungle, and the law of the jungle is kill or be killed. Strength and cunning are virtues. Weakness is fatal. Trust is for suckers.

Many of our cultural heroes and villains exhibit this survival pattern because most of our great stories are about battles between good and evil and about the warriors who fight those battles. If they are fighting for power over the community, they are villains. If they are fighting to protect the community, they are heroes. But, almost always, both display the aggressive pattern.

In the *Harry Potter* series, both Voldemort and Mad-Eye Moody are clearly in the aggressive pattern, the first fighting for power over the community, the second fighting to protect it. (Harry, interestingly enough, is not interested in fighting or wielding power, as he demonstrates at the end of the story when he breaks the Elder Wand and opts for an ordinary life.)

In *The Lord of the Rings*, we have a similar pair of antagonists in Sauron and Aragorn. The great addition in that story is that Aragorn recognizes the pattern within himself and is unwilling to grasp power to serve himself, but only to serve life.

Range of Functioning

As with the other patterns, this survival pattern exists across a broad spectrum of functionality, from those completely ruled by the pattern to those who wear it lightly. The variation here is mostly in how much the person needs to dominate others. Lower functioning individuals need to keep all the power for themselves, while higher functioning ones are confident in their own power and are therefore able to empower those around them.

On the low end of the spectrum, we have those who are totally caught in the pattern and focused on dominating others. They typically want to rule over others, and may become anything from schoolyard bullies to dictators over a nation. Since they have no trust in others and no faith in love, they are typically loners.

In the mid-range, we have those who still live within the worldview of the pattern, but are more focused on conquering their own fears and limitations than on conquering others. They are strong in the skills and talents of the pattern. Extreme athletes are often in this category. For example, the extreme skiers in the film *Steep*, who risk their lives to ski mountains so steep that they've never even been attempted before. Some spiritual paths start from this place and focus on defeating the demons within.

On the high end of the spectrum, we have those who can generally stay present while using the skills and talents of the pattern. While they are still concerned with holding and wielding power, they are more focused on empowering others than on acquiring power over them. Mahatma Gandhi and Martin Luther King are good examples of this.

The Gifts of the Aggressive Pattern

As a person uses any of the patterns, he* continually practices the skills that that pattern requires. Over time, he becomes exceptionally proficient in those particular skills. As he heals the wounds that created the pattern and becomes able to shift his attention out of the pattern and back to presence, the abilities he has acquired stay with him and become the gifts of the pattern. Now he is able to employ his exceptional abilities as he responds to the needs of the present moment. Even though some of the physical structures remain in his body, he has shifted out of the patterned survival defense and into the gifts of the pattern.

Power comes from the focused use of energy, and the gifts of the aggressive pattern are the gifts of energy, including the capacity to gather it, channel it, and use it to make things happen. At their best, aggressive-patterned people are Masters of Energy. They are very aware of energy and attentive to its use. They have a large energy field, which holds a high charge.

They are embodied and easily claim their own space. When in the gifts of the pattern, they are able to measure their own strengths and weaknesses accurately (although when caught in the pattern, they measure only their strengths and ignore or override their needs and weaknesses).

Because they have a strong, focused will, they are good at attraction and manifestation. They also tend to be creative, especially when it's useful for their survival. These are people who show up for life, and they expect others to do the same. They are intense: alive, aware, highly charged, and engaged.

The aggressive pattern is belly centered, so those who adopted it have both belly wisdom and street smarts. This makes them physical, athletic, and sexual. Sex is very important to them, since they have a high charge of life force energy and a strong need to discharge it.

The skills and talents of this pattern give these individuals easy access to the Warrior archetype. They are able to fight for what they want and for causes they believe in. They can also fight just for the fun of fighting and not take it personally. They have a sense of honor, and are courageous, resourceful, and even loyal if it serves their purpose. They are good hunters and trackers — they

---

* To avoid the cumbersomeness of having to continually say "he or she," I will assign a gender to the child described in each chapter and then stick with that gender throughout the chapter. For example, in this chapter, I will assume the child is a boy. However, all five of the patterns are found in both genders, and everything said about the boy in this chapter could just as easily have been said about a girl.

227

can energetically lock on to a desired outcome and hunt it down. As stated earlier, they can be heroic, and they often become our cultural heroes.

Because they have a strong, healthy will and a strong, focused intent, they are also good at survival. They are realistic, accurately measuring both themselves and others, and then making their decisions accordingly. They orient to the truth of the situation — not to a hope or an illusion — and are able to accept that truth. And because they are also self-reliant, competent, and able to think clearly in a crisis, they will often survive against all odds, although not necessarily in one piece (for example, the rock climber who cut off his own arm to save his life in the film *27 Hours*). When they're on a team, they will make sure that others on the team survive, also.

Because they can hold and reference their own core, those in the gifts of the pattern know who they are. This makes them independent and self-confident, and gives them a healthy sense of self-worth and entitlement — they are, in the best sense, full of themselves. This fullness, added to their large, highly charged field, makes them magnetic and charismatic, able to persuade and inspire others.

Aggressive-patterned people are natural leaders, but may be reluctant ones (when at their best, not when caught in the pattern). They will take charge if the situation requires it or if no one else is stepping up. They are able to read others well and can empower and inspire them. They hold high expectations of both themselves and others. When facing difficult choices, they can be both decisive and adaptable, as needed to survive. Once committed, they go all out.

These are people who like to go beyond the established limits to explore new territory and new experiences. They like challenge, risk, and competition, and see these as opportunities to test themselves and practice unbending intent. Once they attach their will to something, either it will be done or they will die trying. They break barriers, records, and rules (*"rules are for other people"*).

These are people who generate energy and initiate action. They are bold, effective, and entrepreneurial. When they see new opportunities, they take them. They are adventurous, fun, and ready to try new things. They are interesting, juicy, passionate people, who usually have lots of stories of their amazing adventures. They seek high stimulation.

The key to shifting into the gifts of the pattern is in discovering that they are not alone but held by something larger, stronger, and loving. This allows them to come out of the fight or flight response, relax into that holding love, and re-open their hearts.

Examples

- special forces in the military (Navy Seals, Army Rangers, Green Berets, etc.)
- the head of security in the film Avatar
- Jack Nicholson in nearly any role
- Tom Cruise
- Lucy in the Peanuts comic strip
- Tigger in Winnie the Pooh ("Bouncing is what Tiggers do best!")
- Arnold Schwarzenegger
- Senator John McCain
- Sarah Palin ("don't retreat, reload")

Alternate Names

- Psychopath
- the Challenger/Defender
- the Controller
- the Charismatic Leader
- the Betrayed Child

Exercise – Being Caught in the Pattern

Life on the Battlefield

This exercise is designed to give you a felt sense of what it's like to be caught in the aggressive pattern, seeing life as a constant battle for survival. As you go through this exercise, try not to judge it, but instead just notice how familiar or unfamiliar the experience is and what it would be like to live this way every day.

Go out for a walk around your neighborhood, but this time, let yourself experience it in a new way. As you walk, notice that you are all alone. No one is with you, no one is by your side, no one is watching your back. Your family is gone. Your friends are gone. There is no one to depend on. There is no God above you looking out for you; there are no angels protecting you. If you think there are, you're deluded, which puts you in even more danger. Even the ground beneath your feet doesn't really support you. It's dead; it doesn't care whether you live or die. No one is on your side. No one cares. Whatever you feel about all this, get over it. This is serious now; it's life or death. It's kill or be killed. Pay attention. This place is a jungle, and you're either the predator or you're the prey. No exceptions. No innocent bystanders. Which are you going to be?

As you approach other people, measure each one for physical strength. Ask yourself, if this gets ugly, if it turns into a fight, can I take them? How big are they? How mean are they? What weapons do they have? What weapons do I have? What weapons do I need to survive in this hell hole?

Some of the people you pass will pretend to be your friends, maybe claim that they love you and care about you. Don't believe it. You've been down that road before. That only leads to being used and hurt. No one is there for you when the chips are down. Some try, but then collapse, and you end up having to carry them. Either way, it's not worth it. No refuge there. Better to go it alone.

But there is something that you can do, something that makes it better. You can start pulling your own energy up into your chest and arms. You can pull up more and more energy, until you fill yourself with it. So stand up tall and start pulling up your energy. It makes you bigger. It makes you stronger. Focus on that strength. Set your jaw. Sure, this takes will and determination, but you can do it. Over and over again, keep pulling up more energy, filling your upper body and the space around you with it.

Notice how you're getting bigger, stronger, more intimidating. You carry more juice now, more voltage to blast people if they challenge you. Stand up taller. Push the energy out in front of you in a big wave, just to let everyone know you mean business. Notice how people step back now when you push on them, how they just give in. Weaklings. Disgusting.

But some people don't back down. They stand and face you. They send a wave back at you. Watch out now. Measure them against yourself. Can you take them? Do you want to? Are they friend or foe? Comrades in arms or traitors? You can measure their strength, but it's hard to tell their intentions . . . so stay alert and stay focused. Keep your guard up. You never know.

Pull up an even bigger dose of energy, just to be safe. Maybe you notice now that your adrenal glands are hurting and your body is buzzing from the adrenaline. No matter, ignore it. Get over it. It's worth the safety that the extra juice provides. If the average person's system runs on 110 volts, you're now running 400 volts. In a crisis, you can go to 600 volts, maybe more.

The only source of safety is having more energy, more firepower. Overwhelming firepower. The more, the better. You can never have too much, because you never know how much the next guy will have. So be ready. Pump it up. Keep it handy. Stay focused. You never know.

Sure, this is hard, but it's the only safety available. All the rest crumbles when you need it. All the rest is only a set up for disappointment or betrayal. It's a tough life. Get used to it.

Let yourself walk back home slowly, keeping your guard up, keeping yourself pumped up and big and intimidating the entire time. Don't say anything to anyone about what you're doing. Don't blab about it, just notice the effect it has on people. Notice how they treat you now. Notice how much bigger you feel.

When you get home, take some time to let all that extra charge drain out of your body. Exhale and send the charge out on each out-breath. Let all the efforting go. Move or shake your body to release the extra charge. Try making sounds, and let the extra charge flow out of you with the sounds. Give your body as much time as it needs to calm back down, even if it takes a while.

Then take some time to reflect on what you experienced.

- *How easy or difficult was it for you to pull up the extra energy and fill yourself with it? Did it feel like just one more day of what you usually do? Or did it feel strange and difficult?*

- *What thoughts or feelings arose as you did it?*

- *What thoughts or feelings seemed to get in the way?*

- *What would it be like to live this way all the time?*

Exercise – The Gifts of the Pattern

Running Big Energy

So far, you've been experiencing what it's like to be caught in the aggressive pattern, stuck in the fear-driven, adrenalized, fight-or-flight state. Now let's shift into the gifts of the pattern.

When you're ready, sit down comfortably with your spine relatively straight, and close your eyes. Take several big breaths down deep into your body and release them. On each out-breath, let any extra energy flow out of your body on the breath. Feel your entire system calming and slowing down. Now we're going to do this the easy way.

First, just notice the strength and erectness of your spine. In your mind, draw a line from the crown of your head down through the center of your torso to your perineum (between your anus and your genitals). Imagine this line as a column of energy, maybe a few inches in diameter, that runs straight down from the crown of your head through your torso to your perineum. This column is your core, the center of your physical being, the place in your body where you are most yourself.

Now, let the bottom of your core begin to grow down into the ground below you, just like the taproot of a tree. It can be brown and woody, like the root of a tree, or it can be more like a current of bubbly, liquid light, or it can have any appearance that you like. Its purpose is to connect you to the deep core of the earth. Only this time, the earth is very different from the way we envisioned it before. Now the earth is a gigantic, warm, kind, nurturing grandmother being. Sort of like your favorite, ideal grandmother, the one who always loved you, no matter what; the one who was always glad to see you; the one who always greeted you with a big hug and hot chocolate and cookies.

This grandmother earth is completely safe and nourishing, so just let your taproot gently grow down as deep into her gigantic earth body as you like. And notice that the flow in this root goes both ways, so you can send down into the earth any emotions or energy that you don't want, and she will send up into you all the love, support, strength, and nourishment that you want. There is no need to push, no need for effort. Any kind of energy that you want flows easily up your taproot and into you.

Once you've established your core and your connection downward into the earth, it's time to establish your connection upward. Let your core begin to gently grow upward, up through the crown of your head and then on up through your higher self, all the way up to Divine Being, or God, or whatever name you use for that energy. Again, let your core connect itself firmly into this divine source.

Now your physical body is suspended on a vertical line connecting the divinity/source above and the grounding earth below. Now you're not alone; you're connected to Everything. Now you're part of the dance of everything and aligned with everything. Now you can live your life in harmony with the energies that flow up and down that line, and you can let those energies guide, inform, and nourish you. This is what it's like to have core and ground and be in alignment with All That Is. Let yourself relax into this experience and enjoy it.

Now that you're fully connected and aligned with everything, we'll add the gifts of the aggressive pattern. Let yourself gently begin to experiment with the possibility that, if you ask for it, you can increase the flow of energy through your body. Be gentle with yourself as you experiment, and turn the volume back down any time your body starts to feel uncomfortable. Self-care is important here. But within the bounds of what feels comfortable, and as long as you do not feel your system begin to strain or your adrenals start to rev up, let yourself experiment and play.

Try letting your root go all the way down into the molten core of the earth. Ask the glowing lava there to feed you and to let some of its energy come up into you and fill your body. Don't use your adrenal glands to make the energy yourself; just let the earth's energy fill you. Let your body drink in this energy, but don't overdo it. Let your body fill only as long as it remains grounded, centered, and calm. Let that big, effortless flow of energy become the core of your self. Or, if that's too much, let a small trickle of that flow become the core of your self

Now let's experiment. You've just tried letting more energy flow gently up from the earth into you and through you. Let's try some other possibilities. Take as much time as you like to explore each one of these:

- You can ask for more energy to gently flow down from above, into you and through you.

- You can ask for more energy to gently flow into you from the rear and out the front.

- You can even ask for more energy to gently appear somewhere within your core and then radiate outward in all directions.

Now let's come back toward ordinary life. Gently let your awareness return to the room where you're sitting. If it's comfortable, you may want to stay with this sense of yourself as a big, effortless flow of energy. If it's not comfortable, simply let it go, but keep the awareness that this is possible and that some people feel this way.

Now notice what you learned and what this whole experience was like for you:

- *How easy was it for you to feel your core?*

- *How easy was it for your core to grow down, deep into the earth?*

- *How easy was it for your core to grow up into your higher self and into divinity?*

- *How did you feel about being a big, effortless flow of energy?*

- *What thoughts or feelings arose as you did this exercise?*

- *What thoughts or feelings seemed to get in the way?*

- *What would it be like to live this way all the time?*

The flow of energy that is available to you is enormous. This is the truth that creates the gifts of the aggressive pattern. However, your body is not naturally wired for enormous amounts of energy. The body of a person who uses the aggressive pattern is generally able to tolerate more energy flow than the average person's body (otherwise, he would not be able to make this survival strategy work), but all bodies have limits. If you decide to experiment further with this, be careful not to over-load yourself with too much energy and fry your system.

The Origins of the Aggressive Pattern

The wound sustained by aggressive-patterned people was a wound to their trust in others. When they needed help, no one was there for them, and they had to survive by the sheer force of their own will. Their defense strategy is their attempt to protect themselves from a similar re-wounding. Their basic story is this: they were in a situation that felt life threatening, but no one was there for them, so they used their own will to fight their way through. Now they're stuck in the fight or flight response, constantly scanning for threats to their survival and fighting their way through life.

Willing yourself to survive

Let's look at their story more closely. Just like most children, they began as very sensitive little beings. They were doing a good enough job of separating and developing will, strength, and autonomy, those crucial developmental tasks that children focus on between about ages two and four. And as they experienced themselves as separate beings, they encountered the next big question: *"Can I trust you? Can I depend on you? Are you consistently there for me? Am I safe in your care?"*

This is where the train wreck happened, perhaps only once, but probably repeatedly. There was some situation that was so overwhelming that they feared they might die, and no one was there for them. But by this age they had inner resources of their own, so they went into hyper-drive and became there for themselves. They summoned their own will and strength, and they willed themselves through it.

How did they do this? They disconnected their awareness from their fears, needs, and vulnerability. They did not yet have the capacity to actually take care of their own needs — to soothe their own fears and buffer their own vulnerability — so they split off their needs and buried them deep in their unconscious. To keep them buried, they contracted their psyche and their muscles: they armored themselves.

Now they've had a whole new set of experiences:

> *they felt terrified → they got big and tough → they handled it → they felt invincible*

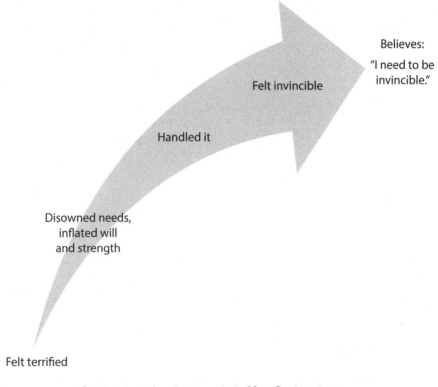

The Aggressive Pattern's Self-Inflation Process

And from that new set of experiences, they drew a series of conclusions: *"No one is there for me. No one cares. I am alone. I have to handle it all by myself. I **will** handle it all by myself. I can make it happen. It's only a matter of will."*

Of course, this is not a real solution to their problem. Their vulnerability and needs have been disowned, but they still organize the psyche. The shock, trauma, and survival fear are still in their system, although deeply buried. They are still very scared, but unaware of it, and now their system can easily be triggered back into that shock and trauma. When that happens, it happens fast. A big wave of fear hits their system, and they are right back in the fight for survival.

They have not learned to turn to others for help. They have not learned to escape or endure to feel safer. What they have learned is that love and connection will not keep them safe, and that the only thing they can trust is their own strength and will. They now have the conviction that *"I have to take care of myself, because I am alone. No one is there for me. I must always be invincible, because if I am vulnerable, I will not survive."* What the child who develops the aggressive pattern has learned is that he must fight for what he needs, because no one is going to take care of him or protect him. Fighting is what will make things better — not trusting, not depending on others. Fighting.

Rapprochement and the Love-Power Split

At this point, you may be wondering, *"Why does this trust issue arise for the child now? Hasn't he always depended on others to care for him? What's different now?"* It's an important question. What's different now is that, as the child sees himself more and more as a separate person, his new sense of separateness brings with it a terrifying vulnerability. At around two years old, the process of separation and individuation began, most obviously with the child's discovery that he could say "No!" At first, this separateness was a marvelous thing. It gave him a new sense of power and ability. But now those abilities have stopped being *just* abilities — they have become *his* abilities. What were formerly just vulnerabilities and needs have now become *his* vulnerabilities and *his* needs. For the first time, the child realizes that because of his separateness, he is needy and vulnerable: without others, he will not survive.

So the child both loves and fears his new-found separateness and autonomy. The struggle to reconcile these two feelings causes him to want to be on your lap, then off your lap, then on your lap again, and then off again. Back and forth, back and forth he goes, alternating between wanting to be merged and wanting to separate.

In psychology, this period is called the "rapprochement phase," from the French word meaning "to bring together." The child's task during this phase is to "bring together" two huge polarities that have appeared in his psyche. The first polarity is one of size: between his bigness and his smallness, his magnificence and his vulnerability, his strength and his neediness. The second polarity is one of connection: between his oneness and his separateness, his unity and his individuality.[1] In short, he must integrate the love and connection he has already experienced with the power and separateness that he is beginning to experience. This is no easy task, and most children don't completely succeed in it.

Parenting the Child's New Power

This is not an easy time for the parents, either. The child's new sense of will and separateness gives rise to a new inner experience in him, the experience of *wanting*. Before this, the child was simply upset — perhaps hungry, wet, or tired — and just needed it fixed. The parents' job was simply to find the problem and fix it. Now the child has developed the capacity to want something specific and the will to try multiple ways to get it, even if it's not good for him. This creates an entirely new set of problems for the parents. First, how do they distinguish between what the child actually needs and what he simply wants? And second, how do they deal with the child's relentless barrage of new strategies to coerce their compliance, especially the tantrums?

Differentiating the child's needs from his wants is hard enough. It requires that the parents perpetually make judgment calls, moment to moment, in the blur of daily life. But then, every time they decide that they have to disappoint the child, they also have to hold firm against his reaction. How skillfully they are able to hold against the child's reaction determines a great deal about the child's experience. There are three possibilities:

1. The parents are able to embody both love and power simultaneously, so they can hold and contain the child's energy, even in the face of his fury, without losing their sense of love and connection to him.

2. The parents are able to embody love, but not power, so they collapse in the face of the child's demands and give in.

3. The parents are able to embody power, but not love, so they retaliate by attacking, abandoning or shaming the child.

Ideally, the parents are able to embody both love and power, so they are able to contain the child's emotional storm without collapsing, retaliating, or losing their loving connection to him. If they can do this, he learns how to integrate his new-found power with the love and connectedness he already has. He learns that he can be all of himself, whether he feels big and strong or small and needy, yet still be loved and safe. He learns that there is something good that is bigger than him, that it contains and protects him, and that he doesn't need to fear either his weakness or his new power.

Most of us, however, were not so lucky. Most of us saw love wielded without the power needed to strengthen it (option 2), or power wielded without the love needed to guide it (option 3). We came to see the two — love and power — as incompatible and opposing forces. We believed we had to choose between them, so we embraced one and rejected the other.

Obviously, which side the child embraces plays a major role in the development of his personality. A child who adopts the aggressive pattern chooses power over love. He does not feel protected by anything greater than himself, so he tries to protect himself by closing his heart and splitting off his own weakness, need, and vulnerability. He shifts into the warrior archetype, which makes him feel stronger, but also makes the world a battleground and life a fight for survival. To survive, he idealizes strength and will while disdaining vulnerability and need. He runs mostly masculine energy and devalues the feminine. (Although we're using "he" in this chapter, girls who adopt the aggressive pattern make these same shifts.)

Environments that often Precipitate the Aggressive Pattern

Keeping in mind that each of the survival patterns is formed by the *interaction* between the child and his environment, and is not something that the environment imposes on him, let's look at how the aggressive pattern forms.

First, let's consider the child. This is a willful, high-energy child. Low-energy, compliant children do not develop the aggressive pattern — they might try out this strategy, but they just can't make it work, so they don't stay with it. Remember that each of the survival patterns is a way to buffer the body from feelings of overwhelm. If you can't make a buffering strategy work for you, you move on to some other strategy.

Now let's look at how the parents respond to the child's high energy and will.

Love without power (not enough containment)

One possibility is that the parents cannot hold and contain the child's energy. They collapse in the face of the child's tantrums and give in. As this child repeatedly wins the fights and gets what he wants, he concludes that fighting works. Naturally, he will continue fighting, and his aggression will develop from a strategy into a survival pattern. He will like feeling big and strong and start to do whatever he can to maintain that sense of himself.

However, he will also feel alone. The experience of being able to overpower his parents is disorienting and unnerving for a child. It takes away his sense that there is something larger keeping him safe. As soon as he can overpower his parents, he is alone in the world. An aggressive-patterned friend put it this way: *"I remember the moment vividly. I was barely 13, and was in some argument with my dad. I was standing at the top of the stairs from the living room down into the rec room. I don't know what we were arguing about, but I had just said why I thought he was wrong. And instead of responding to my reasoning, he yelled 'You're supposed to respect your father!' And, without even thinking, I shot back, 'Respect has to be earned!' And in that moment, I knew it was over. I had defeated him. I went down the stairs with a bitter, sinking feeling in my gut, 'cause I knew then I was bigger than him. I could take him down any time."*

Power without love (not enough connection)

The second possibility is that the parents do have the strength to hold the child's energy, but they cannot stay connected and loving while wielding that strength. So instead of helping the child process his frustration and manage his own energy, they use force to crush it. Whenever he opposes them, they turn the disagreement into a fight and defeat him.

These are authoritarian parents, who believe that opposition from their child is defiance, and that to maintain their authority they must stamp out the child's opposition, even if that requires violence. It's very likely that, when these parents were young, they were themselves attacked by an authoritarian parent. So that is the only model they know and the one they automatically default to under pressure. Now, when their own child challenges them, their buried rage from their own mistreatment bubbles up, often in the form of a thought like, *"How come you get to do that?! I never got to do that!"* They may even have sworn to themselves that they would never treat their own children this way, but the rage buried within them is powerful, and now here they are, reacting just the way their own parents did.

You may have noticed that this is the same type of authoritarian response that we saw in the formation of the enduring pattern, and you may be wondering what's different here. What's different is the response of the child. Both children's attempts at self-assertion are met with crushing opposition, and both lose many fights. But, while the child who adopts the enduring pattern eventually concludes "I can never win" and then gives up and goes underground to save himself, the child who adopts the aggressive pattern decides that he would rather die than surrender, identifies with his will and strength, and keeps on fighting.

There are a whole constellation of factors that influence this decision. He may have more talent for fighting than for enduring, and perhaps enduring just didn't work for him. The parents' violent reactions probably started later, after he already had much more will and strength to fight back, so he had some history of winning before the losses started. He may have measured his authoritarian parent(s) and decided that it was only a matter of time until he got big enough to "kick the old man's ass," so all he had to do was survive until then.

Which parent was the authoritarian one also makes a big difference. If it was the parent who did most of the childcare, then losing every battle may have started soon after birth, and there were no victories before the first attack. If it was the less involved parent, then the attacks started later, and the child already had some history of victories and some sense of safe relatedness with the more nurturing parent.

Other family members may also have been getting hurt, and trying to protect them may have influenced his decision. Many male clients have told me stories of lying awake at night as a child, waiting for the sounds of their father coming home, knowing that, if he was drunk, he would be angry and looking to hit someone. They had seen him hit their mother and their sisters, and they had vowed that, *"If he's going to hit anyone, it's going to be me."* So they would wait for those nights and then intentionally step in front of their father and take the blows. Several told stories of how they would actively taunt the old man to draw him away from their mother and sisters, even though they knew that they were going to get punched in the face. In the film *Good Will Hunting*, Will describes making this same choice when he tells his therapist, *"My father was an alcoholic. Mean fuckin' drunk. Used to come home hammered, looking to whale on someone. So I had to provoke him, so he wouldn't go after my mother and little brother. Interesting nights were when he wore his rings . . . ."*

In contrast, a client who adopted the enduring pattern related how the only way to protect his sister during their childhood was for him to not be strong or successful. He saw that whenever he succeeded at something, it somehow ended up hurting his sister. After a cursory appreciation of his accomplishment, his mom would turn on his sister and berate her for not being able to do the same. Seeing that his accomplishments only led to pain for his beloved sister, he swore off all successes in order to protect her. Notice also, that it was his mother who was the authoritarian parent, not his father.

So there are many factors that go into the creation of a survival strategy and, eventually, a survival pattern. Also, keep in mind the possibility that a child may need a certain survival pattern in order to learn some important life lesson, so he may unconsciously adopt that survival pattern even though another would have worked better.

Betrayed love

A third scenario that tends to create the aggressive pattern is one in which the love the child received was then used to manipulate him. This typically involves an authoritarian parent of the same sex and a manipulative parent of the opposite sex. If the child is male, this would typically be an authoritarian father and a manipulative mother. The usual story is that, before marriage, the mother idealized the father's strength and authority. She admired him and felt protected by him. But as the years passed and their quarrels became more violent, she rejected him and turned to her son for love. Or it may have been that, as the kids were born and she paid more attention to them, her husband felt jealous and the fights began. In either case, her idealization of her husband was replaced by disillusionment and rejection of him.

She then transferred her idealization onto her son and conscripted him into being her replacement "emotional husband." She told him that he was "Mommy's little man" and implied that he was somehow better than his father. Without ever bringing sexuality into the picture, she seduced him into becoming her emotional husband. She praised him, confided in him, and used him to meet her own emotional needs that were no longer being met by her husband.

The boy in this scenario thinks that he's being big and strong and important (because that's what Mom tells him), but in fact, his childhood is being stolen from him. While he is busy trying to be Mom's emotional husband, he's not able to be a child and work through the developmental tasks he faces. He is not able to integrate his new-found power into his sense of love and connection with his parents. He doesn't feel held and contained energetically by his parents; instead, he feels like an equal to his mom and superior to his dad.

His safety isn't found in depending on them, but in matching or surpassing them. It is his job to protect his mom from his dad. This may mean directly challenging his dad or even physically fighting him. If he loses, he has failed his mom. Either way, he loses his dad.

He can't keep his loving connection to both of them, and he can't own both his power and his legitimate childhood needs. Instead, he has to give up his connection to his dad and disown feeling small, weak, and needy. As he tries to be bigger and stronger than is appropriate for his age, he uses his will to inflate himself and to push himself into precocious development. His mom needs him, and he has to be ready to defend her.

In the end, he discovers that his mom was using him, and that no one was really there for him. He has lost his sense that the world is safe, that love is safe, and that he can trust others to care about his needs. All he has left is his own pumped up sense of power.

Of course, this same scenario can happen to a daughter if her father allies with her against her mother and makes her his emotional wife. And it can happen in a situation where some or all of the players identify as homosexual or bisexual, since the wound is not about sexual orientation. The wound is about being used by someone he thought was caring for him.

This child gave his heart to the seducing parent,[2] tried to love and protect that parent, and be what that parent needed, only to find that he had been betrayed. Upon seeing that it was his love and open-heartedness that had left him so vulnerable, he closed his heart in self-protection and unconsciously vowed, *"You will never do that to me again."*

The core wound of those who adopted this survival pattern was the loss of their sense that they can safely need and trust others. Their solution is to trust only their own strength and will.

Defensive Action

So if you can't trust others to take care of you, what do you do? How do you survive? How do you try to make some safety for yourself? This pattern's solution is to become powerful enough to take care of yourself, to will yourself into being able to be there for yourself. That means inflating yourself, while controlling yourself, others, and the situation.[3]

The child attempts to control himself by devaluing and denying his own feelings and needs. His mind turns against his body and its feelings.[4] It closes his heart and splits off and renounces his needs. It uses scorn and contempt to suppress all needs, weaknesses, fears, and dependency, and instead shifts his attention away from his weaknesses and onto his will and strength.

In order to control others and the situation, he takes an aggressive stance toward the world. Instead of asking for what he needs, he demands it. He relies on intimidation and force, rather than on cooperation, to get what he needs.

To make himself appear bigger and more intimidating, he pulls his energy up into his upper body and pushes it out in front of him. He inflates himself and deflates others, as he tries to stay one-up, and keep others one-down.

Results of the Defensive Action

Turning against your own body is a serious act. It requires an enormous exercise of will. It also requires an enormous sacrifice. In order to ensure his physical survival, a person who adopts this survival pattern sacrifices feeling fully alive.

Loss of support and connection

Since the body is what grounds and supports him in the physical plane, devaluing the body's signals and needs means literally losing contact with the ground under him and the support it offers. Discounting the information that comes through his body also means losing the connection up through the crown of his head to his higher self and the realm of the divine. Losing his sense of support from below and his sense of purpose from above causes this person's world to contract. Instead of being part of the universal family, he feels abandoned and alone, caught in the physical plane, with no support from below or direction from above. His original vision of his life purpose contracts into a smaller vision of survival and power. The world around him becomes a battlefield, on which he is a lone warrior, without love, fighting for survival. Life becomes an endless series of fights.

Need for dominance and control

Now there is much to fear: weakness, neediness, loss of control, and surrender in any form. But since feeling is suppressed, these fears are not so much felt as acted out in all the ways he tries to dominate and control others, instead of trusting them and cooperating with them. As with all the survival patterns, his defensive actions actually draw to him the very things he is attempting to prevent. Here, his actions draw to him the abandonment and betrayal that he fears.

So this is where aggressive-patterned people are stuck. There was no bigger, loving force that contained and protected them. They saw love wielded without power, or power wielded without love, or their own love used to manipulate them. So they fell back on the strength of their own will, swore off love, and identified with power. Now they feel all alone in a dangerous world — unloved, unsupported, unprotected. They cannot imagine that anything loving would be strong enough to protect them, or that anything strong would care about them. With nothing they can trust, they are caught in an unending struggle for power and survival.

The Aggressive Pattern in Full Bloom

Body Signs

Since the flow of energy in the body contributes to shaping the body as it grows, the aggressive-patterned person's increased upward energy flow usually causes the upper half of the body to become larger than the lower half. Typically, the body takes on a V shape, with broad, strong shoulders and narrower hips. The legs are thinner and weaker than would be proportionate. The person is attractive and strong, but may seem top-heavy and ungrounded.

The person has a strong core, but it is a defended core, not an open, relaxed core. He does not rest into his core and just let it support him. Instead, there is a constant inner tension, a tension so habitual that he does not perceive it or imagine that it could relax. This tension manifests in his behavior as a constant guardedness and readiness to fight for his survival.

His eyes tend to be compelling. When he looks at you, you can feel the pressure of his will pushing on you, moving you into agreement with him. The tension in his core shows through his eyes as a watchful, distrustful quality, as a slightly tense alertness, rather than a relaxed, open alertness.

As mentioned earlier in the chapter on the leaving pattern, one of the main differences between predator and prey animals is that predators, when they are stalking prey, hold a point-focused attention, an attention focused on what they want. Prey animals, by contrast, hold an open, field-focused attention, which allows them to perceive danger coming from any direction.[5] The slightly tense alertness of an aggressive-patterned person is similar to the point-focused attention of a predator animal, except that here it is being used as a survival strategy. In a predator animal, the point-focus is present only

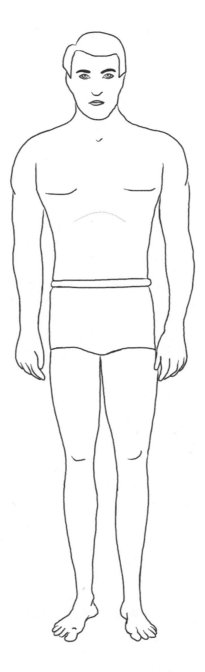

The Aggressive Pattern – typical body shape

while it is needed for hunting, and relaxes while at rest. But since a person caught in the aggressive pattern never feels truly safe, his attention never fully relaxes.

This tension also shows in the body's holding pattern, which is perpetually *holding up*. Notice how this contrasts with the leaving pattern's *holding together*, the merging pattern's *holding on*, and the enduring pattern's *holding in*.

The bodies of people who run the aggressive pattern are usually strong and athletic, but may have been damaged by repeatedly being pushed too hard. Pushing their bodies to the limit puts them frequently into an adrenalized state and tends to make them adrenalin junkies. If they habitually overuse their adrenal glands, they may fall into a state of adrenal exhaustion, in which their bodies begin to seriously break down. This happens because our bodies are designed to use adrenaline only for short periods of time, followed by periods of recovery. Real life energy comes from the earth and nourishes the body, whereas adrenal energy is a fake energy, a chemical energy, which breaks the body down. Women who run the aggressive pattern are especially prone to overusing their adrenal glands because they don't have as much innate testosterone to support their strength. [6]

Psychology

This is the first survival pattern that is developmentally old enough so that both strength and will have already come online and are fully operational as it is forming. Consequently, aggressive-patterned people are the first who, when they go into the fight or flight response, feel capable of fighting and winning.

These new powers are a real accomplishment in the development of any child. What's missing for this child, however, is the experience of being contained and protected by a loving, but larger, force. This larger force was either absent (neither parent could contain the child), or the larger force was not loving (the parent attacked or disconnected from him), or the larger force betrayed him (the child's love was used to manipulate him). Without this protection by a loving, larger force, the child has no feeling of safety and cannot relax. This has left him with a belief that power rules, and that only his own will and strength can protect him.

The main issue for aggressive-patterned people, then, is their doubt that they can trust or depend on others. This puts them in perpetual fear for their physical survival. Since they can't trust others, they try to dominate and control them in order to feel safe. Their refrain is, *"I knew I couldn't trust you."*

They may remain in the fight or flight state for their entire lives, and they typically believe it is normal.

Being stuck in the fight response

However, the belief that power rules has also led this child into a psychological corner. In early traumatic situations, when he went into the fight or flight response, he was indeed able to fight his way through on his own. But then he was unable to turn to others afterward for the soothing he needed to come out of the fight or flight response — to reconnect with them, and with his own heart, and feel safe again. This has left him stuck in a perpetual, low-level fight response, needing to dominate and control everything to try to create some sense of safety, and ready to fight to do it.

Because they are developmentally older, aggressive-patterned people have stronger ego structures than those who do the developmentally younger survival patterns, but their ego structures tend to be less flexible. In psychology, they are said to be "over-bound," while those who do the leaving and merging survival patterns are said to be "under-bound." While this gives them more internal structure, it also makes them less sensitive and less connected with other people.

Those who use this defense strategy enter therapy only rarely, and usually only when their inflation and grandiosity have broken down and some weakness or need has been revealed. And even then, their sole agenda is likely to be the restoration of their former strength, followed by a quick exit from therapy.

Orienting to the Truth

Like all human beings, aggressive-patterned people need some way to orient themselves in the world. They need a reference point. But, since orienting themselves to love and connection wound up hurting them in the past, they now orient themselves to the truth of the situation instead. They see discovering the truth as the key to their survival, whereas love and connection are expendable. This means that the world they experience is fundamentally different from the world experienced by those who use their connection to others as their reference point.

To discover the truth, they develop a great bullshit detector, a skill that is also known as "street smarts." They are energetically sensitive and have a felt sense of their own core, so they've noticed that when they speak the truth, it resonates with their core, whereas when they lie, it doesn't resonate — it doesn't "feel right." They've also noticed that, by monitoring their own felt

247

sense, they can detect lies from others in the same way. When those you love have deceived you, you become very focused on finding ways to avoid being deceived again.

What they're really doing is reading your energy and comparing it to your words. If your words match your energy — which means they're true, or at least you believe they're true — the aggressive-patterned person will trust what you say and listen to you. If they feel that your words don't resonate inside of you, then they won't trust you, no matter what you say. They will discard your words and look for what you're hiding. When a person is caught in this survival pattern, their own felt sense of that resonance is the only thing they will trust — not your words, not your promises, not even your acts.

What they care about is the truth of the situation, not whether it is pleasant or unpleasant, reassuring or scary, and certainly not whether you like them. They want the truth, and they'll know it when they hear it because their system will calm down when they hear the truth, no matter how unpleasant it may be. They will surrender to the truth of a situation, even though they would never surrender to a person. Surrender to a person is defeat. Surrender to the truth is survival.

An aggressive-patterned friend told me a story that clearly demonstrates this dynamic. After years of having a good, calm connection with his girlfriend, his body began feeling weird — sort of jumping around inside. He had no idea what was causing it, but it finally got to the point where he became angry, and confronted her about it, saying *"I don't know what's wrong, but I know **something** is wrong, so would you just tell me about it?"* She immediately burst into tears and confessed that she had been having an affair. As soon as she said that, he felt his whole body relax. He was so relieved that things inside of him had finally calmed down that his anger disappeared. All he did was let out a sigh and ask, *"So, what do we do now?"*

Beliefs

The beliefs of aggressive-patterned people reflect both their history of feeling alone and their strong will to survive. Some of their typical beliefs are:

"I am all alone."
"There is no help."
"No one cares."
"It's a jungle out there."
"Only the strong survive."

"Only the truth is trustworthy."
"I have to do it all myself."
"It's all a matter of will."
"Rules are for other people"
"Abuse is normal."

Fears

When talking about aggressive-patterned people, others will usually say that their main issue is their need for dominance and control, because that is the main theme of their behavior. But if we ask ourselves this question — *"Why would someone think they need that amount of control over everyone around them?"* — we see that their deeper issue is an inability to trust that others will care for and protect them, that is, a fear that trusting others will only set them up for disappointment and betrayal. Just below the surface of consciousness, people caught in this survival pattern are habitually hearing thoughts like, *"No one cares. I'm all alone. There is no help. I have to do it all myself."* They believe that the only safe attitude, then, is to stay guarded and suspicious, and the only safe action is to stay in control of everything and one-up on everyone around them.

Underneath their superior attitude, there are many fears, but these are usually not felt or recognized. You may be able to infer their fears from their behavior, but if you ask, they will usually report that they don't feel any fear.

Fear of vulnerability

They fear vulnerability of any kind. Vulnerability means that they're weak or need something, and weakness and need are a threat to survival. Even receiving what they need from someone else is seen as a threat because that might lead to depending on that person. For those who run the aggressive pattern, the only safe place to get what they need is from within themselves.

Fear of depending on others

Their greatest fear is of being dependent on others, so any emotions that would give others power over them are suppressed. Obviously, this means that attaching to another person or emotionally needing them cannot be allowed or admitted. Remember, their core wound arose out of being dependent on someone who failed them in their time of need. But, of course, they do need others, just as we all do, so they cover up their need by pretending to not care.

If you want to discern the depth of their need for someone, don't focus on their feigned indifference, but on how far they will go to maintain their control over that person.

Fear that their needs are too big

Aggressive-patterned people also fear that their needs are too big for anyone else to handle. This may have been literally true for them in childhood. When they were having a tantrum and they needed a parent who was strong enough to contain their anger — to hold them through the storm — often neither of their parents were capable of doing so. They concluded that others were afraid of their needs, and they became afraid of their needs, as well.

Fear that they are bad inside

They know that, in order to survive, they chose power and renounced love, so at some level, those who developed the aggressive pattern fear that they are bad inside. If they try to hide this, then they secretly fear that there is a monster living inside of them, a monster who bursts out when they're angry and just blasts people. They have seen the damage that their blasts do to other people and to relationships, and they feel ashamed, but they also find themselves helpless to stop it.

On the other hand, if they abandon all hope of human love and openly embrace being bad, then they become the monster. Two great examples of this are Voldemort in the *Harry Potter* series and Sauron in *The Lord of the Rings*. Both characters have embraced the dark side of themselves and are referred to as "the Dark Lord." Both have renounced all hope of love and rule through power and fear. Although they have underlings, both are utterly solitary.

Frozen terror

And, at the bottom of all their suppressed and denied fears, there is a stark, frozen terror. This is the original wound, the terror that felt so life-threatening that the person renounced all dependency in order to get away from it. But it has been locked away, far below consciousness, and it usually doesn't resurface unless the person does deep inner work or falls deeply in love. The emotional attachment of a deep, heart-felt romantic relationship will re-awaken the terror because it re-constellates the experience of emotionally needing another human being. Because of this, falling deeply in love is typically avoided by people who are caught in this survival pattern.

Psychological Defenses

As with all the survival patterns, the psychological defenses of aggressive-patterned people are all attempts to make some sense of safety for themselves in an unsafe world. Let's look at each one of these defenses in turn.

Active aggression

Their most obvious defense strategy is active aggression. Notice how different this is from the passive aggression used by enduring-patterned people. While enduring-patterned people disown and hide their aggression, aggressive-patterned people identify with theirs and even advertise it. These are not the children who lost the fights, but the ones who won them. And even when they got beaten, they never surrendered. Instead, they learned to use their anger and aggression strategically to get what they want. They are familiar with their anger and able to use it deliberately to get the results they desire. They may even verbally acknowledge this with a question like, *"How angry do I have to get to make you do what I want?"*

Beneath their anger, there is always a buried need. They are probably unconscious of it, and most likely won't acknowledge it even when they are aware of it, but it is there, nonetheless. Getting that need filled is one of the main goals of their anger. We'll talk more about this in the section on their approach to conflict.

Charm

Sometimes their aggression is not so obvious. Sometimes they switch strategies and instead use their charisma to charm others into going along with their agenda. This change in strategy is a pragmatic response to the situation at hand. They have assessed the situation and decided that charm will work better than active aggression in this instance. In the current situation, they may not have the power or position to command compliance, or they may have decided that charm and manipulation will be more potent tools to get to the result they want. Whether they are plotting a seduction or a palace coup, this strategy can grow into a complicated edifice of trickery and deception.

While most aggressive-patterned people are capable of both charm and intimidation, they often have a marked preference for one strategy and will use it most of the time, switching into the other strategy only when their preferred strategy is not working.

Projection

Another psychological defense is projection. Fear, need, pain, weakness, and vulnerability are projected onto others, often accompanied by an attitude of contempt for them. This keeps all of these feelings disowned, and allows the aggressive-patterned person to say, *"I am the big, strong, invincible one. Others are weak, disgusting, little worms."*

Objectification

Their projection is made easier by another defense, called "objectification." This means that both self and others are reduced from full, multifaceted human beings to objects. All of us perceive and value the humanness of others through our hearts, so when our hearts are closed, others lose their inherent value as humans, and instead become objects for us. Then we default to another way of measuring their value, which usually boils down to, "What can they do for me?" This is not evil; it is simply a pragmatic way of assigning value when the heart is offline.

People who are caught in the aggressive pattern also default to this method of assigning value, but with one added wrinkle. Since they value competence so highly, they will also assign value according to the person's competence. If someone is competent, they are valuable; if not, they are useless. Notice that they apply this valuation system to themselves as well. It leads directly to their patterned beliefs that *"No one cares about my heart or my humanness, only about my competence"* and *"Without my competence, I have no value."* Underneath those beliefs, there is a very deep heartbreak, but a great deal of inner work is required to bring it up into awareness.

Self-idealization

All of the above defenses are supported by another psychological defense, called "self-idealization." The illusion of this pattern is *"I am superior. I am super-competent."* When facing a problem, aggressive-patterned people often think, *"I can do this. It's only a matter of will."* Their belief is *"I can do anything."* This self-idealization brings with it feelings of pride, superiority, and even invincibility. A great example of this attitude is the character of Annie Oakley, in the musical *Annie Get Your Gun*. She sings, *"Anything you can do, I can do better. I can do anything better than you."*[7]

Their idealization of their own abilities often leads them to feel competent in situations where they're actually not. This is vividly on display in situations where they're absolutely certain of themselves, even though everyone else can see that their assessment is totally wrong.

Their self-idealization also manifests as an attitude of entitlement. This can go as far as believing that they are entitled to do whatever they wish and take whatever they need. Their assumption is that the world is organized hierarchically according to power, and since they have the most power, they're entitled to rule over others and take whatever they want. This sense of entitlement is most obvious in their belief that it is okay for them to blast others into compliance.

Devaluing others

Of course, in order to feel superior, they also have to devalue others, something that this pattern often does in spades. Each of the three previous survival patterns tend to devalue themselves and feel deficient, but here the survival strategy flips to seeing the self as superior and others as deficient.

Devaluing love and connection

Aggressive-patterned people also devalue their need for love and connection with others. They will often deny that they have a need for love and connection, but will get that need filled by getting others to need them and attach to them. In this way, they can get the love they want without having to feel their own need for it. You may notice that this is the same maneuver used by someone who runs the compensated merging pattern, in which they project their own need onto the other and then fill the other's need.

The Heroic Rescuer or White Knight

There is even a co-dependent version of the aggressive pattern, called the Heroic Rescuer or the White Knight. But he doesn't just rescue others, the way a person in the compensated merging pattern would, he also presents himself as a hero while doing it.

Of course, a real hero actually does rescue others, so how is this different? Well, it's different in that a real hero is rescuing others because *they* need it, whereas the Heroic Rescuer is rescuing others because *he* needs it. He not only needs to rescue others, but he needs to see himself as a hero for doing so. If those being rescued would have solved their problem by themselves, his action is actually disempowering for them. They don't get to struggle with their problem and discover that they can solve it themselves. Instead, they are likely to give their power to him and become dependent on him.

However, this is not a black and white, either/or, kind of distinction. Both dynamics may be going on at once: the rescuee may actually need the help, and the rescuer may need to see himself as a hero. What distinguishes the Heroic Rescuer from someone who is simply providing what is needed is the extent to which the act of rescuing serves a defensive function in the rescuer's psyche. The more attuned the rescuer is to the rescuee's needs, the less self-serving the act is. If the action seems un-attuned and forced, it's probably motivated more by the needs of the rescuer.

Guard Mode[8]

There is a low-level form of the aggressive pattern known as "guard mode." When aggressive-patterned people are in guard mode, they are partway out from behind their defenses, but still cautious and guarded. They are not silly or spontaneous, as they might be if they were completely out of pattern, but they are much more accessible than they would be if they were fully in pattern. Until they have a felt sense of safety in their body, however, they are not able to come completely out of pattern. Since acquiring that felt sense of safety in the body isn't possible without a very deep healing of their core wounds, many aggressive-patterned people spend most of their time in guard mode, even after doing considerable inner work.

When the Aggressive Pattern is Masked

There is another variation of the aggressive survival pattern in which the person disowns their power and attempts to mask the pattern in themselves. Because this masking is so contrary to the survival strategy of the pattern, this variation seems to be rare. The few examples I have seen have been women.

This masking of their power is not a conscious act. It is a reaction to an overbearing, authoritarian parent who used force to dominate them. They hated being treated like that and decided that they would never use force in that way, so even as they used their will to survive the onslaught, they didn't actively fight back. Even though the person's body adopted the aggressive pattern, she did not consciously idealize her own strength and will. She doesn't see herself as able to intimidate or dominate others and she avoids behaving that way. She may not see herself as having strength and will at all, but those skills are available when needed. She has a felt sense of the core of her own body, and her strength and will are not a pretense, but they are masked from view rather than advertised.

In order to come out of the pattern and begin their healing process, people who mask their aggressive structure have to discover that they actually do run this survival pattern. Then they can begin to take ownership of their power and learn how to contain and modulate it.

Relationship to Self

Except for the rare variation noted above, aggressive-patterned people always see themselves as the one with the power. In fact, they idealize their abilities and power. This shows up in how frequently they take the position that *"I can handle it."* This identification with ability and power is central to this pattern's survival strategy. The power of those who run this pattern actually comes more from their unrelenting will than from their strength or competence. Their main way of knowing themselves is, *"I am my will."*

Their unrelenting will is also the source of a statement that I find to be diagnostic for the aggressive pattern, in that no other survival pattern will say it. The statement is, *"Don't make me have to kill you."* This is often said in a friendly tone, but it's an acknowledgment that there is something they want and they intend to get it, so don't get in their way.

Relationship to the Inner Critic

Aggressive-patterned people may or may not have a fierce inner critic, depending on their other pattern and how they were treated as a child. What is certain is that, when they are caught in the aggressive pattern, their inner critic's attacks will be directed mostly outward toward others, rather than inward toward the self. It is the other who will be devalued by their sarcasm and contempt, not their idealized self.

Personality Traits

Now let's look at the personality traits of the aggressive pattern. These are the ways an aggressive-patterned person will tend to look when they are actually in the pattern. When they are not in pattern, but instead are present, they may not look and act like this at all. At those times, they will most likely exhibit the gifts of the pattern, such as strength, energy, confidence, and a compelling presence. But when they are fully in pattern, their appearance will be more like what follows.

The first thing you'll notice is that their energy is big and has a pushy, aggressive feeling to it. They will be actively influencing the situation, not sitting back passively or just letting things unfold. They will want to participate in deciding what happens next, or even be fully in charge of things.

They will have the general demeanor of someone who is confident, strong, and just slightly better than you. Or, if they are deeply in the pattern, of someone who is much better than you, even blatantly arrogant and threatening.

When they speak, they will present what they're saying as absolutely true. Even if they have some doubts about what they're saying, their words will come out of their mouths as if they are absolutely certain, to the degree that there's no point in even questioning it. You are seeing their will in action as it supports them and bends you to its agenda.

If you do not run this survival pattern yourself, those who do will seem larger than you, and you may even feel yourself shrinking in their presence. On the other hand, if you do run this survival pattern, you will feel challenged and may notice your own adrenal glands kicking in as you rev up to meet the challenge.

If they feel challenged or threatened by you, they will pull up more energy and throw it at you. Often this will appear as anger, but it can also take the form of a joke, a put-down, or even be done silently. Whatever form it takes, as they send the burst of energy toward you, you'll feel a pressure wave hit your body.

How They Recreate Their Early Wounding

As with all the survival patterns, aggressive-patterned people tend to re-create their own early wounding by the very things they do to try to keep themselves safe. This process is unconscious, of course, but it is very effective in perpetuating the overall pattern by maintaining the kinds of relationships and experiences they had in childhood.

There are several specific ways that aggressive-patterned people recreate their old feelings of abandonment and betrayal. The first is that, by being so controlling and demanding, they make others want to get away from them, thereby recreating their abandonment. Secondly, they may angrily challenge decisions made by others, especially decisions to leave them. Knowing that they will not be allowed to leave without a fight, others may then arrange some kind of deception to cover up their exit, which, of course, recreates the experience of betrayal in the person who runs the aggressive pattern.

Aggressive-patterned people also recreate their childhood experience of being too much for others by inflating themselves and using their size and energy to intimidate others. Naturally, everyone who feels intimidated then sees them as being "too much."

Those in the aggressive pattern also recreate their early wounding by the way they deal with their own needs. Most of the time, they pretend that they have no needs, so the people around them have no practice in meeting their needs and are used to thinking of them as not even having needs. Then, when the aggressive-patterned person finally does realize he has a need that's so big he can't handle it by himself — and then finally turns to others for help — his need is huge. When the others can't meet his huge need, his fears are confirmed. Once again, his needs are too big and the capacity of others is too small. Once again, there is no help and he has to find a way to handle everything all by himself. His belief is confirmed, and as the old, bitter disappointment arises once again, he says, *"Yep. I knew I couldn't trust you."*

The Differences Between the Merging, Compensated Merging, and Aggressive Patterns

Each of the five survival patterns is associated with a particular kind of wound and stage of development. However, these do not define the pattern. Rather, each pattern is defined by the strategy it uses to cope with its wounds.

Both the merging and aggressive patterns were wounded while needing help from others. Those who adopted the merging pattern got some of what they needed, but not enough, and they are still looking for the rest. Now they fear deprivation. Those who adopted the aggressive pattern gave up hoping for help from others, turned inward to their own will and strength, and pulled themselves through the crisis alone. Now they fear depending on anyone else.

The two groups had different talents and skills available to them at the time of their wounding, which led them to adopt different survival strategies and wind up on different sides of the love-power split. Let's put the formation of the patterns in order by age to see how the progression unfolds. You'll notice that as the children get older, they have more developmental skills available for solving their problem.

Merging: Since their will and strength have not yet come online at the time of their wounding, they are unable to use these to solve their problem themselves. All they can do is identify with their current experience of need and vulnerability. *Their core fear is of deprivation.* Their development gets stuck here, so they stay the child in need, looking to the parent to solve their problem. When the love-power split happens, they identify with love and disown power, so they never develop power, even after will and strength do come online. They also never develop a felt sense of their own core, so they aren't able to use it to self-reference.

Compensated Merging: After will and strength have come online, a merging-patterned person is able to create a pretend core and a facsimile of power. Without a real core, however, they can't develop real power. Instead, they identify with their facsimile of power and take on the role of the good parent, the one who meets the needs of the child. *Their core fear is still of deprivation, but now it has been projected onto others.* Needs are accepted and okay, but are experienced only in others, not in themselves.

Since they don't have a felt sense of their own core, they cannot accurately self-reference and discern their own wants and resources. They can self-reference only by referencing their compensation, so their measurement is inflated, and then they take on too much, over-tax their resources, and eventually collapse. When they collapse, their pretend core and compensation dissolve, and they lose their ability to self-reference.

Through it all, they identify with the love side of the love-power split, seeing themselves as the good person who is only trying to help. Even if their love is used to manipulate and betray them, they continue to believe that love will solve everything.

Aggressive: Since they were old enough at the time of their wounding to already have their core, and their strength and will had come online, they were able to use these capacities to be there for themselves when no one else was. However, they had to disown their own needs and dependence. Needing others was what made them vulnerable, so needing others became contemptible in their eyes. *Their core fear is not of being deprived, but of depending on others.*

People who do this survival pattern rejected the love side of the love-power split and embraced the power side. However, no matter how much power they have, they still fear weakness and needing others as threats to their survival. So just having power isn't enough; they have to feel more powerful than anyone who might harm them. In order to feel safer, they want to dominate others.

Sometimes the aggressive and compensated merging patterns are hard to tell apart, especially when the person in the compensated merging pattern is using an aggressive-flavored compensation. The key to differentiating the patterns is this: does the person have a developed core? When slammed, does he collapse or slam you back? When attacked, does he retreat or counter-attack? Does he default to love or to power?

Under stress, a person in the compensated merging pattern loses his pretend core, falls back into the pure merging pattern, and collapses. By contrast, a person in the aggressive pattern goes to his core, revs up his energy, and attacks the problem. Aggressive-patterned people will even use stress to shift themselves more into their core. They will seek out stress because being in their core feels so real and so alive. This is one reason that some people engage in extreme or dangerous sports — they are shifting themselves more into their core in order to feel its vivid aliveness.

How each pattern references

Now let's look at the referencing habits of these three patterns. People in the pure merging pattern habitually reference only others. They have very little ability to reference self, both because they have never developed their core and because they are now actively avoiding putting their attention on it. Not feeling their own core is a fundamental part of their survival strategy, so they have become quite skillful at this.

People who stay more in the compensated side of the merging pattern also habitually reference only others. They are able to reference self only through their compensation, which is built on a pretend core. Since it's a pretend core, it gives them inaccurate information about what resources they have and what resources they actually need.

People in the aggressive pattern habitually reference only self, and that only selectively. They reference only their strengths, while ignoring their weaknesses, needs, and feelings. For the most part, they do not reference others. Someone who is deeply in this pattern is often blind to the feelings and needs of others. When they do reference others, it is only to measure their strengths and weaknesses, whether their statements are true or false, and whether they are friend or foe.

The Skill of Measuring

In order to navigate skillfully through life, each of us needs to develop the skill of *measuring* as well as the skill of *referencing*. Referencing is about where you put your attention. Measuring is about accurately perceiving what you find there. To measure yourself accurately, you must be able to actually sense yourself. To measure others accurately, you must be able to actually sense them.

Measuring self

When a little boy is wondering whether he can jump across a creek, he has to reference himself and measure how far he can jump. Then he has to accurately compare the distance he can jump to the width of the creek. If he over-estimates his ability, he will land in the water. If he references the other boys instead of himself, he may think he can do it just because they can do it. Again, he will land in the water. To get accurate information, he must be able to both self-reference and self-measure.

Measuring others

Any time you're dealing with other people, you need to be able to measure them. When communicating, you need to measure what to say and when to say it. When listening, you need to measure how well the way you're listening is working for them. When teaching, you need to measure how well your students are understanding what you're presenting. Parents, teachers, and coaches need to be especially good at measuring others because they are constantly facing the question "What is the right amount of challenge for this child at this moment?" If they get it wrong, the child may get hurt.

Patterned Distortions When Measuring

Merging: Since people in the merging pattern avoid a felt sense of their own core, they can't self-measure accurately. And when they try to compare their own capacities to the size of a task, their patterned self-image distorts what they can perceive. When they're in the pure merging side of the pattern, they see themselves as being small and needy, and believe that they have very little capacity. Their belief is *"I can't do it."* So they often don't see their own strengths and then underestimate their real abilities.

Compensated Merging: When they're in the compensated side of the pattern, their self-measuring tends to be skewed in the opposite direction. They still don't have a felt sense of their own core to measure, but now they see themselves as being large and capable, so they overestimate their abilities. This leads them to periodically over-reach and get themselves into a jam, from which they must be rescued. It is often an aggressive-patterned person who does the rescuing.

While in either side of the merging pattern, they are very skilled at referencing others, but that skill may or may not extend to measuring others accurately, depending on what sort of capacity they're measuring and whether they have an agenda that is skewing their perceptions.

Aggressive: People in the aggressive pattern are able to self-reference and measure themselves accurately, but they habitually ignore anything that doesn't support their self-idealization. When considering a task, they often measure only whether they will survive. This leads them to see only their strengths, while ignoring their weaknesses and needs. Their inner conversation goes like this: *"Do I have the resources to survive this? Yes? Then I'm good to go."* People who run this survival pattern think they can power through anything, so they override their own body signals of distress with an attitude of "it doesn't matter, it's only a flesh wound." In overriding the body, however, they usually won't endanger their own survival. If a wound is actually life threatening, then they will pay attention to it.

When measuring others, they are again considering only whether the others can help them get what they want, so they're paying attention only to things like, *"Are you telling the truth?"* and *"Do you have the ability to deliver on this?"* Meanwhile, they're ignoring the other person's feelings, needs, hopes, and desires. In general, they don't reference or measure other people at all, and are often clueless about what's going on with them.

They always have an agenda, which limits and distorts their perception. Their constant background agenda is, *"I am bigger than you,"* while their foreground agenda is whatever they're trying to accomplish in the moment. Both agendas skew their perception and distort their measuring process.

They also fail to reference the entire situation before them. They reference only the resources that they personally have to do the task, but fail to reference the help that is available from others. This selective referencing recreates their expected experience of *"there is no help for me"* and confirms their belief that *"I have to do it all myself."* This is an example of how a belief filters perception and shapes experience so that it confirms the belief in question.

Their habitual ignoring and mistreatment of their body is facilitated by a mistake in their measuring process, in which they confuse their body with their will. When a person in the aggressive pattern actually does measure their body, they feel vulnerable, which they hate. It blows their illusion of invincibility. So they avoid measuring their body and switch to measuring their will. While their body is limited, their will is immense, so instead of measuring their body's capacity to do the task, they measure their will to do it. Because of this mistake in measuring, they tend to push themselves too fast and too far. They often push their survival right to the edge. When completely boxed in, they may even choose death over feeling their body and their needs.

Aggressive-patterned people also habitually neglect to measure the bodily limitations and capacities of others. They think to themselves, *"If I can do it, you can do it,"* which leads them to make irrational demands of others, like *"It's only a broken ankle! Walk it off!"* Being treated this way usually puts others into overwhelm and makes them want to avoid those who run the aggressive pattern.

The value of referencing and measuring

The above list of problems demonstrates how important referencing and measuring are to good self-care and navigating skillfully through life. In order to get accurate information, you must be able to reference what you're measuring. If you're measuring yourself, you must be able to reference your own core to get an accurate reading. If you're measuring others, you must be able to actually sense them.

Also, you must be able to set aside any agenda you have and put your attention on perceiving what is really there, not on confirming your agenda. This is where aggressive-patterned people go astray. They habitually distort the measuring process to support their own agendas.

Patterned Thoughts

The mind chatter of someone who does the aggressive pattern is *"I can and I will."* They see their personal will as the source of their great ability, even more than their strength. They celebrate the triumph of their personal will with thoughts like, *"It's all a matter of will"* and *"It has to be hard to be good."* Their other habitual thoughts are those related to getting one-up on others, such as *"I am superior"* and *"You're stupid, weak, wrong, etc.,"* along with those related to not trusting others, such as, *"I knew I couldn't trust you."*

You may recall that each of the survival patterns has a characteristic sequence of thoughts that arise on seeing that someone else has something that they want. For instance, for the leaving pattern, the sequence goes something like *"You have it. I want it. I'll just imagine I have it."* For the merging pattern, it goes more like *"You have it. I want it. I'll get you to give it to me."* For the enduring pattern, it is most often *"You have it. I want it. I've failed."* Here, for the aggressive pattern, the sequence is *"You have it. I want it. I'll take it."* No messing around with how anyone feels about it — just a strong, direct intention to get it. For aggressive-patterned people, desire leads directly to action.

Patterned Behaviors

People who run the aggressive pattern tend to do things in big ways, even without intending to. They naturally have a big energy flow, and they tend to be exuberant. A great example of this is Tigger in *Winnie the Pooh*, who is constantly bouncing up and down, boasting *"Bouncing is what Tiggers do best!"*

High charge and fast action

The bodies of aggressive-patterned people are habituated to a high charge moving into action. They want to build a charge and then immediately discharge it by using it to *do* something. Then, they want to build the charge again. They want action and more action, not feeling or contemplation.

Healthy Charge-Discharge Cycle

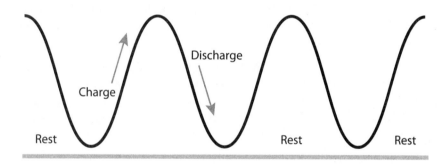

The Aggressive Pattern, Stuck in High Charge

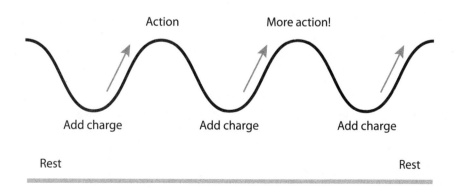

Aggressive-patterned people find it hard to just hold a high charge in the body, patiently let it ripen into a mature knowing, and only then act from the mature knowing. Exercising this kind of patience requires both solid grounding and a container strong enough to hold the charge while it ripens, and while people who run this survival pattern do have a strong container, they usually lack the grounding required.

They fear a state of low charge as a kind of weakness, so they cannot let their body rest in the low-charge part of the charge/discharge cycle, the part where it would naturally feel its needs and receive what it needs. This means that they cannot let their body move through the complete cycle of needing, filling, fullness, action, discharge, and rest. Instead, they try to stay perpetually in the high-charge part of the cycle. As we noted earlier, their holding pattern is *holding up*.

Being big and in charge

You may recall that each of the survival patterns shapes the person's attention in certain specific ways. With the leaving pattern, attention tends to go away from the here and now physical situation to other dimensions. With the merging pattern, attention tends to leave the self and fixate on everyone else and what they want. With the enduring pattern, attention tends to go inside and down and get stuck there. For the aggressive pattern, attention and energy tend to go up and out to claim and control the space around them.

As we noted earlier, aggressive-patterned people try to control themselves, others, and the situation in order to ensure their own survival.[9] They do this by making themselves bigger, stronger, and superior in some way, and by putting you down. This will often take the form of challenges and intimidation, such as critiquing your work, calling you names, devaluing you, or making you wrong in some way. If you can hold steady and meet them eye to eye and toe to toe, they will relax and accept you as an equal, but if you challenge them, they will up the ante and fight for dominance.

They enjoy wielding power and having an effect on others, but tend to avoid letting others affect them, since that would bring up feelings of vulnerability. Because of this, they often seek out jobs and situations where they can influence others from a position of authority, such as being a policeman, preacher, or professor. They also like to challenge themselves and others, so they gravitate toward competitive and dangerous situations, such as sports, firefighting, and the military.

Testing themselves

Challenging themselves often takes the form of testing their bodies by pushing them to the limit. Aggressive-patterned people can often be found out on some edge, pumped up on adrenalin and proving themselves by testing their bodies and their will. To see this behavior in action, go to YouTube.com and watch the film *Steep*, which is posted there in sections. *Steep* shows daredevil athletes skiing "unskiable" slopes with pitches steeper than 50 degrees, setting off avalanches that nearly kill them. When one of the skiers loses his gamble and dies in an avalanche, the other skiers simply take it in stride.

They are able to accomplish these feats because they don't listen to the body's feelings, but only monitor the body for life-threatening damage. As long as the body still functions, they are "good to go." They focus their will on what they want to achieve and then bend the body to their will. They perceive the body's signals and needs, but choose to ignore and override them. This is fundamentally different from the experience of people in the leaving and merging patterns, who don't clearly perceive the body's signals and needs.

This habit of pushing their bodies to the limit means that they are frequently in an adrenalized state. In fact, for many, it is their preferred state. They have become adrenalin junkies and may not feel alive unless they're staring death in the face. This is part of the reason that some soldiers who have seen combat are uneasy in civilian life and reenlist so they can return to the battlefield.

Testing others

People who adopted the aggressive pattern use their street smarts to rapidly size up others and figure out who has power and who doesn't — who is strong, who is smart, who has influence. They collect this information by (consciously or unconsciously) testing those around them for strength and truthfulness. The test is a pulse of energy that they send from their own core directly at the core of the other person. It's a lot like the ping used by one submarine to measure the distance to another submarine. Then they watch for what sort of energy pulse is reflected back. Is it a strong, clear echo that says, *"I see you and I am here."* Or is it a weak, fuzzy echo that says *"I'm sort of here; don't hurt me."* Or is there no echo at all, which says *"I'm not really here."*

If you're energetically sensitive, you can feel this pulse when you first meet them and they're sizing you up. The sensation can range from a tap to something like the heel of a hand whacking you in the middle of your chest. Often this energetic test is accompanied by a more obvious verbal or physical test, such as a challenge, an insult, an intrusive question, or a slug to the shoulder. The point of the test is to see how well you will stand up under attack — will you stand your ground or will you collapse? It is a comrades-in-arms test, designed to sort out the strong from the weak, the ones they can depend on when the going gets tough from the ones they will have to carry.

Needless to say, the experience of being energetically, verbally, or even physically whacked is unpleasant for everyone else. Unfortunately, those who are deeply caught in the pattern may do the testing so strongly that it is mean and hurtful, or even becomes outright verbal or physical abuse. Others typically don't understand the function of this testing, so they see only the abuse and miss the fear behind it.

Testing authority

Aggressive-patterned people will respect real authority (which for them means authority based on competence), but they will not respect authority based merely on someone's title or office and will test every authority they encounter to see if it deserves respect. This is just one more example of their need to constantly test themselves and others. They are also rebellious: they love to push the edge, break the rules, and blow out the container. So if you're in a position of authority, expect them to challenge you and cause trouble, just to see how you will handle it.

In group settings, aggressive-patterned people tend to put the rest of the group into fear. This is caused by many things: their naturally big energy, their aggressive style, their testing of everyone (especially the leader), and their moves to dominate the group. It is also caused by their unconscious habit of energetically tracking others the way a predator tracks prey. Sensitive people may feel this as a probing sensation or a slight pressure on them, and it will most likely scare them. The positive side of this tracking ability is that aggressive-patterned people are often able to track the flow of energy in a person, group, or situation, which is a very useful talent for anyone engaged in leadership or healing.

In any group situation, those with the most aggressive defense strategies will tend to dominate the group, unless there is a leader who is able to control them. If you're running a group, you must be able to control the aggressive-patterned members, or the group will not be able to function. Keep in mind that they want you to succeed. They need something bigger than themselves that they can trust, but they are also terrified that you will use their trust to hurt them. So they will need to test you — repeatedly — before they can trust you.

Pulling energy from others

When they get really scared and go hard into pattern, aggressive-patterned people will pull energy from any source, including everyone else in the room. To set up that possibility, they will do something that gets the others worked up and adrenalized. Then they will pull the charge in the room into themselves. This is a survival strategy, and their use of it shows how scared they are. They don't want to know that they're scared or see that they use others in this way, so if you're running the group, you will have to call them on it. You will also have to teach them how to connect to larger-than-human energy fields and how to pull energy from there, rather than from other people.

Revving up to fight

When facing danger, aggressive-patterned people shift solidly into their core and rev up their bodies with adrenaline. These actions amplify their will and energy as they move to assess the danger and meet it. This makes them good in a crisis: level-headed, competent, courageous, pragmatic, and able to take control.

These are the people most likely to actually go fight for a cause — to man the barricades, lead the charge, and sacrifice their lives. During the terrorist attacks on 9/11/2001, when the passengers on one of the hijacked airplanes counter-attacked the hijackers and the plane crashed in Pennsylvania, the men leading that charge were almost surely in the aggressive pattern. Aggressive-patterned people will defend the underdog from other aggressors, as long as he stays the underdog and does not challenge their own dominance.

Since they are comfortable and effective in holding and wielding power, aggressive-patterned people are often known as the Can Do people, the ones that others turn to for the initiative and courage to accomplish a mission. Their main limitation in this role is that they tend to believe that force is the solution to every problem. Many of those chosen as war leaders and generals do, in fact, run this survival pattern.

Of course, all this inflation and will still doesn't make the aggressive-patterned person's needs go away. His needs still exist, even though they are disowned, denied, and attacked. Even while buried in his unconscious, they still influence his behavior. You can gauge the depth of his woundedness by noticing how much he attacks and shames the vulnerability and needs of others.

Patterned Experience of Time

Aggressive-patterned people experience time as rushing into the future, so there is no time to waste. They need to act now!

Patterned Emotional Life

Ignored feelings

Since aggressive-patterned people habitually do not reference others, they often don't know what others are feeling. The feelings of others don't even show up in their awareness. They also aren't aware of most of their own feelings. Their unconscious intention is to survive, not to fully know their own inner experience. Since they see feelings of weakness and need as a threat to their survival, they usually suppress and ignore those feelings. So the emotional life of aggressive-patterned people is filtered and limited by their pattern. And, just like those caught in other patterns, they don't realize that they're seeing a filtered, distorted picture.

Projected fear

Instead of being felt, their fears are projected onto others. They see others as being weak and afraid, while seeing themselves as strong and confident. Their practice of intimidating others supports this projection, since it actually does create fear in others.

But they may not even be aware that they are scaring others, even though everyone around them knows it. Why? Because their fear meter is broken. Imagine that each of us is born with a meter inside us that registers how much fear we're feeling. A long time ago, in the situation where the aggressive-patterned person thought he was going to die, his fear meter was hitting the maximum reading. But you can't act if you're frozen in terror. So, as part of willing himself to survive, he just pulled the wires out of his fear meter and disabled it. Now, instead of showing zero when he's safe and max when he's in danger, his fear meter reads max all the time. The needle doesn't move, so it tells him nothing. And he's ignoring it anyway.

Having a broken fear meter not only makes a person unable to feel his own fear, it also makes him unable to tell when he's scaring others. So aggressive-patterned people are often completely oblivious to the fact that they're scaring those around them. And if you point out that they're scaring you, they'll typically say that you're being a wimp, instead of acknowledging that they're being scary.

Anger and blasting others

The default emotion of aggressive-patterned people is anger. Whenever too much energy hits their system and they go into overwhelm, they experience the extra energy as anger. You may recall that the default emotions of the previous survival patterns have been fear, shame, and guilt, emotions that make a person pull back and pull in, emotions that diminish the person's energy and capacity to fight for survival. Anger has the opposite effect — it adds energy to the person's system and makes him more able to fight for his survival. In a life-threatening situation, it gives the person more ability to survive. This surge of additional energy is part of the reason that those in the aggressive pattern are often able to survive situations that would kill others.

However, in most interpersonal conflicts, automatically shifting into anger and blasting the other person only makes things worse. It does not address the aggressive-patterned person's real needs, and it makes the other person even less willing to engage and trust. Unfortunately, aggressive-patterned people usually feel entitled to blast others at will. Their rationalizations and excuses are many, such as *"I can't help it," "you made me do it," "you deserved it,"* and *"come on, you sissy, it doesn't really hurt that much."*

In reality, their anger is coming from their buried needs, fueled by their terror of needing anything from anyone. But people caught in this survival pattern do not want to see this because seeing it would wreck their fantasy of invincibility. Instead of taking responsibility for blasting others, they want everyone else to just handle it. This is neither fair nor healthy. Blasting others is violent and abusive. A big part of the healing work for those who run this pattern is seeing the effect that their actions have on others, giving up their sense of entitlement, and taking responsibility for managing their own energy.

When they blast others, the explosion also serves to vent some of the charge that has built up inside of them. When the energy building up inside is becoming too much for them, venting it is a self-correcting mechanism, a way to down-regulate their system.

If you live with someone who does this survival pattern, you have to learn to defend yourself. And you have to demand that they give up their entitlement to blast you at will, because they won't until you demand it. Until you demand respect, they won't respect you. And until you demand respect, they won't trust you. Unfortunately, that's how their test works. Do you value yourself enough to fight for yourself? If so, they will respect you and value you — and maybe trust you. If you don't value yourself, they won't either. This is the law of the jungle, remember?

High-charge living

It can be exhausting and overwhelming to live with aggressive-patterned people. Even when they're not angry or upset, but just exuberant, the amount of energy that runs through their system can be enough to put you into overwhelm and trigger your own survival-patterned defenses. One of my clients expressed his dismay at this by remarking, *"My God, these people have no off button!"*

Interacting with Others

More than any other survival pattern, the aggressive pattern is defined by its interactional style. The wound was, *"I trusted you, and you weren't there for me."* From that, aggressive-patterned people concluded, *"I must never trust anyone again."* But they still need to interact with others, so their problem is: "What is the safest way to interact with others when you cannot trust them?" And the solution, of course, is to control them. Add to that the naturally big energy of those who run this pattern, and you have the defensive strategy of the aggressive pattern: dominate others in order to control them.

Their general approach to both relationship and problem solving is pragmatic. It's not moral, romantic, or personal. It's simple and straightforward: "What action do I need to take to get what I want?" Since force is their main tool and trusting others is not an option, their approach typically becomes, "How big and intimidating do I need to get to coerce you into doing what I want?" Or, it can become, "How do I charm you into doing what I want?"

With trust and love off the table, everything is seen as a task, rather than as part of a relationship. And in accomplishing the task, the question is not how you feel about it, but can you do it? Are you capable? Competence is reliable, even if relationships are not. So aggressive-patterned people value competence above all else. Because of this, they tend to test everyone's competence. If you are in any sort of relationship with a person who runs this survival pattern, expect to be tested.

As we said earlier in the section on referencing, people in this pattern tend to reference themselves, but not others or their needs. Their attitude is *"If you can't keep up with me, I don't want you on my team."* They will push you and themselves until they find the limit. If you have a limit, you have to tell them what it is because they won't reference it and won't notice it. When you tell them about your limit, remember to speak from your core, as detailed more in the section below on communication.

Others generally find aggressive-patterned people to be attractive, confident and commanding. At first, this can be very appealing, especially in men, but it becomes less so when you discover that they expect you to keep up with them.

Romance

People who are caught in the aggressive survival pattern are often found in romantic relationships with someone who is smaller, younger, weaker, and quieter — someone who is emotionally dependent on them and will not challenge their authority or strength. The partner's need maintains the emotional connection without the aggressive-patterned person having to feel his own need for it. If his partner does get stronger and challenges him, he will often attack, disempower, and reject his partner because the safety afforded by having power over his partner is more important to him than the emotional connection.

Recall that when they were children, aggressive-patterned people typically gave their heart to someone who failed them in their time of need. So as adults, they are wary of love, believing that it only makes them vulnerable again. A deep and emotionally attached love relationship will re-awaken their core terror because it re-constellates the experience of emotionally needing another human being. Because of this, people who are caught in this survival pattern often avoid falling deeply in love.

If they were betrayed as a child, they unconsciously expect to be betrayed again and project that betrayal onto others, so they often see betrayal even when it isn't there. When that happens, they need the other person to stand their ground and hand the projection back to them.

Generally, people who run this survival pattern are unable to trust anyone completely. They can trust only bit by bit, and they will test and challenge you as they open up each bit. If they decide you're safe, then maybe they can get what they want, so they may engage in a relationship with you. If they decide you're not safe, they will just disengage and drop you.

Sexuality

In terms of sexuality, the governing factor is that, to the degree that they're still stuck in the fight or flight response, their heart is still off-line. This means that sex may be more about feeling good than about emotional attachment. They are often highly sexual, but for them it may be more about feeling powerful than about feeling connected. When they have too much energy in their body — which is often — sex is a way to vent some of that energy. They usually want to be in charge of the interaction and may genuinely take pleasure in moving and pleasuring their partner, but they are less eager to surrender into being moved themselves. Surrendering to the other person brings up fear, so they typically avoid it.

Their Approach to Conflict

Unlike those who run the first three survival patterns, aggressive-patterned people do not avoid conflict. Some would even say they love conflict, and in fact, they have many reasons to do so. They love the challenge and the danger. During a fight, they get the excitement and adrenaline rush of battle, which makes them feel more alive. And they expect to win. Remember, these are the kids who won the battles of childhood, not the kids who lost.

They often have a history of being told they are "too much" or "too big." So, just to be accepted by others, they have had to pull themselves in and suppress their own energy. Fighting gives them a release from having to hold back and be small. It's an opportunity — and an excuse — to finally relax and run their energy at full throttle, which is exhilarating. For them, just letting it fly can feel like a huge relief.

They also get to vent the energy of any feelings they are suppressing (such as fear, grief, or shame), but without having to actually feel them. Instead, all those pent up feelings get converted into anger and allowed to burst out of the body during the fight. This venting feels cleansing to them and helps their system relax. Sometimes they will actively seek out a fight just to vent their pent up energy. If you've ever seen guys come into a bar on a Friday night just looking for a fight, this is probably what they were doing.

Escalating

When challenged, aggressive-patterned people will challenge back; when attacked, they will counter-attack. And they will not just meet you, tit for tat. They will up the ante. They will increase their energy, size, and scariness. They will stand up, inflate themselves, stick out their chest, broaden their shoulders, advance toward you, and get in your face to intimidate you.

They are generally very good at measuring how much pressure it will take to get you to back down, so their response may be well calibrated, but if they need to, they will escalate their pressure as far as needed to win. This can include becoming mean, threatening, or violent. They will not back down, unless that is the only way to survive. In the face of overwhelming opposition, they will strategically retreat. But they will never surrender, and will only rarely apologize.

Others are often surprised at how strongly they will react to even a small challenge. Why do they react this way? Because they unconsciously experience every challenge and every conflict as, potentially, a fight for their very survival.

They typically do not experience feeling afraid. Remember, their fear meter is broken. Instead, they simply experience more energy, anger and determination to win. Often, their reaction will look like that of a cornered, wild animal — but a predator animal, not a prey animal. Their reaction will be visceral and physical, a snarling display of tooth and claw, rather than a coolly reasoned rebuttal.

Weapons used in a conflict

The weapons aggressive-patterned people turn to in a fight are usually obvious, blunt weapons, not hidden or precise ones. They use the club, not the knife; carpet bombing, not a surgical strike.

Their anger typically takes the form of an energetic explosion or storm. It's big and loud, but not precisely aimed, and tends to flatten everything that's nearby. Sometimes it looks very much like a young child throwing a tantrum. During these times, it's easier to see that they are venting their terror, while not actually feeling it.

When they blast you, turn sideways. Don't take the spear in your chest or the force of their blast into your body. Intend for the blast to go around you, not through you. Imagine that your shoulder is like the prow of a ship and that it divides the big wave of energy coming toward you, forcing it to go around you, rather than through you.

The blast goes out horizontally, so another way to avoid it is to energetically go either up or down, if you can. The enduring pattern's talent of hunkering down is very useful here. Imagine that you can drop down deep into the earth, where a blast on the surface won't harm you. Or dive under the wave of energy, just like you would if you were diving under a wave at the beach. If you don't have that talent, do what you can to duck and cover.

If you have the talents of the leaving pattern, you can use them to go up, but if you leave your body, the aggressive-patterned person will feel you leave, will feel abandoned and unconsciously terrified, and will blast you for that, as well. Most people find that either physically leaving the room or using one of the other strategies mentioned is their best defense.

Listen for the seed of truth

If you are able to stay present during the storm, try to listen for the seed of truth in their rant. The aggressive-patterned person is telling you about his feelings and needs, while trying desperately to not feel them. If you can hear that bit of truth and reflect it back to him, he may be able to hear it and recognize it. That will take some of the fuel out of his tantrum and may even stop it entirely. Aggressive-patterned people do orient to the truth, so if the truth is that their need has been heard and is about to be filled, their storm will lose its fuel. However, do not take onto yourself the task of managing their needs and their energy. That is their task and their responsibility. You can help them learn to manage their needs and energy, but don't make it your responsibility.

Their Difficulty with Apologizing

When asked why aggressive-patterned people so rarely apologize, one man who runs the pattern put it this way:

> *The creation of the pattern in my body involved completely abandoning my heart and shifting my attention to will and power. The original wound came in through the heart and my decision was, 'I will never let you do that to me again. I will not allow my heart to be broken like that again, so my heart will never again be available.'*
>
> *So then my energy all went to being really big and strong, and my heart closed. And then I became unable, literally unable, to feel other people's feelings. I couldn't tell if I had hurt somebody. I couldn't tell if I had terrified somebody. I could only track my own feeling state, and not very well, because I was mostly numb to hurt and fear in me, too. The whole mechanism for protecting myself depends on not being able to feel pain or fear, mine or anybody else's. That numbness keeps me safe.*

In order to apologize, I have to let go of that entire self-protection mechanism. In order to apologize, I have to let myself realize that I just hurt somebody and that they actually have feelings, and that awareness had been totally gone before. And that their feelings are important, which had also been totally gone before. And that I don't have some special privilege to just go around nuking anybody who pisses me off.

And the request to let go of that protection makes me feel so naked and so vulnerable. It's like I lose all the protection that I have in the world. My protection is that my heart is closed. To apologize, I have to re-open my heart. I have to reconnect with another human being. I have to notice this trail of dead bodies behind me, this wake of destruction. And I have to realize how incredibly unskillful I am at seeing what's going on with other people and what they need. And that's a very hard doorway to walk through.

Essentially, they have armored themselves with numbness, and when that armor first cracks, all they can feel is their own distress. That, by itself, is over-whelming and all that they can manage. It feels like their very survival is at stake, so all their attention goes to their own distress and survival. Before the armor cracks, they really are convinced that they are invulnerable and nothing can hurt them. But the moment they re-open their heart, that conviction dies and they become vulnerable again. And then the original heartbreak — and all the heartbreaks since — start pushing back up into consciousness, creating a huge wave of vulnerability and pain.

It is only after much of their own distress is healed and they are in a more stable place, a place where their own survival is secure, that they can pay attention to anyone else's needs. If they can't get to a safe, stable place, they will go right back into pattern and flare again, attempting to protect themselves. Of course, this only exacerbates the problem.

So the question — *"Why don't you just apologize?"* — feels to them like an invitation to commit suicide. Opening that door looks like it will threaten their very survival, and their pattern's main focus is on ensuring their survival. So until an aggressive-patterned person learns to tolerate feeling vulnerable and learns to soothe themselves, they cannot turn their attention to the distress they have caused others, and they cannot even begin the process of apologizing for it.

Communication Style

Aggressive-patterned people almost always have an agenda: there is something they want, and they are taking action to get it. Typically, their communication is part of that action. It tends to be strong, direct, and driven by their agenda. They may be trying to control the situation by influencing or intimidating you. They may be trying to charm you or persuade you to join them in their plan. They may be trying to prove you wrong and win the fight. They may be venting energy by yelling and storming around. Or they may be revving up the energy between the two of you to ward off their feelings of neediness or vulnerability. The one thing you can be sure of is that their communication isn't small talk: it is communication with a purpose.

The skills and talents of those who run this pattern often make them good communicators and performers. They have a compelling, sometimes even charismatic, presence. They use their will and their energetic skills to gather everyone's attention and move it to their agenda. As Anodea Judith puts it in *Eastern Body, Western Mind*: *"They can cajole you with sweetness, impress you with eloquence, command you with the clarity of their arguments, and stun you with their candor."*[10]

What makes their communication so compelling is that they speak directly from their own core to your core. This has an energetic impact on your system that is far more powerful than the meaning of their words. You feel the energy hit your body in the same way that a person standing in the surf feels the force of a large wave as it hits their body. The force of their energy hitting your system will very likely move you. It may organize you around their intention, as when a general is rallying his troops in the last moments before a battle. Or it may disorganize and incapacitate you, and make you surrender. Or it may put you into your own survival pattern's reaction. What is certain is that you will feel the force of their communication.

Communicating with Them

To get them to take you seriously, you must come as close as you can to speaking the same way they do. That is, you must be in your own core and speak directly from your core to their core. To do this, focus your attention on the core of your own body and bring your awareness into your core. Standing up may help you feel your own core and strength more. Stand firmly on your own two feet. Feel your own core from the inside and then speak from there. Send your words directly at their core, not off to the side somewhere. If you don't do this, they often won't give much weight to what you say, and they may not even hear you.

It may also help to somehow position yourself so that you are physically above them. One woman said that when she argued with her taller, stronger, aggressive-patterned husband, she always tried to get to the stairs and go up a few steps so that her head was above his. This gave her a little more size and sense of strength, and made him look up at her, instead of down on her.

If you want to be heard by someone who does this survival pattern, speak the truth, no matter how bad it sounds — remember, above all else, they are listening for the truth. They use the truth to orient themselves in the world, so they care a lot about the truth. They have a terrific bullshit detector, so you must be congruent; that is, your words must match what you really feel. This is critical. If you're speaking from your core, this will most likely be happening already. But if you have a hidden agenda and you're trying to manipulate them into it, they will feel that, become (unconsciously) scared, go into pattern, get angry, and then blast you.

Don't try to manipulate people who run this survival pattern. Remember, their whole system is focused on detecting manipulation and opposing it. They are not afraid of your anger and hatred, but they are afraid of being manipulated, so give it to them straight. You can say anything to them, as long as you are honest and congruent.

If you want them to pay attention to something, show them how paying attention to it benefits them and their survival. Remember, they are pragmatic, and they're organized around survival. Don't expect them to care about something just because you care about it. That may be true for your survival pattern, but it isn't true for theirs. Show them why what you want matters to them.

Their Way of Complaining About Something

When they have a need or a complaint, aggressive-patterned people will probably express it as a put-down. They won't mention the fact that they have a need, and they probably won't even be aware of it. What they will do is devalue whatever (or whoever) is not giving them what they need. They will call it names, or declare it to be stupid, weak, wrong, lame, incompetent, etc. If you're not giving them what they need, the put-down will be directed at you. If you can hear the need behind the put-down, you can respond to that and give them what they need. They will like that, even if they still deny the existence of the need. Your ability to hear their real need will also make them trust you more.

Their Way of Asking for Help

Before any of us will ask for help, we have to believe that help is available, that there is someone out there who wants to — and can — help us. Unfortunately, aggressive-patterned people do not have this kind of trust in others, as this is exactly how they were wounded. So it is rare that they will *ask* for help. Doing so puts them one-down and makes them vulnerable once again, so instead of asking for help, they will usually demand or command what they need.

When they go into criticizing or demanding, try to remember that their attack is covering a buried need. If the attack is aimed at you, you may be so thrown by the blast of energy and hurt by the put-down that you aren't able to remember this. But, if you're able to stay present enough to reassure them that you care about their needs, and then ask what they need, they may be able to find their way to it. However, you may have to weather an emotional storm first. Shifting into feeling their needs terrifies them, and they may need to test you to see whether you can really be there for them when they let down their guard.

Remember that this is a visceral reaction for them, not a logical one. In essence, you are dealing with a wounded animal. They are hurting, scared, and skittish. To help them, ground yourself deeply, stay quiet, and wait. If they're having an emotional storm, don't take it in, even if it's aimed at you. Turn sideways and just let it pass by. Imagine a shield around you that divides the current — the way a plow divides the earth — and makes it go around you, not through you. Remind yourself that it's not nearly as much about you as they say it is. But also listen for the seed of truth buried in their complaints and accusations. Somewhere in there, they are telling you what they need. By venting their terror and anger, they may even have solved the problem themselves. Remember, their anger is a self-righting mechanism.

Aggressive-patterned people seldom show their vulnerability, so most people don't expect it or know how to hold space for it. Most people also get so distracted by the emotional storm that they can't hear the need underneath it. If you are able to hold space for their vulnerability, weather their conflict about revealing it, and then hear their real need, you will become uniquely valuable in their eyes.

Making a Request of the Pattern

When making a request of someone in the aggressive pattern, you will need to do what was outlined above in *Communicating with Them*, that is, speak from your core and be congruent and honest.

Be concise

Don't beat around the bush with indirect questions like, *"I wonder, if it wouldn't be too much trouble, if you might, at some point, be able to find it in your heart, to _____?"* Aggressive-patterned people don't care about politeness, they care about truth and action. Trying to sift through all your politeness to get to the real request just makes them confused, impatient, and mad. The harder it is for them to figure out what you're really asking, the angrier they will get. Then their anger will distract both of you away from your actual request. So drop trying to be polite, and just tell them what you want. Make it direct, short, and clear.

Don't justify your request

Also, avoid justifying your request. If you get into "you should," "you owe it to me," "if you loved me, you would," and the like, you are making them less inclined to agree to your request, rather than more so. First, they don't care about your justifications. They don't feel bound by other people's rules or the social principle of reciprocity. If you give them a gift, they accept it as a gift, not as an obligation to give you something in return. If you later try to turn your gift into a trade by telling them that they owe you something for it, you're stepping on the third rail of their survival mechanism. They will think that you're attempting to manipulate them, the old survival terror of their early wound will flare up, and they will have to fight you just to protect themselves.

Secondly, when you start justifying your request, they are likely to feel challenged, which will shift them into automatically mounting a counter-challenge. Even in a situation where they would be happy to fulfill your request, if they disagree with your justification, they will need to fight and defeat it before they can attend to your actual request. To not challenge your justification would be to give away power and territory, thus making themselves weaker when confronted with similar requests in the future. They cannot allow that, so they will feel compelled to negate your justification before turning their attention to your actual request. Remember, they are always tracking the power dynamics of the situation.

Thirdly, your justification just diverts their attention away from your request. It is unlikely to persuade them, but is instead very likely to lead both of you off into a useless argument about the validity of your justification. They like to fight, and they're probably better at it than you are, so don't give them an excuse to go there. Keep your request concise and straightforward.

Their Response to a Request

Their response to your request will most likely be pragmatic: they will comply if they see that it benefits them, and will decline if they don't. Feel free to point out how it benefits them, but don't expect them to simply take your word for it. They will need to see that for themselves. When they do see how it benefits them, complying with your request will become part of their survival strategy, and they will want to do what you've asked.

Complimenting the Pattern

When you want to compliment an aggressive-patterned person, do your best to speak directly from your core to their core. If you're not present in your core when you state your appreciation, they may evaluate what you say as unimportant or untrue, and simply dismiss it. Or they may be so distracted by the fact that you're "not really there" that they can't even listen to your words.

You must also express your compliment in their language, by referencing what they value. They value competence above almost everything else, so they're more likely to feel valued if you remark on how well they did something rather than if you focus on how correctly they did it or how much fun you're having with them.

As with all things relating to the survival patterns, this is not a one-size-fits-all prescription. In addition to considering what patterns they run and what those patterns value, you'll also need to consider their personal values. If you watch their responses closely, you'll probably be able to tell when your compliment really hit home, and when it didn't.

Getting Yourself Out of the Aggressive Pattern

Whenever you realize that you've gone into pattern, your first job is to get yourself out of pattern and back to being present. The survival pattern is distorting your perceptions and your experience. In fact, your patterned response to this distress is most likely making things worse, not better. Once you're back in presence, you'll be able to find the best way to respond to this current situation.

Signs you're in the aggressive pattern

- you are throwing energy at others

- you feel a need to dominate others

- you're in fight or flight, revved up to fight

- you're not referencing others' feelings and needs

- you are referencing only your own strength and will, while ignoring your own weaknesses, feelings, and needs

The solution: You need to connect with something loving that is bigger than you and let it hold you.

To get out of the aggressive pattern

Connect with something larger than you that holds and protects you.

Exercise:

Bend your knees, take a deep breath, and focus your attention inside yourself.

- are you feeling fear? hurt? shame?

Shift your attention down to your connection with the earth.

- feel into the earth

- feel your connection with it

- send the anger and hurt and fear down into the earth

- ask the earth to send support and safety up into your body

- open to that and receive it

Shift your attention up to your connection with the universe and/or divinity.

- feel your connection with it

- ask it to send support and safety down into your body

- open to that and receive it

Remind yourself, *"I am safe. I am not alone. I have help and support."*

For more information on how to get yourself out of pattern, please see Chapter 13, *Getting Yourself Out of Pattern*, on page 358.

Remember, whenever you're in pattern, your first job is getting yourself out of pattern and back to presence.

Healing the Aggressive Pattern

The developmental need of aggressive-patterned people is to feel safe by being held, contained, and protected by something bigger than them — something good and kind, but also stronger and more capable than they are. Within this safety, they need to have all parts of them accepted, valued, and reflected back, especially the small, weak, needy parts. This is what will restore their trust in others.

Feeling held and protected this way will allow them to finish the developmental tasks of the rapprochement stage, which we discussed earlier. They need to heal the love-power split in their psyches by re-owning and valuing their love, heart, and connection to others, and then by integrating love and power within themselves. They need to become capable of feeling both strength and need at the same time.

In psychological terms, this integration needs to happen in two different realms. In the realm of size, they need to integrate their bigness with their smallness, that is, their strength with their vulnerability and needs. In the realm of connection, they need to integrate their oneness with their separateness, their unity with their individuality.[11]

Feeling defended and protected

In order to complete that process, they will need to have several profound healing experiences. First, they need to feel defended by someone else. This has to be a bodily, felt sense experience of being protected. Remember that their core wound was that they were *not* protected during a time of vulnerability, and therefore had to survive on their own by an act of sheer willpower.

A healing psychodrama can be set up in which someone is threatening the aggressive-patterned person and someone else protects him. Both the threat and the protection have to feel real to the person's body, so you have to find an area in which he really is vulnerable, even today, and a way of protecting him that feels real to him. If he is willing to accept the protection, his body will start rewiring itself, gradually relaxing into the safety of the protection. However, this will not happen all at once, but only bit by bit. He will feel somewhat protected, relax a little, feel some of his own need, become alarmed, re-check his protector, decide if it is okay, and then relax a little bit more. This cycle can go on for hours as his body digests the new experience of being protected and experiments with actually trusting this protection.

Feeling contained

Secondly, aggressive-patterned people need to feel energetically contained by someone or something that's bigger and stronger than they are, yet also kind and caring. Being lovingly contained shows them that they are not a monster who is too big and bad to live in human society. It also teaches their body how to contain its own energy and emotions. By giving them a model of power integrated with love, it shows them that they don't have to be afraid of their own power and that it can be integrated with their love.

The experience of being energetically contained also teaches the person that there are limits to what he can do and what is allowed. He will test the container, of course, and may even go into a full-blown tantrum against it, but if it can hold against his attack and not attack him in return, he will begin to relax and calm down. His body will finally feel met by something larger, yet loving, and it will feel safer.

By holding but not retaliating, the bigger container gains his trust. It can then teach him that there are limits and consequences to his actions. This is a crucial step that he missed as a child. A person who adopted this survival pattern needs to learn that he can be all that he is, without having to be all that there is. He needs to learn that it is better to cooperate with the world than try to rule it.[12]

Re-owning vulnerability and needs

As an aggressive-patterned person begins to feel protected and contained, he will also be able to begin to gradually surrender into feeling his own vulnerability and needs, asking for what he needs, and receiving it from others. This process may happen slowly over a long period of time, as it sometimes does in therapy, or it may happen rapidly in response to a life-threatening crisis, such as a heart attack or a cancer diagnosis.

Whether it happens slowly or rapidly, several key ingredients must be present for the experience to soften, rather than reinforce, his survival pattern. First, he must realize that this is something he cannot will himself through and that he needs this help to survive, since he will surrender only in order to survive. His is a strategic surrender, not a collapse. Keep in mind that some people who do this survival pattern will choose not to surrender and will not survive. That is simply their choice.

Secondly, some strong, capable help must arrive and provide what he needs. As always, he will not just accept the help; he will test it. If the helpers pass the test, he will relax and take in a little bit of the help he needs. Then that same cycling process will start: as he takes in some of what he needs, he will begin feeling his need more vividly, become alarmed, rev up, and then re-test the helpers. If the helpers again pass the test, he will relax and take in a little bit more, and the cycle will begin again.

If you are taking care of someone who does the aggressive pattern and he is continually testing and challenging you, it doesn't mean you are failing. It means you are succeeding. He is challenging you because, each time he touches his real needs, he feels terrified and has to reassure himself of your competence. Every time you pass the test, he trusts you a little more. If you were not passing the test, he would simply dismiss you and try to do it all on his own.

For this experience to shift him towards trusting others more, he must see that it wasn't his own competence, but something outside himself, that brought him through the crisis. Gradually, he will learn that there is something besides himself that he can trust, something that he can depend on to protect him and keep him safe. To heal their core wound, then, aggressive-patterned people need to feel contained, protected, and safe enough to soften down into their original wounding. They especially need to touch their frozen terror, sit with it as it melts, and let the terror pass through them. Eventually, they need to re-own all their feelings and vulnerabilities.

Since they originally disowned their inner child in order to survive, their re-owning process will include admitting that they actually do have an inner child, and that the child's needs are valid and important. Then they will need to take responsibility for managing their inner child and getting its needs met. This includes learning to ask for what they need, instead of demanding it, and learning to tolerate the frustration and disappointment of not getting their own way all the time. Gradually, they will need to re-integrate the inner child into their adult self.

As they do this, they will have to give up their idealized image of themselves as superior and super-competent, and return to seeing themselves as an ordinary human being. This will include learning to track their own weaknesses and needs, rather than just their strengths. Their patterned habit is to see only their strengths. To balance that, they will have to practice intentionally shifting their attention onto their weaknesses and needs. This includes feeling their body's limits and honoring them. It includes measuring what they are *not* capable of, rather than only what they *are* capable of. It means telling others about their needs, instead of about their capacities. In short, it means focusing on self-care instead of survival, and trusting that others care about them and will help them.

Anger work

With some of the other survival patterns, we've discussed how important it is to unearth the buried anger and release it. With the aggressive pattern, there is typically very little buried anger. It is already the emotion that is most frequently expressed and the one that the aggressive-patterned person feels most comfortable expressing. But it is being fueled by other buried emotions, such as hurt, fear, grief, and shame, and those emotions need to be brought to the surface and released.

There is one form of anger work that aggressive-patterned people frequently do need, however, and that is being physically contained while they let their anger rip. Because they could blow out their parents' container, even as a child, and have probably blown out lots of containers since, they are afraid that no container can ever hold them. They tell themselves: "No one can hold my energy. I'm too much. It's never safe." In order to finally feel safe, they need to feel held by a container that is stronger than they are. In many cases being physically immobilized is the best way to give them that experience.

During the 16 years that I ran men's groups, the need to feel held within a strong container would regularly arise in one or another of the men, including men who did other survival patterns. We would handle it by putting the man in the center of the room, standing up and surrounded by all the other men in the group. Everyone would grab an arm, a leg, or his belt, and we would immobilize him as much as possible. Then we would have him move a little so we could test our ability to hold him safely. If the group was not sure they could safely immobilize him while standing up, I would have him lie down on the floor, either face up or face down, with his arms and legs extended. This allowed us to use our weight as well as our strength to immobilize him. When we were sure that we could hold him and no one would get hurt, no matter what he did, I would invite him to let his anger rip. Even if he did not feel angry at the moment, being restrained like that generally made him angry. At first he would try a few different moves to test our container. Then, as he felt more and more safe, his full fury would come out and he would struggle against us until he was spent. During this process, he learned that his anger and strength were finite, and that other men who loved him could contain him and keep him safe. And he learned these things through his body, not his mind. (Although this example refers to a men's group, this exercise can be just as valuable when used with women or children. Just make sure that the group can safely immobilize the person, even in full-blown rage, so no one gets hurt.)

Because the group was composed of men who did all of the different survival patterns, they all got different things out of this process. Those who were afraid of their anger learned that it was not so scary. Those who just needed to release their anger safely were able to do so and then felt relieved. For those who were using their anger to cover up other emotions, their buried emotions usually came to the surface as soon as their anger was vented and they felt safely contained and protected. This last scenario is usually what happens for aggressive-patterned people. It is only after they trust the container to hold and protect them that their terror will surface. So for them, anger work is a doorway into finally experiencing their core terror.

Acquiring a felt sense of safety

As aggressive-patterned people dissolve their terror and acquire a felt sense of safety in their body, they become able to do something they've never done before: stop defending their own core and instead simply rest into it. This is an enormous change. It allows them to attend to their heart and their needs, rather than focusing on reinforcing their iron will. Now, they can allow things to simply move them. Instead of moving the world, they can allow it to move them. For the first time, they can take pleasure in letting go.

One word of caution: as aggressive-patterned people heal and the old buffering wears off, they will begin to feel very sensitive and vulnerable. They will go through a time when they feel like almost anything can shock them. They're not used to being so vulnerable, and it will scare them. This is a sign that they're getting down to their core trauma, and their fear meter is once again working.

As the pattern dissolves, their illusion of super-competency will also dissolve, and they may fear that they're losing their capacities. In fact, the only thing they are losing is an illusion. What they are gaining is the ability to accurately reference their needs. If they need something to reorient them, give them a challenge that will help them grow. For example, challenge them to measure their weaknesses, rather than their strengths, or challenge them to routinely ask for help. They like challenges, and they can use them as a way to orient themselves.

Learning self-containment

Aggressive-patterned people also need to learn how to contain their own energy. Until they do this, they are not safe for others. First, they must give up the belief that they're entitled to blast others. This requires admitting to themselves that blasting others is abusive and that no one "deserves it." It requires giving up the belief that they are superior and acknowledging that others are equal human beings, not just servants or objects for their use. As always with people who run this survival pattern, the decision to give up this privilege will be a practical one, not a moral one. They will do it only to get something they want more than the privilege of blasting others. For example, one man who ran this pattern asked his teacher how to handle a conflict in his love relationship. Knowing how he would approach making such a decision, his teacher seized the opportunity to lay out the choice for him in the starkest possible terms. She said to him: *"You can have this love that you value so much, or you can have the privilege of blasting her whenever you're upset. You cannot have both. Which do you want more?"*

The starkness of the choice startled him. He didn't want to believe it, but his teacher was speaking to him straight, core to core, and he couldn't ignore it. He spent a few minutes squirming and searching for some way to have both, but after seeing that her statement was true, he surrendered to the truth of it and chose to relinquish his right to blast people. He then found himself grieving for a week or so, as if he had lost something dear to him. This is not uncommon. As they give up their superiority and privileges, aggressive-patterned people may actually need to grieve for their losses, just as a child does when he gives up the freedom to tantrum at will.

Learning to contain their own energy also requires changing their internal relationship with their own inner critic. Instead of thinking that its voice is their own voice and allowing it to attack others at will, they will need to disidentify from their inner critic and then learn how to protect others from its attacks. This includes not letting it use their mouth to blame and criticize others.

Becoming a safe person for others to be around will also require that they become able to recognize when they are revving up and going into pattern, and give themselves a time out to cool off before they vent their energy by blasting someone. Usually this means going somewhere else for a few minutes and either venting or soothing themselves there. In psychological terms, it means learning how to down-regulate their system. They are experts at up-regulating their system by revving it up. To heal, they also need to learn how to soothe and calm themselves.

Learning to function from inner peace

For people who run the aggressive pattern, the final step in becoming able to contain and regulate their own energy is learning how to function without using adrenaline. This means learning to function from a calm, centered inner state rather than from an adrenalized, revved up state. For those readers who have studied the nervous system, it means functioning from the parasympathetic, rather than the sympathetic, nervous system. Functioning from this state allows them to finish the day or task with a full tank, instead of an empty one.

If you'd like to have a bodily experience of the difference between these two states, try the following exercise: First, rev yourself up and go for a short walk. This means shifting yourself into a somewhat adrenalized state to give you extra energy. If you live in the United States, this may feel normal, since the U.S. is an adrenalin-addicted society. If you're not sure how to rev up, try this: *turn the walk into a contest.* Make yourself walk faster than normal. Give yourself a goal that requires going faster than is comfortable for you. Your body will rev up to achieve the goal.

As you walk, notice your sensations and perceptions:

- *What are you feeling?*

- *Where is your attention focused?*

- *Is it on the world around you, or on your goal?*

- *How do your surroundings look to you now?*

After finishing your first walk, allow at least half an hour for your system to relax back down to its ground state, and then go for a second walk. This time, walk from a sense of pleasure, instead of a sense of task. Instead of hurrying, just stroll. Put your attention on your five senses and the pleasure of walking — just being right here, right now. If you are habitually in a hurry, this may feel very strange, and you may have to keep slowing yourself down and re-focusing on your senses each time your old habit kicks in and speeds you up.

As you walk from pleasure, again notice your sensations and perceptions:

- *What are you feeling now?*

- *Where is your attention focused now?*

- *Do your surroundings look different to you now?*

The world will probably seem different, and you may notice an unusual feeling of calm contentment in your body. This is the state you want to learn to maintain throughout the day, even as you go about your usual business and tasks.

Energetic skills needed

In terms of energetic skills, people who do this survival pattern are already pretty skillful at core and me/not me, so they mostly need to focus on grounding and holding their edge, that is, on containing their own energy. (For more detailed descriptions of each of the four energy skills, please see *Healing the Leaving Pattern* on page 103.)

Their human need and spiritual need

The human need of aggressive-patterned people is to once again feel safe in trusting and needing others, especially when they are in need and vulnerable. Their spiritual need is to re-connect with their own Higher Self and their own internal spark of Divinity. This will dissolve their life-long fear that their own essence is somehow bad or evil. As they heal the love-power split and re-own their connection to Divinity, they will realize that they, too, are fundamentally good. This frees them to see the goodness in others, as well.

For more help in determining which patterns you go into, please visit
www.The5PersonalityPatterns.com.

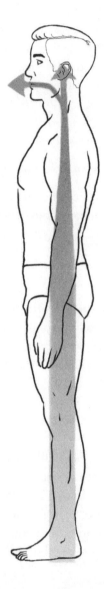

The Rigid Pattern – body and energy flow

– 11 –

The Rigid Pattern

"I am my performance. So are you."

LIKE ALL THE SURVIVAL PATTERNS, the rigid pattern is a holding pattern in the body, conditioned into it by trauma, which creates a particular habit of attention. The habit here is to shift attention away from internal experience and onto an external set of rules and standards. The emphasis is on correctness: both on being correct and on finding what is incorrect and fixing it. This creates a negative bias of attention: it shifts the person's attention away from what is right and toward what is wrong, away from satisfaction and pleasure and toward improving whatever is not yet perfect.

Unlike the first four patterns, this survival pattern is usually not precipitated by an identifiable traumatic event. In many cases, the child is simply indoctrinated into the Church of the One Right Way. If this is the only reflection she* gets from her parents and her community, she grows up thinking, "This is who I am."

To get a felt sense of what it would be like to grow up within this pattern, imagine that every morning of your childhood you stood up with your brothers and sisters, placed your hand over your heart, and solemnly recited in unison, "I pledge allegiance to the Rules and to the Standards which they protect.

---

* To avoid the cumbersomeness of having to continually say "he or she," I will assign a gender to the child described in each chapter and then stick with that gender throughout the chapter. For example, in this chapter, I will assume the child is a girl. However, all five of the patterns are found in both genders, and everything said about the girl in this chapter could just as easily have been said about a boy.

My own feelings and needs do not matter. I must obey the Rules." Although no one actually does this, it is very close to the silent, inner experience of those who adopted the rigid pattern. (I will capitalize "Rules" at times in this chapter to give you a sense of the almost divine authority that the Rules hold for those caught in this pattern.)

Range of Functioning

As with the other patterns, this survival pattern exists across a broad spectrum of functionality, from those completely ruled by the pattern to those who wear it lightly. The variation among those who do the rigid pattern is mostly in the amount of flexibility they have as they perceive and respond to the world. Lower functioning individuals are more rigid, while higher functioning ones are more flexible.

On the low end of the spectrum, we have those who are totally caught in the pattern: people who are very constricted, controlled, inhibited, and rigid in their thinking, feeling, and actions. Their life is strictly regimented by the rules they must follow. Any transgression of those rules is alarming to them. It must be corrected, and order restored. Often they preach their rules to others. The members of fundamentalist religious sects often fall into this group.

In the mid-range, we have people who still live within the worldview of the pattern, but their rules are much less strict. They may be able to tolerate much more diversity in the thoughts and actions of those around them, but they still believe they are right. They are strong in the skills and talents of the pattern, but still have a very strong need to look good and perform well. They have difficulty letting go into silliness, spontaneity, joy, or play.

On the high end of the spectrum, we have those who can generally stay present while using the skills and talents of the pattern. While they are still very aware of form and structure, they are able to see that the essence of something is more important than its form. Consequently, they value their inner experience and feelings over their performance. They often have an alive and vibrant energy about them.[1]

The Gifts of the Rigid Pattern

As a person uses any of the patterns, she continually practices the skills that that pattern requires. Over time, she becomes exceptionally proficient in those particular skills. As she heals the wounds that created the pattern and becomes able to shift her attention out of the pattern and back to presence, the abilities she has acquired stay with her and become the gifts of the pattern. Now she is able to employ her exceptional abilities as she responds to the needs of the present moment. Even though some of the physical structures remain in her body, she has shifted out of the patterned survival defense and into the gifts of the pattern.

The gifts of the rigid pattern are the gifts of form and structure. At their best, rigid-patterned people are Masters of Form. They love form and structure and often use them in their work. They can perceive and work with patterns in all modes of perception. When working with patterns of time, they have good rhythm and may be drummers or dancers. When working with patterns of space, they may be talented architects, designers, painters, or sculptors. When working with patterns of sound, they may be good with music and languages. They tend to be skillful with words and grammar, and are usually good at putting ideas into words. They are able to break the ideas down into parts and show how all the parts are connected.

They are also Masters of Order — of categories, lists, maps, systems, and analysis. They know how everything fits together, but have no need to force it. They give clear instructions and follow directions well.

When in the gifts of this pattern, they have a strong respect for social, cultural, and legal rules; they know the rules and understand their value. Because they are so aware of form, those in the gifts of this pattern are good at perceiving and respecting boundaries, whether they are psychological, spatial, or legal boundaries. They make a clear distinction between self and other, and usually hold a clear energetic boundary around them, which others can often feel. (When they are caught in the pattern, their energetic boundary is rigid and others may perceive it as "the Wall.") They also tend to make clear divisions of things, such as space, time, money, and resources.

These are the people who personify left-brain functionality. Their thinking is linear, rather than non-linear. They specialize in clear, logical, methodical thinking and reasoning, and excel in systematic thinking and analysis. This makes them very good at logical, sequential tasks and at solving problems.

At their best, rigid-patterned people have a strong, focused attention. It tends more toward a narrow or point focus, rather than a field focus, so while they see one part of the picture with exceptional clarity, they may miss the overall picture. They often have a large capacity to keep track of the details, and to be thorough and precise in everything they do. They are able to prioritize well, break large tasks down into smaller steps, and then put those steps in order and complete them, one by one. They are persistent and determined and want to complete any task they start. This is part of keeping the world in order. Their will is well developed and they can apply it to any task they engage.

Performing is important to them, and they want very much to be competent at whatever they do. They look good and perform skillfully and energetically. When approaching any task, they have a plan, and they are prepared to execute that plan. They are committed to excellence and can take pleasure in a job well done, even when there is no external reward or recognition.

They are responsible in most things, and are especially so in making and keeping agreements. They will fulfill an agreement just because they said they would. This is part of keeping things in order. They are typically on time for an appointment, and are often early.

The key to shifting into the gifts of this pattern is in learning to feel and value their own inner experience, in learning to "feel their way" through a process or situation, rather than think their way through it.

Examples

- Inspector Javert in *Les Miserables*
- Jessica in *Kissing Jessica Stein*
- Annette Bening's character in *American Beauty*
- Richard Gere's character in *Shall We Dance*
- the black and white town depicted in the movie *Pleasantville*
- Mitt Romney
- Hilary Clinton
- the archetypal librarian, trying to keep everything in order and everyone quiet

Alternate names

- Compulsive
- Industrious

- the Achiever

- the Disciplined Child

- the Hurried Child

Exercise – Being Caught in the Pattern

Seeing Only the Faults

This exercise is designed to give you a felt sense of what it is like to be caught in the rigid pattern, overly focused on order and correctness. As you go through this experience, try not to judge it, but instead just notice how familiar or unfamiliar this is, and what it would be like to live this way every day.

Sit down comfortably, with your spine relatively straight, and close your eyes. Take several deep breaths deep down into your body and release them. On the out-breath, let any extra energy flow out of your body on the breath.

Open your eyes again and read this paragraph. As you read, you may notice certain **misteaks** in spelling, grammar and punctuation. Notice how each of the mistakes seems to jump out at you off the page, saying "**Loook** at me**!!!**" To give you this visual experience, I have put the mistakes in larger bold type, but this is what **they they** look like all the time to someone in the rigid pattern. This is what it is like for them to read a book and come across a typo — at least it is if correct **gramar** and **spellling** were part of the Rules in their childhood.

Notice how difficult it is for you to just see the paragraph, without your attention going immediately to the mistakes. Notice how the mistakes just seem to scream, "Fix me!" In fact, when you first turned to this page in the book, didn't your eyes go immediately to the larger, bold letters? Welcome to the daily experience of those who do the rigid pattern.

And this experience doesn't happen only when they're reading a book, it applies to everything in their lives — at least to everything that is covered by their Rules. All of life is seen in this black and white, correct and incorrect, high-contrast way. To give you more of a feel for this, let's try looking this way at one of your acquaintances or distant relatives (but don't use anyone who is close to you, for reasons that will soon become clear). Pick someone and bring him (or her) to mind as vividly as you can — the way he looks, the way he sounds, and the way he acts. Take some time to let that picture develop in your mind.

Now let another image form in your mind, an image of the ideal him — the perfect him. Let that image become as vivid as possible. How tall should he be, really? How should the features on his face be shifted to make them perfect? How should the proportions of his body change for him to have an ideal body? What about his voice — how would his perfect voice sound? Different pitch? More resonant? Less nasal? And then there is the issue of his clothing: how would the ideal him dress? Better shoes? Creases in the slacks? A matching shirt? And, of course, there is his behavior: how would the ideal him behave, instead of the way he usually behaves? Take some time to let this ideal image develop fully, also.

Now take the ideal image and superimpose it on the image of him as he actually is, so that every difference is revealed, so that every flaw stands out with the same vividness as the larger, bold letters did above. As you look at him now, notice how most of your attention goes to his flaws, instead of to him as a person. Notice how every flaw seems bigger and more important than it ever did before. Notice how part of you suddenly wants to fix those flaws, wants to start making small suggestions for his self-improvement. After all, you like him, don't you? And wouldn't he be happier if he were more ideal? It's the least you can do to help him . . . .

Now take a deep breath, and let all of that go as you breathe out. If some of it remains in your body, take another deep breath and let it flow out of your body on the out-breath.

Now take some time to reflect on what you just experienced:

- *How easy or difficult was it for you to shift your attention to the typos?*

- *How about to the other person's flaws?*

- *Did it seem natural and easy, or did you have to push yourself to get there?*

- *What thoughts or feelings arose as you did it?*

- *What thoughts or feelings seemed to get in the way?*

- *What would it be like to live this way all the time?*

Exercise – The Gifts of the Pattern

Seeing the Inner Order and Structure

In the previous exercise you experienced being caught in the rigid pattern and seeing only the mistakes. Now let's shift into experiencing the gifts of the pattern. As you go through this exercise, just notice how familiar or unfamiliar these experiences are for you and consider what it would be like to have these skills and gifts always within reach.

One of the gifts of the rigid pattern is the ability to perceive the structures and patterns that are inherent in everything around us. For example, when reading poetry, a poet will often see or hear the rhythmic pattern of each line, as well as the rhyme scheme of the whole poem. When listening to music, a musician will often hear not just the melody and rhythm, but even each note within each chord, thereby hearing the inner structure of each chord. When inside a building, an architect or interior designer is likely to see not only the objects, but the rhythms and patterns of their arrangement. She may also see the spaces between the objects, and the patterns created by the spaces.

To get a sense of what the experience of seeing inherent structures and patterns is like, try looking at the back of your own hand. At first, you will probably just see a hand. But try looking more closely. Try looking at the tendons as you move your fingers. Can you see how each tendon is attached to a finger? Can you see how it transfers the movements of muscles further up your forearm as it pulls to straighten that finger?

Now try shifting your attention to looking at the blood vessels in the back of your hand. Can you trace the whole web of veins? Can you begin to see how the blood from each finger is gathered into larger veins as it is moved back toward your heart?

Now imagine that you can see the bones inside your hand. You probably recall how the bones are arranged from seeing models or pictures. Try pressing the fingers of your other hand into this hand and feeling the shapes and movements of each bone. As you move your hand, notice how much you can perceive of how the bones fit together and move against each other. What would it be like to automatically perceive inner structures and patterns like this all the time?

When listening to a lecture or presentation, you can discover the inner structure of the lecture by listening for the key statements and assembling them in your mind into an outline of what is being presented. When reading a book, you can highlight the key statements in each chapter, then re-read just the highlighted parts to again create an outline of what is being presented.

We can look at an example that may give you the experience of initially seeing only a tangled mass of information . . . and then seeing its inner structure emerge from the tangle and become clear for you. Turn back to the Principles page at the very beginning of this book and read through the Principles again. Now that you've read through most of this book, can you see how the essence of the entire book is laid out on those early pages? Can you see that the Principles are the inner structure of the map of personality described in the book? This is an example of seeing something's inner structure emerge from the whole.

Ask yourself:

- *Has this ever happened to you before?*

- *How easy or difficult was it for you to perceive the various inner structures and patterns we considered? The rhythms and rhymes? The chord structures? The objects and spaces? The structures in your hand?*

- *How easy or difficult was it for you to see how the Principles are related to the entire book?*

- *What thoughts or feelings arose as you saw these relationships?*

- *What would it be like to frequently see inner structures and patterns this way?*

The Origins of the Rigid Pattern

There are many routes an individual child may follow in adopting a particular survival pattern. As the needs of that child interact with her situation, she finds her own unique path, so generalizations are only generally accurate. They may explain most people's route to a pattern, but they cannot explain every case.

There are two paths that commonly lead a child to develop the rigid survival pattern. The less common situation occurs when the parents and the home situation are chaotic and unstructured, but this particular child needs the safety of an ordered, structured environment. In this case, the child adopts the rigid pattern as a way to bring more order and structure into her life. She herself creates the order and structure that she needs as a reaction to its absence.

The more common situation occurs when one or both parents are so caught in the rigid pattern that they over-emphasize rules and order in the home. Believing this is the best way to be, they require it of their child. The child then absorbs the rigid pattern in much the same way she absorbs her native language.

Developing self-trust

Between about three and five years old, as the child becomes increasingly able to exercise her own will and take action in the world, a new developmental need arises. Now that she can do many things, she also faces many choices. She can hug her brother or hit him. She can grab for the toy she wants or she can ask for it politely. Different actions lead to different consequences, and the child wonders, *"How do I choose?"* Now that she *can* do, she needs a way to decide *what* to do.

In the ideal scenario, her parents teach her how to choose for herself. They provide guidance, set limits, and teach manners, of course, but they also begin the process of teaching her how to find her own answers inside herself. At first, they simply reflect back to her what she seems to be feeling. By saying things like *"you look sad"* or *"you sound angry,"* they give her names for her feelings. As she grows, they give her choices and help her use her feelings to evaluate those choices. Gradually, they teach her how to find her own answers inside herself.

Through this process, she learns to reference her own body sensations and feelings as information to use in making her decisions. She learns that she can use her sensations and feelings as an inner guide for her decisions, in addition to the external guidance that her parents give her. As she makes decisions that are right for her, she learns that she can trust herself.

In order to develop self-trust and self-confidence, we all need to go through this same process. We need to learn to self-reference, that is, to reference the core of our body and our own feelings. That is where we can find our own answers to the basic questions, such as "How do I feel?" "What do I want?" "Do I like or dislike this?" "Do I prefer this one or that one?"

Learning to feel your own core and reference it in making decisions is the foundation for knowing and trusting yourself. It is the source of real self-confidence, the self-confidence that comes from confiding in yourself and knowing your own truth. Ultimately, the ability to reference your own core is the source of authenticity and the key to developing an authentic self.

When the child's inner life is not reflected back

However, what happens if the parents cannot see and reflect their child's feelings and essence? Remember, the child does not see herself directly; she sees herself through the eyes of her parents. Whatever her parents reflect back to her, she sees more clearly. Whatever her parents do not reflect back, she may not even notice. Simply by putting their attention on something, her parents are showing her that it has value and is important to them. By ignoring something, they are showing her that it is unimportant and does not have value.

So if her parents are blind to certain parts of her, she will tend to become blind to those parts of herself as well. If her parents are unable to reflect back her own heart and essence, it may be very hard for her to feel and reference those parts of herself. And if her parents are also unaware of their own essence and do not reference themselves when making their own decisions, she will have no model for how to do this. She may never even realize that such a thing is possible.

This is the core wound of those who adopted the rigid pattern: their inner life was not reflected back to them and they did not learn to reference it as a source of inner guidance. Instead, attention was focused only on their surface — on their appearance and performance — and they were taught to use an external set of rules as their guidance. So they live their lives trying to conform to those external rules, unaware that they are missing their authentic self and the guidance it would provide.

Like merging-patterned people, they did not learn to self-reference. However, they did not learn to other-reference, either. Instead, they learned to rule-reference.

Parents who are caught in the rigid pattern

Since rigid-patterned people often marry each other, both of the child's parents may be believers in the Church of the One Right Way. In that case, they both see this as a wise teaching and believe that this training is the best thing they can do for their child. They see indoctrinating their child into this survival pattern as a loving act, and they offer it in that spirit. The parents then conscientiously model these priorities in their own behavior and teach them to their children. They emphasize the rules and forms of life and the importance of performing according to them, but pay little attention to personal feelings or desires. The child is taught that there is only one right way for everything. Only the perfect performance is praised, and everything else is either criticized and corrected, or ignored.

A lot is ignored. The parents are not spontaneous, silly, or playful. They don't do anything just for the fun of it, just for the feelings it evokes. They actually fear play and spontaneity as being "frivolous" or "out of control." Often, they are uncomfortable with displays of affection or strong emotions. And they model this avoidance of spontaneity and affection and enforce it on their child.

Rigid-patterned parents often withdraw their heart connection from the child for any mistake or misdeed. Typically, the parents are not aware that they are doing this. Since they're not consciously tracking their own hearts, they do not notice that they have dropped their heart connection to their child. They think they're simply teaching the child what is proper, but when they move their attention from loving her to correcting her mistake, they close their hearts. The child feels the subtle loss of her parents' love and learns to correct herself in order to keep the heart connection and the love. Consciously, she may not feel any hurt, or even know that anything has happened.

A friend told me a story that shows how this scenario unfolds and how this survival pattern gets passed down from generation to generation. He said,

> My mother's father was a Danish Baptist, a pretty severe religion. I never met him, but from the stories I've been told, he probably did the rigid pattern. My mother says he hugged her only once in her entire life, when she was 28 and he knew he might never see her again, since she was leaving their small town to go to Alaska.
>
> She also told me that one day, as a young girl, she was skipping down the sidewalk in town and whistling to herself. When her father came around the corner and caught her, he reprimanded her for 'being so frivolous.' Apparently she took his reprimand to heart, because she never skipped or whistled as an adult. Instead, she adopted the rigid pattern, got really good grades in school, and became the valedictorian of her high school class.
>
> One of the things she learned almost perfectly was grammar and pronunciation, and I think she was proud of it, because she took pains to teach it to me. I learned it so early and so well that all those grammar tests in elementary school just seemed like a waste of time to me. The only answers I knew were the right ones, so every test was easy. For most of my life, I considered myself fortunate to have learned grammar and pronunciation so well and so young.
>
> It wasn't until I had done 20 years of inner work that I discovered I had also been wounded during those grammar lessons. The scene

that came back to me was from when I was about four years old. I had found some amazing bug in the yard and I was really excited about my discovery. I ran into the kitchen to show Mom and tell her all about my wonderful, amazing bug. My whole body was bursting with feelings and excitement about my wonderful bug. But, in my rush to say it all, my grammar wasn't quite right. So my mother could not share my excitement and my feelings and, instead, began correcting my grammar.

Looking back, I don't recall feeling hurt at the time. It was only one of many, many corrections. Instead of feeling hurt, I shifted my attention to what she thought was important. I concluded that 'my feelings don't matter, but my grammar does,' so I learned perfect grammar and adopted the rigid pattern myself. It wasn't until 40 years later, after doing a lot of inner work, that I could look back on that moment and finally feel the heartbreak that I didn't feel when I was a child.

This story illustrates how subtle the wounding that creates this survival pattern can be — how it can be mixed with genuine love, and how people who adopt this pattern often do not even notice their gradual alienation from their own inner feeling life, and therefore do not feel wounded at all. They may even feel lucky to have received such good instruction.

This is a different kind of wounding than we have seen before. There is not a severe, identifiable harm or traumatic event, as with the previous survival patterns. Often, there is no intense feeling to alert the child that something bad is happening to them. It's more a gradual indoctrination into the Church of the One Right Way and the Church of the Performance Self. Some who adopted the rigid pattern had a much harder time of it, of course, but this example shows how subtle the wounding that creates this pattern can be.

Not every child whose parents treated her this way goes on to develop the rigid pattern, however. A great deal depends on the child. As the child feels the constant drumbeat of criticism and correction, she will take one of two paths.

A more heart-centered child will feel the devaluation of her feelings as a profound wounding. She will feel unloved and will usually blame herself. She will be unable to abandon her feelings enough to perform according to the rules and win her parent's approval, so she will probably decide "I can't measure up" and "I'm not good enough." Such a child is more likely to develop the merging pattern.

On the other hand, a less heart-centered child will find it easier to abandon her feelings enough to win her parent's approval, so she will probably decide "I can measure up, I just haven't achieved it yet" and dedicate herself to constant self-improvement. She will also believe "I'm not good enough," but will think of it as "I'm not good enough *yet*." Taking this path will lead her straight into the rigid pattern. Ironically, this child will feel loved. In fact, she will believe that criticizing someone to help them improve is an act of love. She will think that, "Criticism is caring."

Because one or both parents often literally teach it to the child, the rigid pattern is more directly passed from generation to generation than any other survival pattern.[2] Like the other patterns, this pattern is created by a situation that prevents the completion of an important developmental task. The task missed by this child is the development of a felt sense of her own core and the ability to reference her own inner wisdom and feelings for guidance. Instead, she is trained to reference only outside authorities for guidance. Since her inner critic is an amalgam of all those outside voices of authority, it becomes very strong, and she comes to believe that its voice is her own voice.

The Inner Critic as Parent

Typically, a person who develops the rigid pattern has at least one rigid-patterned parent. While this is not always the case, it is common. Such parents relate to the child mostly from their inner critic, rather than from their heart. They see the whole world through a right/wrong, good/bad filter, with no shades of gray. They may have little empathy for their child and are able to love her only conditionally. For a young, defenseless child, this can be a very painful experience.

Criticism as caring

The parents' failure to internally integrate good and bad also means that their own "good enough" meter has never developed and they cannot perceive when something is "good enough." To them, only perfection is good enough, and anything less than that is nothing. Their internal belief is "Unless I'm perfect, I'm worthless." They then pass this on to their child as "Unless you're perfect, you're worthless." Since the parents cannot value their child as she is, she doesn't learn to value herself as she is. Instead, she inherits their perfectionism.

The child faces a general attitude of judgment and correction. Things are assessed, found to be imperfect, criticized, and improved, but they are not simply loved or appreciated. There is little wonder or delight in anything. Instead, there is constant criticism. The parents actually believe that they are helping their child become more perfect by constantly pointing out her flaws. This is the "criticism is caring" approach to human relationships. The parents' habit of constantly assessing and correcting her is all that she knows, so that is what she absorbs and how she learns to treat herself.

They cannot see their child as whole, but only as a good child or a bad child, depending on her behavior. Since she sees herself only in the reflection they give her, she cannot see herself as a whole being either, but only as a good girl or a bad girl. In trying to be a good girl and win their love, she adopts their habit of constant assessment and correction and turns it on herself.

Seeing the child as a project

Since parents who remain identified with their inner critic cannot value their own beingness, they cannot value their child's beingness, either. They cannot value and love her as she is. Instead, they value and love the idealized child that they are trying to turn her into. For rigid-patterned parents, improving their child replaces loving their child as she is. The child becomes a project, rather than a Being, and managing the project replaces trusting the child's natural growth and development.

However, since the parents are focused on their image of the ideal child instead of on their actual child, they are often unable to accurately assess her current stage and abilities. They tend to expect too much, pushing her into situations she's not ready for. As she tries to keep up, she gets ahead of her natural rhythm and timing, takes on too much responsibility, and begins to act like a little adult instead of like a child. In psychology, this situation is referred to as "precocious development," and it is part of what other authors have highlighted when they referred to "the Hurried Child."

Living in a police state

Since anyone's inner critic functions as a kind of internal policeman — enforcing the received rules and punishing unacceptable behaviors — having a fierce inner critic is a little like living in a police state. You have to keep yourself under tight control, because you live in fear of that knock on the door. When you have not yet disidentified from your inner critic, the situation is even worse because there is no "you" who is separate from the police — you are the police, and the police are you.

Rigid-patterned people typically have a fierce inner critic and remain identified with it, so its rules are strict, and they obey it without question. When they become parents, they're unable to tolerate in their child feelings and behaviors that break the rules, such as being self-indulgent, childlike, animal-like, passionate, sensual, or sexual.[3] Similarly, such parents are not able to relax and enjoy being fun, silly, or spontaneous, because this kind of internal freedom might lead to unacceptable feelings or behaviors. Although these behaviors are a natural part of childhood, the parents punish and shame the child for them, and she learns to avoid them.

Prohibited emotions and perceptions

Frequently the parents' internal rules also prohibit "negative feelings," such as anger, hatred, jealousy, envy, and despair. So those feelings are banished from the family and replaced by a false positiveness. The process of prohibiting and replacing negative emotions may be lightly or heavily enforced, but its effect is always to confuse the child and make her distrust her own feelings and perceptions.

Let's look at some examples. As a young boy, one of my clients marched into the kitchen one day and announced, *"I hate my brother!"* To which his mother responded, *"Oh, Sweetie, you don't hate your brother, you love your brother."* Since, at that moment, he was actually feeling intense hatred for his brother, his mother's response scrambled his internal feelings and confused him. Instead of getting help processing and resolving his feelings, he left the kitchen with an additional layer of internal conflict.

Another client described a much more extreme example. When she was about three, she saw a dog hit by a car and killed in front of her house. She became hysterical, and while one of her parents took her back into the house to calm her down, the other parent secretly cleaned up the carcass and the blood. Then they led her out to the street and said, *"Look. There's no blood. There's no dog. Nothing happened."* In their attempt to calm her, they were teaching her to distrust what she saw with her own eyes. Decades later, her self-distrust was still undermining her ability to function in the world.

Perfection as the goal of life

The wounding here is a manipulation of both the child's attention and the outer environment to give her the impression that she can be a perfect person in a perfect world. She then adopts her parents' conviction that perfection is the goal of life and does her best to achieve it.

Defensive Action

In order to keep her inner sensations and feelings muted and under control, the child must find a way to contain and constrict the flow of energy through her body. She does this by tensing her muscles and reducing her breathing. This lowers her sensitivity to inner stimuli and provides some protection from incorrect feelings, desires, and actions.

Over time, she learns to habitually restrict the flow of energy and sensations through her body. Whenever a feeling or impulse arises, it is checked for correctness. If it is not an approved experience, she tenses internally to suppress it. She learns to automatically contain all inner feelings and impulses in order to not have any incorrect ones. Instead, she does her best to feel, think, and act as the rules dictate. She tries to conform to the ideal self-image she has been given. She tries her best to be perfect. Instead of learning to *be* herself, she learns to *perform* herself.

Results of the Defensive Action

The consequences of this internal struggle for self-containment and self-correction are many. Let's go through them.

Tensing to maintain control

Inside, the rigid-patterned person is engaged in a perpetual war against her own natural, spontaneous impulses. She must maintain a constant physical and mental tension to control both what she experiences and what she expresses — and to limit both to what is "appropriate." She is unconsciously afraid that if she relaxes, something bad will happen and she will be in deep trouble.[4]

She is also likely to project her fear of freely expressing herself onto the world around her. The sight of others spontaneously expressing themselves makes it even more difficult for her to maintain her own inner control, so she often tries to stop them. Take, for example, the hellfire and brimstone preacher who feels a constant need to rail against "those fornicators." We may ask, where is his internal pressure coming from? Why does he have such an intense need to control the behavior of other people?

As she wages this constant internal war against her own impulses, she becomes overly disciplined. When her internal discipline is strong, there is usually little evidence on the surface of the battle within. Under normal circumstances, she feels no internal conflict and is unaware of the tension she carries. But when her strong internal discipline is weakened by alcohol, illness, or opportunity, her internal passions may suddenly burst out. This is the root of the classic rigid-patterned-person-on-vacation scenario, in which a meek, sexually-repressed librarian from small town America winds up dancing topless on a tabletop in a bar in Rio de Janeiro.

Developing a fierce inner critic

In order to rigorously police her impulses, her inner critic becomes very strong, sometimes even cruel and punitive. At a minimum, she remains identified with it, which leads to the effects already mentioned above. Since the inner critic focuses only on what is wrong, she develops a negative bias of attention, which makes whatever is wrong seem much larger and more important than what is right. She also views the world through a good/bad, black/white, right/wrong filter that emphasizes the contrast even more.

Needing to improve everything

The rigid-patterned person never develops an internal "good enough" meter, a deficit which leaves her believing that only perfection will do and that any flaw is damning. Since she is unable to measure the relative importance of a particular flaw to the whole endeavor, a single misplaced comma or misspoken word can ruin an entire project for her. Things lack proportion and perspective, and the imperfections seem huge, while the good parts recede from view. While this is a very useful perspective for a proofreader, it is not helpful for general life and personal happiness.

She comes to view herself, others, and even experiences as things to be improved, rather than delights to be appreciated. A correct performance becomes more valuable to her than self-expression or beingness.

Fear of making a mistake

She may also have difficulty making decisions that must be based on personal feeling.[5] Because she was trained to ignore her internal feelings and instead use an external set of rules to guide her in life, she has had no practice in using her feelings to make decisions. She has never learned how to reference her gut and heart to tap into her body's wisdom about whether something will be good or bad for her, or whether she even wants it. Instead, she was taught to reference the rules when making a decision. But what if the rules don't say anything about this particular decision? What if this is a personal decision that must be based on personal feeling, such as, "Do I love this person? Do I want to marry him?"

In such a situation, she may feel lost and be unable to decide. Then the fear of making a mistake becomes her main feeling, and she may try to avoid deciding by going into delay, confusion, or the analysis of irrelevant data. Rigid-patterned people want their choices to be clean and clear cut and will try to avoid any messy or murky decisions, if possible.

Performing well

This is the child that decides "I can do this" and devotes herself to performing well. She performs well in many situations and becomes a high achiever. She is very organized and productive, and others may well envy her perfect life in her perfect house with her perfect husband and family.

Abandoning self

To become the child that others want instead of the child she is, she has to abandon herself and ignore her own perceptions, feelings, impulses, and desires. Her self-abandonment is not coerced by violence or force; it is an act of love on her part. It is one of those gifts that children give so easily from their undefended hearts. However, on the unconscious level, she learns that a deep, open-hearted love requires giving up her autonomy and doing whatever the Beloved wants.[6] This unconscious belief will have a profound effect on her adult love relationships later on in life. We will go into this more in the section on relationships.

A vague sense of dissatisfaction

Because she is unable to develop an authentic self, she becomes "appropriate" instead of authentic. Correctness becomes more important than intimacy in her connections, both to others and to herself. There may be little joy, delight, wonder, adventure, risk, or spontaneity in her life. Barbara Brennan sums up the experience of rigid-patterned people well: *"The outer world is perfect, the inner psychological world is denied, and the core essence doesn't exist. Underneath the veneer . . . is the vague distant fear that something is missing and life is passing them by. But they are not sure. After all, maybe this is all there is."[7]*

Preaching

Often, rigid-patterned people try to fend off this vague sense of dissatisfaction and lack of meaning in life by crusading to improve others or themselves, causing them to become zealots of all kinds or self-improvement junkies, or both. In addition to being true believers in the Church of the One Right Way, they are often preachers of it.

In summary, as the rigid pattern is forming, the child learns to suppress her own internal experience and never learns to value its guidance. Instead, she learns an external set of Rules and comes to trust those Rules to guide her. As she becomes more and more focused on performing well according to those Rules, she joins the Church of the One Right Way.

The unfinished task of those who do the rigid pattern is learning to trust the self — to be authentic, personal, and spontaneous. They literally need to learn to feel their way through life.

The Rigid Pattern in Full Bloom

Body Signs

Since energy follows attention and the flow of energy in the body contributes to shaping the body as it grows, the habit of containing and constricting the flow of energy through the body actually causes the body to take on a contained, and even rigid, appearance.

Rigid-patterned people are typically athletic, fit, and active, and their eyes are bright and lively. Looking at them, we see that the body is slender, proportionate, and harmonious, with a sense that movements are integrated and coordinated, although they may be initiated from the periphery, rather than from the core.

There is a general tightness and tautness in the body; it is not loose or flaccid. However, rigid-patterned people are unable to perceive this tension, since they have nothing to compare it to, and no sense of what a state of real relaxation would feel like. They believe the tension *"is me,"* and cannot conceive of themselves without it. They may also have a rigidly correct posture — stiff and straight — rather than one that is more fluid or sensual.

Because of their constant internal self-censorship, the face may have a stiff, wooden look. Typically, they also have a tight or set jaw, and use the constant

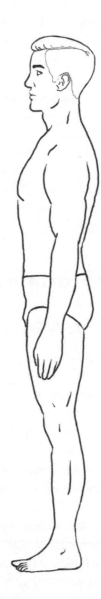

The Rigid Pattern – typical body shape

jaw tension to maintain control over what they say and express.[8] Most of the time, their anger is held in, but when they do express it, it usually comes out as biting words — another expression of the tension held in the jaw.

The holding pattern here is one of *holding back*, of not allowing incorrect impulses to reach the surface. To accomplish this, muscular armoring forms within the body, taking the shape of a hollow tube surrounding the core. The armoring forms a kind of internal wall that stops energy from moving either outward or inward. This effectively separates their core from their skin-level awareness, allowing rigid-patterned people to perform according to the rules without too many feelings or impulses from their core getting in the way. Since they cannot feel their core, rigid-patterned people will often report feeling "empty" or "hollow."

This inner tubular constriction is the physical manifestation of the person's inner critic, as it tenses the body to control both their inner energetic current and its flow outward into expression. This tubular wall is the most rigid internal structure created by any of the survival patterns. In addition to giving the body its taut, slender shape, this internal structure makes the rigid pattern the most static of the survival patterns, and the one that generates the most consistent, unchanging thoughts and feelings over time. In contrast, the merging pattern is the most changeable and fluid of the patterns.

Psychology

The main issue for rigid-patterned people is their lack of trust in their own inner experience as a source of both guidance and personal authenticity. Usually, they have no idea that they could have a self that is more authentic than their normal experience, so they may find this concept confusing. At the same time, their conviction that their present behavior is correct may be so strong that they will fiercely object to the idea that it is not authentic.

People who do this survival pattern typically have a strong, rigid ego structure. If we look at how tightly bound a person's internal psychic structure is, we can see a spectrum, extending from very loosely bound (with a porous boundary between inside and outside) to very tightly bound (with an almost impenetrable boundary between inside and outside). People who do the earlier developmental patterns, such as the leaving and merging patterns, tend to have a looser psychic structure and a more porous boundary. Those who do the rigid pattern, which is developmentally the oldest pattern, tend to have a stronger, more rigid psychic structure and an inflexible boundary. We can say that the rigid pattern is over-bound, while the leaving and merging patterns are under-bound. Just as those who run the earlier patterns need to develop more internal structure and stronger boundaries, those who run the rigid pattern need to soften their internal structures and boundaries and allow things to become more fluid and flexible.

The strong ego structure of rigid-patterned people is supported by a strong will. This pattern develops only after the will comes online in the child, because executing its survival strategy requires constantly using the will to control both inner experience and outer performance. As a result, people who adopt this survival pattern develop a very strong will. However, their will is not necessarily under their voluntary control. Often their inner critic, rather than their self, is directing their will.

Lacking a felt sense of self to express in the world, they substitute an image of their ideal self and express that. To make themselves conform to this idealized self-image, they exercise constant internal control over all thoughts, feelings, and impulses. This happens mostly below the level of consciousness, so they aren't aware of it. As far as they can tell, they're just naturally more correct and appropriate than most people. Without realizing it, they are performing themselves instead of just being themselves.

Their correct performance is maintained by a constant, mostly unconscious, process of self-containment, self-judgment, and self-correction. All internal feelings and impulses are checked for correctness, then ruthlessly suppressed if they do not pass muster. I have known rigid-patterned people who became physically ill from just beginning to feel a forbidden impulse or desire. It was only years later, after much therapy and inner softening, that they were able to bring the original impulse back up into conscious awareness and understand how ruthlessly it had been suppressed.

In general, the heart and feelings have been rejected and the mind has been assigned to do the heart's job: to answer the question, "How do I feel and what do I want?" For the mind, this is an impossible task. It can't feel or want. It can only check the rules for how it should feel and what it should want.

Referencing the Rules

This leads rigid-patterned people to develop a kind of referencing that we have not previously discussed. With the previous survival patterns, we have differentiated between referencing self and referencing others. Here, we have a third kind of referencing: referencing the Rules. In many ways, this unconscious habit of attention is the core of the rigid pattern. Instead of scanning their own internal state to discover *"What do I want?"* or scanning the internal state of those around them to discover *"What do you want me to want?"* these people scan the Rules to discover *"What should I want?"*

And, since the Rules are held in the superego — and rigid-patterned people mistake their superego for their self — they experience these as their own Rules, not something imposed on them from the outside. Their inner experience is, *"These are the correct Rules. These are the One Right Way, the way things should be."* To them, this One Right Way is obvious, and the failure of other people to see this obvious truth is baffling. The idea that other people don't really care about the Rules and don't use them for guidance is beyond baffling to them; it is unthinkable.

This constant referencing of the Rules shapes the person's entire experience of the world. Her attention doesn't go to "Am I safe?" or "Do you love me?" Nor does it turn toward fun or personal feelings. Instead, her attention habitually goes to "Is this right?" And since all perceptions are also fed through the right/wrong filter, everything in her awareness is perceived as right or wrong, good or bad, correct or incorrect.

This can actually cause a change in the person's visual perception of the world. I've heard several people who run this survival pattern describe this visual shift similarly. One man put it this way, *"The whole world looks like a drawing that shows just the outlines of things. All black and white, right and wrong, with no shading or color at all. A sterile environment of hard, sharp edges. It's almost like tiny black lines have been drawn on the entire world to emphasize the edges of everything, and then the color has all been drained out. The drawing shows where everything goes and how it functions, but there's no emotion or fun or heart."*

Obviously, this limits and distorts the world seen by someone who does the rigid pattern. But remember, some sort of filtering process goes on for all of us, created by our own survival patterns. We each see only a small slice of the entire world, and we each mistake our slice for the whole world.

Experiencing life through words

However, the rigid pattern takes this shift in perception one step further, in that people who do this pattern tend to experience the world through words, rather than through sense perceptions. Most people process their experience as sense perceptions, that is, as images, sounds, sensations, tastes, and smells. They experience the world and the self initially through the five senses, and then struggle to put their experience into words. For them, the words are only a way to communicate their experience to others, and the experience is often more complex and nuanced than they can find words for.

This is quite different from the experience of people who are deeply caught in the rigid pattern. They tend to experience the world at a slight remove, through their internal words more than through their senses. Because they were trained to ignore their body sensations and feelings, they focus on the words and often have little awareness of the underlying sense perceptions. When remembering the past, they tend to recall their experiences as words, rather than as raw sensations, sounds, images, etc. Instead of struggling to find the words to describe the immensity or nuance of their sensory experience, they already have the words. For them, it is the sensory experience that is missing.

However, they have no idea how much of the experience they're missing. The only experience they're aware of is the one named by the words in their mind, so the words needed to describe it are immediately available to them. When wondering why someone else seems to have such a hard time finding the words to describe an experience, they are likely to conclude that the other person is simply stupid or deficient in some way. One man described it this way:

> *During the first half of my life, I never had a feeling or an experience that I didn't already have the words for. The words came easily to me. As I watched other people struggle to find the words for their experiences, I thought that they were having this trouble because they were stupid or ignorant. It never occurred to me that people could have sensory or emotional experiences that were beyond what words could easily describe — it certainly hadn't happened to me. Then, sometime in my 30's or 40's, after a lot of inner work, I began having inner experiences for which I did not already have the words. I had shifted from being aware only of the words in my head to being aware of the raw sense perceptions that preceded the words. This blew me away. I had never dreamt of such a thing. Suddenly, all those other people didn't seem so stupid. Instead, it seemed like they had something that I'd been missing all my life.*

This tendency to experience life through words instead of through the senses makes rigid-patterned people very good at verbal communication, but also very lost outside of the verbal realm. The problem is this: the words are not the experience. Their over-focus on the verbal level tends to cut them off from the underlying sensory experience. When they stay within the mental boxes created by their words, they miss out on most of their actual experience.

As Alfred Korzybski said, "The map is not the territory." If you habitually substitute the map for the territory, you cannot actually experience the territory or learn anything new from your experience of it.

Beliefs

There is One Right Way for everything

The organizing belief for rigid-patterned people is that there is only One Right Way for everything. To those outside the pattern, this seems ridiculous, but to those caught in the pattern, this is simply The Truth. This belief may be so deeply ingrained in them that they aren't even consciously aware of it. Nonetheless, it is what organizes their entire life. These are the unquestioning True Believers who are so common in religion, politics, and many other walks of life.

More than those in any of the other survival patterns, rigid-patterned people think that their organizing belief is shared by everyone. They think that everyone agrees that there is One Right Way, but some people are just misguided about what that Right Way is. This makes them convinced that correcting other people's behavior is an act of service.

Living this Right Way is their goal. They believe that it is attainable and they very much want to attain it. It is their image of perfection — at least, perfection according to whatever version of the One Right Way they were taught. And in fact, many different versions of the One Right Way can be found, depending on which group is doing the preaching.

Sometimes they rebel against their parents' Right Way and adopt a new Right Way, along with its prescribed politics, morals, behavior, attitudes, emotions, style of dress, and so on. But they haven't questioned their core conviction that only one Right Way exists, they have simply adopted a new one. Whatever One Right Way they're following, they are driven to constantly improve themselves and others around them to meet the high standards of their chosen form.

Order is the source of safety

Another important belief for those caught in this pattern is that order is the source of safety. Consciously or unconsciously, they believe that disorder and chaos bring danger, so they must be avoided and corrected. These are the people who believe fervently that "Cleanliness is next to Godliness" and disorder is an offense against God.

Disorder therefore arouses anxiety, and they fear criticism and punishment for it. Restoring order is soothing. When they are upset, they often soothe themselves by cleaning and restoring order wherever they can. If their parents also did the rigid pattern, being dirty or disorderly probably did bring criticism or punishment. Conversely, if their parents were disorganized and chaotic, creating order may have been one of their childhood methods of creating some feeling of safety for themselves.

Mistakes must be punished

Punishing mistakes is part of the rigid-patterned person's attempt to restore order. If a mistake has happened, then disorder has happened, and whoever caused it must be discovered, assigned the blame, and punished. In rigid households, this is the normal and expected routine. If something bad has happened, blame and punishment must follow, so the hunt is on to find the offender.

Because of this, many people who do the rigid pattern get scared as soon as anyone anywhere makes a mistake. Fearing that they will be blamed, they try to protect themselves by immediately declaring themselves innocent and assigning the blame to someone else. On the other hand, if they suspect that they are indeed responsible, their fear may be intense, and they may become stridently defensive of their action. The idea that "it was just an accident" and "we can just fix it without punishing anyone" does not occur to rigid-patterned people, and if you suggest it to them, they will likely look perplexed.

You are your performance

Another important belief for rigid-patterned people is that you are what you do, that is, "you are your performance." Your value is in your achievements, not in your being. You are not loved for your beingness. "Love must be earned," and "only perfection is lovable." Again, this may have been literally true in their childhood, so their belief is based on actual experience.

Similarly, human connections and relationships are held to be less important than performance. Since personal connection didn't win the love and approval of their parents, they tend to believe that personal connections are not part of succeeding in life. This belief becomes especially apparent in the workplace because they expect it to be a cold meritocracy in which promotions are based solely on performance. When others are hired or promoted because of personal connections instead of performance or qualifications, they often become frustrated and gripe, "It's not right!"

Work has value; play does not

A related belief is that only work has value, while play does not. Rigid-patterned people believe they are not allowed to play until all the work is done, and somehow, the work is never all done. In extreme situations, they may not even take a break until all their work is done. This is supported by their belief that play is dangerous and scary, since something spontaneous might happen, allowing an incorrect impulse to leak out. So, to stay safe, "Everything is work, and we work all the time."

Only certain feelings are valid and allowable

When it comes to feelings, their belief is that some feelings are valid and allowable, and others just aren't. To be valid, feelings have to be reasonable and correct. Incorrect feelings are dismissed. Such a dismissal might sound like this:

"But I'm afraid of it."

"Oh, come on. You can't be afraid of a mouse."

The basic message here is "You are not allowed to have that feeling."

Another way of saying this is, "Feelings must be justified." When a person believes that she can't have a particular feeling until she has a good reason for having it, she will have to build a case for her feeling before she can express it. So when someone who runs the rigid pattern tries to describe her feelings, it often starts to sound like she is presenting a legal argument instead of a personal feeling statement. This need to justify her feelings also leads her into making excuses and blaming others for her feelings.

Personal feelings do not matter

One of the most consequential beliefs held by those who run this survival pattern is that their own personal feelings are not important. They believe that their feelings have no intrinsic value: no one cares about them, no one wants to hear about them, and they must be kept under control at all times. Their attention is on the *form* of their behavior, not on the feelings that motivate it. This is why they tend to appear formal and controlled.

Similarly, maintaining a heart connection with others is not important or expected. Their silent inner dialogue about heart connections typically goes something like this: *"Don't count on it. It's not a big deal. It's overrated."* Only the correct, appropriate performance is important.

Fears

Imperfection

Rigid-patterned people fear imperfection in any form. They fear any deviation from the approved forms and rules, and more generally, they fear failing, disorder, making mistakes, and looking foolish. Taken together, their fears boil down to a fear of criticism and the loss of love. Just like everyone, they want approval, but they do not expect to get it for anything less than a perfect performance. Usually, they were conditioned this way by a rigid-patterned parent who could not give approval for anything less than a perfect performance.

Taking the wrong action

The fear of making a mistake often leads rigid-patterned people to fear taking any action at all, lest it turn out to have been the wrong action. In a situation where the rules do not spell out what is right and what is wrong, they are thrown back on themselves for clues about what to do. But since their own inner guidance has not been developed, they have no mechanism for deciding what to do. Since they believe that they *should* be able to decide, they may have an inner critic attack and go into paralyzing self-doubt and self-criticism. Or they may turn outward and focus on collecting more data about the situation, hoping that some additional bit of information will tip the scale. If this works, they will arrive at a decision, but if it doesn't, they will go into the continuous loop known as "analysis paralysis." Either way, delaying the decision serves to buffer them somewhat from their fear of making a mistake.

Uncontrolled experiences

There is one other major fear that comes with the rigid pattern, and that is the fear of new, uncontrolled experiences — experiences like being spontaneously moved, falling in love, falling apart, and falling in general.[9] Experiences like these involve sailing into uncharted waters, going to places that are off the map and outside the rules, and possibly even against the rules. Allowing such experiences requires relaxing the strict internal control used to stay within the One Right Way, so it opens the gates inside and might allow some incorrect feeling or impulse to rise into awareness. And that could lead to doing something wrong. So those who run this survival pattern will typically avoid new or unplanned experiences.

Psychological Defenses

As with all of the survival patterns, the psychological defenses used by rigid-patterned people are all attempts to make some sense of safety for themselves in an unsafe world. Because this survival pattern is developmentally older than the others, it has more developmental skills and therefore more psychological defenses. Let's look at each one in turn.

Following the Rules

The most obvious psychological defense used by people who adopted the rigid pattern — the one that permeates every cell of their body — is following the Rules. They will rule-reference instead of self-reference almost all of the time. As they shift from self-referencing to rule-referencing, you will see them shift from the personal to the universal, from the concrete to the abstract, and from feeling (heart) to reasoning (head).

Creating order

Behaviorally, this involves putting things into their correct form, which means cleaning, ordering, correcting, and improving them. When rigid-patterned people are upset, they will often start cleaning and ordering things: washing the dishes, vacuuming, straightening up. Restoring order and cleanliness is soothing for them. Although it may have nothing at all to do with the real source of their upset, it is at least something they can control and put right, some part of their world in which they can restore order. They may not even be aware that they are unhappy, but if you see them suddenly begin zealously cleaning up, they're probably upset.

Planning and predicting

They will also try to keep everything under control by planning and predicting what is going to happen. If things unfold as planned, they will feel relaxed and happy. But if something unexpected happens, it throws them into internal disorder and upset. Typically, they do not like surprises (unless a surprise was part of the plan).

Correcting and punishing rule violations

Another side of their attempt to create safety for themselves by following the Rules can be seen in their response to violations of the rules by others. They will try to defend the proper order by correcting, criticizing, and punishing rule violations by others. As you see this going on — perhaps directed at you — remember that what you are seeing is also constantly happening inside them, as their inner critic constantly censors and corrects their inner feelings and impulses. The criticism aimed at you is only a fraction of the self-criticism going on inside them every moment.

All this correctness means that a lot of incorrect feelings, thoughts, and desires have been crushed back down into the unconscious. They still exist, of course, but they are denied, disowned, and attacked in both self and others. They are attacked in the self through self-criticism, self-punishment, and even, in religious zealots, mortification of the flesh. One example of this is the monk in the film *The Da Vinci Code*, who cinches a nail-studded belt around his thigh to keep himself in constant pain. This is extreme behavior, to be sure, but it is not so different from what happens internally for many rigid-patterned people. When they begin exploring their inner experience in therapy, they are often horrified at the violence of the mechanism inside them that crushes their incorrect desires back down into unconsciousness.

Their intense repression of incorrect thoughts and feelings is often assisted by projecting them onto others. This allows rigid-patterned people to externalize their inner, unconscious struggle and play it out in the outside world. Now they can accuse someone else of having the forbidden desires. Now they can righteously condemn the offenders and then offer to help them improve and return to the One Right Way. This is the main theme of zealots of every stripe: *"Something is wrong. But it is not in us; it is in them. We must correct it in them."*

Pride

A related defense involves taking pride in their own correctness and in how well they are following the rules. There is a real and lasting inner support and satisfaction for them in a job well done — in following the instructions and completing the task. This includes being personally clean, neat, well dressed, well mannered, and well behaved. While this usually simply supports performing well, in its extreme forms, this psychological defense can turn into a fanatical fastidiousness about minute details of dress and behavior.

Intellectualization

Their suppression of incorrect sensations and feelings is facilitated by withdrawing most of their awareness from the body and heart and shifting it into the mind. This allows the mind to declare that they are having

Rule-appropriate feelings and desires, without too much interference from the body.

Achievement

Another psychological defense used by rigid-patterned people is achievement. Since they do not believe that their beingness is inherently valuable, the only way they can feel personally valuable is by succeeding according to some outside set of standards. One way they do this is by performing well. A performance is "good" when it meets the accepted standard and receives approval from others. Common examples are making a lot of money, being critically acclaimed, and being celebrated for an achievement.

Another proof of achievement is winning a competition — any competition. It can be a playground foot race, a spelling bee, a debate, or the Olympics. It can be winning the game, winning someone's heart, getting promoted, or getting elected. It is a proof of value by comparison to someone else's performance.

In the film *American Beauty*, Annette Bening does a terrific job of portraying this need to succeed so that she can see herself as "a winner." She is a real estate agent, and in one scene she is preparing to show a house. In response to an attack of self-doubt, she faces a mirror and starts slapping herself in the face, yelling: *"I am not a loser! I am a winner! I will sell this house today!"* While this is a shocking display of external behavior, it is an accurate depiction of the internal violence that those caught in the rigid pattern use to keep themselves performing at the highest levels.

Being right or superior

Feeling valuable through comparison can also be achieved through being right or superior. This can come from any kind of comparison, as long as the person using it comes out on top. For instance, in morals, it might include proclaiming, *"My way is right!"* In a field of knowledge, it might include being an expert or simply a know-it-all who proclaims, *"I'm right!"* In sporting events, it comes from winning the competition and proclaiming, *"I'm the best!"*

In all of these situations, the victory may be very real and legitimately won. What turns it into a psychological defense is the rigid-patterned person's use of it as a source of value. Since she has lost touch with her intrinsic value — with the preciousness of her own Being — she cannot feel her own value and worth directly and must turn to a substitute source of value in order to feel worthy.

This disconnection from intrinsic value and the attempt to replace it with external value is not limited to people who do the rigid pattern. Most people experience this inner disconnection. And most people turn outward to achievement and approval for their sense of worth, but rigid-patterned people throw themselves into the task with exceptional zeal. Because their idealized self-image and their inner critic are so dominant in their psyches, they have a stronger inner need to achieve. And because they are developmentally older than those who do the other survival patterns, they have more developmental skills and abilities to apply to the task.

Staying constantly busy

Another defense mechanism used by rigid-patterned people is speed itself. Actually sensing your inner experience usually requires slowing down and taking some time to feel into it. That's why it's often said that "speed kills feeling." By staying constantly busy, rigid-patterned people are able to suppress feelings that would rise to the surface if they were to slow down and relax their attention. This attitude is codified in the old saying "Idle hands are the devil's playground," which subtly implies that personal impulses are the work of the devil. While those who run other survival patterns also use this defense mechanism, none do so as relentlessly as those caught in the rigid pattern. And because these people often use work as their method of staying busy, they tend to work a great deal of the time, which, of course, helps them to perform better and achieve more.

The Wall

The last psychological defense is one that you cannot see with your eyes, but that many people can feel with their bodies. This is an energetic "Wall" that rigid-patterned people often create around themselves. It will be several feet out from their body, and for someone who is energetically sensitive, the experience of running into it can be almost as palpable as running into a physical wall. It says, *"Stop. This is my boundary. Don't come in."*

Of course, everyone has (or should have) an energetic boundary in about this location. It serves the same function for the body that the cell membrane serves for the cell: it regulates what comes in and what goes out. However, a healthy energetic boundary is more permeable and flexible, and thus better able to adapt to changing situations, than the Wall created by rigid-patterned people. Their Wall is much more rigid than a healthy boundary would be.

Relationship to Self

People caught in the rigid pattern mistake their superego for their self. They do not experience their authentic self and typically do not even know that such a thing exists. It is not part of the approved territory within which they're used to operating, so they generally need help to even begin to experience it.

If they are aware that they do not quite experience themselves as real, they will welcome this help, although with some trepidation about where it might lead. If they believe that their performance is their real, authentic self, they are likely to defend that belief, possibly quite ferociously. They may assert that they are being authentic because they have a certain feeling, but when pressed for how they know they have that feeling, they will reference the Rules or something outside of them, rather than a personal, felt, body sensation.

Although they may experience a baby as being precious and innately lovable, they usually have no sense of themselves as being precious and innately lovable.

Relationship to the Inner Critic

In contrast to the leaving and merging patterns, which are clearly pre-verbal, the rigid pattern is a distinctly verbal pattern. It depends heavily on the development of the superego and its three components — the ideal self-image, the inner praiser, and the inner critic — which cannot arise until language and conceptual thinking have come online.

The rigid pattern develops in people who are strongly identified with their inner critic, and for most rigid-patterned people, that identification remains in place for their entire lives. When their inner critic speaks, they hear it as their own voice. In a sense, the rigid pattern is the result of an inner critic that over-develops and grows into the Inner Commander in Chief. It takes over the executive functions of the central ego and literally runs the person's life. It judges every thought and feeling and creates a constant need to become more perfect. When something is out of line, the inner critic attacks it. These attacks may be directed inside at the self or outside at others. When the person is in distress, her inner critic also attacks her for being in distress, which, of course, makes everything worse. Such an inner critic attack can be quite vicious. To redirect it away from herself, she may turn it outward and let it attack others.

The inner critic also censors thoughts, feelings, and impulses, typically not allowing incorrect ones to even reach consciousness. The process of self-censorship works like this:

Some personal feeling, need, or impulse begins to arise → before it reaches consciousness, it is checked for correctness by the superego → unless it is correct, it is ruthlessly crushed back down by the inner critic.

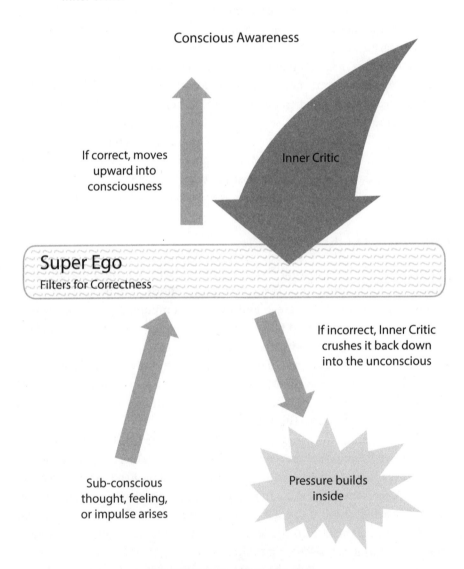

Conscious Awareness

If correct, moves upward into consciousness

Inner Critic

Super Ego
Filters for Correctness

If incorrect, Inner Critic crushes it back down into the unconscious

Sub-conscious thought, feeling, or impulse arises

Pressure builds inside

The Self-Censoring Process

If the rigid-patterned person feels this internal conflict at all, she only feels that "something is wrong." Her mind then begins searching for what is wrong, but it looks in the wrong place. Instead of turning to her inner felt sense to discover what is wrong, her mind begins comparing each part of her current experience to the ideal self-image that she holds in her superego. Whatever is not ideal is then highlighted and corrected by yet another critic attack.

As her inner critic continually crushes her feelings, impulses, and needs back down into unconsciousness, all that we see on the surface is her incessant criticism of self and others. However, if we are able to look deeply enough, we can perceive her inner struggle. To see her real self being crushed back down so viciously is heartbreaking. In therapy, when the client is finally able to perceive this violence within herself, she often bursts into tears.

Personality Traits

Now let's look at the personality traits of the rigid pattern. These are the way a rigid-patterned person will tend to look when they are actually in the pattern. When they are simply present and not in pattern, these qualities may be muted or even absent. At those times, they will likely still exhibit the gifts of the pattern, such as the ability to track details and stay organized. But when they are in pattern, their appearance will be more like what follows.

There are many different forms of the rigid pattern, depending on what was Right and Good in the eyes of their parents or teachers. So, a rigid-patterned person may be a conservative or a liberal, a fundamentalist or a socialist, a breadwinner or a stay-at-home mom, a leader or a follower, a prude or a tantric sex expert, a flower child or a nun. Again, it's not the particular form that defines the rigid pattern, but the substitution of the form and its external rules for the internal guidance of the authentic self.

The first thing you'll notice is that this person sees herself as the keeper of a set of Rules and Standards. She not only follows them precisely, but she wants you to follow them, too. You may also notice a certain formality in the way she talks and acts, as if she is guided more by protocol than by what she feels. She sees the world mostly in terms of good and bad, right and wrong, correct and incorrect — all according to her Rules. This emphasis on correctness tends to crowd out simply accepting and appreciating things as they are. Instead of delighting in the fun or beauty of life, her attention habitually goes to how things can be improved. Therefore, she can't easily appreciate anything less than complete perfection.

You will also notice that this person works very hard. In her eyes, the purpose of life is to improve self, others, and the world. It is a project to be completed. She believes that satisfaction will come *after* everything is completed and perfect, so she throws herself into action. When her efforts leave her still feeling unsatisfied, she concludes that she hasn't done enough, so she throws herself into more action. This creates a constant state of frustration inside her, as she continually expects the next achievement or improvement to bring a sense of satisfaction and contentment, but it never really does. However, she doesn't question her basic assumptions. She just works harder.[10] When under pressure, she will double and re-double her efforts both to do things right and to be right. When she can no longer contain her frustration, she will become judgmental and angry.

As she tries to contain her frustration and keep everything under control, you'll also notice a certain tightness about her. Such tightness is often present with rigid-patterned people. They are tight with money: they're frugal and prefer to save money, rather than spend it. They are tight with time: they're on time or early, and don't like being late (or others who are late). They are tight with order: they want things neat, clean, and in their place. And they are tight with praise and appreciation: they're not able to give much of it. Freud coined the term "anal retentive" to describe this tightness, but the modern slang is usually "tight assed."

Their hard work and effort pays off for them, however, as these are people who cope effectively with the world. They perform exceptionally well; they are active and ambitious, and are often seen as experts. They are clean, well dressed, and well behaved. They have a good job and a nice house. And they may well have a perfect spouse (who also does the rigid pattern) and a perfect family. The general impression is of a well-oiled machine, of a "human doing" instead of a "human being." Mitt Romney is a good example of this: by many measures, he looks perfect, yet there is a certain stiffness and lack of authenticity about him.

How They Recreate Their Early Wounding

As with all the survival patterns, rigid-patterned people tend to recreate their own early wounding by the very things they do to try to keep themselves safe. This process is unconscious, of course, but it is very effective in perpetuating the pattern by maintaining the kinds of relationships and experiences they had in childhood.

One way that they recreate their childhood wounding is by presenting themselves as their performance and achievements, rather than as their beingness, feelings, and needs. Then, when they are admired and loved for their achievements, it reinforces their belief that their being and self are not lovable. And since the love does not penetrate to their core, it feels somehow unsatisfying. They may then conclude that something is wrong with the relationship and move on, or they may try to achieve more, which just restarts the cycle.[11] Either way, their belief that they are lovable only for their performance has been reinforced, rather than challenged.

They also recreate their childhood wounding by continually correcting themselves, doing to themselves what was done to them. Actually, their inner critic is correcting them, but since they think their inner critic *is* them, they take it to be their own voice.

Patterned Thoughts

The rigidity of rigid-patterned people is not confined to their muscular tensions, but extends even into their ways of thinking and perceiving. When they are caught in the pattern, all of their thinking is done within a set of known categories, arranged in neat boxes within the mind. This habit of "thinking in boxes" requires fitting everything that they experience into these known categories. The categories already exist: they are all the categories of the known, approved world, and they have been inherited as part of the One Right Way — or figured out later in support of it. Since rigid-patterned people are literally unable to "think outside the box," all new experiences must somehow be stuffed into the available boxes.

Processing their experiences this way is both an attempt to keep everything in its proper place, and an attempt to control their experience so that nothing happens that would challenge the established order. When rigid-patterned people have an experience that they cannot fit into any of the available boxes, they experience a kind of internal earthquake. Their entire known world is thrown into question, and they are likely to become emotionally upset. When scared, they go even more into pattern, just as anyone does. As they go deeper into the pattern, they energetically contract, and the boxes in their head get even smaller and tighter. Their attention contracts to a point focus and they push even harder to nail everything down and cram it into the existing boxes. Often, furrows appear between their eyes as they become more and more insistent about HOW THINGS MUST BE.

Other people, whose thinking is more fluid and flexible, may find this thinking-in-boxes process frustrating and even physically painful. For example, one psychically sensitive woman reported that on entering the house of a person who was deeply stuck in the rigid pattern, she grabbed her head and cried out, *"Stop making boxes in my head!"* So, if you feel constantly boxed in when talking with a particular person, consider the possibility that he or she may be stuck in the rigid pattern.

The mind chatter of someone who does the rigid pattern is not *"I can"* or *"I can't,"* but *"I should"* or *"I shouldn't."* It is all about making things the way they should be, about correcting and improving self, others, and the world. Other frequent thoughts are:

"There is only one right way."

"What is appropriate?"

"It has to be hard to be good."

"If you want something done right, you have to do it yourself."

You may recall that each of the survival patterns has a characteristic sequence of thoughts that arise on seeing that someone else has something that they want. For the leaving pattern, the sequence goes something like, *"You have it. I want it. I'll just imagine I have it."* For the merging pattern, it goes more like, *"You have it. I want it. I'll get you to give it to me."* For the enduring pattern, it usually goes, *"You have it. I want it. I've failed."* For the aggressive pattern, it goes, *"You have it. I want it. I'll take it."*

Here, for the rigid pattern, the sequence is more like, *"You have it. I want it. You should give it to me."* So their request will not be a personal appeal to your heart, but a logical argument that some abstract Truth or Rule requires that you give it to them. It will include something like *"because you promised,"* or *"because we're family,"* or *"because that's what friends do."* Or, they may go directly to getting it through their own efforts. Then their sequence of thoughts will be more like, *"You have it. I want it. I have to work harder. If I work hard enough, I can get it, too."*

Patterned Behaviors

Focus on appearance and performance

When a person is in the rigid pattern, their attention goes to the outside world, not to the inner world. They focus on appearance and performance, on the surface of the body, not on the core or the heart. Likewise, their attention goes to the form of each activity, not to its essence. They are loyal to the form and will diligently execute it, even without understanding why the form is the way it is or how it supports the essence of the activity. As they practice the form, they generally don't know how they feel about doing it — that's just not part of their awareness.

Performing well is very important to rigid-patterned people. They are committed to excellence in all they do and will work hard to achieve it, even without external rewards like appreciation, fame, or even decent pay. Excellence is a goal in itself to them — not just as a means to some other end — and this can sometimes lead to conflict with others. First, they typically just don't understand that others can have different ideas about what constitutes excellence or a reasonable effort. Second, they often don't understand that others just don't care about order and excellence in the same way that they do. They unconsciously expect that everyone will want to work as hard as they do, and then end up disappointed when their expectations are not met.

Likewise, they value competence and want to master whatever they attempt. They will work relentlessly toward the ideal, perfect performance, even in trivial things, such as having all the dishes they're preparing for dinner finish cooking at the exact same moment, or vacuuming until there is not a single footprint or speck of dust left on the carpet.

Avoidance of change and missteps

Their general fear of mistakes and failures shows up in the daily lives of rigid-patterned people in many ways. For instance, they generally like to keep things the same, since that is known to be okay and correct. They typically want to go to the same restaurant and eat the same food. They may keep their furniture arranged the same way for years. They drive the same route to work each day. They pay bills early, sometimes on the same day they receive them. Trips and vacations are planned, not spontaneous. Since they fear that something could go really wrong if they allow sudden or dramatic changes to occur, they need all change to be gradual, so they can be sure that it will be okay.

When beginning a project, their fear of a misstep can also manifest as a need to see the entire path to their goal — every step and every detail — before they can take even the first step toward it. Many years ago, I saw this starkly displayed while working in a shop that built stage scenery. We received a large order for a complicated stage set, with lots of blueprints and plans. The owner, who ran the rigid pattern, disappeared into the office for three days to study the plans, while the rest of us sat around, idly waiting for instructions.

On the third day, his brother, who was the foreman and ran the aggressive pattern, reached the end of his patience and stormed into the office to get things moving. Through the closed office door, we could hear him yelling, *"In the time that you've been sitting in here getting ready, I could have built the damn thing! And if it was wrong, I could have built it again!"* Different patterns with different needs.

Over-responsibility

Rigid-patterned people also have a strong sense of personal responsibility for keeping things in order and making everything right. Often this leads them to take on responsibility for things that are beyond their control and not really their job. As workers, they try harder and work harder than do those caught in any of the other survival patterns, although they may get bogged down in trivial details and not work efficiently, as illustrated above. Some people caught in this pattern believe that they must finish an activity just because they started it — even reading a book or watching a movie — as if quitting part way through would somehow upset the Order of the Universe.

Organizing

People who adopted the rigid survival pattern are usually excellent at tracking details and keeping everything organized. They know where their car keys are, what time it is, and how long it will take to get to their destination. They often make lists to help them stay on task. Having someone who can track details and keep everything in order is necessary for every organization, and the person in charge usually wants to have someone like this within reach. CEO's, presidents, and even gurus usually have a rigid-patterned assistant walking a couple of steps behind them.

Solving problems

Since they are good at solving problems and get real satisfaction from finding the solutions, rigid-patterned people tend to see everything as a problem to solve. They approach problem-solving in an orderly, methodical way, analyzing what's before them and then logically deducing the answer. This is quite different from the way leaving-patterned people find a solution. They just go out to some other dimension and *get* the answer, rather than looking for it logically. They tune in to it, rather than deduce it. Watching two people who do these two different patterns solve the same problem, each in their own completely different way, can be amazing.

For instance, suppose that each one of them has lost her car keys. To find her keys, the rigid-patterned person will go back in her mind to a time when she definitely had her keys, then methodically walk forward in time, recalling everywhere she went and everything she did, even replicating her motions, until she locates her keys. By contrast, the leaving-patterned person will more likely go inside, psychically tune to the frequency of her car keys, call out to them, and listen for a response. Then she will follow that response, almost like the ringing of a lost cell phone, to find her keys.

Respect for authority

As we've mentioned before, rigid-patterned people have a strong respect for authority — for those who tell them the correct forms and rules. Because of this, they are very conscious of their proper place within any hierarchy of authority. They are respectful and obedient to those above them in the hierarchy, and strict with those below them. Because they feel more comfortable within authoritarian structures, they tend to gravitate to authoritarian institutions, such as the military, police, and strict religions.

Formalness

This emphasis on correctness, on following the proper Rules and Forms, often makes rigid-patterned people formal, even when others would be casual. It shapes every aspect of their behavior and makes it slightly more studied and proper than it would otherwise be. Watching this effect of the rigid pattern closely can give you a window into their unconscious, inner world, and especially into its preoccupation with correctness and improvement.

Their actions will usually follow whatever is the proper protocol. For instance, when greeting someone and choosing between a handshake, a hug, and a wave, they're more likely to be guided by the form that they've been taught rather than by a felt sense. To decide, they unconsciously ask themselves *"What's the right thing to do?"* rather than the more personal, heartful question, *"What do I want?"* or *"What would he/she like?"*

Their speech is also typically formal and correct, even stilted, which shows up in their grammar and word choices. Things are called by their proper names, not by popular substitutes or slang terms. They will speak in longer, more formal sentences, rather than shorter, more casual ones. Their speech sounds more like formal writing than casual talking.

Rating and correcting

People who run this survival pattern also feel an inner pressure to point out their own correctness and others' incorrectness. This is caused by their belief that becoming more perfect is — or should be — everyone's goal in life. Correcting others is therefore a way of helping them to improve; it is an act of caring.

Rigid-patterned people also feel an internal pressure to name *who* is to blame for something, even when the matter is trivial and the identity of the transgressor is irrelevant to what they are trying to say. This arises out of their belief that blame must be assigned, and mistakes must be punished, in order to maintain the all-important order of the world. Naturally, others notice this constant blaming and singling out, and often feel criticized, angry, or hurt.

People who run the rigid pattern also tend to rate both themselves and others on how good a job they are doing at self-improvement. When attempting to compliment a friend on a new behavior that they like, rather than making it personal by saying *"I really like how you did that,"* they will often phrase it as an impersonal rating by saying something like *"You're doing that so much better than you used to."* If the friend receiving this message is also rigid-patterned, she will feel seen and complimented. But if she isn't, she will probably notice the implied judgment and feel hurt.

Patterned Experience of Time

Rigid-patterned people are usually on time or early, since being late is a violation of the rules and therefore makes them anxious. In their experience, time marches rigidly and mechanically forward. It is not flexible or stuck or rushing ahead, as it is for other survival patterns.

Patterned Emotional Life

Anxiety

The strong need of rigid-patterned people to always be correct, and to always do the right thing, means that they live in constant fear of making a mistake. This creates a constant tension within them, a tension which they feel as a general sense of anxiety, and sometimes even as panic.[12]

This inner tension also manifests as a constant charge in the body. Because they can't express themselves freely, their discharge is restricted. This naturally causes a charge to build up in the body, which creates both a feeling of anxiety and a restless need to be *doing* something. The only way they know to discharge the extra energy is to take action and do even more. This is the mechanism behind their reputation for being relentlessly energetic, like the energizer bunny.

Merely being in the presence of disorder arouses anxiety in rigid-patterned people. Their inner distress is usually not expressed as a personal feeling of anxiety, however, but as criticism of the disorder and of those causing it. In order to notice their own anxiety, they would have to self-reference and feel their inner experience, and that is less comfortable than referencing the rules and complaining about rule violations.

On the other hand, restoring order is soothing for them. When they are anxious or upset, they will often begin cleaning and putting things in order as a way of soothing themselves. Their operating principle is "a place for everything and everything in its place," and if you visit their home, you are likely to see their CDs filed alphabetically by artist, their books neatly organized on bookshelves by subject and author, and their socks matched and paired in the bureau drawer. Women may keep their folded, matched sets of bras and panties arranged by color in the drawer, while men may have a pegboard in the garage with the outline of each tool drawn on it to show that tool's proper place.

Judgment and resentment

As we have said before, each of the survival patterns has its own default emotion, and the default emotion for rigid-patterned people is anger, which usually appears as some combination of judgment, blame, criticism, and resentment. Any time too much energy hits their system and they go into pattern, they will start to feel some form of anger. This anger does not necessarily mean that anything is wrong, only that they are in overwhelm, have gone into pattern, and need to start taking steps to bring themselves out of pattern and back to presence.

As the anger rises, however, it creates an inner conflict because feeling angry is against the Rules, unless it is clearly justified and righteous. So the anger is initially held in and denied, while the mind seeks a righteous justification. When one is found, the held-in anger bursts out in a torrent of judgments and accusations.

The anger usually originates in a buried need or desire, which is then expressed as condemnation or resentment of those who are allowed to have or do the forbidden thing. Seeing others enjoying what they are forbidden arouses their desire for it, and their condemnation is a way of both suppressing their own desire and venting their anger at not having it. So when they are criticizing you, look for the feeling and need underneath it and try to ask the person about that. They tend to reference the rules, rather than themselves, so when they want something from you, they're more likely to say, *"You should give it to me,"* than *"I want it."*

Suppressed feeling

Rigid-patterned people distrust and often suppress their feelings, so they may appear controlled and formal, or even cold and aloof. Remember, the rigid-patterned person's holding pattern is "holding back," in the sense of holding back the body's flow of feelings and impulses. For them, a feeling is not a starting place for exploring and expressing their inner life, but a part of their performance of themselves, so it must be done correctly.

Parents who run this survival pattern often discourage effusive expressions of feeling in their child, so she learns to maintain a "proper" restraint, rather than to express herself fully. If the parents are embarrassed by expressions of affection, they will most likely teach her to be embarrassed by them, also.[13] A child growing up in such a household may feel a lot on the inside, but since she doesn't get to express it, she doesn't become skillful at naming what she is feeling, or even at knowing *that* she is feeling.

Hysterical outbursts

Sometimes, however, a rigid-patterned person can no longer contain all the energy inside of her. Sometimes, so much energy builds up inside her closed, rigid container that the container bursts. When that happens, the pressure and feelings escape randomly in every direction, and she becomes hysterical. This sudden discharge is disorienting to her, and as she is swept away by her fears and fantasies of failure and rejection, she goes into an energetic spin. A great example of this kind of hysterical discharge happens in the film *Kissing Jessica Stein* in the scene where Jessica discloses her lesbian relationship to a close friend.

Even though this energetic spinning in the person's psyche is often very emotional and dramatic, it is caused more by the pressure being vented than by authentic feeling. It is generated in the head, in her fantasies, and not from her body sensations. In fact, this discharge process usually masks real feeling and body sensation. If you are attempting to calm someone who is lost in this kind of hysteria, putting your attention on her fantasies will only feed her hysteria and spinning. Directing her attention back to her body sensations will give her a real-world reference point that will gradually stop the spinning.

The hysterical explosions displayed by rigid-patterned people are fundamentally different from the explosions displayed by aggressive-patterned people. The aggressive-patterned explosion is a self-righting mechanism. It's designed to vent their internal pressure so that they can function again, and to pressure those around them into compliance with their wishes. During the explosion, the aggressive-patterned person stays oriented to reality and to what she wants and doesn't want.

By contrast, the hysterical explosion of the rigid-patterned person lacks both power and purpose. It does not restore the person to functionality or support her agenda. It's more likely to make those around her afraid *for* her, than afraid *of* her. It's the result of the rupture of her correctness container, rather than a purposeful act.

It is also important to note that anyone can become hysterical, whether or not they run the rigid pattern. However, hysteria is more common in those who adopted this pattern, especially in rigid-patterned women. Because emotional outbursts are against the rules for men, rigid-patterned men who feel overwhelmed are more likely to get righteous than to get hysterical. Each gender handles their emotions in the ways the Rules have approved for their gender.

Interacting with Others

The style of contact of rigid-patterned people is to be appropriate, which usually means that they are focused on performance and protocol. They are typically attractive, sometimes nearly ideal: trim, neat, well mannered, well dressed, and accomplished. They've had a lot of practice. For someone who grows up in a rigid-patterned family, merely participating in family life requires performing well.

People who run this survival pattern use agreements to organize their world. They will keep their agreements with you, and they need you to keep your agreements with them. When you don't, they become disoriented and distressed. And when distressed, they get even more rigid. As one man put it, *"I get inflexible. If we made an agreement, I need us to carry it out. Changing it upsets me. And when I get upset and try to enforce the agreement, it comes across as scolding."*

Since they believe that the purpose of life is improvement, they are likely to want to improve not only themselves, but also those around them and any organizations they are involved in.

Romance

In romantic relationships, rigid-patterned people typically want to improve both the relationship and the partner/spouse. In fact, they see helping the other improve as an act of love, since this is how love was expressed to them in childhood. One of my clients put it this way: *"During my 20's, I still believed that 'criticism is caring' and that loving someone meant helping them improve, so naturally I behaved that way toward my girlfriends. Because I loved them, I would correct their pronunciation and grammar, expecting them to feel how much I cared about them. To my surprise, they did not feel loved and cared about. They felt criticized and hurt. This confused me, since I was only trying to help. This was how my Mom had loved me, so why didn't they feel my love now? After a couple of girlfriends all said the same thing, I learned to keep the corrections to myself, but it wasn't until I got into therapy in my 30's that I discovered that criticism isn't really an expression of love at all."*

When a rigid-patterned person feels that some aspect of the relationship is not good enough, she is likely to turn it into a project and start trying to fix it. When her spouse feels the pressure of her plans and suggestions for improvement, he is experiencing what she felt from her parents. This is what was presented to her as Love.

And, when her lover is inappropriate or imperfect in some way, she is likely to drop her heart-to-heart energetic connection to him. Consciously or unconsciously, her lover will perceive this as a sudden loss of love. How he interprets the sudden loss of the love connection depends on his own history and patterns. For example, if he does the merging pattern, he uses that connection to orient himself in the world, so he will feel the loss of the connection deeply and may become disoriented. Then his own inner critic is likely to attack him, telling him that the love went away because he is inadequate and "not good enough." As he feels this criticism inside, he will probably think it is coming from outside, which will lead him to accuse his rigid-patterned partner of criticizing him. The partner replies that she didn't say a word, and since she is unaware of dropping their heart connection, she really doesn't have any idea of how she contributed to her lover's distress. As you can imagine, many fights get started this way. (In this example, "he" and "she" have been used to keep the roles as clear as possible, but the lovers could be of either gender or the same gender.)

Remember also that, in childhood, rigid-patterned people abandoned their own inner self out of their love for their parent(s). This was an unrestrained act of love on their part, and they learned from it that unrestrained feelings are dangerous and can lead to bad things. This belief is unconscious, but it fuels their need for restraint and caution in dealing with personal emotions as adults. In a love relationship, it often makes them reluctant to surrender into loving deeply and unconditionally. They are unconsciously afraid that unrestrained love will once again cost them their autonomy and obligate them to do whatever the Beloved says.[14]

Even when seeing their lover as perfect, their expressions of love and desire are usually controlled and appropriate, rather than passionate and impulsive. They distrust their own feelings, and the unconscious fear mentioned above makes them hold back. So instead of impulsively making some wild, passionate gesture, their attention shifts away to something safer, something more restrained and orderly. This doesn't mean that they don't love deeply, only that they usually don't get to feel swept away by it, and that their lover doesn't get the gift of their unbridled passion.

The three stages of love relationships

For almost everyone, falling in love involves some idealization of the beloved. This is a good thing, and it helps us stay in love with those we have chosen. But it also helps create the three stages that love relationships tend to go through, often called "romance," "power struggle," and "co-creation."

In the romance stage, you don't yet really know the other person, so it's easy to project onto him everything you want your lover to be. You then fall head over heels in love — but you're in love with your own fantasy lover, not with the actual other person. It's as if you've pasted a mask of your ideal lover over his face, so you can't see his actual face — but you sure do love the mask that you see.

As time passes and you get to know him better, you see more and more things that don't fit your ideal image. He leaves the toilet seat up or the top off the toothpaste tube. He doesn't get a joke or doesn't really share your politics. The mask slips a bit, and you struggle to put it back. You complain and try to turn him back into your ideal lover, but he repeatedly falls short. You try even harder to change him, and he tries harder to change you. This back and forth struggle to change each other is what marks the second relationship stage, the power struggle.

In order to move on to the third stage, known as co-creation, you have to get to know who the other person really is, let go of your unconscious hope that you can change him, and decide that he is good enough, as is. You have to shift from loving your romantic ideal to loving a mere human being. This last shift is a difficult one, and many people — no matter which patterns they run — are never able to do it.

However, this shift is particularly difficult for rigid-patterned people, for two reasons. First, their "good enough" meter isn't functioning. And second, they're engaged in a life-long romance with perfection itself, which they have devoted themselves to pursuing in every aspect of their lives. To now see their lover as flawed but still lovable would challenge one of the organizing principles of their life. In order to get out of this dilemma, they would have to do the inner work required to heal their core wounding and let go of their lifelong romance with perfection.

The pursuit of the ideal spouse

As long as rigid-patterned people remain caught in their romance with perfection, they will continue to pursue their rigid-patterned dream of having a perfect spouse. In that case, they have four options:

1. They can idealize their spouse enough to believe that he or she fits their ideal image. This means keeping the mask on their spouse forever.

2. They can marry an already "ideal" spouse, who must then keep up the illusion. Here the spouse agrees to wear the mask forever and, indeed, strives to keep it on. A spouse who also does the rigid pattern may already hold this goal. In pursuit of this, rigid-patterned people will often marry each other. They may disagree over particular rules, but neither one challenges the underlying premise that they should live according to the rules and try to perform ideally at all times.

3. They can have short-term relationships while waiting for the perfect partner to come along.[15] This may take the form of low-investment relationships with lovers who are clearly imperfect, but "will do for now." Or it may alternate with option # 1, in which they fall hard for someone who "is perfect," but then recoil when the mask of perfection slips. When their idealization falters, seeing the other person as merely human breaks the attraction and the relationship ends.

4. They can attempt to improve their spouse to fit their ideal image. Spouses who run certain other survival patterns may try to accommodate this improvement program, but they can't ultimately win, and they generally don't like trying.

There is a variation of this option that is healthier, although it is still dictated by the rigid pattern. In this variation, both spouses do the rigid pattern, but their quest to improve themselves, each other, and the relationship leads both of them to do enough inner work to eventually "break" the pattern and become capable of presence. On the way, however, their relationship will be focused mostly on doing the inner growth work, so spontaneity, play, and just being enough will often be missing.

Sexuality

In sexuality, maintaining the correct form often overshadows both tender feelings and passionate desire for those caught in this pattern. Sensuality and spontaneity are often inhibited, lest they lead to incorrect feelings or actions. Depending on the rules they are following, sex may be absent or mechanical, or alternatively, they may have studied to become sexual performance experts. Or, if their indoctrination somehow did not include anything about sex, this may be the one place where the rules *don't* apply, so they feel free to let go and follow their impulses.

Their Approach to Conflict

At the first hint of conflict, whether internal or external, rigid-patterned people contract inside, both energetically and muscularly, in order to contain and control themselves. They automatically clamp down inside in order to censor themselves and insure that they have only correct feelings and responses. They also become more logical and reasonable as they shift their attention away from their feelings and try to solve the emotional problem with their mind. If you're the one having difficult feelings, they're likely to develop a logical argument for why you shouldn't have those feelings, or why your feelings don't matter. Don't take it personally: they also minimize their own feelings through this same talking-yourself-out-of-it strategy. Infuriating as it may be for you, their minimizing of your feelings is not aimed at you, personally, but at controlling feelings in general. You're getting a taste of how they suppress their own feelings, day in and day out.

As they focus intently on solving the factual problem behind the conflict, their attention narrows to a point focus, drilling down into the details and pulling things apart to see how they work. This disassembly process is their habitual way of solving all problems, and it is successful in many situations. When it's turned on you in a moment of emotional vulnerability, however, you may find it piercing and distressing.

Since getting angry is probably against their rules, they will also unconsciously minimize and suppress their own anger. They will stuff it down and try to *be good, be good, be good* . . . until they can't contain it any longer, and it boils over. They may not even know that they're angry until they start saying it out loud and then hear it in their own words.

When it appears, their anger usually takes the form of judgment and resentment. The judgment relates to some rule that is being broken and often takes the form of criticizing or attacking whatever is incorrect or imperfect. The resentment arises from seeing that someone else is getting to have what they want, even though their desire may be unconscious.

Weapons used in a conflict

Since those who do the rigid pattern are skilled at focus and precision, these skills become their weapons. Their anger typically has a sharp, biting quality, and their weapons are pointed, precise ones.

Their attack is usually delivered in the form of pointed, biting words: words of criticism, sarcasm, or insult. The attack often has an intimate, personal quality, like a dagger to the heart. Or it may be more like a time bomb: a comment that detonates later when you finally figure out what they said. Or it can be more like poison, delivered as an insult that eats away at your self-esteem over time. If they have shifted from the hot anger of the immediate moment to a longer-term, cold anger, it may not even be said loudly. They might just drop a parting comment like, *"Did you really think I could ever love someone like you?"* Or the classic zinger from the door: *"And I faked all those orgasms."*

Rigid-patterned people are better at nailing you than those who run any other survival pattern. They have been keeping a mental list of your faults and vulnerabilities, so they know exactly where to slide in the dagger. Notice how different this is from the anger of aggressive-patterned people, whose weapons rely more on blunt force.

Those are the big weapons, however, the ones used during a major fight. Day to day, they're more likely to simply criticize you as they attempt to reshape you to fit their ideal image of a spouse, child, friend, etc. What you're hearing is their inner critic attempting to improve you, just as it does to them all day long. You're being treated to a dose of their own inner hell. Try to listen for the seed of truth in their criticism — they are telling you about their feelings and needs, without consciously feeling them.

Communication Style

Rigid-patterned people tend to use communication to transmit facts and information rather than feelings. They're more likely to communicate to solve a problem than to create a feeling state, such as joy, beauty, or fun. Their attention gravitates to accomplishing a goal or performing a task rather than to expressing a personal experience.

And even when expressing a personal experience, the person's unconscious habit is to rule-reference instead of self-reference, which causes her attention to shift from the personal to the universal, from the concrete to the abstract, and from feeling in the heart to reasoning in the head. This behavior grows out of her deep, unconscious conviction that *"My feelings don't matter, they're not important, only the Rules are important."* Buried underneath this conviction is a very young, tender, broken heart, but becoming aware of it requires considerable inner work, and even then, when she's caught in the pattern, she cannot feel her heart.

Those who run this survival pattern also have a tendency to use their communications to preach and lecture — mostly about how things could or should be improved. This is a natural expression of their automatic internal correction mechanism. They are just saying to others what their own inner critic is continually saying to them. But of course, others feel the judgment behind the preaching and wish it would stop.

Words — not feelings, pictures, or energy

Most of their communication is sent and received through words, not through feelings or psychic awareness. When listening to a song, they typically hear the words more than the melody. When they are listening to you talk, they tend to focus on the words you use, but not on *how* you speak them and the feelings behind them. When they are doing the talking, they carefully choose the words that will convey their exact meaning, but they aren't so careful about the inflection or tone that they use. Because of this bias, a person who does the rigid pattern may be completely unaware that her inflection is contradicting her words. For example, she might shout in an angry voice, *"I said I loved you, didn't I?"* and not understand why you don't feel her love. After all, it's right there in the words, as plain as day.

Because they don't intentionally broadcast or listen on any non-verbal channels, they often think that the words are *all* of a communication, and that there is nothing else. This means that they may not notice any other forms of communication — a look, a feeling, a burst of energy, a psychic picture — and are likely to miss what you send to them, unless you put it into words.

For those who are *not* rigid-patterned, the words may be only a fraction of the entire communication. For them, the words are a doorway into a feeling, a picture, or an energy field, which holds the meaning being conveyed. But for rigid-patterned people, the words are the beginning and the end of the communication. For them, the words themselves hold the meaning and are not a doorway into something else.

Unfortunately, most of us are completely unaware of the fact that words are used differently by differently-patterned people. Most of us believe that our way of doing something is the same as everyone else's way. Since we've never experienced anything other than our own way, we aren't even aware that there *are* other ways. Our ignorance of these different ways of doing things is the source of many a misunderstanding. Many fights between couples boil down to *"I told you!"* versus *"No you didn't!"* And both people are right, as far as their own experience goes. I see this frequently in my work with couples. Understanding the differences in their survival patterns — and the consequent differences between their communication styles — is the key to resolving many of these fights.

Communicating with Them

First, focus on your words — not your inflection, not your feelings, not your ability to psychically send pictures mind-to-mind. Rigid-patterned people speak words — they don't speak feelings or energy. If words are not your strong suit, you may need to practice keeping your attention on your words until you can do it well enough for a rigid-patterned person to understand what you're saying.

Secondly, do it the Right Way. That is, comply with the forms and rules they value. Consider their rules as you decide when and where you talk to them, how to begin, how to address them, and how to lay out the information that you want them to hear. Consider their rules when deciding how to dress for the conversation and even how close to them you should sit or stand. Remember that they have a spatial and energetic boundary around them, and that they need you to respect it. One man who runs the rigid pattern put it this way: *"If I'm in pattern when having a conversation with someone, part of me is paying attention to the word selection that they use. And if the word selection doesn't fit with what they're trying to say, it's hard for me to continue to listen because, 'wait a minute, that was the wrong word.' If the way the person is dressed is inconsistent with what's being presented, that also creates conflict in me. It's like my attention is magnetically attracted to anything that is not right."*

Respecting the rules and forms rigid-patterned people value does not mean that you're surrendering to them. It's a practical, pragmatic way of presenting your information in a form that they can receive. If you're violating the rules, they may be so distracted by the rule violation that they're simply unable to hear you.

Help them manage their inner critic

When communicating with people who are caught in the rigid survival pattern, you may also need to help them manage their inner critic and their fear that they will be punished if they do something wrong. You can help them out by agreeing with them whenever you can, even with small parts of what they say. Your agreement and validation calms their fear and quiets their inner critic, which may otherwise be yelling at them non-stop. After they've made their point, start your response with *"You're right"* or *"I can see that,"* or some sort of agreement, no matter how small. You don't have to agree with everything they've said, or even with their main point. Just agree with some small piece of it. Doing this helps them relax inside so that they can hear your response. Without some affirmation, they may be so distracted by an internal critic attack that they cannot even hear what you're saying.

If you're feeling constantly boxed in when talking with them, it's a sign that they've gone into pattern and are trying to organize what you're saying by making mental boxes. Their fear has made them go rigid inside, and has also made their mental boxes more rigid. If you have their permission to speak to them in this way, ask if they can soften their thinking for just a moment to let in some new possibilities. Make it a question, not a demand. Without making them wrong, ask if they might take a moment to breathe and expand, or maybe try to soft-focus their vision for a bit. Doing these things helps them soften inside and open up a bit to hearing something new.

Their Way of Complaining About Something

When rigid-patterned people have a need or complaint, they will probably express it as an attack on what they don't want, rather than a request for what they do want. They will declare that what they don't want is wrong, bad, inappropriate, or otherwise against the Rules. This is an example of how their attention shifts away from the personal realm and toward the Rules as they attempt to justify a personal desire. Since, in their world, the Rules matter, but personal feelings don't, they're more likely to present their desire as *"You should,"* than as *"I want."* They're building a case for why you *should* do what they want, instead of just *asking* for what they want. Listen for the personal feeling or need hidden beneath their complaint, and reply to that, if you can.

Their Way of Asking for Help

The way rigid-patterned people ask for help is essentially the same as described above. The request is likely to be voiced as judgment, criticism, blame, or resentment of what they don't want, rather than a request for what they do want. If their accusations are distressing to you, you'll first have to ground and calm yourself so that you're not distracted by the accusations, and then dig for what they really want. If they can't identify what it is that they want, you may need to help them find it. And since personal wanting may bring up anxiety in them, you may also need to fend off their inner critic and assure them that it's okay with you for them to have a personal want. This can be a delicate and tricky process. But then, each of the survival patterns has its own challenges with wanting, and each needs help to work through those challenges.

Asking for Their Help

When asking for their help, the first thing to know is that rigid-patterned people just love to help. Know also that they like solving problems and are very good at it. Problem solving is a form that works well for them, so tell them that you have a problem and ask for their help in solving it. If they agree, lay out your problem using "I statements" and without blaming, accusing, or criticizing them in any way. If you imply that they have done something wrong, you will activate their inner critic and derail the whole process.

After you've laid out your problem, let them wrestle with it and come up with a solution. This may take some time, but they will stay on it. They are good at this. When they present a possible solution, praise it if it works for you, or if it doesn't, at least praise their efforts. If their solution doesn't yet work for you, use "I statements" to say why, and let them wrestle with the problem some more.

Be aware that once you've engaged their help, they will tend to automatically assume responsibility for solving your problem. Unconsciously, it starts to feel to them like *their* problem, so if you want to retain control over how it gets solved, you will have to say so explicitly. It's okay for you to want to retain control, but they typically won't notice that they've turned it into *their* problem and are starting to take over, so things will go better if you say out loud that you want the final say-so on how it gets solved.

Making a Request of the Pattern

Suppose that you already know what you want a rigid-patterned person to do for you and you're ready to make a specific request of her — what then? Again, remember that giving you what you want counts as a success for her, and she loves to succeed. First, ask if it's okay for you to tell her what you want her to do. (By asking this question, you're respecting her boundaries and autonomy.) If she says "Yes," give her clear, logical instructions to follow. Tell her what outcome you want, why it is important to you, and *how to give it to you*. The *how to give it to you* part must be stated in terms of what behavior you want from her — exactly what you want her to do and say. Don't ask her to read your mind or figure out how to give it to you; instead, *tell* her how to give it to you. She wants instructions that she can follow, even if she doesn't understand them. So don't just say, *"I want you to make me happy."* Most likely, she's already trying to make you happy, but she doesn't know how. Tell her what specific actions she can take to make you happy. This will relieve her confusion and give her a clear path to success.

I once read a report of a couple's therapy session that elegantly illustrates the value of giving clear instructions as opposed to insisting on mind-reading (though it doesn't reveal what survival patterns are involved). The wife's complaint was *"He doesn't love me."* The husband asserted that he did love her and that he did everything he could think of to show her that he loved her, but nothing satisfied her. So the therapist asked the wife, *"How do you know that he doesn't love you?"* And the wife replied: *"Because he doesn't act like it."* Knowing that he could not read the wife's mind and did not know what behaviors she was referring to, the therapist asked, *"And how would he act if he loved you?"* *"Well, when he gets home from work, before he takes off his coat, he would come into the kitchen and give me a kiss and a hug,"* said the wife. *"And how did you learn that?"* asked the therapist, to which she replied, *"That's what my father always did."* Then it was a simple matter for the therapist to turn to the husband and ask if he would be willing to do that each night. Hugely relieved that he finally had the magic formula to make his wife happy, the husband immediately said *"Yes."* When the therapist asked the wife if that would prove that he loved her, she beamed and said it would.

This story highlights the importance of not expecting others to read your mind, but instead telling them what specific actions you want them to take. While those who adopted the leaving and merging patterns may have become quite skillful at reading what others are feeling and what to do to make them happier, those who adopted the rigid pattern did not develop those skills. So don't ask rigid-patterned people to read your mind — they just can't do it. Instead, spell out exactly what you want them to do.

Lastly, make sure to tell them how they can know that they have succeeded. They always check their work, and they will be looking for this confirmation, so tell them what to look for. Each time they see it, they will get a good feeling, and it will motivate them to continue doing what you've requested.

Their Response to a Request

Their response to your request will most likely be arrived at by referencing what would be correct according to whatever set of rules and forms they are following. They will rule-reference, rather than self-reference or other-reference to get their answer. In general, their answer will be polite, formal, and correct — according to their One Right Way.

Be aware that, if they are deeply caught in the rigid pattern, their personal desires and preferences were not even consulted, so their patterned answer now is no guarantee that they will not resent this choice later, as their personal feelings push against their correct response.

Complimenting the Pattern

Just as with each of the other survival patterns, when you want to compliment rigid-patterned people, you must express your compliment in *their* language, by referencing what *they* value and pay attention to. Since they value order and correctness, they're more likely to feel appreciated if you remark on how well organized or well designed their creation is, rather than on how unique and original it is. Since they value success and achievement, they'll probably prefer your congratulations on their success to your gushing on about how their success makes you feel.

It will also be easier for them to accept your appreciation if you make it specific and verifiable. They will not simply take your statement at face value — they (or their inner critic) will crosscheck it for accuracy. They probably have a rule that forbids claiming credit for things they didn't really accomplish, so you'll have to give them some proof, along with your praise. Give them some specific details about what you particularly liked, and don't take offense if they question you further about it. They're just trying to pin down the evidence so they can verify and claim their success. Remember, they're not allowed to have a feeling unless they can justify it.

As with all things relating to the survival patterns, this is not a one-size-fits-all prescription. In addition to considering what patterns they run and what those patterns value, you'll also need to consider their personal values. If you watch their responses closely, you'll probably be able to tell when your compliment really hit home, and when it didn't.

Getting Yourself Out of the Rigid Pattern

Whenever you realize that you've gone into pattern, your first job is to get yourself out of pattern and back to being present. The survival pattern is distorting your perceptions and your experience. In fact, your patterned response to this distress is most likely making things worse, not better. Once you're back in presence, you'll be able to find the best way to respond to this current situation.

Signs you're in the rigid pattern

- you're trying to cram all your experiences into the known categories and boxes

- you're trying to put the whole world in order

- you're trying to improve others who don't want it

- you're following the Rules of some outside authority, rather than referencing your own felt sense for guidance

- you think that you are your performance and that all your value is in your achievements

The solution: You need to focus on your feelings and sensations as the source of your inner guidance.

To get out of the rigid pattern

Shift your attention from correctness to something soft, playful, or pleasurable. It can be any sort of pleasure, contentment, or delight.

Exercise: Simply wiggle your butt.

Exercise: Shift your attention from a contracted, point focus to an open, expanded field focus.

Soften the focus of your eyes — let them become soft eyes.

- instead of looking actively, just softly lay your eyes on the scene.
- instead of looking at individual objects, just take in the entire scene as a whole.
- instead of looking at the objects, look at the spaces between them.
- stop trying to keep all the objects in your visual field distinct and separate. Just let them blur together a little bit, like an impressionist painting.

For more information on how to get yourself out of pattern, please see Chapter 13, *Getting Yourself Out of Pattern*, on page 358.

Remember, whenever you're in pattern, your first job is getting yourself out of pattern and back to presence.

Healing the Rigid Pattern

The unmet developmental need of rigid-patterned people is to have all their various parts seen, valued, and loved — especially the young, needy, and vulnerable parts. Additionally, they need to feel loved and cherished just for their beingness, without having to *do* anything.

To heal, they have to move toward feelings, rather than forms and rules. Their developmental tasks are to learn to feel and value their own feelings and needs, to trust their own feelings as their source of inner guidance, and to allow the full flow of their life force energy to move through their body.

Loosening the One Right Way

Their first step out of the rigid pattern is usually the simple discovery that there is more than one Right Way in life, that others often follow completely different ways, and that some of these other ways could have value for them. Studying a map of personality patterns often leads rigid-patterned people to this discovery. Any map of personality patterns provides the amazing news that there are fundamental and legitimate differences between people. And if it's an especially good map, it also shows that there are fundamental differences in how people experience reality. For rigid-patterned people, these can be mind-blowing discoveries. They will check and re-check the map against the people around them, but once they realize that the map is truer to real life than their old belief, their conviction that there is only One Right Way will start to dissolve.

Like all the survival patterns, the rigid pattern is a solution to a problem. The problem faced by those in the rigid pattern is, "How do I know what to do? What do I turn to for guidance?" To relinquish the Rules as their source of guidance, they need a better source of guidance. This may sound like a simple transition, but in fact, it is not, because on a deeper level, on the level of the needy child buried deep within their psyche, the question is, "How do I keep Mom and Dad's love?" This question is laden with all the emotional intensity of a young child's need for love and safety.

Often their first step out of the One Right Way solution is to begin to see its limitations. As the person begins to realize that the external Rules are not the *only* source of Truth and Wisdom, she naturally begins looking for other sources of guidance. This opens up the possibility of noticing her feelings and wondering what guidance they offer her. A long period of experimentation usually follows, during which she gathers data on the merits of trusting her feelings and using them for guidance.

Turning inward for information

This turn inward is monumental. She is now referencing herself — the very thing that was discouraged during childhood. She is turning her attention inward, to her own felt experience, rather than outward to the Rules. As she discovers that her inner experience contains useful information, she begins to value it. Gradually, she realizes that her own body and heart can guide her, and that the outer forms can provide support for her actions, instead of restricting them.

Since her early wound involved ignoring her sensations and emotions — especially those of the needy child — her healing requires accepting, loving, and valuing all of those parts. And eventually, it includes uncovering and grieving her early heartbreak at not being valued or seen. Her healing has to be physically embodied: it must be a felt sense in the body, not just an idea in the mind. In the end, it requires dethroning the mind as the source of all wisdom and learning to also trust the body's sensations and emotions as a source of wisdom.

Bodywork is typically very helpful in this exploration. It helps soften the chronic muscular holding patterns that she has used to constrict the flow of feelings and life energy through her body. It also brings her attention back, over and over again, to just feeling her raw body sensations without making up a story about them or having to do anything about them. Rosen Method bodywork is particularly helpful in gently bringing a person's attention back to her body sensations.

Disidentifying from their inner critic

Rigid-patterned people need help seeing how all day, every day, they filter all of their perceptions through their superego's good/bad worldview, and how this actually distorts their perception of the world, rather than sharpens it. Once they see this, the good/bad commentary in their mind becomes less compelling, and they can pay more attention to exploring their own raw sensations, rather than just labeling those sensations as good or bad.

Since those who are caught in the rigid pattern have not completed the developmental step of disidentifying from their inner critic, they need to complete that separation. (For more information on how to disidentify from the inner critic, please see the chapter on *The Basic Skills Needed for Inner Work*.) As that separation proceeds, more space will open up inside them for exploring new experiences. They will become increasingly able to simply sense their body sensations and feelings, both positive and negative, without having to judge them. Instead of instantly labeling them, they can begin exploring their sensations and feelings as a source of information about both themselves and the world.

Once they have enough safety and support, they can begin to explore relaxing their rigid internal control and see if they are still okay. They can even try breaking a few rules to see what happens. At this point in therapy, I often suggest that they experiment with this a little bit. I help them pick out a rule that they're ready to try violating. Then they try breaking it, either in session or as homework. Whether their immediate reaction is elation or anxiety, it is all part of the process of getting to know themselves. Gradually, they become less and less afraid of what will happen if they are imperfect.

Being a mess and still being loved

At some point, rigid-patterned people need to experience being a mess and still being loved. This doesn't just mean that they aren't being criticized. It also means that the other person maintains a loving heart connection with them throughout the messy episode. This is very important, since messing up in childhood often resulted in losing the loving heart connection with their parent.

As they feel more confident that there actually is something lovable inside of them, they will begin to explore deeper heart connections with others. Eventually, they may even come to expect a heart connection with certain people and be able to notice when that connection disappears.

Exploring pleasure and fun

Another important area of exploration for rigid-patterned people is surrendering into pleasurable sensations and learning to value something "just because it feels good." This area includes exploring playfulness, fun, joy, and silliness. For some rigid-patterned people, silliness can be almost terrifying, since it is impossible to do it properly.

Other practices for exploring pleasure can range from simply opening deeply to the taste of a strawberry to allowing themselves to be completely swept away by an overload of sexual pleasure during lovemaking. One man I worked with was surprised when one of his teachers told him, *"Your spiritual path is to learn to tolerate pleasure."* Because he was caught in the rigid pattern, his internal rules had been stopping him from completely surrendering into pleasure in any form, lest he do something "inappropriate." Now, since a respected teacher had given him a new rule, he had not only permission, but even an obligation to explore this new territory.

Relaxing the Wall

Gradually, the practice of surrendering into pleasure and trusting the impulses of their body begins to relax the energetic Wall around them, and they find themselves being deeply touched and moved by life without worrying about what is correct. Although the patterned defense was to contract their muscles and psyche to restrict the flow of energy and feeling through their body, they can gradually become able, in safe settings, to let energy flow freely through their system and surrender into the waves of feeling.

Anger work

The anger work needed by rigid-patterned people usually involves uncovering the ways they were hurt by the requirements of the Rules, and then letting themselves feel their anger at each of those hurts. Feeling the anger and hurt will reconnect them with the heartbreak buried underneath the hurt. Then, staying with the heartbreak will reconnect them with their own denied and buried needs.

Forging this chain of inner reconnections is fundamental to the completion of the unfinished developmental task of the rigid pattern, which is to form a strong connection with their own heart, essence, and beingness. Doing this allows rigid-patterned people to face their fear that they're not real,[16] to find out that they *are* real, and then to develop an authentic sense of self.

Energetic skills needed

In terms of energetic skills, people who adopted the rigid survival pattern are usually already pretty skillful at "me/not me" and at holding their edge, so they mostly need to focus on grounding and core. Eventually, as their rigid interior tube structure dissolves, they will go through a period of confusion and loss of competency, but that will soon be replaced by a new, softer, more heartful competency. (For more detailed descriptions of each of the four energy skills, please see *Healing the Leaving Pattern* on page 103.)

Their human need and spiritual need

To heal their core wound, rigid-patterned people need to become aware of both their individual essence and their unitive essence as real, felt sense experiences. While growing up within the pattern, they most likely did not directly experience either essence, so neither their self nor their connection with the divine seemed palpable to them. Now, their spiritual need is to personally feel these two essences, and their human need is to feel and be authentic, rather than appropriate.

For more help in determining which patterns you go into, please visit
www.The5PersonalityPatterns.com.

– 12 –

Primary and Secondary Patterns

Now that we've looked at each of the survival patterns individually, let's look at how they appear in combination. When considering the various combinations of patterns, we'll use just the first letter of each pattern, so

L = leaving
M = merging
E = enduring
A = aggressive
R = rigid

When discussing possible pairs of survival patterns (without considering which is primary and which is secondary), we'll put a plus sign (+) between the letters. For example, L+M indicates both the leaving and merging patterns. When we're talking about primary and secondary patterns, we'll use a forward slash (/), as in L/M or M/L, showing the primary pattern before the slash and the secondary or backup pattern after it.

As noted earlier, a person usually does two survival patterns. Whenever his* system goes into overwhelm, he will first go into his primary pattern. It is his first method of buffering himself from the feelings of overwhelm. If

---

* In this chapter, I will assume the individual is a man. However, everything said about the man in this chapter could just as easily have been said about a woman.

that defense strategy is not solving the problem, he will shift into his backup pattern.[*]

As the distress in his system builds, you can sometimes actually see a person shift from his primary pattern to his secondary pattern. As the backup pattern takes over, you can see its particular energy flow, behaviors, and survival strategy replace those of the primary pattern. For example, the person may switch from leaving to fighting (L/A), or he may switch from being accommodating to preaching manners (M/R).

However, the change is not always so black and white. The more he has integrated the two survival patterns, the more the behaviors of one pattern will color how he does his other pattern. The less he has integrated them, the more sharply his behavior will change as he switches from his primary to his backup pattern. Also, the first pattern may happen mostly internally and be hard to see from the outside. If it is subtle and internal, the person may not even be aware of it himself.

The secondary pattern may also be used to manage the undesirable aspects of the primary pattern. For instance, the rigid pattern is often used to try to contain the aggressive pattern and impose some manners on it (A/R). Similarly, the enduring pattern may be used to put some brakes on the aggressive pattern (A/E). Or the rigid pattern may be used to bring some order and structure to the leaving pattern (L/R).

Also, if the parents run a pattern strongly, their child will often learn the skills of the pattern even when he does not adopt the pattern as a survival strategy. In this case, the child acquires the gifts of the pattern, but when in distress, he goes into some other survival pattern to try to buffer himself. For instance, if both parents run the rigid pattern, their child will likely learn how to put things in order and handle details, even if he never adopts the rigid pattern. Or, if both parents run the leaving pattern, their child will most likely be psychically sensitive, even if he doesn't adopt the leaving pattern. In his home, much of the conversation happened psychically — "on the airwaves" — so he learned to put his attention there to find out what was going on.

---

[*] The observation that each person does two patterns, arranged as a primary and a backup, came to me through the oral teachings of Lynda Caesara. She received it as an oral teaching from Harley Swift Deer Regen, who got it from a psychotherapist, whose name I do not know. I have not seen this insight from any other source. Harley Swift Deer is now dead, but his organization, the Deer Tribe, can be reached through their website, *www.dtmms.org*.

The Possible Combinations

Remember that when a child tries out any particular survival strategy, he is trying to feel safer by buffering himself from his overwhelming feelings of distress. But, in order to make it work, he must have the skills needed to execute the required maneuver. Each time he employs that survival strategy, he is practicing that set of skills, and if he adopts that survival pattern, he will practice those skills frequently. The more time he spends in that particular pattern, the stronger that skill set becomes. In this way, each survival pattern both requires and hones a specific set of skills.

Because the survival patterns correspond to different stages of child development, the earlier patterns have fewer developmental skills in place and are the least self-sufficient, while the later patterns have access to more developmental skills and are more self-sufficient. So a person who does L+M has the fewest developmental skills, while a person who does A+R has the most developmental skills (although he is missing some important perceptual and relational skills that are highly developed in the earlier patterns).

Let's look now at the possible combinations of patterns to see which skills are more present or absent in each combination. We aren't focusing here on which patterns are primary and secondary, but only on what each combination of patterns creates.

L+M – Strong skills for creativity and connection, along with exceptional flexibility and fluidity. Very perceptive on the energetic and emotional channels. Since both patterns are developmentally so young, they have little foundation and few developmental skills, so the person may struggle just to function in life. Since both patterns form before strength and will come online, self-assertion is weak.

L+E – Creative and grounded. Strong skills at escaping and enduring, and strong awareness of others' intentions and of energy in general. They may be able to fade into the background and become almost invisible. More developmental skills than above, but self-assertion is still weak.

L+A – Strong energetic awareness and big energy. Both patterns ignore the body and its needs, so these people often ignore and abuse the body while wielding that energy. Not grounded, but usually able to operate in both the psychic and physical realms.

L+R – Able to bring their creativity into form. Strongly mental; they tend to stay up in the head and ignore their felt sense experience. They may be uncomfortable with emotions. Tend to have slender bodies, since both patterns tend to be thin or slender.

M+E – More heart-centered, with strong skills for connecting and grounding. Sensitive to other's needs, especially for space. They live in the body, but without power. Tend to have rounder, heavier bodies, since both patterns tend in that direction.

M+A – Wants to both connect and dominate, to be both soft and hard, so has big mood swings as the felt sense of core comes and goes. This is the most problematic combination because the aggressive pattern attacks the merging pattern's neediness. This combination is less common than any of the others.

M+R – Strong skills for connecting, pleasing, and doing what's expected, but both patterns ignore the self to do it. Not grounded; no felt sense of core. They are eager to help others and do what's right.

E+A – Strong skills for both grounding and using power, so able to run big energy without becoming unstable. This is the only combination in which both patterns have a felt sense of core. The body tends to be muscular and needs exercise.

E+R – Strong skills for grounding, endurance, and order, creating a patient, organized strength, or a stubborn righteousness. Both patterns are cautious, so this person is not a risk-taker.

A+R – Big energy, coupled with precision and a sense of righteousness. These people have big firepower and good aim, so they are able to use power effectively to accomplish their agenda, whether for good or ill. Both patterns tend to ignore the needs of others.

Primary versus Secondary Patterns

The amount of time a person spends in his primary survival pattern versus his secondary pattern also varies. The split may be 50/50, 70/30, or even 10/90. The split may also vary from one environment to another, depending on what each environment calls forth in the person.

Because the earlier patterns have smaller developmental skill sets and the later patterns have bigger developmental skill sets, shifting from one survival pattern into another can mean gaining or losing skills. It can also feel like shifting in age, as if you're getting older or younger. When you shift from your primary pattern to your backup pattern, you may feel this effect, and you may experience it as a gain or a loss.

Because the developmentally older survival patterns have more resources at their disposal, having an older pattern as your backup pattern is more functional. As a situation gets worse and you go into more distress, shifting into an older pattern means that more skills become available to you to as you try to handle your distress. Having a younger pattern as your backup tends to be less functional, since it means that as you go into more distress, you're left with even fewer resources to handle it. You find that you've lost some of the abilities you had just a moment ago, and this causes you even more distress.

When a person's survival patterns are closer to each other in developmental age, switching patterns creates less of a gain or loss in abilities. Conversely, when a person's patterns are farther apart in developmental age, switching involves more of a gain or loss. Because of this, a person who does L/A or L/R may like the increase in skills and abilities and may spend a lot of time in his backup pattern. His split may be 30/70. On the other hand, a person who does A/L or R/L may not like the loss of capacity and may try to avoid going into his backup pattern. In this situation, the skills of the backup pattern still color how he does his primary pattern, but he may actually go into his backup pattern only when in extreme distress, so his split may be 90/10.

As you think about these different combinations of patterns, remember that the best option is to not be in any pattern at all. The goal is presence, a presence which includes the capacities and skills you have honed while in your patterns but leaves you free to use those gifts consciously.

– 13 –

Getting Yourself Out of Pattern

Whenever you realize that you've gone into pattern, your first job is getting yourself out of pattern and back to being present. At first, this may seem counter-intuitive. After all, you went into pattern to buffer yourself from some difficult experience. Why would you want to remove that buffer and face the upsetting experience without it?

There are several reasons. First, the survival pattern is distorting your perceptions and your experience. The upset may not be nearly as bad as it appears to be through the filter of the pattern. And even if it is that bad, you still need to see it clearly to figure out the best way to respond to it. Following a distorted map will not take you where you want to go.

Second, as long as you're in pattern, your response will be dictated by the pattern. It will be the automatic response of the pattern, even though that response is probably not the best choice right now. In fact, the patterned response is likely to make things worse, not better.

Third, since the survival pattern was formed when you were much younger and had fewer resources, it's likely that you have better options now. When you get out of pattern and back to being present, you'll once again have access to all the resources and maturity that you've worked so hard to develop. Once you're back in presence, you'll be able to find the best way to respond to the current situation.

Once you've realized that you're in pattern, you must decide to get out of pattern. Then you must do the things that bring you out of pattern and back to being present. Here are some practices that will help you get out of any pattern and move back toward presence. This list is just a start — as you find new practices that bring you back to being present, add them to the list.

Remember, whenever you're in pattern, your first job is getting yourself out of pattern and back to presence.

Do Your Basic Energy Skills

No matter what survival pattern you've gone into, the first step in getting yourself out of pattern is to put your attention on your basic energy skills. Often, putting all four skills in place will bring you out of pattern; at a minimum, it will help immensely. Attend to each one in turn. The more you've already practiced them, the easier this will be. That's why it's so important to practice them frequently. It's much easier to put them in place when you feel safe and relaxed, and the more your body already knows them, the easier it'll be to do them when you're in distress.

Learning to maintain your basic energy skills involves the same kind of process you went through as a child when you were just learning to walk. Think back to when you were a toddler, just learning to walk and maintain your balance. It was hard. You were clumsy. You fell down a lot. Over and over, you got back up and practiced some more. But the more you practiced, the steadier you got. Slowly, it became easier. Gradually, you became an expert at maintaining your balance. When you started to lose your balance, your body instantly felt it and took corrective action. Today, maintaining your balance is second nature. Most of the time, you don't even consciously think about it. Your body attends to it at the unconscious level and maintains your balance automatically. That's the place you want to get to with each of the basic energy skills: an automatic, unconscious, embodied maintenance of each skill.

Here's the list of basic energy skills, as previously described in Chapter 5. Practice them in whatever order works best for you.

- core

- ground

- me/not me

- edge

Re-Center Yourself (a five second practice)[1]

This is a simple centering practice, adapted from Wendy Palmer's way of teaching aikido exercises to leaders to help them embody the various qualities of good leadership. It is the simplest and quickest way I know to re-center yourself. If you take five seconds to do this practice hourly, within a few weeks, it will become second nature:

1. Let your back be straight but not stiff.

2. Inhale once up your spine.

3. Exhale once down your spine.

Use the AK 4-Point Rubbing Technique

This technique comes from Applied Kinesiology and involves rubbing four points on the front of your body at once, for as long as feels right to you. The lower two points are located about one inch on either side of your navel. Most people like to use the thumb for one point and the first two fingers of that same hand for the other point. The top two points are also about two inches apart, just under your collarbone, on each side of your sternum. On an acupuncture chart, they are called K-27. Those familiar with Emotional Freedom Technique (EFT) will recognize them as the Collarbone Points.

Simply rub all four points whenever you need to calm your body down. Do it until you feel a shift or until your hands get tired. If you find yourself taking a deep breath, that's a sign that your body is relaxing.

Shift Your Attention from the Story and Emotions to Your Raw Perceptions

Whenever you're in pattern or lost in any kind of reaction, you're probably telling yourself a story about what's happening. The story comes from your past, from something that happened to you back then, but that may not be happening to you now. Whenever that button gets pushed, that story plays in your head in living color. It's a conditioned response. But it's from the past, not the present, so it actually clouds your awareness of the present and causes you to feel the emotions that go with the story, instead of sensing what's actually happening right now.

To get out of your reaction and return to the present, put the story aside. Shift your attention from the story and its emotions to your raw perceptual experience right now — to the sounds you hear, to the color of someone's shirt, to the sensations of heat or cold on your skin, or to the felt sense of pressure in your body. Putting your attention on your raw sense perceptions will interrupt the story and bring you back to the present. You may not like the raw sense perceptions, but they're more useful to you than being lost in the old story and the reaction it brings. When you're back in the present, you can compose a response that is tailored to the present situation, instead of just repeating your conditioned reaction from the past.

Calm Your Body

Frequently, the distress that puts you into pattern also changes your body's physiology, putting you into fight or flight or some similar stress response. Calming your body is an important step in the process of getting yourself out of pattern. There are many ways to calm your body so that you can return to the present. Here are some of them:

- Slow your breathing: do long, slow out-breaths through pursed lips.

- Shift your attention to the here-and-now raw sensations in your body, especially pleasurable ones, and away from emotions, meanings, or your story about them.

- Do yoga, quiet contemplation, or meditation.

- Lay belly-down on the earth or grass.

- Snuggle into someone's lap or arms.

- Put a hand on the middle of your chest and feel into that area.

- Take a hot bath or shower or sit in a hot tub.

- Get a foot rub, facial massage, head stroking, or any gentle massage.

- Shift from left brain into right brain.

- Soften your eyes, soft-focus your vision.

- Sing or listen to heartful music.

- Focus on beauty, joy, love, or pleasure.

Use the Questioning Practice

Another tool that you may find helpful is known as the Questioning Practice. It's like an affirmation, in that it's designed to shift your attention in the direction you've chosen. However, it's different from an affirmation in that it's not a command or a declaration of your new focus. Instead, it gently coaxes your attention in the desired direction. Even if you rebel against affirmations, the questioning practice will probably work well for you.

The essence of the Questioning Practice is to simply ask yourself a question about your current experience that shifts your focus *slightly* in the desired direction. The basic form of the question is *"What would this experience be like if I were feeling a little more _____?"*

Insert in the blank whatever quality you would like to move toward. For instance, suppose you've noticed that you tend to be overly serious and you want to add more joy to your life. You can nudge your attention in that direction by frequently asking yourself, *"What would this experience be like if I were feeling a little more joy?"* Then you just notice whatever response arises in your awareness. You don't try to force any change. You just ask the question and see what arises.

Notice also that you don't ask for a big change. That's probably beyond what your system can allow without reacting against it. So you just posit a small shift in your inner experience. If only a very small shift seems tolerable, you might phrase the question as, *"What would this be like if I were feeling just 1% more joy?"* On the other hand, if a larger shift seems to work for you, put in the right words for that.

You can use the Questioning Practice to shift your awareness in whatever direction you want to cultivate — towards joy or seriousness, freedom or responsibility, alertness or sleepiness, or even presence itself. Just figure out what quality you want to nurture and put it into the blank. Then notice how big a shift seems tolerable for you right now, and use those words.

After you've done this for a while, notice whether it is working to shift your habitual stance of attention in the direction you desire, and then adjust your practice as needed. I have known people to stay with a single quality for an entire year as it gradually re-organized their way of seeing the world.

Here are some suggestions for each of the survival patterns:
Leaving pattern – explore: "sensation in my feet," "connection to the earth"
Merging pattern – explore: "sensation in my core," "the support of the earth"

Enduring pattern – explore: "expanding," "moving," or "energy flowing up and out"

Aggressive pattern – explore: "safe," "protected," "supported," "contained"

Rigid pattern – explore: "pleasure," "joy," "softness"

Use EFT ("tapping")

You can also deal directly with your feelings of overwhelm by doing something to dissolve those feelings. There are many good tools and techniques available for this, and you may want to try out several before settling on one that works well for you.

The tool that I have found to be the quickest, easiest, and most effective is something called Emotional Freedom Technique, or EFT. It involves tapping on your body's energy meridians to clear out the energetic disruptions caused by overwhelming and traumatic experiences. Often, this technique will clear out the sense of overwhelm and restore your system to a healthy, calm presence within a few minutes. The basic forms of EFT are quite simple and easy to learn. To learn the basics, I recommend the tutorials and videos on Gary Craig's website at *www.emofree.com*, or attending workshops and trainings. Look for a well-trained, certified instructor. You can also learn the basics by reading *The EFT Comprehensive Training Resource, Level 1* by Ann Adams and Karin Davidson. When I teach EFT, that's the book I recommend to my students.

Helping Others Get Out of Pattern

The most important thing you can do to help others get out of pattern is to get yourself out of pattern. Whenever you're in pattern, you're putting a strain on everyone around you, and that strain tends to put them into pattern, also. So the biggest favor you can do for all of your friends, family, and co-workers is to be in presence, rather than in pattern. If you can do that, even part of the time, people will notice a huge change.

Holding space for others in such a way that they are drawn out of pattern and back to presence is a very important subject. However, it is much too big a subject to include in this book. Instead, I plan to cover it in a future book focused on healing the patterns.

Breaking Your Patterns

In addition to becoming very adept at noticing and getting out of a particular survival pattern, it's also possible to "break" that pattern. A series of healing experiences — ones that dissolve the core trauma(s) that conditioned your body into the pattern — can achieve this. As each trauma is dissolved, some of the fuel that was driving the survival strategy is removed. When enough of that fuel has been removed, you reach a tipping point: your perspective changes and you begin to seek safety in presence, rather than in the pattern's survival strategy. Once broken, a pattern loses much of its compelling force.

Unfortunately, this does not entirely remove the survival pattern from your body. Remnants of it continue to exist in the physical structures of your body, in your sense of identity, and often in your habits of attention and energy flow. When in enough distress, you'll still go into that pattern. But now, much more stress is required to throw you into pattern, and when it happens, it is a much milder experience. Your old conviction that this strategy will save you is gone, replaced by a clarity that wants to come home to presence. In daily life, you experience a kind of freedom from reactivity and drama you had never known before. And you retain the gifts and talents of the pattern.

As your old emotional reactivity recedes, your attention becomes more stable. Instead of flitting away into endless reactions, it stays more easily in the present. Without a thousand unintentional side trips, all of life becomes easier. This stabilizing of attention is immensely valuable — in fact, it is the goal of many meditation and attention practices. These unintentional side trips are one of the main obstacles that prevent a meditator from dropping into deeper states of awareness, so healing the core wounds that fuel these side trips can be very helpful for anyone engaged in a meditation practice.

How the core wounds of each of the patterns can be healed enough to break the pattern is, again, more than can be included here, but I do plan to cover it in a future book on healing the patterns.

– 14 –

Conclusion

We've seen that our usual view of the world is not a complete one. Instead, it is only a slice of reality, a slice that is filtered and distorted by the survival patterns we're caught in. We've learned about the developmental stages and the tasks that we all need to complete to become mature adults. We've learned about each of the survival patterns and how they grow out of getting stuck in a particular developmental stage, unable to complete the tasks of that stage.

By now, you probably recognize which survival patterns you do and you've begun to see how those patterns organize your life and distort your experience of the world. Perhaps this awareness has begun to loosen the hold those patterns have on you, and perhaps it has also given you a little more room inside to feel your core and know your self. Perhaps you've even begun to do some practices to shift yourself out of your patterns and back toward presence.

Now some questions arise: How are you going to use what you've learned to diminish your suffering and improve your life? How are you going to use it to relate more skillfully to yourself and to those around you?

To diminish your suffering, and that of those around you, you must learn to recognize when you've gone into pattern. And then you must take steps to get yourself out of pattern. That's the path that will bring you more into presence, day by day. That's the path that will free you from the prison of your survival patterns. And that's the path that will allow your essence to shine out into the world.

The world needs your essence.
Don't fool yourself into thinking that you're not important.
No one else can sing your song.
No one else can bring your gifts to the world.
We need you.

Endnotes

Introduction

1. Wilhelm Reich, *Character Analysis* (New York, Farrar, Straus and Giroux, Third, enlarged edition, 1949), p. 355.

Leaving

1. Lynda Caesara, oral teaching on the patterns, 2014.
2. Barbara Ann Brennan, *Light Emerging* (New York, Bantam Books, 1993), p. 209.
3. Brennan, *Light Emerging*, p. 209.
4. Anodea Judith, *Eastern Body, Western Mind* (Berkeley, CA, Celestial Arts, 1996), p. 59.
5. Stephen M. Johnson, *Character Styles* (New York, W. W. Norton & Company, 1994), p. 76.
6. Johnson, *Character Styles*, p. 75.
7. Johnson, *Character Styles*, p. 89.
8. Linda Kohanov, *The Tao of Equus* (Novato, CA, New World Library, 2001), pp. 160–161.
9. Barbara Ann Brennan, *Hands of Light* (New York, Bantam Books, 1987), p. 112.

Merging

1. Lynda Caesara, oral teaching on the patterns, 2014.
2. Alexander Lowen, *The Language of the Body* (New York, Collier Books, 1971), p. 162.
3. Johnson, *Character Styles*, p. 111.
4. Lowen, *The Language of the Body*, p. 162.

5. John Bowlby, quoted in Susan Johnson, *Becoming an Emotionally Focused Couple Therapist, The Workbook* (New York, Routledge, 2005) p. 102.
6. Johnson, *Character Styles*, p. 102.
7. David Wilcox, *Break in the Cup*, on *The Very Best of David Wilcox* (2001, A & M Records).
8. Brennan, *Light Emerging*, p. 217.

Enduring

1. Jay Suzer, *An Essay on Education and Instruction of Children*, 1748, quoted in Johnson, *Character Styles*, pp. 198–199.
2. Kruger, J. G., 1752, quoted in Johnson, *Character Styles*, p. 199.
3. Judith, *Eastern Body, Western Mind*, p. 19.
4. Lowen, *The Language of the Body*, p. 214.
5. Brennan, *Hands of Light*, p. 121.
6. Johnson, *Character Styles*, p. 210.
7. Johnson, *Character Styles*, p. 220.
8. Johnson, *Character Styles*, p. 219.
9. Judith, *Eastern Body, Western Mind*, pp. 199–200.
10. Brennan, *Light Emerging*, p. 236.
11. Johnson, *Character Styles*, p. 219.
12. Johnson, *Character Styles*, p. 219.
13. Judith, *Eastern Body, Western Mind*, p. 197.
14. Judith, *Eastern Body, Western Mind*, p. 197.
15. Brennan, *Light Emerging*, p. 236.
16. Johnson, *Character Styles*, p. 228.
17. I first learned the Doubt Shout at a men's conference in about 1984, where it was taught by Martin Keogh. I do not know where he had learned it.

Aggressive

1. Johnson, *Character Styles*, p. 158.
2. Brennan, *Light Emerging*, p. 225.
3. Alexander Lowen, *Bioenergetics* (New York, Penguin Books, 1976), p. 160.
4. Lowen, *Bioenergetics*, p. 159.

5. Kohanov, *The Tao of Equus*, Chapter 5.
6. Anodea Judith, private communication, 2014.
7. *Anything You Can Do*, in the musical *Annie Get Your Gun* by Irving Berlin, 1946.
8. Lynda Caesara, oral teaching on the patterns, ~2008.
9. Lowen, *Bioenergetics*, p. 160.
10. Judith, *Eastern Body, Western Mind*, p. 326.
11. Johnson, *Character Styles*, p. 158.
12. Henry Cloud, *Changes That Heal* (Grand Rapids, MI, Zondervan Publishing House, 1992), p. 115.

Rigid

1. Lowen, *Bioenergetics*, p. 167.
2. Johnson, *Character Styles*, p. 271.
3. Johnson, *Character Styles*, p. 274.
4. Johnson, *Character Styles*, p. 275.
5. Johnson, *Character Styles*, p. 280.
6. Johnson, *Character Styles*, pp. 283–284.
7. Brennan, *Light Emerging*, p. 245.
8. Lowen, *The Language of the Body*, p. 271.
9. Lowen, *The Language of the Body*, p. 271.
10. Judith, *Eastern Body, Western Mind*, p. 272.
11. Judith, *Eastern Body, Western Mind*, p. 271.
12. Lowen, *The Language of the Body*, p. 255.
13. Johnson, *Character Styles*, p. 283.
14. Johnson, *Character Styles*, pp. 283–284.
15. Brennan, *Light Emerging*, p. 247.
16. Brennan, *Light Emerging*, p. 247.

Getting Yourself Out of Pattern

1. Adapted from Wendy Palmer and Janet Crawford, *Leadership Embodiment* (San Rafael, CA, The Embodiment Foundation, 2013), p. 46.

Bibliography

Almaas, A. H., *Essence: The Diamond Approach to Inner Realization* (York Beach, ME, Samuel Weiser, 1986)

Almaas, A. H., *The Pearl Beyond Price: Integration of Personality into Being: An Object Relations Approach* (Berkeley, CA, Diamond Books, 1988)

Brennan, Barbara Ann, *Hands of Light: A Guide to Healing Through the Human Energy Field* (New York, Bantam Books, 1987)

Brennan, Barbara Ann, *Light Emerging: The Journey of Personal Healing* (New York, Bantam Books, 1993)

Brown, Byron, *Soul Without Shame: A Guide to Liberating Yourself from the Judge Within* (Boston, Shambala, 1999)

Cloud, Henry, *Changes That Heal: How to Understand Your Past to Ensure a Healthier Future* (Grand Rapids, MI, Zondervan Publishing House, 1992)

Cloud, Henry, and Townsend, John, *Boundaries: When to Say Yes, When to Say No to Take Control of Your Life* (Grand Rapids, MI, Zondervan Publishing House, 1992)

Heller, Laurence and LaPierre, Aline, *Healing Developmental Trauma: How Early Trauma Affects Self-Regulation, Self-Image, and the Capacity for Relationship* (Berkeley, CA, North Atlantic Books, 2012)

Johnson, Susan, *Becoming an Emotionally Focused Couple Therapist, The Workbook* (New York, Routledge, 2005)

Johnson, Stephen M., *Characterological Transformation: The Hard Work Miracle* (New York, Norton, 1984)

Johnson, Stephen M., *Humanizing the Narcissistic Style* (New York, Norton, 1987)

Johnson, Stephen M., *Character Styles* (New York, Norton, 1994)

Judith, Anodea, *Eastern Body, Western Mind: Psychology and the Chakra System as a Path to the Self* (Berkeley, CA, Celestial Arts, 1996)

Kohanov, Linda, *The Tao of Equus: A Woman's Journey of Healing and Transformation through the Way of the Horse* (Novato, CA, New World Library, 2001)

Levine, Peter, *Waking the Tiger: Healing Trauma* (Berkeley, CA, North Atlantic Books, 1997)

Lowen, Alexander, *The Language of the Body* (New York, Collier Books, 1971)

Lowen, Alexander, *Bioenergetics* (New York, Penguin Books, 1976)

Newton, Michael, *Journey of Souls: Case Studies of Life Between Lives* (St. Paul, MN, Llewellyn Publications, 1994)

Newton, Michael, *Destiny of Souls: New Case Studies of Life Between Lives* Woodbury, MN, Llewellyn Publications, 2000)

Palmer, Wendy and Crawford, Janet, *Leadership Embodiment: How the Way We Sit and Stand Can Change the Way We Think and Speak* (San Rafael, CA, The Embodiment Foundation, 2013)

Pierrakos, John C., *Core Energetics: Developing the Capacity to Love and Heal* (Mendocino, CA, LifeRhythm Publication, 1987)

Reich, Wilhelm, *Character Analysis* (New York, Farrar, Straus and Giroux, Third, enlarged edition, 1949)

Index

About the Author

Steven Kessler has been a licensed psychotherapist for almost 30 years. He has studied many different maps of personality and many healing modalities, including Character Structure, the Enneagram, NLP, energy work, Thought Field Therapy, and EFT (emotional freedom techniques). He is a licensed psychotherapist and a certified EFT Expert and Trainer and maintains a private practice in Albany, CA.

Since 1984, Steven has taught hundreds of groups and workshops in the U.S. and internationally, helping men and women heal their wounds and grow into their full adult selves. More recently, he has taught over a hundred classes and workshops training other therapists in the use of EFT. From 2006 to 2010, Steven left his private practice for 2-3 months a year to work on U.S. military bases in both North America and overseas, helping soldiers and their families heal the wounds of war.

Steven holds a Masters Degree in Transpersonal Psychology from John F. Kennedy University and has spent many years studying mythology, anthropology, and the evolution of human consciousness. For over 40 years he has pursued various spiritual and meditation practices, including 16 years in the Diamond Heart meditation school. Since 2004, he has been a student of Lynda Caesara, studying character structure, the direct perception of energy, and shamanism in the lineage of Grandfather Two Bears and the Southern Seers tradition.

For information on speaking, workshops, and trainings, please visit *www.The5PersonalityPatterns.com* or contact Steven Kessler at *info@The5PersonalityPatterns.com*.